ART THERAPY
In Theory and Practice

ART THERAPY

In Theory and Practice

Edited by ELINOR ULMAN
and PENNY DACHINGER

Schocken Books · New York

First published by SCHOCKEN BOOKS 1975

10 9 8 7 6 5 4   82 83 84 85

Library of Congress Cataloging in Publication Data
Main entry under title:

Art therapy.

Selected articles from the American journal of art therapy.
1. Art therapy—Addresses, essays, lectures.
I. Ulman, Elinor. II. Dachinger, Penny
RC489.A7A78   616.8'916'5   75-10610

Manufactured in the United States of America

ISBN 0–8052–3596–5

For Claire and Bernie

Contents

Introduction

The character of the material available for this collection has been determined by thirteen years of editorial policy in the selection of articles for the *American Journal of Art Therapy*. From the *Journal's* start in 1961, we defined our work as "assisting the crystallization of a body of knowledge and ideas concerning the visual arts in education, rehabilitation, and psychotherapy." To this end we aimed to provide "first and foremost a forum for the vigorous discussion of ideas," and asserted our belief in "rigorous intellectual debate as the only road to meaningful consensus."

The writings included in this book testify to our acceptance of articles with theoretical underpinnings that range from Freud to Montessori, and the work described therein extends from the predominantly educational to the predominantly psychiatric, including much that lies between. However, we have at times declined to publish writings that would tend to subvert our fundamental beliefs about the nature of art and the nature of therapy. Two articles by the senior editor of this book ("Art Therapy: Problems of Definition" and "Therapy Is Not Enough") and three articles by Edith Kramer ("Art and Emptiness," "The Problem of Quality in Art," and "Art and Craft") reflect those beliefs more directly than do most of the other articles included.

In this collection will be found studies whose main emphasis is on diagnosis; studies dealing with the treatment of disturbed children, of the elderly, of schizophrenics, of drug abusers, of the retarded, and of troubled family groups; descriptions of work done in hospitals, community mental health centers, treatment homes, special educational settings, and ordinary classrooms. The research reports include both systematic clinical observations and the analysis of data collected under controlled conditions. Some contributions to theory seek to make general definitions of the field of art therapy applicable in any time or place, while one gives searching attention to social developments belonging specifically to the third quarter of the twentieth century. The case material discussed was accumulated in a wide variety of therapeutic and educational groups as well as in individual therapy sessions. There is an article offering a number of useful art therapy techniques and another that presents a psychiatrist's analysis of a series of pictures by a patient he had not treated—indeed, the pictures themselves were never used in treatment.

Within the scope permitted by the economics of publishing, it was hard to choose the articles to be included. Colleagues involved in selecting the contents agreed that there was already available in the back issues of the *Journal* enough excellent material for a second volume. Choices were particularly difficult in the area of case studies, and a book consisting largely of case studies could be prepared readily, should the demand warrant it. In the space available, we tried to strike a balance among the types of material the *Journal* had invited from its start—articles of "broad theoretical import . . . information about existing programs, techniques developed, and the ideas on which they are based. . . the analysis of experience: thoughtful consideration of what happens in ordinary working programs as well as the results of more formally organized research."

This defintion of the range we wanted to cover was published in our first issue, and, in the main, the implied policies remain the same. However, in the course of writing this introduction the editor came to realize that additional, unstated considerations have guided the choice of material. She welcomed expression of opinions contrary to her own, but found herself refusing to publish anything she did not fully understand. Unclear statements that seemed to contain deeply buried gold were discussed at length with their authors until the hills or mountains of overlying verbal dross could be edited away. Asked about the intellectual and professional level of the audience to which the *Journal* was directed, the editor searched for the honest answer and declared, "The *Journal* is directed to me."

Probably every editor whose sifting of contributions has neither a commercial nor a manipulative purpose might make a similar observation: the editor, like the artist, is his own first audience. Both of them make myriad choices shaped solely by a determination to come as close as possible to fulfilling their own demands and meeting their own standards.

This occasion for looking back over the *Journal*'s history also makes us keenly aware that in 1961 when (under the title *Bulletin of Art Therapy*) the *Journal* was born, the notion that a public for a collection of articles such as this might come into existence in a mere dozen years would have seemed like a pipe dream. At that time, we were elated to have acquired two hundred subscribers before our second issue went to press. Each time our printing deadline approached we wondered whether an article worthy of taking the lead position would materialize, and once a year for the first three years we had to use reprinted articles to fill the gap. Today it is hard to keep abreast of the backlog of worthy new material that awaits attention.

Even in 1961, however, art therapy had to its credit an honorable history of more than twenty years. In the United States, Margaret Naumburg, Loretta Bender, Paul Schilder, and Edith Kramer had already published at book length, as had Adrian Hill in England. On the Continent, in the late nineteenth and early twentieth centuries, there had been important precursors—Prinzhorn, Simon, and Lombroso. From the start we aspired to continue this distinguished tradition.

The production of this volume, long urged by Edith Kramer and Bernard Levy, Ph.D., was sparked by the interest of the junior editor, Penny Dachinger, when she was a master's degree candidate in the art therapy program of The George Washington University. In the selection of articles, Ms. Dachinger made sure that items of particular interest to students in training as art therapists received full consideration. Ms. Kramer and Dr. Levy joined the editors to constitute an informal selection committee.

All of us involved in the work on this volume welcome the almost overwhelming growth of interest in art therapy during the past four or five years. This book has been compiled with the belief that it will help meet a demand for ideas and practical information about art therapy on the part of an audience extending far beyond the profession itself. We feel sure that the time has come when much material in back issues of the *Journal* known mainly to our long-time subscribers will prove illuminating to many whose interest in the field is of more recent origin. We welcome the opportunity to make these articles more readily available in book form.

ELINOR ULMAN

Part I

THEORY OF ART THERAPY

Art Therapy: Problems of Definition

ELINOR ULMAN

It is always hard, sometimes impossible, to find the ideal name for any complex and subtle discipline. The title "art therapy" can easily be dismissed as inadequate or inaccurate, but I have not found a better one. Doubtful implications can only be resolved by careful, evolving definition. The purpose of this paper is an opening move in that direction.

"Art therapy" is currently used to designate widely varying practices in education, rehabilitation, and psychotherapy. Directors of special schools, psychiatrists, and even (in at least one case) the United States Civil Service Commission, refer to certain professional and volunteer workers as art therapists, even though no similar educational preparation, no set of qualifications, nor even any voluntary association binds these people together. Possibly the only thing common to *all* their activities is that the materials of the visual arts are used in some attempt to assist integration or reintegration of personality.

Yet competing and mutually exclusive definitions of art therapy have already been published by art therapists. At least one psychiatrist, objecting to the looseness with which the term is used, has attempted to tighten up its meaning. Psychiatrists also have suggested various combinations of new names to designate special uses of art materials in psychotherapy.

Art therapy is the only one of the many activity therapies to attract this kind of attention from psychiatrists. This, I believe, implies something important about the peculiar nature and potency of our medium. There is a considerable body of literature describing the therapeutic use of patients' graphic and plastic projections in psychiatric practice.[1] A number of these

---

[1] See for example H. G. Baynes, *The Mythology of the Soul;* Baltimore, Williams and Wilkins, 1940.

Gustave Bychowski, "The Rebirth of a Woman"; *Psychoanalytic Review,* 1947, vol. 34, pp. 32-57.

Nolan D. C. Lewis, "The Practical Value of Graphic Art in Personality Studies"; *Psychoanalytic Review,* 1925, Vol. 12, pp. 316-322.

Ainslie Meares, *The Door of Serenity;* Springfield, Ill., Charles C. Thomas, 1958.

books and papers antedate the important publications of such art therapists as Naumburg and Kramer. Since art therapists have begun to publish, some psychiatrists imply that the term is being used to denote territory that belongs rather to themselves.

Direct attempts by art therapists to define art therapy demand first consideration. Whatever its deficiencies, our two-word title at least indicates the two main trends in existing practice and theory: some art therapists put the emphasis on art and some on therapy. The art people tend to exclude procedures where completion of the creative process is not a central goal; the therapy people often explain that preoccupation with artistic goals must be minimized in favor of a specialized form of psychotherapy. In the United States the second group — emphasis on therapy — found its spokesman earlier in the person of Margaret Naumburg. They are the ones who afford us the unique privilege of colliding squarely with psychiatrists who encourage their patients to communicate not only with words but with paint and clay. Among them also are the few who claim that art therapy can be an independent as well as an auxiliary technique in psychotherapy — a claim made, as far as I know, for no other activity therapy.

"Symbolic Speech"

Naumburg's theory has undergone considerable evolution since the early 1940's; only a recent formulation will be quoted. Naumburg designates art therapy as analytically oriented, saying that it "bases its methods on releasing the unconscious by means of spontaneous art expression; it has its roots in the transference relation between patient and therapist, and on the encouragement of free association. It is closely allied to psychoanalytic therapy. . . . Treatment depends on the development of the transference relation and on a continuous effort to obtain the patient's own interpretation of his symbolic designs. . . . The images produced are a form of communication between patient and therapist; they constitute symbolic speech."

Naumburg cites the advantages of introducing painting and clay modeling into analytically oriented psychotherapy as follows: First, it permits direct expression of dreams, fantasies, and other inner experiences that occur as pictures rather than words. Second, pictured projections of unconscious material escape censorship more easily than do verbal expres-

———, *Hypnography;* Springfield, Ill., Charles C. Thomas, 1957.
———, *Shapes of Sanity*; Springfield, Ill., Charles C. Thomas, 1960.
John Weir Perry, *The Self in Psychotic Process;* Berkeley, University of California Press, 1953.
Max M. Stern, *Free Painting as an Auxiliary Technique in Psychoanalysis,* in *Specialized Techniques in Psychotherapy,* edited by Gustav Bychowski and J. Louise Despert; New York, Basic Books, 1952.
———, "Trauma, Projective Technique, and Analytic Profile"; *Psychoanalytic Quarterly,* 1953, Vol. 22.
The list would be much longer if literature devoted mainly to the diagnostic value of painting and sculpture were included.

sions, so that the therapeutic process is speeded up. Third, the productions are durable and unchanging; their content cannot be erased by forgetting, and their authorship is hard to deny. Fourth, the resolution of transference is made easier. "The autonomy of the patient is encouraged by his growing ability to contribute to the interpretation of his own creations. He gradually substitutes a narcissistic cathexis to his own art for his previous dependence on the therapist."[2]

An informal inquiry made in 1960 revealed that of 30 art therapists working in the United States and Canada a substantial majority believed that a therapeutic endeavor where spontaneous graphic and plastic projections serve primarily as "symbolic speech" was an important goal of their own practice. About half of these, like Naumburg, minimized any other special contribution of art activity to the treatment of the mentally ill. Independent private practice appears to be rare;[3] most of these art therapists work as members of psychiatric teams. Conditions vary widely and technique is modified in many ways. It is worth noting that Naumburg and others have applied similar methods both in individual treatment and in group therapy.

Naumburg's procedures overlap those described by psychiatrists who use painting and clay modeling in the course of psychoanalysis or analytically oriented therapy. These doctors share most of her convictions about the advantages gained by introducing these special materials and techniques, though in their reports I have found no mention of any change in the problem of handling transference. Max Stern and Ainslie Meares make it abundantly clear that they regard the interpretive use of patients' spontaneous productions in paint or clay as an integral part, but only a part, of their own basic therapeutic practice. W. L. Meijering assigns "expressive therapy," characterized as intensive and interpretive, exclusively to the "expert psychiatrist."[4]

Healing Quality of the Creative Process

The conflict here implied can be discussed better after considering another important theoretical formulation. Edith Kramer emphasizes art in defining the art therapist's special contribution to psychotherapy. In 1958 she became the second member of our nascent profession in the United States to publish at book length and to attempt rigorous definition.

---

[2] Margaret Naumburg, *Art Therapy: Its Scope and Function,* in *The Clinical Application of Projective Drawings* by Emanuel F. Hammer, et al, Springfield, Ill., Charles C. Thomas, 1958.

[3] See Margaret Naumburg, *Psychoneurotic Art: Its Function in Psychotherapy;* Grune & Stratton, 1953.

This is the only published report I know of. Lucile Rankin Potts, describing *Two Picture Series Showing Emotional Changes During Art Therapy,* does not mention referral source or other psychiatric treatment of patients in her groups. International Journal of Group Psychotherapy, 1958. Vol. 8, No. 4.

[4] See footnote 1, also W. L. Meijering, *La Thérapie Créative;* talk delivered at 3rd World Congress of Psychiatry, Montreal, 1961. Mimeographed.

The healing quality inherent in the creative process explains, in Kramer's view, the usefulness of art in therapy. "Art," she says, "is a means of widening the range of human experiences by creating equivalents for such experiences. It is an area wherein experiences can be chosen, varied, repeated at will. In the creative act, conflict is re-experienced, resolved and integrated. . . . The arts throughout history have helped man to reconcile the eternal conflict between the individual's instinctual urges and the demands of society. . . . The process of sublimation constitutes the best way to deal with a basic human dilemma, but the conflicting demands of superego and id cannot be permanently reconciled. . . . In the artistic product conflict is formed and contained but only partly neutralized. The artist's position epitomizes the precarious human situation: while his craft demands the greatest self-discipline and perseverance, he must maintain access to the primitive impulses and fantasies that constitute the raw material for his creative work.

"The art therapist makes creative experiences available to disturbed persons in the service of the total personality; he must use methods compatible with the inner laws of artistic creation. . . . His primary function is to assist the process of sublimation, an act of integration and synthesis which is performed by the ego, wherein the peculiar fusion between reality and fantasy, between the unconscious and the conscious, which we call art is reached."[5]

The complete artistic process thus exemplifies victory in the continuous struggle imposed on man by his basic nature. Therefore the arts have special value in the treatment of the mentally ill, but by themselves they cannot repair seriously damaged capacities for sublimation. No art therapist who places the emphasis on art considers art therapy a possible substitute for psychotherapy in the more conventional sense. Most agree with Kramer about a few salient qualities that distinguish the art therapist from the art teacher. In therapy the product is more clearly subordinated to the process than in teaching. Even more than the teacher must the therapist offer acceptance and respond to the special needs of every patient. His psychodynamic understanding shapes attitudes and actions in ways too subtle for brief recapitulation, enabling him to contribute both to the therapeutic program and to the understanding of each patient's total personality.

Of the 30 art therapists previously mentioned, a majority consider that providing adequate conditions for the creative process is an important part of their job, but only a small number appear to believe that it is their whole job. About twice as many aim only at the use of graphic and plastic productions as "symbolic speech." The largest single group — about half of those responding — believe in both these two main ways of using art.

Psychiatrists' Definitions

No psychiatric writer lays claim for himself to the area defined by Kramer. Stern, who does not concern himself with the problem of defining

[5] Edith Kramer, *Art Therapy in a Children's Community;* Springfield, Ill., Charles C. Thomas, 1958, pp. 6-23.

art therapy at all, writes as a psychoanalyst addressing himself to other psychoanalysts. Meijering, on the other hand, does define the artist-therapist's role, but he purposely avoids the term art therapy; "creative therapy" is his name for the broad spectrum of mental hospital practices involving the more or less creative use of paint and clay. Within this field he distinguishes between "expressive therapy," "creative therapy proper," and "artistic activities."[6]

Expressive therapy centers on the expression of emotion within the framework of the therapeutic relationship. It is an integral part of psychotherapy and should be strictly the doctor's province, for it is often so profoundly revealing to the patient as to be extremely dangerous in any other hands. Simple, easily handled art materials best serve the purposes of expressive therapy, and the psychotherapist conducting it need have little specialized knowledge about media and art techniques.

Creative therapy proper is the concern of the "creative therapist," who has his own area of competence. He must know a great deal about art materials and their use, and above all must have such a first-hand knowledge of the artistic process that he can avoid interfering with the patient's determination of his own expressive goals. While the creative therapist must understand psychiatric principles, his main concern is with helping the patient find a means of imaginative expression rather than with the content of expression. Interpretation is purposely avoided, for this is "no longer part of a psychotherapeutic process. . . . It is rather a task to execute than a liberation of feeling." Meijering's brief description of the "integrative" role played by creative therapy implies considerable understanding of the artistic process and its potential service to the personality. However, he sees the development of the patient's relation to the *outside* world as the main contribution of this isolated phase of treatment.

Creative therapy proper is distinguished from "artistic activities," the name given by Meijering to the recreational use of art materials in the treatment of chronic patients. The leader's role is here conceived as much more directive than that of the creative therapist. Artistic activities apparently serve to strengthen defenses; in contrast to the "uncovering" function of expressive therapy and the "integrative" function of creative therapy, artistic activities are designated as "covering." Curiously Meijering likens artistic activities rather than creative therapy proper to "creative activities" outside the hospital where "there is no question of psychiatric treatment," and where "artistic norms" prevail. An American can only wonder whether this identification reflects the state of art and of art education in Holland.

Meijering is aware that in practice his three forms of creative therapy cannot always remain strictly separated. His treatment of the subject demands serious consideration because his distinctions are reasonable and

---

[6] W. L. Meijering, *Op. cit.* Translation mine. Meijering speaks in the name of a committee of psychiatrists consisting of himself and Drs. Vaessen, Zitman, and Palies, which in 1959 undertook formulations based on existing practices in the mental hospitals of Holland.

impose some order on a semantic chaos.[7] I would hesitate, however, to identify the art therapist's role with the creative therapist's role as he delineates it. The dictionary meaning of his terms appears to me too broad and the meaning he assigns to them too narrow to serve our purpose.

Meares, who has invented such cumbersome terms as hypnography, plastotherapy, and hypnoplasty to designate the psychiatrist's various uses of art materials, does use the term art therapy, and sets very strict limits to its meaning. Not only is the art therapist excluded from the doctor's territory, but bits and pieces arbitrarily assigned to occupational therapy and recreation nibble away a good deal of what is left. As if this were not enough, he creates a sort of no-man's-land called "integrative therapy," where the enforcement of literal realism and something vaguely termed "good craftsmanship" are artificially isolated. The domain of "aesthetic" concern that remains as the province of his so-called art therapy is not only extremely narrow but it is poorly and superficially defined.[8] Meares' opposition to the sloppy use of the terms "art" and "art therapy" in psychiatric writing is admirable. In *The Door of Serenity* he demonstrates exquisite sensibility in regard to his schizophrenic patient's graphic expression; here and in *Shapes of Sanity* his remarks show that he knows the difference between good art and bad. But in both books it becomes clear that his understanding of sublimation and the creative process as a whole is not equal to the worthy task he set himself.

The Role of Sublimation

Though many artists, art therapists and art educators do not agree, I believe that only on the basis of sublimation can the function of art and the full potential of art therapy be adequately understood. In sublimation, as Kramer uses the term, "instinctual behavior is replaced by a social act in such a manner that this change is experienced as a victory of the ego. . . . Artistic sublimation consists in the creation of visual images for the purpose of communicating to a group very complex material which would not be available for communication in any other form. . . . Every work of art contains a core of conflicting drives which give it life and determine form and content to a large degree."[9]

Too often sublimation is talked about loosely, as if it were the fruit of a benign deceit practiced by parents, teachers, and therapists upon unsuspecting children and patients — a harmless dissipation of steam that might otherwise cause an explosion. The steam of instinctual energy is indeed dissipated in neurotic symptoms; in sublimation this same energy drives

---

[7] Another psychiatrist, H. Azima, striving for precise terminology, contributes to our embarrassment of verbal riches. He prefers "projective therapy" to his own earlier "analytic art therapy" to designate an aspect of *Dynamic Occupational Therapy*. Diseases of the Nervous System, Monograph Supplement, 1961. Vol. 22, No. 4.

[8] *Shapes of Sanity*, pp. 4, 453-464.

[9] *Op. cit.*, pp. 12-16.

an engine that does useful work. The metaphor is, of course, too mechanical; but labor is an unescapable part of the creative process, in science and in art as in life itself. The marvel is that out of inevitable inner conflict, out of the same primeval forces so easily turned to violence and destruction, springs man's capacity for civilized living and the greatest cultural achievement.

The situation is not entirely within our control: art itself refuses to stay within the rigid boundaries that Meares and even Meijering set for it. Meares observes that clay modeling integral to psychotherapy often provokes intense anxiety. Elsewhere plastic expression is, he says, always safe and pleasant, relationships with auxiliary therapists are always positive, after the first try patients always look forward with eager delight to using art materials. In my experience it just doesn't happen that way. I will also wager that in "creative therapy" new self-awareness sometimes develops, whether or not Dr. Meijering wishes it so, whether or not the deep unconscious content of paintings is interpreted. The "how" and the "what" of expression in art simply cannot be torn asunder.

More readily subject to choice and regulation is the question of who should do what in the area of intensive, analytically oriented therapy mediated by the expressive use of paint and clay. I think it is easier for art therapists and psychiatrists to divide and share this moot territory in practice than in theory. There are enough art materials to go round; Dr. Stern can use them in his psychoanalytic practice and nobody reading his papers could possibly mistake him for an art therapist. Margaret Naumburg is not only an art therapist but a psychologist; she is equipped for a kind of practice few, if any, other art therapists now qualify for. In institutions many patterns of collaboration between art therapists, psychiatrists, and psychologists have been developed and continue to evolve. Thus art therapists step over the border into Dr. Meijering's "expressive therapy," playing a more or less central role under the supervision of psychiatrists.

Stern points out that the primitive, pictorial form of thinking used in therapeutic painting is alien to the ego; this arouses the resistance not only of the neurotic patient but of the analyst. It is 36 years since Nolan D. C. Lewis described this auxiliary technique,[10] ten years since Stern offered more detailed exposition, yet its use by psychoanalysts has not spread like wildfire. Perhaps the art therapist can rush in where the analyst fears to tread; regression to preverbal modes of thought is not as alien to the artist's ego as to the intellectual's. Art therapists may, therefore, be of service to psychiatrists who do not find non-verbal communication techniques congenial, even when the art materials and processes used are so simple that no specialized help would appear to be called for.

Collaboration between psychoanalysts and art therapists, working separately with the same patients, occurs and perhaps will increase as qualified art therapists become available. Sometimes associative work begun with the art therapist is carried further in sessions with the doctor.

---

[10] *Op. cit.*

A few accounts have been published[11] but not much has yet been told about how the therapists handle problems that arise in their relationship with each other.

Art therapists defining their own role are naturally less apt than psychiatrists to atomize the creative process or try to fit it into a strait-jacket. To Naumburg, the often embattled pioneer, we shall always be deeply indebted. Starting more than 20 years ago to survey the boundaries of newly explored territory, she had to distinguish sharply between her own sensitive, dynamic procedures and the stultifying misuses of art materials all too common both in occupational therapy and (despite much enlightened theory) in art education. As Naumburg's practice evolved, so did her theory. From the treatment of behavior problem children in a mental hospital, she moved on to work with psychotic adults, and later into the treatment of neurotic patients outside the institutional setting. Gradually she put less emphasis on sublimation, more on bringing unconscious material into awareness by analytic procedures. More and more emphatically she warns that premature concern with artistic achievement is bound to interfere with maximum therapeutic exploitation of "spontaneous art expression."

Two Approaches to Analytically Oriented Therapy

Both Naumburg and Kramer base their formulations on psychoanalytic theory. They are generalizing, however, from two very different kinds of experience. While Naumburg worked mainly with individuals, or with groups in a sharply circumscribed setting, Kramer found ways to make art a living, profoundly civilizing force in a community of disturbed delinquent boys. She did this by being "at once artist, therapist, and teacher," by developing in breadth and depth the aspect of art therapy that Naumburg only touched on in her earlier work. Emphasizing that the process of sublimation is the art therapist's main field of action, she is at pains to differentiate his role from that of psychologists and psychotherapists who use drawings and paintings as an aid in diagnosis and therapy. Psychiatric procedures where "artistic values are of secondary importance" are not, according to Kramer, art therapy.

By Naumburg's recent definitions, Kramer is an art teacher rather than an art therapist. Into Kramer's ideological scheme, Naumburg fits as a psychotherapist, not an art therapist. This is an extreme statement of the cleavage between those art therapists who operate near the peripheral area of psychotherapy at the one side, and those who operate near the peripheral

---

[11] See for example Florence Cane, *The Artist in Each of Us;* New York, Pantheon Books, 1951, pp. 303-368.

Hanna Y. Kwiatkowska and Seymour Perlin, *A Schizophrenic Patient's Response in Art Therapy;* U. S. Dept. of Health, Education, and Welfare, U. S. Government Printing Office, 1960.

Margaret Naumburg and Janet Caldwell, *The Use of Spontaneous Art in Analytically Oriented Group Therapy of Obese Women;* Acta Psychotherapeutica, Basel (Switzerland) and New York, Supplement to Vol. 7, 1959.

area of art education at the other. When representatives of the two trends meet they are apt to treat each other and each other's ideas with a rather gingerly politeness, so that it is hard to tell where catholic acceptance leaves off and veiled difference about important convictions begins. Yet for all their serious and overt disagreement, even between two such strong personalities as Naumburg and Kramer the conflict in practice is not absolute.

Naumburg points out that patients with no art experience except their work with her sometimes develop a capacity for producing aesthetically satisfying forms.[12] There is good reason for this; projecting "spontaneous images" is as significant to creative art education as to analytically oriented art therapy. Naumburg gives way to a patient's demand for direct instruction in picture-making only when she feels this is necessary to keep the therapeutic process in motion. But she has willingly undertaken to help artists liberate, through art therapy, their blocked creative capacity, and has developed special methods of dealing with this difficult problem.[13]

Kramer as art therapist understands the need for accepting sterile constriction and temporary regression in painting that no art teacher need tolerate. In her own practice, art became an integral and important part of the therapeutic milieu. Often artistic experience directly complemented individual psychotherapy, by bringing unconscious material closer to the surface, and by providing an area of symbolic living wherein changes were tried out, gains deepened and cemented.

Naumburg's art therapy and Kramer's art therapy meet the criteria set forth at the end of this paper. I want to underline that the selection of Naumburg and Kramer as spokesmen is mine. There are art therapists, some of them doing excellent work, who would reject their formulations for the very reason that I find them adequate: that is, their basis in psychoanalytic understanding.

Unanswered Questions

Several topics are so closely related to the subject of this paper that their omission calls for a word of comment. One of these is the relationship, actual and potential, between art therapy and occupational therapy; another is the art therapist's role in the use of free art expression to assist psychiatric diagnosis. The diagnostic value of patients' art products is widely acknowledged; the art therapist's part in handling such material, has not, as far as I know, received a great deal of attention. This could well be the subject for another paper. I believe also that the area where art and occupational therapies come close together can be discussed more

---

[12] See *Schizophrenic Art: Its Meaning in Psychotherapy;* N. Y., Grune & Stratton, 1950, p. 37; and *Psychoneurotic Art: Its Function in Psychotherapy,* pp. 6-7.

[13] See *The Power of the Image: Symbolic Projections in Art Therapy;* (catalog) Annual Meeting of the American Psychiatric Association, 1960.

profitably after the newer discipline has taken more steps to map out its own territory.

Two other important questions have been implied but can scarcely be answered here. First, what kinds of patients are more apt to benefit from art therapy than from other available means of treatment? An adequate answer depends on more exhaustive investigation and formulation than has yet been undertaken. Such investigations should lead eventually to refinement in the choice of art therapy media and methods best suited to the needs and capacities of the individual patient.

Last of all, the definition of art therapy is intimately intertwined with the definition of art therapists. Who are they? How did they get to be what they are? If we were in a position to start training art therapists, what disciplines would we ask them to undergo? I hope that this paper will stimulate thinking and writing along these lines.

Synthesis

Throughout this discussion I have been indicating dissatisfaction with definitions that seem to me too narrow to cover functions that are and should continue to be fulfilled by art therapists. I believe the realm of art therapy should be so charted as to accommodate endeavors where neither the term art nor the term therapy is stretched so far as to have no real meaning. This implies well-defended boundaries (some day we may be strong enough to take the offensive) separating art therapy from all misuses of art material that are basically anti-art. Some other practices not in themselves noxious can be called "therapy" only by misplaced courtesy; these I shall first attempt to designate and exclude.

Therapeutic procedures are those designed to assist favorable changes in personality or in living that will outlast the session itself. The vagueness of this statement is not accidental. When we talk about cause and effect, art therapists are in the same boat as the rest of psychiatry — mostly at sea. If favorable changes occur we don't know exactly how much an aesthetically valid painting or how much a dramatic new spoken insight did or didn't have to do with it.

We do know that therapy aims at "favorable changes in personality or in living." Therefore, specialized learning that leaves the core of the personality untouched is not part of therapy as we are here using the term, even though mastery of specific skills has an important place in rehabilitation. Thus, formal art instruction that stresses technique, instruction not guided by understanding of the whole personality's needs, has its own place but that place is not in art therapy.

Therapy aims, we have said, at a relatively durable effect. In this it is distinguished from activities designed to offer only distraction from inner conflict, activities whose benefits are therefore at best momentary. The art therapist often must tolerate defensive or escapist uses of art materials, but this is never his goal. In some so-called recreational uses of art materials, on the other hand, such superficial satisfaction of immediate wishes is actively encouraged. Such programs are not art therapy. We can go further, and say that the use of art materials in them creates needless confusion, builds special resistances, and is not even very effective (a pack of cards would generally serve better).

Finally the definition of art therapy hinges on the definition of art. The psychological forces and mechanisms involved in artistic creation are closely akin to those that underlie the development of human personality as a whole; they are no less complex, no easier to describe. Nevertheless I must offer a very brief statement about what is essential to art activity. **Its motive power comes from within the personality; it is a way of bringing order out of chaos — chaotic feelings and impulses within, the bewildering mass of impressions from without. It is a means to discover both the self and the world, and to establish a relation between the two. In the complete creative process, inner and outer realities are fused into a new entity.**

The spontaneous projections encouraged in therapy-oriented art therapy are not art in the complete sense, but neither are they anti-art. They are vital fragments of the essential raw material from which art may evolve. (This helps explain both the immediate fascination of much "psychiatric art" and its ultimately thin, boring character.)

Concern with the visible world may also set the creative process in motion. In this process the self gives form to material in order to grasp some aspect of reality; subject and object are alike indispensable. (This explains why photographic imitation has not even a brief flicker of vitality.)

If exact reproduction is set up as an ideal, then even the great art of drawing can be perverted into anti-art. American business genius has perfected special media whereby the element of choice is eliminated and anti-art is guaranted. Ceramic moulds, for example, which are an old invention, have been brought to new heights of vulgarity and ugliness. Kit-craft has drained the life and meaning from many of the great traditional media. With numbered paintings it appears that the ultimate in by-passing and falsifying the creative process has been achieved — unless invention beyond the imagination of a mere art therapist is still in store for us.

The proportions of art and of therapy in art therapy may vary within a wide range. The completion of the artistic process may at times be sacrificed to more immediate goals. Stereotyped, compulsive work used to ward off dangerous emotions must sometimes be permitted. Communication and insight may take priority over development of art expression. On the other hand, where no fruitful consolidation of insight can be foreseen, the exposure of conflicts may be deliberately avoided in favor of artistic achievement. But anything that is to be called art therapy must genuinely partake of both art and therapy.

*Therapy Is Not Enough: The Contribution of Art to General Hospital Psychiatry**

ELINOR ULMAN

If we use the word therapy to designate anything that does people good, we have to hope that it's enough, because what else is there? In calling my paper "Therapy is not enough" I am thinking of therapy as more narrowly defined, i.e., psychotherapy which depends largely on verbal exchange. The kind of art therapy where the art work is regarded primarily as a springboard for the patient's verbal association falls within the latter definition. Though it undoubtedly has a place in general hospital psychiatry, I have two reasons for stressing aspects that depend more strictly on the nature of our medium, *art.* First, therapy aiming at verbally expressed insights mediated by art is more often spoken and written about, and is therefore more widely understood. Second, I believe the arts can make a contribution that nothing else

---

*This article and the discussion which follows it are based on material presented in January 1966 at a symposium, "Art Therapy and General Hospital Psychiatry," which took place in Boston, Massachusetts. The symposium's sponsors were the Harvard Medical School Psychiatry Service at Boston City Hospital; the Massachusetts Association for Mental Health; and the Northern New England District Branch of the American Psychiatric Association.

can, and this *unique* value lies partly outside the area where art therapy and verbal psychotherapy so largely overlap.

When I speak of general hospitals I refer of necessity to my own experience in a 200-bed psychiatric unit of the city hospital of the District of Columbia, which is also a teaching hospital. In essence it is a receiving hospital. This is where the courts send men and women accused of crime to determine whether they are capable of taking part in their own legal defense; the juvenile court refers some of the children who come before it accused of crime or merely declared by their parents to be "beyond control"; the police bring would-be suicides, alcoholics in the d.t.'s, and others whose behavior suggests acute mental illness; custodial and correctional institutions for children send those whose behavior appears bizarre; and in recent years the hospital has been required to provide a treatment program for narcotics addicts.

However, a majority of its patients enter voluntarily. Many of them stay only a few weeks; of these, some are discharged back to the community, with or without outpatient follow-up, and others, clearly in need of long-term hospitalization, are moved to Federal or State mental hospitals. A few stay for several months of short-term treatment, and a still smaller number are kept for about a year of intensive treatment because they have been selected as teaching cases. Then there is always the tiny minority who somehow get lost in the disposition mill and remain for many months because nobody has decided what to do about them.

While this description would by no means fit the psychiatry departments of some other general hospitals, one thing about this particular psychiatry service is, I believe, typical. It is now in a state of transition, in the course of being transformed into a Community Mental Health Center. The outlines for its future are not yet entirely clear, but the general concepts on which it will one day operate are fairly well defined. For part of the city it will provide comprehensive mental health services, including not only full-time residential care but day-hospital service for some patients, night-hospital only for others, and outpatient clinic treatment both as follow-up to residential care and for patients who may never need hospitalization.

Such plans are a sign of widespread awareness that traditional services must be radically changed to meet more effectively the needs of the thousands who come to general hospitals for psychiatric help. The idea of comprehensive services offered by single, relatively small units close to the homes of patients is considered promising both in cities and throughout State mental hospital systems.

No new administrative setup will by itself bridge the gap between the many mental patients who belong to the working class and have limited education, and the psychiatric residents in training, most of whom are preparing for practice with middle-class patients. Many training hospitals traditionally designed their programs with first consideration given to the doctors' needs. Today there is enormous pressure toward resolving this dilemma in favor of the patients, but to do so will demand major changes of attitude and many modifications of treatment method. Possibly those who understand both dynamic psychology and the artistic process are particularly well equipped to take part in this formidable undertaking.

New Therapeutic Approaches

Freud himself foresaw that psychoanalytic *techniques* could not be used with the masses of the mentally ill. Analytic *insights* can, however, reveal other ways of tackling the massive problem of mental illness—and the search for applicable techniques is the immediate concern of all the mental health disciplines. I believe that analytic *principles* will provide the key, and these principles are not discredited by the many mistaken attempts that have been made to apply psychoanalytic methods inappropriately.

Like other members of the psychiatric team, art therapists have contributed their share of unhappy examples. I have good reason to look with sympathy on the first-year resident intrigued by the textbook-like verbal outpourings of semi-literate schizophrenics well entrenched in their psychoses; as a neophyte in general hospital art therapy I too was misled into false hopes of dynamically oriented therapeutic victories. Schizophrenic patients are also very obliging about producing spontaneous pictorial imagery from the unconscious, and it is only natural for the beginner to believe that this can somehow be translated into conscious insights that will in turn have a favorable influence on behavior and mood. It takes a while to learn that the psychotic patient may rather need our help in building defenses against this wealth of unconscious material that threatens to overwhelm him.

Freud, of course, is rather strong medicine, so the revisionists have had their day, mixing Freud with water and adding sugar to taste. Until recently it was, however, customary to acknowledge that Freud's thinking was the source of all our modern understanding of psychology. But today it is stylish to say that Freud is old hat, that psychoanalysis has proved useless as a therapeutic technique. It is not altogether clear what we're supposed to go forward to, or back to, and it is not from this anti-Freudian direction that I have heard voices crying in the wilderness. The men who are searching out and trying out imaginative new ways to meet the psychiatric problems of our day are not only thoroughly grounded in their understanding of psychoanalytic principles, but loyal to them. I think of psychologists such as Fritz Redl and Frank Riessman and psychiatrists such as Philip S. Wagner. While these men have not addressed themselves specifically to the problems of either art therapy or general hospital psychiatry, they have begun to explore the same area of community mental health where we must all try to function.

Riessman and Wagner (working separately) have demonstrated a twofold approach to the problem of making psychiatric services effective with the masses.[1] On the one hand, therapists must modify techniques that were developed in practice with middle-class intellectuals. In one sense they must be more directive, in another they must be less direct. The working-class patient, on the other hand, must be taught to modify his assumptions. He must learn, among other things, that change does not just come from the outside, and he must accept the non-directive nature of psychotherapy to some degree. Investigators see possibilities for compromise and rapprochement in techniques where words and concepts are subordinated to nonverbal and motor activities. They observe that much "insightless change" takes place, and conclude that emphasis on insight, free association, and resistance analysis should be reduced. Emphasis should be placed rather on catharsis and emotional reeducation in its broadest sense.

Margaret Naumburg's recent teaching is in line with these new trends; we find that she is still the pioneer of our profession. She now works with students from various disciplines, helping them to understand graphic communication so that they can react constructively to its content, implied as well as overt. People so equipped are in a position to offer treatment that stops short of deep analysis, but still produces insightless change. Such techniques can be of enormous value in the general hospital, since they may meet the needs of patients who cannot be reached by purely verbal approaches.

Riessman and Wagner both emphasize the value of drawing patients' families quickly into the therapeutic endeavor. Hanna Yaxa Kwiatkowska, director of the art therapy program at the National Institute of Mental Health, has developed effective methods for involving families quickly in purposeful joint art activity. Investigators working with blue-collar patients have found that "diagnosis should take place concomitantly with preliminary treatment," and that meetings from the start should be "cathartic, supportive, and informal." Mrs. Kwiatkowska's approach eminently meets these criteria. Further possibilities for broad applications of family art therapy are seen in the work of Rachel Levine, a social worker, who has taken to multiple-problem homes simple games, cards, and clay, and engaged family members in activity. Conflicts that arise are discussed and worked with right on the spot.

We have come a long way from the era when, as Fritz Redl has remarked, reaction to fantasy was considered somehow deep while reaction to behavior was supposed to be somehow superficial. Today most of us would agree with Redl that this idea is "crazy." Another writer, June Mazer, noted that "according to the literature of the 1930's and 1940's nothing in a psychiatric hospital seemed to occur on a conscious level." [2] During the same period, says Redl,

---

[1] The ideas cited here and below were expressed by these two speakers at a panel discussion on "Mental Health Programs in Industrial Settings" held at the 1963 annual meeting of the American Orthopsychiatric Association. Direct quotations are from mimeographed materials distributed by Dr. Riessman.

[2] *Producing Plays in the Psychiatric Hospital,* unpublished M.A. dissertation, The Catholic University of America, 1964.

a mistaken view prevailed that for institutionalized patients the therapy hour was crucial, while the other 23 hours of the day were of little significance.

By now most observers acknowledge that the attitudes of auxiliary personnel can have as important an influence as the doctor's skills. Furthermore, the therapy hour's effectiveness depends on the quality of life during those other 23 hours of the day. Edith Kramer has demonstrated in several treatment homes and hospitals what therapeutically oriented art programs can offer the younger members of the very population we must serve.

The importance of art in the therapeutic milieu should scarcely need arguing, but it does. Only in our own very recently developed industrial society have the arts lost their place as a normal, taken-for-granted part of human social experience. It is strange that some of the best chances for restoring this vital element should occur in those places where the poor and the emotionally sick are segregated. By making art activity available to those who can use it and works of art available to the entire institutional population (staff as well as patients), the therapist whose medium is art makes a far-reaching contribution. Some artists are, I believe, rightly attracted to careers in art therapy because here there is a freer opportunity to nourish genuine artistic development than in most ordinary teaching jobs, where art is apt to be forced into a curriculum strait-jacket, reduced to artificial units of design, illustrations for courses in social studies, providing decorations for school parties, and the like.

Art Therapy in a General Hospital

The absence of precedents and specific requirements does not make for absolutely smooth sailing. Rehabilitation centers and mental hospitals are not immune to the false artistic standards of the world around them. At D. C. General Hospital it took some years to get away from the occasional talent-and-hobby show, which usually included competition for prizes, and substitute a constant, shifting display throughout the hospital of genuinely expressive work by both gifted and ordinary patients. Doctors who feared that work by the depressed might be depressing, or thought that a psychiatric ward was the one place in Washington where psychopathology must not be displayed on walls were won over by the vitality of the work and the patients' often surprisingly charitable responses to each other's efforts.

Some narrower contributions of art therapy are perhaps more generally understood. In my own first years of trials and errors in a general hospital, diagnosis was the first area where I began to find a clear connection between my own work and that of the medical staff. I had to learn to formulate my impressions succinctly enough so that people unaccustomed to looking at pictures could focus on the revelations contained in this kind of material. The auxiliary therapist must learn to speak to psychiatrists in their own language and at the same time maintain the special character of insights derived from his own area of expertness.

Later, at the urging of the chief psychologist, I developed a procedure for collecting data in a single session, to illuminate not only pathology but the resources of the whole personality.[3] Analyses of such material, based on dynamic psychological concepts, will, I believe, continue to have a place in general hospital psychiatry. A similar method, expanded and refined for use with families, has been developed by Mrs. Kwiatkowska.

Another service which may have potential usefulness elsewhere was a series of training conferences on "Communication through Art" for first-year psychiatric residents. After a few lectures about art in diagnosis and treatment, I invited the first group of residents to discuss paintings of patients —and drew an almost complete blank. The young doctors didn't see any relationship between the pictures their patients painted and the patients as they knew them from other sources. It gradually came to me that they didn't see the pictures at all. Therefore I tried having them paint and look at their own and each other's work, and talk about it. This enabled them to *look* at pictures and respond to what they saw there. For many good reasons I tried to prevent these meetings from turning into group therapy sessions, but such is the power of art that, in the view of an occasional resident, therapy did sometimes occur despite my best efforts.

While we occasionally held individual sessions for patients in intensive treatment, this was only a minor part of our work. More often we worked with groups, but mainly in the sense that there were a lot of people in the room at the same time. Individuals worked at many different levels, on their own, and we tried to meet their various needs.

Patients came on referral, some eager, some reluctant. We exercised a certain amount of pressure to try three art sessions on the doctor's say so. Sometimes unlikely looking candidates became deeply absorbed in very expressive work, but a few others who did not become involved dropped out, so that a certain amount of self-selection took place. I believe that this kind of art therapy will find a prominent place in the community mental health services that are gradually taking shape.

Organized group art therapy, where patients make pictures and then discuss the work and its implications, can only succeed if it is possible to compose reasonably homogeneous groups which are likely to stay together for a predictable period of time. In my general hospital experience these basic requirements could seldom be met. We also found that working class adults do not readily make use of the conventional organized discussion period. I did learn something, however, from our attempt to develop this style of treatment with a group of dope addicts who were for a time a captive audience. They permitted me to cherish briefly the illusion that I was rather clever at getting psychiatric ideas across in the common tongue. I was cured

---

[3] For details see "A New Use of Art in Psychiatric Diagnosis." *Bulletin of Art Therapy,* Vol. 4, No. 3, April 1965.

of that notion when one of the men said, "Maybe you don't think we get what you're saying but we do; sometimes you talk like a psychiatrist." A younger man agreed, very seriously saying, "That's *right*. What she say don't make sense."

One perceptive observer remarked that the art room was the one place in the hospital where the patients had a chance to show their craziness a little, where they could relax, and be for the moment accepted, pathology and all. Under present trends patients are being asked to give up their symptoms very fast; soon after admission they must behave in a socially acceptable manner or be tranquilized into a stupor. Art therapists too have limits as to the amount of crazy *behavior* they can tolerate, but it is easier for them to accept frankly sick *art* than false artistic attempts to pretend health.

Teacher or Therapist?

Possibly my emphasis on particular aspects of art therapy will be better understood in light of the way my own career and ideas evolved. When I started working in a psychiatric clinic in the early 1950's, I envisioned myself as a potential art *teacher,* not as an art *therapist*. Guided by the new approaches to art education enunciated by such writers as Florence Cane [4] and Henry Schaefer-Simmern,[5] I wanted to try to be the kind of art teacher I wished I had had. Margaret Naumburg stood alone at that time as the spokesman and advocate of psychoanalytically oriented art therapy. I did not feel qualified to follow in her footsteps, but I was pleased and excited when some of the clinic patients led me a little way along that road. A much larger number of patients, however, did not try to translate the symbolic content of their pictures into words, yet it seemed to me that they too were getting something valuable from their work in art that nothing else could supply. People began to call me an art therapist and I even began to call myself one, but I was not sure that the title fitted me.

It was eight years later that Edith Kramer's book *Art Therapy in a Children's Community* [6] was published. In addition to describing the development of art as a significant feature of a therapeutic milieu, this author analyzed from the vantage point of Freudian theory the place of the arts in the emotional economy both of the individual and of society. The subtle relationship between psychoanalytic and artistic insights began to come clear to me, and I was provided with theoretical backing for my unarticulated feeling that my functioning as an artist-teacher and as an art therapist were not so far apart.

---

[4] *The Artist in Each of Us*. New York, Pantheon Books, 1951.

[5] *The Unfolding of Artistic Activity*. Berkeley and Los Angeles, The University of California Press, 1948.

[6] Springfield, Ill., Charles C. Thomas, 1958.

In 1961 I attempted my own synthesis of the two main trends in psychoanalytically grounded art therapy represented by Naumburg and Kramer.[7] In this present paper I am emphasizing the aspect of therapy that depends on values inherent in art, values that are the same for sick and well, for professional artist and for serious amateur. Therefore I will quote at this point my own already published formulation of what is essential to art activity: "Its motive power comes from within the personality; it is a way of bringing order out of chaos—chaotic feelings and impulses within, the bewildering mass of impressions from without. It is a means to discover both the self and the world, and to establish a relation between the two. In the complete creative process, inner and outer realities are fused into a new entity."

Once I put it more simply, when I was sharing the confusion of a group of acutely psychotic men on a ward at D. C. General Hospital. Some of them had been asking me the purpose of their work with me, and my feeble answers about the potentialities of art therapy were falling on sterile ground. One of them said, "Miss Ulman, what is art, anyway?" "Art," I answered, "is the meeting ground of the world inside and the world outside." Suddenly things began to fall into place; patients who had insisted that they were only doodling began to find personal meaning in what they were doing. Although the outlines can still be seen only dimly, incidents such as this confirm my belief that through art which by its nature contains many opposites—among them action and contemplation, impulse and control—ways can be found to bridge the gap between middle-class therapy and working-class patients.

When art is understood in this way, the subtlety of the art teacher's role becomes evident. I have often been baffled by hospital visitors who asked, "Do you teach them art or do you let them express themselves?" Apparently many people assume that art excludes self-expression and self-expression excludes art. Unfortunately there are some teachers and therapists who give lip service to both and understand neither. For example, the staff of one art therapy installation assured me that the purpose of all the work was self-expression. On the walls there were, among other things, about 30 copies of the Mona Lisa hand-painted with oil paint. It is almost impossible to prevent self-expression altogether; there were simple schizophrenic Mona Lisas, paranoid Mona Lisas, delinquent Mona Lisas, and Mona Lisas ranging in intelligence from deficient to superior. The few pictures in the room not copied from art reproductions or magazine illustrations were more-or-less slick abstract smears. Such an experience is sad but it provides convincing evidence that a therapist who understands art and art teaching really *does* make a difference in the patients' expressive range.

[7] "Art Therapy: Problems of Definition."

Figure 1

The true *teacher* of art, then, must find ways to help people set their own goals and use their own vision. As a *therapist* he will offer technical help only when it is both needed and wanted. Paradoxically, it is only those who know a great deal about art and about art teaching who know how to not teach art at the wrong time or in the wrong way.

Two Illustrative Cases

In my experience with art therapy at a public clinic and in a general hospital, patients did gain insights: what happened in their art work was spontaneously appreciated by them as a sample of living. Insights were thus derived from experience of an artistic process more often than from verbal translation of symbolic imagery.

Janet, for example, was an outpatient at an alcoholic clinic, intelligent and well-read. She was sophisticated enough to share some common misapprehensions; she started in art therapy by debating whether she should "study art" or "try to express" herself. She quickly proved to herself how false this distinction was.

Figure 1 is her first painting. She was severely critical of it, thought it looked like a candy-box cover, saw it as over-precise in some areas, too vague in others. Most of all she was distressed that in spite of all her reading in the theory of perspective she had still failed to depict depth.

Figure 2 is the first picture Janet made by projecting imagery into a scribble. Working intuitively she had achieved the three-dimensionality that eluded all her studying and plotting. She called the mermaid-like figure a "sky-maid"; but her interest in the picture's symbolic content was subordinated to her exhilaration over its formal success. She said, "Now for the first time I really understand what my therapist means when she says I must learn to trust my feelings."

Figure 2

Figure 3 shows how Janet's new-found freedom carried over when she abandoned the scribble technique. The cold, lonely park certainly partakes of self-expression, and it is clear that Janet at the same time had learned a good deal about artistic technique.

The next picture was painted by Margaret, a schizophrenic patient in remission, who had spent her early childhood on a farm, then grown up in an orphanage. She had very little formal education and showed no signs of unusual intelligence. Figure 4 shows one of her childhood stereotypes, the only thing she brought to the renewed experience of using art materials. She was probably never aware of the reverse perspective (tiny automobiles in the foreground, immense birds in the sky) which may have been symptomatic of her illness, but she later became very critical of rigidity in her work.

A few weeks and many drawings later she achieved a delicate flower painting, Figure 5. Ecstatically she declared, "It's the first thing I've ever done in my life that isn't *neat.*" She told how when she was a waitress she and her colleagues drove each other frantic because she became so upset if the salts and peppers she had lined up in a certain way got disarranged.

Figure 3

Figure 6 shows some of the expressive ability Margaret developed. She did not recognize the pathetic self-portraiture in the poor, exposed goldfish with their paranoid eyes, but she was proud of the originality and effectiveness of such pictures, made without models or assistance. "I wish my ex-husband could see these pictures; he never thought I could do anything," she said. "He took my mind away from me. But it started in the orphanage. In the orphanage everything was thought for us, even time. I have no meaning of time."

Margaret was discharged from the hospital with plans for placement in a vocational rehabilitation program, but the slow unwinding of red tape left her idle and she was too fragile to stand this period of waiting. She returned to the hospital in an acute paranoid schizophrenic state. Figure 7 was painted in response to my request for her to make a picture for a research project we happened to be conducting at that time.

As she worked she took purposeful measures to prevent this picture from being what she called "too proportionate" and to make it expressive of the "softness" which, she yearned to believe, underlay her "hard" exterior. The final product is in some ways less clearly symptomatic than her first picture, made when she was in remission. Margaret also retained some of the autonomy she had found, perhaps for the first time, in her earlier art therapy experience. At first she refused my request that she draw, and only acceded at the last minute, explaining that she first had to search her mind

Figure 4

to decide whether she would be doing this only because I asked or because she really wanted to.

Thus we see that Janet learned from painting a little about the value of her feelings, and Margaret caught through her art a glimpse of her own worth and capability. For neither of them did the meaning of art therapy

Figure 5

See also color plate I.

Figure 6

depend upon analysis of imagery spontaneously projected from the unconscious. Undoubtedly, however, both of them had been able to use energy that came from unconscious sources, and had exercised more spontaneity than they were yet able to muster elsewhere in life. This is the nature of successful art work for anybody, anywhere, any time. On a conscious level

Figure 7

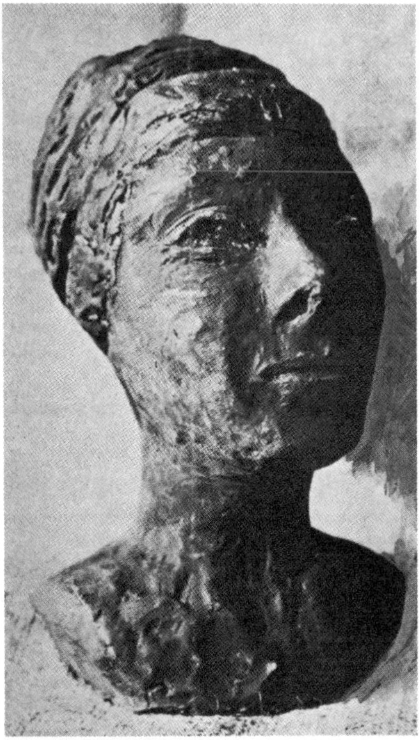

Figure 8

they were trying to make the best pictures they could, and I was supporting their efforts to the best of my ability.

Future Prospects for Art Therapy

In looking to the future it appears that long-term hospitalization is on the wane. The candidates for sustained treatment with art therapy are apt to be outpatients, and their attendance will be largely voluntary. Art therapists need not expect to cater to all comers. They should encourage self-selection, acknowledging that an important part of their contribution will be to offer the same kind of satisfactions that *good* art classes offer the normal population.

Art therapists can stand ready to carry out many recommendations made by the pioneers of psychiatric help for the working class, who point to the urgency of offering services that meet real needs and to the useful effect of deflecting pathology into endeavors giving social returns and satisfactions. They point out also that involvement in problems and activities outside the self may bring about rather than follow internal change.

Should we then merely try to duplicate art classes already existing in the community? The answer is no. The well-equipped art *therapist* should be able to offer more than an art *teacher*, however expert and sound, is able to. The therapist's understanding of sick people, what you can demand of them and what you cannot, should enlighten a myriad of split-second decisions. The therapist will know when conventional art school methods make sense, when they do not, and much more.

An example can be drawn from my own well-intentioned ignorance, still recalled with pain. In my early days at D. C. General Hospital a mentally defective adolescent girl had drawn the same house, the same tree, the same sun perhaps 100 times. It was not wrong of me to try to interest her in change, to suggest that she might show what was going on inside the house as well as outside it. But when she persisted with her formula, some of my irritation at my own failure spilled over onto her, and I cannot forget her look of hurt bewilderment. Had I recognized the meaning of her security operation, which I would even then have accepted easily enough from a younger child, my behavior would not have been destructive.

Another illustrative experience is probably common to many therapists. Their knowledge of developmental stages tells them that several children messing with clay and water should be handled in entirely different ways. For a compulsively clean child this may be a triumph we should share and applaud. Another child doing the same thing may be acting out aggressive impulses and tacitly begging for limits to be set. Yet another may be enjoying an appropriate experience yet ready for encouragement to move on to the stage where he can let the clay take form and shape it expressively.

Here as in the art teaching aspect of art therapy, a little learning may be worse than none. Our understanding must be well digested if it is to inform lightning decisions. Just as it is only the true teacher who knows when and how to teach and when not to, only the therapist deeply versed in psychoanalytic theory knows when to use this knowledge directly, when to hold it in abeyance. Most dangerous is the semi-informed auxiliary therapist who rushes to ape what he thinks psychiatrists do, at the many unsupervised opportunities that occur in institutional settings.

Art Therapy and the Talented Patient

My last illustrations are representative of the occasional patient who in art therapy discovers an extraordinary talent. Kathy is a constant truant, sexually promiscuous, and her slender arms are often covered with fresh scars from self-inflicted wounds. If one looks hard one can see that she is a pretty girl. Usually she is either hidden behind an exaggerated mask of make-up, or goes around looking like a slob.

She was not quite 16 when she made her first work in clay, Figure 8. There is self portrayal here and in the other female heads to be illustrated, but it is portrayal of Kathy the sensitive young artist, not of the faces she

Figure 9

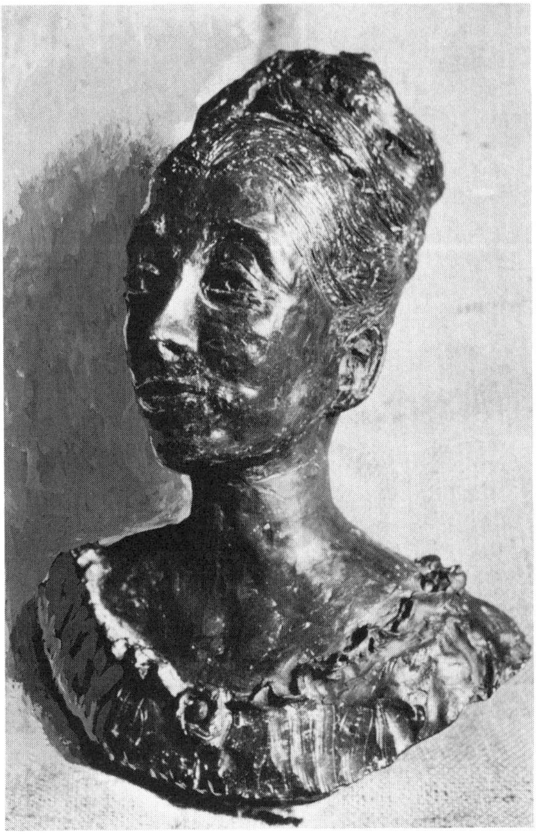

showed the world. Figure 9 is her third work in sculpture; she designated it as the head of a woman about 40 years old.

Kathy never worked from life; in her own phrase, she got her subject "all imagined out" before she started to model. She used people present and a mirror only to check on anatomical detail. Figure 10 demonstrates that her imagination carried well beyond self-portrayal. She asked me to suggest a title for this head and I came up with "The Old Bastard." Kathy liked that but felt that it would not make people respect her work. After checking in the dictionary she accepted our other art therapist's suggestion, "The Old Reprobate." Kathy said he reminded her of a stepfather she had once. She had had many.

Figure 10

Figure 11, her fifth piece of work, again suggests Kathy the artist herself. While she was working she was like Dr. Jekyll and Mr. Hyde—at one moment her face alight as she moved with the natural grace of a born craftsman. A moment later her distorted face might be almost unrecognizable as she snarled obscene threats at a child who teasingly came too near her work.

The art therapists offered Kathy something that nobody else in the hospital could. We were an appreciative but discriminating audience, and able to give the technical help needed to assist the unfolding of an artistic talent infinitely greater than our own.

Kathy's craft work in occupational therapy was in its way as remarkable as her sculpture. Her designs were original and their execution exquisite. Her extraordinary ability was of course not an undiluted blessing; it earned her the envy not only of her peers but of many adult staff members as well. Yet when the young occupational therapist assigned to work with her made a half-hour report on Kathy, she never mentioned a word about Kathy's craft performance. Misguided by her elders, she was so busy trying to practice

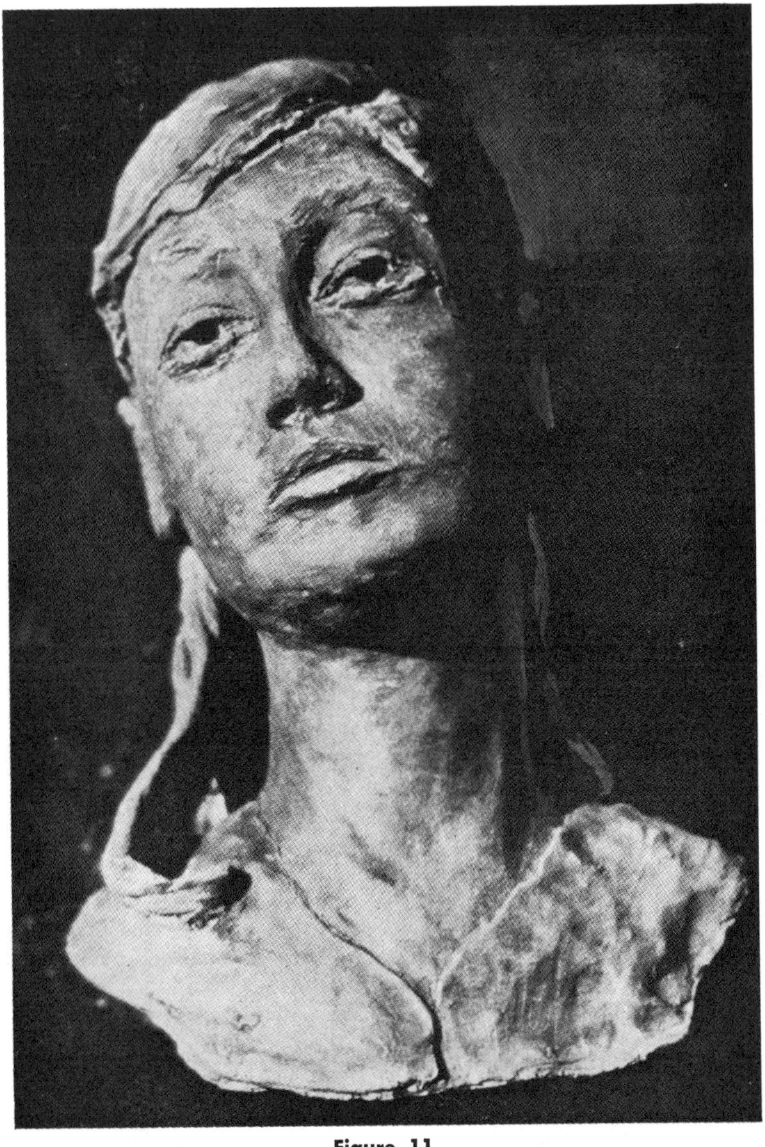

Figure 11

verbal relationship therapy that the significance of the intense relationships Kathy formed to and through the things she created completely escaped her.

Conclusion

Therapists can deserve and gain respect only if they themselves respect their medium. Everybody in a general hospital—doctors, social workers, psychologists, nurses, scrubwomen—can offer patients a chance to *talk*. If we really believe in the value of nonverbal communication, we will not feel like second class citizens when we relate to patients through their work rather than through words.

Some of what patients do with art materials is a direct expression of feeling, which can and at times should be translated directly into words. On those rarer occasions when the artistic process is completed, the artist-patient has created a new form which in some way exemplifies a human process or understanding. It can be *talked about* but it cannot be *translated* into words.

Though I called my paper "therapy is not enough," I am well aware that art is not enough, either. Five years after she painted the sky-maid, Janet still needed psychiatric support, still bewailed her inability to trust her feelings. Margaret's psychotic break was not her first, but it was more severe than any she had previously suffered. Kathy left D. C. General Hospital for a State mental hospital where she did not belong, but her home was impossible, and there was no money to place her elsewhere. She vegetated for a few months, then as usual ran away.

In the community mental health center of the future, there will still be more than enough need to go round, and art therapists of all persuasions should be able to get as large a share of it as they can handle. Trends in psychotherapy and hence in art therapy appear to be toward methods that rely more on experience than on rumination; toward greater tolerance of differences, with less demand that the patient meet the therapist's middle-class standards. Therefore flexibility must stand high among our values; we must be ready to use our diagnostic understanding to make the immediate therapeutic response.

Nevertheless, there will always be some patients amenable to therapy concerned with profound changes in personality, and to treatment methods that rely as much on talking as on doing. Thus there is likely to be a place for each art therapist to use the approach he is best equipped to use, for each to take pride in functioning as effectively as his own peculiar abilities permit.

Our young profession still has a chance to avoid getting caught up in the artificial values of the psychiatric snob system, where talking stands at the top because doctors deal in words. We are perhaps lucky that the system as a whole faces at this moment profound challenges. Art therapists who hold fast to their belief in the power of art may bring a special competence to bear on the problems of our day.

Art and Emptiness: New Problems in Art Education and Art Therapy:

EDITH KRAMER

The fundamental problems of artistic creation are forever the same. Art is always menaced from two sides: primeval chaos and stereotyped order. The balance between the two forces is never static. At any time form may stiffen from a living container of emotions and experience into a dead screen which hides and perverts meaning, or direct inarticulate discharge of passion may break and destroy the form. It is the goal of all creative art teaching to bring about the synthesis of emotional freedom and structured expression. The same principle remains the guiding idea also where creative activities serve more general goals of education, rehabilitation, and therapy. Even though the basic difficulties of art remain the same, specific problems change. Our modern art-teaching methods were created in a struggle against established academic stereotypes of the Victorian age. Since then changing times have brought about new problems. In this article I shall describe certain difficulties in work with underprivileged children and adolescents which seem to touch upon more universal problems of our time and culture.

The Gains of Progressive Art Teaching

The revolutionary discoveries of modern art teaching are based on two main ideas: first, the understanding that children's art develops in a typical and predictable manner. Representation of space, human figures and objects, grows according to inner laws which should not be disturbed by superimposed adult ideas. This discovery freed children from the constraint of having to attempt the impossible: to render the world through the eyes of their adult teachers. It brought about the blossoming of children's art as an independent form. This in turn opened the way to creative work with untutored adults who usually retain child-like ways of representation and can develop only when this primitive style is accepted and allowed to grow and change at its own pace.[1]

The other important discovery, or rather re-discovery, was the recog-

[1]Franz Cizek, *Children's Colored Paper Work;* New York, G. E. Steichert, 1927.
Viktor Lowenfeld, *Creative and Mental Growth;* New York, MacMillan, 1952.
Henry Schaefer-Simmern, *The Unfolding of Artistic Activity;* Berkeley, University of California Press, 1958.

nition of the role of unconscious and preconscious processes in artistic creation. To counteract exclusively intellectual planning, playful activities which can be considered forerunners of art were encouraged. Such exercises helped stimulate greater emotional freedom and imaginative work. Another avenue to greater emotional depth and intensity was opened by exercises in concentration, where outside stimuli were deliberately shut out, and the student concentrated upon inner experiences, memories and moods.[2]

All these approaches, which lead toward greater self-awareness, or help make repressed unconscious material available for creative work, are particularly helpful in work with those emotionally disturbed children and adults who are too preoccupied with their acute conflicts and obsessions to be receptive to impressions and stimulation from the outside. Such persons may become productive when unconscious material belonging to their central emotional problems finds symbolic expression in art. Philosophy and methods of modern art teaching complement and parallel the development of modern psychology and psychotherapy. In this interchange, art teaching has become infinitely more flexible and adaptable to different needs and situations. Creative experiences are today within the reach of almost anyone who is at all receptive to them, no matter what his training, age, or state of physical or mental health may be.

New Stereotypes

No new discovery or method is exempt from the menace of mechanization, perversion into its opposite. The ever-present longing for easy prescriptions, the fear of the unpredictable, only change aspect as times change. It is interesting to observe how methods, developed to stimulate creative work, have been perverted into ways of circumventing and avoiding the creative act.

Let us examine the fate of the scribble first. Originally it had several functions. To begin with, radical departure from stereotyped drawing habits. The student was encouraged to do the forbidden and the childish, to produce random shapes or perhaps express a mood or feeling, but represent no specific object. The second step—finding an image in the scribble—was based on the recognition that images projected on random forms almost invariably touch upon central preconscious and unconscious fantasies. The last phase—completing the image, elaborating the idea—

---

[2]Florence Cane, *The Artist in Each of Us;* New York, Pantheon Books, 1951.

Viktor Lowenfeld, *The Nature of Creative Activity;* New York, Harcourt Brace, 1939.

Margaret Naumburg, *Studies of the "Free" Art Expression of Behavior Problem Children and Adolescents as a Means of Diagnosis and Therapy;* New York, Nervous and Mental Disease Monograph, 1947, 71.

———, *Schizophrenic Art: Its Meaning in Psychotherapy;* New York, Grune & Stratton, 1950.

———, *Psychoneurotic Art: Its Function in Psychotherapy;* New York, Grune & Stratton, 1953.

constituted the creative work proper. Only now was the material brought forth by playful activity, accident and projection, transformed into genuine artistic communication. Free play with paint and other materials had a kindred function. Again the breaking of tabus (getting dirty, wasting material, enjoying primitive, childish pleasures, creation of non-stereotyped configurations, projection of latent fantasies) finally led up to the making of a picture by conscious effort.

If we compare this complex process with the conventional scribble designs that decorate many of our classrooms, we see that the idea has suffered total perversion. To begin with, the scribble is no longer an adventure but routine; no longer created by free rhythmic body movement but by random motions of the hand performed without pleasure or conviction. The second phase—projecting an image into the scribble or identifying with a mood or feeling—is left out entirely. The third step—completion of the image—is replaced by coloring-in the mechanically produced areas. It is busy-work, comparable to the traditional coloring book except that coloring books may stimulate fantasies about the story which is depicted, while the scribble is totally meaningless.

Playful activities with paint and other materials are somewhat less barren. Children are stimulated and excited by the interesting colors or textures they produce, but again the activity stops short of creative work. The children are taught to make patterns by dropping color-saturated strings on paper, by making Rorschach-like color blots, by innumerable failure-proof tricks that assure easy success even to the most unimaginative child. Evolving pictures from these experimentations is not encouraged.

Another element in modern art teaching was the introduction of a greater variety of materials. Using the conventional media, the student found that the expressive possibilities of any medium are infinite (a piece of charcoal, three colors, a lump of clay—each suffices to create a whole world). With the addition of unorthodox materials they learned that one medium can stand for another. Bits of colored tile, paper or cloth may replace paint; sculpture can be created from cardboard, wire, stone or wood as well as from clay.

This education towards artistic economy and resourcefulness has been perverted into a search for novelty. Exploration of the infinite possibilities of each medium is supplanted by superficial acquaintance with a multitude of techniques. Children become greedy for new sensations and are impoverished among a wealth of goods which they have not learned to use creatively.

My description is no doubt one-sided and exaggerated. Art teaching as a whole is more enlightened today than it was 25 years ago. In every society there will be some abuse and perversion of good ideas. However, the specific quality of such perversion is always determined by the basic problems and contradictions of the culture. Our time has brought forth a strikingly new phenomenon. The ancient polarity of the two enemies of art—chaos and stereotype—has been replaced by a composite: stereotyped chaos.

It seems as if the discovery of the role of unconscious processes and primitive, instinctual drives in artistic creation has led to a lack of distinction between cause and effect, a confusion of the source of energy with its end results, based on the misunderstanding and oversimplification of psychoanalytic theory. Let us illustrate the confusion with a present-day fantasy in the Swiftian manner:

On his trip to Laputa, Gulliver inspects the Academy of Prospectors in the land of Balnibarbi. There he meets a scientist-gardener who has come to the following conclusion: No plant life can exist above ground without being fed by roots deep in the earth. Ergo root and flower are the same; indeed because of its dependence on the root, all growth above ground is negligible and worthless. Consequently our gardener decorates his house with roots only, and cuts all sprouting buds as they appear above ground, because their growth might deplete the all important roots. The consequent withering of his roots he combats by ever-increasing vigilance in the destruction of any growth that might still appear in his garden. The desolation and waste he has created are to him signs of new and wondrous developments below the surface.

Like this gardener, modern art educators using the techniques we have described understand something about the inception of creative activities but inhibit their fruition. Common to all these pseudo-art activities is acceptance of primitive, unstructured, playful use of art materials. Regression is accepted, indeed it is induced. This means that one of the necessary conditions for creative work is well provided for.

Temporary regression is a necessary phase in every creative act. The transition between regression and the reintegration of unconscious and preconscious material into ego-controlled creative work is usually fluid and hard to discern. The process becomes dramatically apparent either when repressed unconscious material is recovered so that there is a sudden spurt of inspiration and heightened creative power, or when regression leads to disruption of creative sublimation through direct acting out. When access to preconscious and unconscious material is blocked, the educator or therapist may be justified in inducing controlled regression by the various methods we have described.

Whatever the situation may be, one basic rule is essential to all education and therapy. Stimulation and help towards maturation must be given even while regression is encouraged or tolerated. Acceptance and understanding should never be confused with a deficient standard of values or sense of direction.

Because of failure to make clear distinctions between the function and value of infantile play, aggressive acting out, and creative work, the art activities which are criticized constitute a subtle form of seduction. When the adult abdicates his function as guide and helper in creative maturation, he seems to join forces with the very powers which threaten the child from within. When classroom walls are covered with images of unredeemed chaos, temptation to regress replaces stimulation towards creative communication. The emptiness pervading the art activities and their products tells of the dissolution of inner structure, the depletion of the ego, which is the result of seduction.

At this point we must remark that we are doing grave injustice to teachers and educators. What we describe may be perpetrated in the classroom but it does not originate there. Not just school art, but most of the pseudo-art of our time has the same quality of stereotyped chaos. Emptiness and seduction pervade large areas of our cultural life.

The use of scribble designs or other foolproof ways of manufacturing products that can pass as art work, and attempts to create interest by introducing new art materials, are often the last resort of a desperate teacher confronted with an ever-increasing number of children and adolescents who are empty, bored, and chronically dissatisfied. The fact that these teaching methods feed the very evils which the teacher strives to overcome constitutes a trap in which teacher and students alike are caught.

The art therapist who works with children and adolescents encounters much the same difficulties. While the traditional defenses in drawing and painting such as stereotyped houses, trees and flowers, and copies from magazines, have not disappeared, resistance increasingly takes the form of endlessly repeated scribbles, or aimless, destructive play with paint. It almost seems as though those children who scribble and mess with materials are even a little harder to reach than those who produce traditional stereotypes. This is surprising. Modern art activities, even in their mechanized, stereotyped form are closer to art or at least to the origins of art than are the senseless teachings of the old school. Yet any one who has tried to induce a resistant child of the modern school to develop a picture from a color blot or a scribble, knows that he is often confronted with a wall of incomprehension, a solid unwillingness to make any step in the direction of a personal statement. The resistance seems more unshakable than the old fear of abandoning the safety of the traditional house and tree or the three tulips, for more adventurous work. The question arises: are the difficulties in the art room only a symptom of changes in today's troubled children and adolescents which make them unresponsive to the challenge and appeal of the creative arts?

The Underprivileged Spoiled Child

If we compare today's underprivileged disturbed children of New York City with the children of 10 or 15 years ago, we find a subtle change in the character of the disturbance. Certain qualities exist frequently among the very poor, which we used to associate rather with the emotionally deprived rich child who is brought up by indifferent paid help and offered material goods as a substitute for human relationship: distrust of the motives of adults who make friendly overtures, the conviction that all kindness has ulterior motives, a cynical readiness to exploit this situation, insatiable hunger for material goods and a compulsion to destroy and waste such goods as soon as they are obtained.

This similarity is caused by kindred experiences. Today's neglected unloved children, rich or poor, are brought up, comforted, instructed and amused largely by paid help. They have in the TV entertainer an ever-available slave who will help them to endure loneliness, anxiety, and isolation. In the service of his sponsors the entertainer establishes a pseudo-relationship with the child. He necessarily resorts to ingratiation and seduction since he must please the child and stimulate his desire for more without being able to establish genuine relationship. Even the least perceptive child soon learns to distrust the flattery of TV and knows that the entertainer's statements are full of exaggeration and lies. The neglected child thus learns to depend for comfort on people whom he does not trust.

The experience of being bribed with material goods is also no longer the privilege of the wealthy. Mass bribery directed against all children includes even the destitute. A child who eats breakfast is, for example, supplied with an abundance of toys and trinkets; since these goods are not symbols and tokens of affection but bait, recognized as such by the child, they cannot give satisfaction. Instead their possession stimulates greed, which operates in the interest of the manufacturer.

We see that whenever genuine satisfactions are missing, ersatz is available. As with all flattery such offerings are based on a shrewd understanding of children's needs and of their weaknesses. Often the substitute is almost indistinguishable from the real thing, so that gratification of basic needs, distrust, and disappointment become inextricably mingled.

Today's disturbed underprivileged children and adolescents in our large cities are not only deprived of love, understanding, space to live and play in, and exposed to the brutality of the streets; they have also been bribed, seduced, and left empty. They are in a sense all addicts, dependent on synthetic gratifications which destroy their capacity to seek genuine satisfactions for their emotional needs. Today's delinquent gives the impression of being both deprived and spoiled. He is not only violent and destructive but also capricious, convinced that he can get something for nothing, and that desirable experiences can be had without effort.

The task of rehabilitation has changed. With the diminution of publicly condoned brutality against children, the average underprivileged child is somewhat less afraid of cruelty from the adult in authority. Instead, he suspects his sincerity and sees in him a salesman who will cheat and disappoint him. It no longer suffices to satisfy unfulfilled needs. We have to withdraw injurious ersatz satisfactions. We not only have to prove that we are not monsters and brutes but also that we are not lying salesmen.

Art, Defense, and Maturity

This digression into analysis of change in the character structure of modern city slum children was undertaken because it occurred to us that the trends in the perversion of modern art teaching might have more than one cause. Besides the misinterpretation of psychoanalytic theory and the general tendency of all revolutionary ideas to harden into rigid systems, there is a change in the students' type of resistance to art. Stereotypes are never merely imposed by authority; they arise to fill an ever-present need to ward off the emotional upheaval which creative work may cause. They help guard the individual's equilibrium against the emergence of unwelcome or dangerous feelings and knowledge by a system of avoidance, denial and lies. (Not every individual nor every society fears the same thing.)

This need for defense was previously fulfilled by set standards that determined choice of subject matter and manner of representation. Reality was falsified and censored. Passion, conflict, hostility, ugliness, and other unwelcome facts and feelings were not permitted expression. The conventionally accepted stereotypes were intricate: their execution required time, patience and dexterity. Such a system satisfied the needs of people accustomed to obedience, who possessed well-established inhibitions and defenses, and whose aggressions were mostly turned inward in the form of guilt or channelled into constructive, often compulsive work. We see that this form of defense depends on a relatively high level of maturity and integration.

The modern version fulfills the need for the avoidance of creative work in a simpler way. Reality is not censored or falsified but negated and overlooked. There is no false standard of perfection but an indiscriminate acceptance of any and every product that avoids the very concept of standards. Awareness of unwelcome feelings and facts is prevented by avoidance of intelligible statements and preference for amorphous, incoherent expression. This solution corresponds to the character structure of the spoiled underprivileged child who is incapable of obedience to a complex system of inhibitions, restrictions, and standards of perfection, because he is accustomed to flattery and persuasion rather than to authority and criticism. It does not help to ward off specific forbidden or dangerous ideas or emotions, but rather expresses a universal fear of reality on the part of young people who have been fed on substitutes until they have lost the capacity to respond to direct experiences. When such a child is confronted with a blank piece of paper and the invitation to make a statement on it, he becomes aware of a great and frightening emptiness. The lack of a solid self and the absence of relationships has emptied the world of substance and meaning. While these children are relatively free of anxiety caused by guilt, they are defenseless against the older nameless fear of being overwhelmed and annihilated by primeval impulses of rage and desire.

Confronted with a new mechanism, we may ask: How well does it help young people to control impulses, reduce anxiety, and maintain equilibrium? We find that the fear of nothingness and emptiness is alleviated by producing something, however inadequate it may be, but because the products remain anonymous and amorphous they cannot serve as valid self-representation. Since scribbling and splashing retain a strong flavor of violence, they can be useful as a way of letting off steam but they have little enduring power to bind aggression. In the strict sense they are not mechanisms of defense but primitive forerunners that have the quality of stereotyped repetition and of substitution that belong to defense but retain more elements of direct instinctual gratification.

We see that they can be helpful in an emergency situation but are too primitive to have lasting effect.

It is interesting to observe how each culture, as it develops specific mechanisms of defense also develops tolerance against certain weaknesses that are inherent in the defense system. The Victorian age had great tolerance toward hypocrisy and lies, indeed demanded them from children. We have developed tolerance toward expression of violence both in words and deeds but we do expect greater truthfulness from our children.

How should we work with young people neither severely retarded nor psychotic who use scribbles and splashes as defense? As in psychotherapy, the basic rule of acceptance is valid. We have to accept the scribble as we accept the three tulips or anything else the child offers. We cannot, however, expect the scribble to have the liberating effect which it has for the inhibited child. At times it may be possible to transform the mechanical scribble into a creative activity by helping the child to see images in his productions and to complete them. However this will be possible only when the child has developed a sufficient store of structured mental images to be able to project and recognize them in random forms. When there is too great a vacuum the scribble or color blot remains a butterfly or an explosion or a "design," and that is as far as it goes. As one boy put it, "You make something, it don't look like nothing, you call it a design: that's modern art." The task then is not so much to free the child from inhibitions (although there are usually also constrictions and perfectionism) as to help chaotic fantasy develop into imagination, and to revive an atrophied faculty of observation and self-observation.

The difficulties are enormous, our old methods are inadequate, and there is great need for experimentation. Our task is also less immediately rewarding than it used to be. When we liberate a person from inhibitions, we lift depression and are gratified by immediate change of mood. When we try to build up structure, we take away direct instinctual gratification. When there is success, increased mastery and ego strength eventually produce a feeling of victory and elation, but the process is more strenuous and rewards come slowly.

There is no way to bypass the crucial moment when the making of a picture becomes an independent act, when the young painter confronts a blank surface with the will and desire to make a statement and the inner strength to overcome the fear of committing himself. This desire and this fear are at the core of all creative work. We can give support, encouragement and help, but we cannot deny the difficulty and should not try to circumvent it.

Growth and development in art remain unpredictable. Sometimes hidden vitality begins to bloom as soon as conditions are favorable, and a child will go rapidly through all missing developmental phases and soon produce according to his age and potential. With another child, all efforts may bring only meagre results.

The emphasis on building up structure in art parallels the course recognized as necessary for treatment plans in general. The controlled behavior of the youngsters we have described is a thin veneer supported by a flimsy structure which gives way readily under stress. Rehabilitation begins by strengthening the ego, cementing relationships, fostering identification and internalization of values. Uncovering work has to be handled cautiously and slowly.

Conclusions

A long analysis of difficulties and their possible meaning has been followed by rather meagre suggestions for changes or remedies. The observations and conclusions are controversial and open to discussion. Indeed this essay was written in the hope that it will stimulate discussion in this new publication. I want to make it clear that I do not mean to denigrate any insights or discard methods that have proved valuable. This would be as absurd as it would be to advocate return to corporal punishment or castration threats because their abandonment has not solved all the problems of child rearing. I only want to add one more cause to our old ones, to define new threats to creative growth which are felt by many but not yet well-described or understood. We must learn to recognize emptiness, even in stereotyped chaos where it bears superficial resemblance to art or to the stuff art is made of.

We have found three interlocking factors which contribute to the spreading of emptiness: the oversimplification and misinterpretation of psychoanalytic theory[3] which results in seduction to regression; the mechanization of progressive teaching methods; and the increase of synthetic experiences in daily life. The first two evils can be combatted within education; against the third evil we have at present no direct weapon.

If ersatz gratifications are recognized as serious threats to the mental health of deprived and unloved people it will be possible to attempt pro-

---

[3] Cultural lag accounts for this in part. The discovery of unconscious processes, of the nature of the id and the pathogenic effects of repressions, preceded understanding of the function of the ego as central organizing force in the emotional household, and the role of the mechanism of defense and of sublimation in ego development. More widespread understanding of these newer ideas should lead to better practices in art education and art therapy.

For the change in emphasis from id psychology to ego psychology see: Anna Freud, *The Ego and the Mechanism of Defense;* New York, International Universities Press, 1936.

——, *Mutual Influences in the Development of Ego and Id,* in *The Psychoanalytic Study of the Child,* Vol. VII; New York, International Universities Press, 1952.

Heinz Hartmann, *Notes on the Theory of Sublimation,* in *Ibid.,* Vol. X; 1955.

——, Ernst Kris, and Rudolph Loewenstein, *Comments on the Formation of Psychic Structure,* in *Ibid.,* Vol. II; 1946.

Ernst Kris, *Psychoanalytic Explorations in Art;* New York, International Universities Press, 1952.

——, *Neutralization and Sublimation,* in *The Psychoanalytic Study of the Child.* Vol. X; 1955.

tection in those areas where a therapeutic milieu is being created, in day-care centers, treatment homes, and hospitals. The difficulty will be the same we encounter in all milieu therapy.

It is a basic rule that any disturbed person should be protected carefully from those situations which caused the initial injury. A child who has been harmed by brutality needs more careful protection against even slight corporal punishment than a normal child; a child who has been abandoned should be protected from repeated separations. We also know that it is almost impossible to create such an environment because every disturbed person is under the compulsion to re-create the situation which led to his illness. A child who was driven to distraction by nagging will force the adult to nag him; a brutalized child will force the adult to beat him. By the same token, children who have been impoverished and corrupted by substitute gratifications force the environment to give in to their addiction. Attempts to replace substitutes with substance, passive consumption with active participation, meet with resistance. In a milieu which recognizes the problem and works toward its solution, art therapy can do its share to give depth and meaning to the children's lives.

My own experience in various situations has taught me that art therapy can function under all sorts of difficulties. It can endure heat, cold, lack of space and facilities, disorder and violence, but it cannot well endure emptiness. When people's lives are too consistently filled with synthetic living art does not survive easily. But if the battle against emptiness seems hopeless at times, we must remember that 25 years ago the battle against well-entrenched academicism may often have seemed equally disheartening to those who fought and won it.

The Problem of Quality in Art[1]

EDITH KRAMER

This is one of a series of articles concerning the relationship between psychological processes and qualitative aspects of art.[2]

In art therapy and education we use the word art to denote a great variety of products that have not much more in common than that form has been given to matter with the intent of making a symbolic rather than a useful object. This does not mean that we are blind to the enormous qualitative differences between these products which, for want of a better word, we call art. Indeed the question arises whether it might not be better to coin a new word free of the value judgment implied in the term art, that would encompass the objects created in those art sessions that are conducted with the principal aim of alleviating suffering or of bringing about beneficial personality changes rather than with the intention of training artists.[3] In this article I will not propose any new terminology. Rather I will describe various kinds of pictorial products and attempt to elucidate the psychological processes that enter into their creation, calling them all art for the time being.

---

[1] The case material and some of the ideas developed in this article were presented at the Third International Congress of Psychopathological Art, Antwerp, Belgium, July 1962, in a paper titled "Emotional Discharge and Formed Expression."

[2] See Edith Kramer, "Art and Emptiness: New Problems in Art Education and Art Therapy"; *Bulletin of Art Therapy,* 1961, vol. 1, no. 1, for the author's treatment of a related topic.

[3] For previous discussions in the *Bulletin of Art Therapy* bearing on this problem, see Elinor Ulman, "Art Therapy: Problems of Definition"; 1961, vol. 1, no. 2; and M. L. J. Vaessen, "Art or Expression? A Discussion of the Creative Activities of Mental Patients"; 1962, vol. 2, no. 1.

The practicing art therapist or educator finds that he necessarily orders the great variety of art products which he encounters into a number of loosely defined categories. He distinguishes work that is predominantly formless and chaotic; art that is conventional and stereotyped; pictographic communications that can be understood only if the painter explains their meaning; and complex, esthetically valid creations that possess to a greater or lesser degree those qualities which we associate intuitively with art in the full sense of the word.

Such categories can never be rigid nor is it always easy to discriminate between the various kinds of products. For instance, certain seemingly unrestrained chaotic pictures reveal themselves upon closer examination as stereotypes in the modern manner, characterized by the kind of tame banality which we associate more readily with conventional pictures of flowers and fruit. On the other hand, a picture may seem stereotyped at first glance because subject matter and composition follow a familiar pattern, while actually the artist has filled this conventional form with fresh and vital experience. But, though no foolproof method of distinguishing between various kinds of art can be devised, and though judgments remain subject to error and controversy, we cannot doubt the validity of such categories. We feel intuitively that scribble, stereotype, pictograph, and artistic creation differ not merely in intensity but in kind, though all four may be manifestations of related processes.

In practice our responses show that we appreciate these differences. For example, we may feel that uncovering the secret meaning of a schizophrenic's pictograph constitutes a therapeutic victory. We know, on the other hand, that it would be nonsensical to apply the same kind of literal translation of symbols to an esthetically conceived work of art. And when a scribbler attributes very special meaning to some element in one of his scribbles, we would see this as an act of projection comparable to response to Rorschach blots. The projected idea would interest us, but we would not mistake the scribble itself for a pictograph made with the intention of expressing meaning.

Underlying our actions and attitudes are certain general assumptions which we can accept as self-evident in the majority of cases. For instance, we can safely suppose that paintings or drawings consisting entirely of chaotic colors or lines are created at a time when impulses have ascendance over controlling forces. Beyond this no conclusion can be drawn. Unless we know more about the specific situation, we cannot guess whether the artist purposely abdicated his controls and permitted the impulsive elements of his being full reign, or whether he was overpowered by an upsurge of emotion. Assuming that he was overpowered, we must remember that a weak ego may be overwhelmed by a relatively slight increase of aggressive energy, while even a strong ego may be thrown off balance by an infuriating or devastating experience. And again, areas of strength and weakness differ. A person who in art easily resorts to angry gestures may have considerable self-control in other situations, while the opposite may be true for another.

We can also be reasonably certain that the balance is reversed in stereotyped, conventional work and that such painting serves mainly as a defense mechanism. The painter of stereotypes confirms this by his attitude, for he is usually happiest about those pictures which deviate least from his chosen prototype, thus revealing least his own personality. On the other hand, there are painters who make a conscious effort to be original and nevertheless end up copying someone's else manner. We suppose that in such persons an unconscious need for defense is stronger than the conscious wish for self-expression. As before, we cannot tell without further information why the stereotype was painted or what function it serves. A stereotype may have been painted because any departure from conventional norms arouses anxiety in the painter, or it may have been manufactured to please a public that prefers conventional art, or for a variety of other possible reasons.

Pictographs are important but it is hard to make generalizations about them. They are intended to convey meaning, but in each instance a key must be found before that meaning becomes intelligible.

Finally there are products more complex than chaotic expression, more original than stereotypes, more immediately intelligible than pictographs, that possess to some degree the quality of art in a narrower sense. Again we may ask whether we can discern properties common to all such products, and try to guess their function in the artist's emotional household.

The Elements of Art

From the outset it begins to appear debatable that specific underlying processes distinguish true art from other forms of pictorial expression. Art, it can be argued, is always emotionally charged; it arises from and evokes feeling. An emotional outburst captured on canvas or paper may be deeply moving both to the artist and to the spectator. Where then is the difference between art and a passionate scribble? And where should we draw the line between stereotype and art, when it is virtually impossible to create art that is not influenced by tradition and convention? Finally, may not the same process that leads to the making of simple pictographs also contribute to artistic creation? For every work of art holds within itself a secret story, matter concealed even from the artist's awareness, which influences the choice and arrangement of pictorial symbols.

The arguments are persuasive, yet we are convinced that art is an entity, however elusive, however subject to controversy and open to error, that is distinct from all other forms of pictorial expression. Art is characterized by economy of means, inner consistency, and evocative power. Beyond such very general description, art defies definition. Prominent critics of the past and present have admired rubbish and condemned great art, and whole societies have been blind to the merit of certain schools of art. Even the critic with faith in his own judgment knows that he can never absolutely trust his evaluation of any single work of art. It almost seems as if the quality of art were entirely subjective, and yet we feel certain that beyond error and subjective feeling there exists a core of objective truth, and that it is therefore worth while to seek insight into the quality of art by investigating the psychological processes that are active when art is made.

I shall begin by presenting three instances where I have had the good fortune to observe more closely than is usually possible the transformation of experience into picture. In each case I shall discuss not only the psychological situation that led to the painting of each picture but also the relationship between the formal elements of each finished painting and the story of its creation. I observed the incidents closely and was well acquainted with each of the three children and with his environment, but had no further information derived from psychotherapy. Particularly in view of this limitation, it is understood that the story of the making of three children's pictures does not constitute sufficient evidence for building new theoretical concepts. Furthermore, inferences from processes observed in children cannot be applied to adults without taking the greater complexity of the adult mind and world into account. I believe, however, that analysis of these examples will illuminate existing theory, and should stimulate further thinking in this area.

"The Mountains of New Hampshire"

Eight-year-old Mary was an energetic, highly intelligent child who suffered from a great variety of neurotic disturbances. She was given to impulsive behavior, crying spells, and temper tantrums. Because of her talent and interest in art, painting sessions were arranged in Mary's home, mainly as a supportive measure. At the time the picture (Figure 1) was painted she was struggling, not very successfully, to gain some degree of self-control.

Mary began the art session by mixing colors without deciding on a subject. At first all went well; Mary was pleased as she found new and exciting colors and color combinations to use in her picture. But soon this total freedom became too much for her. Mixing colors more and more wildly, she soon reduced most of her paint to a brownish mess. Her mood became destructive. One could foresee that Mary would soon cover not just the paper but also the furniture and herself with muddy brown paint. Unless something was done quickly, it would all end in tears and a tantrum.

Mary had covered about two-thirds of her paper with splashes of different shades of brown interspersed with red and orange spots. I made her stop painting and look at her picture for a moment, saying, "To me this looks like the mountains of New Hampshire in the fall." I had visited Mary in the mountains and knew that her stay there had been happy. Indeed the wild

Figure 1

See also color plate II.

splashes of color on her paper reminded me of the blazing, turbulent colors of the New England autumn.

Mary's expression changed. She declared yes, she would paint the mountains. Now she acted without hesitation. She bounded the rise and fall of her masses of color with a strong, deliberate brush-stroke which defined the mountain range. Then she added bright spots of yellow and light grey-blue to bring out the fall colors. Finally she very calmly and carefully painted a blue sky and a yellow sun, taking pains to keep the blue paint from turning the sun green. When the painting was completed, Mary was radiant and proud.

How can we explain what happened? Working with color, especially in the absence of form, is exciting. Mixing and splashing paint, and the appearance of more and more brown color led to an upsurge of anal-aggressive impulses, which in Mary were ever ready to come to the surface. Her feeble controls were about to be swept away.

When the teacher made Mary stop her wild splashing and reminded her of her beloved mountains, Mary was able to link her inner turmoil and the turmoil she had created on the paper to a memory that contained some of the same qualities but that was charged with positive feeling. As she transformed her wild and messy painting into the image of autumn mountains, chaotic, aggressive energy was channeled into constructive action. Mary finished her painting by adding sky and sun, graphic expressions of the calming, reassuring forces that had gained ascendance in her mind.

Why was all this possible? A teacher's request to stop destructive action and reflect is not always heeded; the invitation to see an image in a mess of paint is not necessarily accepted. We presume, and there was evidence for the presumption in the child's behavior, that Mary was ready to make the step, and that the teacher only supplied the extra push necessary to bring it about.

An interesting element in the story is the association of the mountains, which was offered spontaneously by the teacher and picked up so eagerly by the child. This is unusual. More often a teacher makes many suggestions, and the child, stimulated by the many choices offered, picks up one among them or finds his own image. Because the teacher's association fitted so perfectly, Mary may have felt very close to her, and this feeling may have contributed to her successful painting.

We also note that the teacher took on both ego and superego functions. By inhibiting destructive action she supported the superego. When she helped the child find a satisfying alternative to destructive behavior, she became the ally of her ego.

To what extent did the history of the picture's creation determine its final form? What would we see and feel if we did not know the story behind the painting? The picture is altogether alive: the brush-stroke which outlines the mountains and separates them from the sky is the most dynamic element of composition. This line, we recall, marked the transition from random activity to creation. There is a marked contrast between sky and sun, painted in a conventional, childlike manner, and the mountains which seem at first glance to be painted in a more mature style. However, sun and sky are not altogether conventional. The shape of the sun is childlike, but its position, rising above a sudden dip in the mountain, is unconventional and dramatic.

The seemingly greater maturity in the painting of the mountains is in part deceptive, since in splashing paint Mary had obtained accidental effects. Later, however, some color was put in deliberately. In addition, although Mary had not planned all her effects, she was able to appreciate the visual possibilities of the accidents, and utilize them.

There is, then, a clear connection between the picture and its history. The decisive creative act became the most important element of composition. The balance between destructive and constructive forces is manifest in the kind of balance between earth, sun, and sky. Form and content have become one. Although no one could guess the specific events which led to its creation, the painting expresses, in the universal language of form and color, the quality of the conflict and its resolution.

"The Burning Tree"

The next picture (Figure 2) was painted in direct response to a dramatic event. A group of children at camp were painting in a little cabin on a hot, sultry summer day when a violent thunderstorm broke out. As the rain poured down, the whole group ran out into the open to roll in the wet grass. Only nine-year-old Lillian, seeming rather frightened, stayed indoors. I invited her to paint a picture of the storm. Thereupon she chose a tan-colored paper, and on it painted a tree struck by lightning.

Figure 2

See also color plate III.

The picture is constructed entirely of rhythmic lines. The dark-brown tree, burning with red and yellow flames, reaches out diagonally toward the middle of the paper. There it is cut off by the lightning which streaks across in the opposing diagonal direction. Its motion is repeated and emphasized by white scribbles. Only the green grass growing straight up, and the black raindrops falling down counterbalance the dramatic movement of tree, flames, and lightning.

The painting depicts not the actual storm but a much more destructive and violent fantasy, "A tree is struck by lightning and burns up." We can surmise that the violent outburst in the sky found an echo in Lillian's own fantasies of violence and passion, and aroused fear of their uncontrollable power. The symbolic shape of the tree, the position of its branches, the red flames that are densest in the crotch which divides the tree's crown in half, all strongly suggest a bloody, violent, sexual fantasy. The specific meaning of the fantasy in Lillian's life cannot, of course, be guessed. But here we are not primarily concerned with uncovering unconscious content; we are interested in the quality of Lillian's picture, and how she was able to paint it.

Being frightened by the storm, Lillian might have done a number of things. She might, for instance, have decided to be a brave girl and go out into the rain with the others. To do this she would have had to override her fear, probably by denying that she was afraid; she would have repressed perception of her inner world. On the other hand, Lillian might have helped herself by shutting out the storm, perhaps by concentrating on a picture that had nothing at all to do with storms. In this case she would have repressed part of her perception of outer reality. Finally, she might have succumbed passively to her anxiety.

When Lillian moved from passive endurance to action, creating her own storm on the paper, perception both of her inner world and of the outside world was heightened. Unconscious material could come close to the surface, and find symbolic expression without endangering the child's necessary defenses. Lillian could allow herself to be moved by the drama and grandeur of the storm outside without being flooded from within by unmanageable excitement. Her response to stress was the most economical one. In painting she retained full command over her power to perceive, to imagine, and to act. She had transformed a potentially upsetting experience into creative adventure.

The teacher's role is not as decisive this time as it was in the story of the mountains. Her presence probably gave the necessary security, and her suggestion to paint the storm may have given an extra push toward creation. More important were the child's previous experiences in art. Not only was Lillian talented, but she also had been given much encouragement and understanding. It was quite natural for her to turn to art under stress.

Again we can ask how much of all this would come through if the story of the picture were not known. While no one could guess that the painting was made in direct response to a storm, it can be seen that the picture is carried by a swift, powerful, inner rhythm. We can feel that the painter responds strongly to moods in nature, and observes well. No layman would connect the burning tree with the primal scene, but violent drama is visibly expressed in line and color. The picture does not tell how anxious Lillian felt at the beginning, or how pleased she was with her finished work.

This young painter's capacity to integrate a subject that contains great tensions is impressive. In a painting that includes opposing forces—fire, lightning, and rain—one of them might easily overpower and obliterate the rest. Fire might consume tree, rain might drown fire, lightning might tear the paper. In Lillian's painting a balance is maintained wherein each force is given full play.

"The White Whale"

The third example, Moby Dick (Figure 3), was painted by Gordon, a twelve-year-old emotionally disturbed boy, during an art therapy session where only he and his friend John were in the room. In the course of the session the two boys embarked on a bout of so-called "slipping" or "playing the dozens," a ritual of mutual insult where each boy accuses the other's mother and grandmother of every conceivable and inconceivable kind of sexual perversion and promiscuity.

Figure 3

This exchange of vituperation constitutes a conventional social pattern among slum children whose mothers are in fact promiscuous. It can be embellished with all sorts of colorful inventions, but the crowning insult remains the disdainful declaration, "You don't even have no mother." Both partners to the abusive exchange get relief through projection. While the child could not possibly accuse his own mother of desertion and immorality, he can freely accuse another child's mother, and have the accusation thrown back at him. Such loaded banter may remain playful among friends, but more often it ends up in a fist-fight.

This time peace prevailed. While insults were passed back and forth almost mechanically, Gordon began a large painting of Moby Dick (its actual size is one-and-a-half by four feet). The subject gave occasion for additional obscenity over the double meaning of the word Dick. One might expect that a painting created while such talk was in the air would at best be crudely obscene. Instead, there emerged a powerful, beautifully executed image of evil that comes close to embodying the symbolic meaning of Melville's masterpiece.

The white whale is floating on the surface of a light-blue sea, spouting a blue jet of water. The sky is indicated by lose blue brush-strokes. The whale's body is painted in subtle shades of grey, with dark-grey accents. The light, silvery atmosphere of the painting contrasts sharply with the whale's evil expression. His mouth is open in a crooked sneer, baring a dark-red cavity surrounded by sharp, white teeth. There is a sly, evil look in his small, black eye. The whole body conveys a feeling of nakedness.

The sexual symbolism of the painting is obvious. We see a composite of male and female elements. The whole whale can be interpreted as one gigantic penis, conceived as a dangerous weapon with teeth. The whale's mouth, on the other hand, can also be interpreted as a vagina dentata, devouring the male organ. The whale as a whole also recalls a woman's body, with the forked tail standing for her thighs and vulva.

In other words, the painting symbolizes a composite of dangerous, evil sexual fantasies, the kind of fantasies that haunt the masturbation of a boy whose experiences do not correct but rather confirm his most confused, primitive sexual theories. Yet in spite of all its contradictory symbolism, the painting remains a well-integrated picture of Moby Dick, the white whale.

It was impressive to see the intensity with which Gordon painted the whale's body. Again and again he brushed over its surface, adding more and more subtle shading. Although his way of painting was reminiscent of masturbation, it did not become obsessive or purely repetitive. Gordon never lost command over paint and brush; he knew what he was doing and when to stop. He was proud of the completed painting, and his friend and slipping-partner was filled with admiration. The session ended in a spirit of contentment.

If we compare the meaning of the talk that had accompanied the work with the symbolic meaning of the painting, we find that they both relate to the same painful situation: the boys' unfulfilled longing for mother, their rage over her unfaithfulness, shame over her behavior, and guilt and shame over their own degraded desires and fantasies.

On the surface all this seems to be expressed more directly in the boys' talk. "Your mother," it implies, "is promiscuous, she is indeed no mother at all; furthermore you, her son, are ready to degrade her by attacking her sexually." When we listen closely to the merciless words, we find that the abuse is quite impersonal, uttered so mechanically that it becomes meaningless. Talk circles endlessly around the boys' most profound longing and grief, but it brings no insight or relief. The longing for mother is denied, drowned in the flood of mutual abuse.

When Gordon paints a gigantic image, half fish, half mammal, frightening, fascinating, and unfathomable, he creates it out of the same ambivalent feelings, the same fears and pressures that drive him and his schoolmates to relentless vituperation, threats, and fights, but he is no longer obsessed, forced to repeat stereotyped behavior with no will of his own. By transposing his conflicts from the narrow confines of his life into the wider world of imagination and adventure, he frees himself from meaningless repetition. Painting does not alter the nature of his trouble. He is too deeply injured to make an image of goodness. He can only make a monstrous composite of love and hate, male and female, but in making it he has ceased, at least for the duration of the creative act, to be the helpless victim of his conflicts.

Again, how much of what we have constructed by using several sources of information is actually visible in the painting? Most striking are the proportions, roughly 3:8, an unusual, extravagant length suitable for the whale, which indeed fills the paper completely. This conveys a feeling of hugeness and power that comes through even in the much reduced reproduction. The obsessive, overpowering emotions the white whale symbolizes are expressed in the spatial organization of the picture.

Next there is the tactile quality of the body. This whale is no decorative symbol; it is a three-dimensional living thing. More than any specifically symbolic shapes, this quality makes the whale sensual and sexually charged. Finally there is the evil expression, the half-open mouth which is the more menacing because of the tactile quality of the painting. The whale invites touch, but at the same time threatens to bite. While the picture does not reveal the exact circumstances of its inception, it does express obsessiveness, ambivalence, aggression, and sexual excitement.

Discussion

Returning to our initial quest for qualities that characterize the creative process in art, a number of factors common to our three examples can now be identified.

In each of them, there is evidence of strong emotions pushing toward direct discharge. In the story of the New Hampshire mountains it was Mary's anal-aggressive fury, expressed by angry smearing. In the thunderstorm, Lillian's anxiety was the danger signal which indicated that the storm had activated some highly charged instinctive material in her. While the white whale was being painted, sexual excitement mixed with rage and despair were being expressed in vituperation that verged toward a fist-fight.

In each case, direct discharge was inhibited, but none of the three children repressed his dangerous feelings altogether. Instead, each child linked his emotional state to a pictorial idea with similar qualities: a mood in nature, the New Hampshire mountains; a dramatic event, the burning tree; a figure from a story, Moby Dick. Out of this linkage the child created an image that contained and symbolized his emotions. In each instance, it was possible to trace in detail the transformation of emotional content into pictorial form. We observed how the union of form and content brought about the qualities essential to art: inner consistency, economy of artistic means, evocative power. In this process, the constellation of inner forces was so altered that the child's ego gained control at least temporarily, over energies that originally belonged to the impulses.

Emotional conflict was linked to an analogous pictorial theme in each of these three pictures. So much is certain. Whether or not each step that occurred in our examples is an indispensable part of the creative process in general, these events can be classified as examples of sublimation.

The Concept of Sublimation

The concept of sublimation is controversial. In my opinion the controversy is complicated by confusion about the meaning of the term. I will therefore define the concept as it is understood in this paper.

Man can never unconditionally obey his instinctive drives or his primitive affects. The instinctive safeguards which direct the animal's behavior having atrophied in man, he depends for survival upon continuous appraisal of and adjustment to reality. Those forces which assure the survival of more primitive organisms are in their unmodified form a constant source of mortal danger to man.[4] At the same time the drives remain man's chief source of energy, and the gratification of instinctive needs his basic source of pleasure.

The dilemma is inescapable. According to Freudian theory, it has brought about the division of man's personality into two areas, the original primitive id and the ego. The ego develops anew in each individual, and to it are ascribed all highly organized functions, such as the capacity to perceive and manipulate reality, to postpone gratification, and to maintain unity of personality. Ultimately the ego serves the needs of the instincts,

---

[4] Konrad Lorenz, *King Solomon's Ring: New Light on Animal Ways;* N. Y., Crowell, 1952.

which, through the ego's efforts, obtain the gratification which could never be achieved through the impulsive discharge which is all the id is capable of.[5]

The ego could not fulfil its manifold and contradictory tasks of controlling impulses, avoiding dangers, warding off anxiety, and obtaining pleasures without the aid of simple repression as well as the various more complex mechanisms of defense. We often tend to think only of the dangers inherent in certain defense mechanisms, forgetting that basically they are indispensable to the maintenance of emotional health.[6]

Sublimation is the most economical of the mechanisms of defense. It is a process wherein direct instinctive gratification is relinquished and a substitute activity is found which permits symbolic gratification of the same need in a socially productive way. An essential feature of sublimation is the large amount of genuine pleasure which the substitute activity affords. Sublimation is expansive; it permits movement away from the original source of conflict, and fosters the capacity for modulated, flexible behavior. It can bind great quantities of anxiety and aggression. Because ego strength and autonomy increase in the process, we surmise that a shifting of energy from id to ego occurs and that aggressive and libidinal energy is neutralized.[7]

The beneficial qualities of sublimation are of course limited. Ultimately it remains a mechanism of defense, based on renunciation of instinctive gratification, a compromise albeit an advantageous one. If we accept the theory, sublimation is seen to be an important part of the artistic process.[8]

Sublimation and Symptomatic Behavior

To classify our three stories as examples of sublimation gives only a general idea of their import. So we return to our detailed study.

Comparing the original raw material with the emotional content of each picture, we find that the emotions and conflicts we observed or could infer appear with little or no change in two of the finished paintings. Lillian's

---

[5] See *The Standard Edition of the Complete Psychological Works of Sigmund Freud;* London, Hogarth Press, 1953-. "Formulations on the Two Principles of Mental Functioning"; vol. 12, pp. 213-226; and "The Unconscious"; vol. 14, pp. 159-215.

[6] See Anna Freud, *The Ego and the Mechanisms of Defense;* New York, International Universities Press, 1936; and "Mutual Influences in the Development of Ego and Id" in *The Psychoanalytic Study of the Child,* Vol. VII; New York, International Universities Press, 1952.

[7] See Heinz Hartmann, "Notes on the Theory of Sublimation" in *The Psychoanalytic Study of the Child,* Vol. X; New York, International Universities Press, 1955.
———, Ernst Kris, and Rudolph Loewenstein, "Comments on the Formation of Psychic Structure" in *Ibid.,* Vol. II; 1946.
Ernst Kris, "Neutralization and Sublimation" in *Ibid.,* Vol. X; 1955.

[8] For a different theory of creativity, see Lawrence Kubie, *Neurotic Distortion of the Creative Process;* Lawrence, University of Kansas Press, 1958.

burning tree expresses the violent passion which had made her anxious; Gordon's Moby Dick expresses ambivalence and sexual excitement more vividly than did the obscene talk which accompanied its production. Evidently the neutralization of aggressive and sexual energy which we associate with sublimation does not extend to the emotional content of these pictures. Mary's mountains, on the other hand, do not express her initial mood. The painting, which began as an expression of anger, ended with the restitution of a loved object wrought from chaos and destruction. Mary's submerged positive feelings found expression in the act of painting.

In all three cases, emotion reaches a high pitch, and the threshold of repression is lowered. It seems that the lowering of the threshold of repression depended on two conditions: inhibition of direct action, and the substitution of a subject which, because of its kindred qualities, could serve as a symbol for the repressed material.

Such symbolic substitution alone does not, of course, automatically lead to sublimation. When conflict is merely shifted from one area to another, this usually leads to symptomatic behavior which impairs ordinary functioning in the area which has become the new battleground for conflict. For instance, the "slipping" of Gordon and John is symptomatic behavior that both expresses and wards off ambivalent feelings toward mother. While the boys swear at each other they cannot listen. Language is reduced to automatically uttered gibberish. The habit of "slipping" thus reduces the capacity to use language for communication.

The following incident illustrates the point. In a home for dependent children a group of adolescent boys, among them several orphans, engaged in a bout of "slipping." At the appropriate point in the succession of insults, one of the orphans uttered the climactic stock phrase of the game: "At least I got a mother, you don't even have no mother." Thereupon a boy, who had not previously spoken, said very quietly, "My mother died of cancer when I was three years old." There was total silence. Brought up short against the real implication of their talk, the boys could not go on with the game.

Destructive processes of this kind cannot be called sublimation, even though symbolic behavior is substituted for direct gratification. This kind of substitution frequently impedes productive work. Let us suppose, for example, that Gordon while painting Moby Dick's body had been unable to stop adding more and more shading because the act of painting had become a direct substitute for masturbation. (We recall that his painting of the body actually did to some extent resemble masturbation.) Gordon would have ended up by ruining his picture. There would have been symptomatic behavior, not sublimation.

We can speak of sublimation because the intense personal feeling Gordon put into his white whale enhances the painting's evocative power. Likewise, the symbolic impact of Lillian's tree makes her picture of a thunderstorm more alive; and Mary's dramatic change of mood came across in the dramatic quality of her mountains. In each instance private meaning and universal message intensify each other. This process widens horizons and opens avenues of growth beyond the confines of personal conflict. (There is, of course, no guarantee that what happened while the pictures were being painted will continue or be carried over automatically into other aspects of life.)

Sublimation and Form

Substitution of an analogous subject for the original source of conflict facilitated sublimation, but it was only the beginning. Beyond the finding of the artistic theme, dramatic as it was, lay the struggle of execution. Here a division sets in. While the picture may contain any kind of emotion, no matter how disturbing or negative, the act of painting must be carried out in relative calm and serenity. Mary can paint her mountains only when she stops furiously hurling colors. We admire Lillian's discipline as she handles lightning, fire, and rain without excess. We are impressed when Gordon restrains himself from being carried away by the excitement of painting the whale's body.

The neutralization of aggressive and sexual energy characteristic of sublimation occurs in the area of artistic execution. No matter what emotion he expresses, toward the act of painting and toward his medium, the painter must maintain a positive feeling equally removed from obsessive sexual excitement and from aggressive fury. This state of serenity is not easily maintained. It is constantly menaced by untamed drives on the one hand, and on the other by the ego's tendency to apply radical, stifling mechanisms of defense.

As therapists we are more accustomed to failure than to success. We are used to seeing paintings of volcanoes become a mess of red and black because explosive feelings were not depicted but acted out. We see carvings end up as slivers of wood because the act of cutting unchains aggressive drives that cannot be confined within a given shape. Before our eyes, drawings turn into tangles of half-erased lines because ambivalence paralyzes the capacity for making decisions. We see symptomatic behavior more frequently than we see sublimation.

Our three examples are exceptions. The process of production is too smooth. We see that form and content became one, but we observe no struggle for form. We do not really know why all went well when all might as easily have gone wrong. These are a few of the miracles one hopes for but seldom experiences. Obviously we cannot develop theory solely on the basis of stories selected because they fit existing theory so nicely. In subsequent articles I shall approach the same problem by analyzing failures, examples where the creative process broke down.

Summary

We began with the observation that the various products we encounter in art therapy and art education fit into several loosely defined categories. We can roughly distinguish products that are chaotic; products that are stereotyped; cryptic pictorial signs that can be called pictographs; and last, products which possess to some degree those qualities proper to art in the full sense of the word.

True art defies simple definition. Chaotic impulse, traditional form, pictographic symbolism—none of these is alien to art yet none encompasses it. After analyzing three children's paintings which fall within our last category, we can attempt some description of the relationship between works of art and simpler kinds of pictorial expression.

Art derives emotional impact from the same primitive energies which find direct expression in the impulsive manipulation of art materials. But the artist imposes form upon these raw emotions, and when he does so, his work is linked to the same mechanisms of defense which are active in stereotyped art. However, whereas the painter of stereotypes employs established techniques, symbols, and conventions to ward off and deny conflict, the very same means are employed by the artist to contain and express conflict. Finally, there are in most works of art traces of personal meaning that can be understood only through uncovering techniques such as free association. So art is also linked to the simpler pictograph, but while pictographs mainly satisfy the need to state a private meaning, in the work of art any element which contains private meaning is so integrated that it contributes to the universal message of the painting. Thus instinctual drives, defense mechanisms, and unconscious symbolism combine with each other in many different ways.

Implications for Art Therapy

Complete unity of form and content, of private and universal meaning is seldom attained. In educational and therapeutic practice it would often be futile to distinguish rigidly between the various kinds of products we deal with. The moment when scribble, stereotype, or pictograph may turn into art can never be predicted. However, it is worth pointing out that some kinds of therapeutic application are almost of necessity inimical to art.

Whenever pictorial expression is used primarily for communication in psychotherapy, it is unlikely that the product will be art. Insofar as psychotherapy seeks to uncover the hidden core of the individual's behavior, it is opposed to that aspect of the artistic process which leads from the private to the universal. Pictorial communication in psychotherapy has served its purpose when meaning is understood by patient and therapist. Often the most abortive pictorial signs serve this purpose best.

When manipulation of art materials is encouraged mainly to help break down rigid defenses and permit the emergence of pent-up emotion, the result will usually remain too disorganized to become art. Finally, when therapy is limited to strengthening defenses, the patient may use art activity chiefly to negate some unbearable truth. Even if his products are the antithesis of art, the therapist may have good reason not to intervene.

Therapeutic situations favorable to art are those designed to provide areas of symbolic living that help the restitution of a more economically organized personality. Since the artistic value of the work produced is a sign of successful sublimation, the quality of the work becomes a measure (though not the only measure) of therapeutic success. Insight into the psychology of artistic creation shows that the formal qualities of a product make manifest processes of great significance to the therapist.

When products of therapeutic creative activities attain the esthetic qualities of art, this fact is too often neglected in psychological evaluation. Sometimes this is because art has been relegated to a vague field of cultural interest, or is thought of as just another hobby, beyond the realm of therapeutic interest. This attitude can be an unfortunate consequence of recognizing that much of what is made out of art materials in therapy is not art. The recognition is accurate, but to imply that there must be a sharp division between therapeutic creative activities and art activities is mistaken.[9] Indeed, insofar as the therapeutic situation fosters honesty, it is more conducive to true art than are situations where pretense is encouraged so that status may be upheld.

We can draw no further conclusions from analysis of only three examples. They have been presented and discussed in the hope of stimulating interest in an area where psychological investigation may illuminate problems of therapy, education, and esthetics.

---

[9] See Ainslie Meares, *Shapes of Sanity;* Springfield, Ill., Charles C. Thomas, 1960.

*Fostering Growth Through Art Education, Art Therapy, and Art in Psychotherapy**

SANDRA PINE

In recent years I used art with children in three entirely different settings. I was an art teacher in an urban elementary school, an art therapist in a residential school for psychotic children, and a psychotherapist in an outpatient psychiatric clinic. In this study I will describe these dissimilar settings and discuss my function and the goals I envisaged for myself in each of them. I will select individual children from each setting, show samples of their work that illustrate their development, and describe how they used art materials. I will try to analyze how their artwork reflected and influenced their inner life.[1]

The setting in which an activity is conducted largely defines and limits the leader's role, but the leader's personality and philosophy are nevertheless important. The quality of a child's artwork and his emotional growth depend not only on these two factors but, finally, on the characteristics of the child.

Since the leader's philosophy vitally affects the goals of the program, I must here state my orientation. Viewing the child, his work style, and his products from the psychodynamic point of view, I am interested in understanding what conflicts are at the root of his difficulties in order to be able to set goals and to know how best to work with him. I view pathology in developmental terms and as having its roots especially in the disturbances of early childhood. I am interested, above all, in emotional growth—for a child's intellectual growth remains forever linked to his emotional readiness for cognitive experiences. In my use of art materials with children I have come to appreciate the enormous value of creative experience in furthering emotional growth and development.

---

*This paper is based on a thesis accepted in 1972 by the Bank Street College of Education as partial satisfaction of the requirements for a master's degree in special education.

[1]For similar observations, see Edith Kramer, *Art as Therapy with Children*. New York, Schocken Books, 1971.

Art Education Geared to the Individual in a Public School

I ran an art program in an urban elementary school that served an area still referred to as a "melting pot." The children came from Puerto Rican, Cuban, Greek, Yugoslavian, and Chinese backgrounds, with a few black and a few middle-class white children as well. My art program was geared as much as possible to the individual child. I attempted to give the children the freedom and opportunity to be truly creative, and I was ready to make the experience therapeutic wherever the need arose. I functioned, however, in a milieu that was largely authoritarian. The art program was low in the order of priorities because the school's reading scores were below the city and state mean.

As long as there was an art program and some visible evidence of its existence in the form of art shows, parents and administration were satisfied. The emphasis was placed on the product. There was little or no awareness of how important creative experiences are for children and how the resultant feelings of satisfaction, ease, and self-worth may help learning in other areas. While the administration paid homage to the abstract ideal of "creativity," little was done to develop the concrete educational techniques and the kind of environment that would foster it.

As part of the school curriculum, art education fitted into a 45-minute period once a week. Only two-thirds of the classes in the school participated in the program because there was only one art teacher for 900 children. The children were from 5 to 13 years old, and the classes ranged in size from 26 to 33.

Given massive and rapid student turnover in the art room and given an environment not geared to self-expressive activities, one must develop a specific technology that will make possible individual work in this mass-oriented setting. One must find ways to make the art room into a nonjudgmental place where a child can feel expansive, where defenses can be relaxed, and yet where others are treated with consideration and respect.

How could I meet the needs of each individual when there was one teacher to 30 children and within 45 minutes the children had to be seated, aproned, presented with a lesson, given time to work and time to clean up, and, in addition, the art room had to be made ready for the next class? It was indeed quite a feat to organize the program, particularly for painting.

I had 30 sturdy aluminum lunch trays. On each tray was a can of water, two or three brushes, a sponge, and a bendable plastic ice-cube tray with seven large compartments arranged in single file; these were filled with poster paints in the following colors: red, yellow, blue (space), black (space), white. (I have also used 2-inch glass casters that can be stacked, thus keeping the paint from drying out.) The trays were lined up on a counter near the sink. Extra ice-cube trays filled with paints were ready so that the muddied paints of the messy child could be discarded and clean paints set in their place for the next class. If only the white was muddied one could easily bend the ice-cube tray and pour out the white paint alone and replace it. A lunch tray with open jars of fresh paint and teaspoons stood ready for the child who needed a refill. There was plenty of space on each child's lunch tray for mixing colors. Cleanup was expedited by having the children wash their brushes in their own cans of water, wipe their trays and tables with their own sponges, and then bring the trays back to the counter. A few children stayed to change the water and wash the sponges before the next group entered. Paintings were laid on the window sill. It had heat vents that helped speed up drying so that the next class could put their paintings on top of the first class's paintings. At the end of the day the pictures were sorted out,and the ice-cube trays were washed and readied for the next day.

A high degree of organization strictly adhered to was necessary in order to carry this through successfully; one might wonder whether the advantages of such a system outweigh the difficulties. I am firmly convinced that they do. Painting can have no therapeutic value at all without it. Naturally, it is far easier to put children around a table and have them share the same muddy paints and muddy water, depriving them of the experience of creating their own palettes. But consider, in contrast, the potential of a setup in which each child has his own paints. Consider the good feeling it engenders at the start, especially in children who have little that they don't have to share, who in school are always treated as one of a group and rarely recognized as individuals. If the program is to enhance creativity we must recognize and promote individuality. If we wish to encourage responsibility and self-determination in our children, we must give each child a chance to decide for himself how to use his own paints.

Thus, the neat, fastidious child can use his paints as he wishes without having to contend with the anxieties he experiences when having to share with a child who has an intense need to mess. The impulsive, aggressive child or the child who needs to overcome his inhibitions can mess until he is ready to make a painting that isn't all muddy and undifferentiated.

Many kinds of art materials were explored, but the main emphasis of the program was on painting, drawing, and sculpture. I sought to open the children's eyes to the world around them, to teach them not to take anything for granted but to look again and to see their world from the point of view of recreating it or restating it in their own way.

To make for the most productive use of the brief time in a large group, it was necessary to provide a single motivating theme. I worked to help the child feel and recall and try to capture on paper or in sculpture the movement of his own life. We talked about walking, running, jumping, leaping, throwing a ball, catching a ball; we talked about the light of day, how it changes; we tried to capture the mood of it all. At times we talked about how we felt. I tried to foster an awareness of the child's own environment and to make the emotional atmosphere of the art room such that a child was not afraid to explore and to express, a place where he would come to enjoy working with art materials.

Such an atmosphere is therapeutic in the broad sense of the term. When I began this art program, as soon as the children touched the brush or attempted a line the perpetual cry was "I can't" or "I made a mistake." I emphasized over and over that there was no such thing as a mistake in art, that almost any line could be used, that they were masters of the paint and clay, that they were all capable of expressing themselves, and that there was nothing to fear. I worked very hard to break through the inhibition springing from the fear of making a mistake. Dirty water and waste materials were used to try new things that in the end, to their surprise, turned into beautiful pictures.

One important way of encouraging the children to have confidence in their own ability was to mount and display their work attractively, backed with black construction paper or framed with felt strips. This gave even the simplest pencil sketch dignity and power to command a respect that the children otherwise never had accorded to their work.

There were times when my role was strictly that of an art teacher and other times when my role came closer to that of a therapist. I spent every minute possible working with one child at a time. Some children had great difficulty achieving any success in the art room because they were so disorganized that they could not apply themselves to anything. Some found the impulse to mess hard to resist and had to be helped to establish control. There were those who appeared to fear the empty white paper; at times this seemed to me to be because of an inner turmoil, particularly in preadolescents, that was seeking expression. And, of course, some children just needed a kind, encouraging word in order to blossom.

Figure 1

There were healthy children and disturbed children, retarded children and bright children. Everyone could take something from a teacher receptive and open to the needs of the individual child.

Caroline

I had the opportunity to get to know individual children quite well through their work. Caroline, in particular, had great talent. In fifth grade her paintings were still of the latency period. The figures (see Figure 1) were childlike, full of movement, fresh and happy. In sixth grade she began drawing incessantly, often copying book illustrations.The figures were much more mature and rich, and had a somewhat masculine appearance (see Figure 2). At this time, if there were more than one figure in a painting, each was alone, facing off in a different direction (see Figure 3). The paintings became more somber in tone as the year progressed. A painting that seemed to epitomize her loneliness was never finished. It had but one figure in it, with black surrounding it, and a bleak atmosphere.

The paintings were expressions of the problems she was coping with at this time. She grew more and more difficult to motivate. Her stance was dejected, and she often slumped in her chair. Often her head was down, eyes downcast. Indeed I cannot recall a smile.

Unfortunately, I do not have much personal information on this child other than that she had a stepmother who was rather harsh, demanding, and unloving. Caroline increasingly indicated her need for therapeutic help as she moved from latency into puberty. This was not only evidenced in her artwork but also was noted by her classroom teacher.

To the adults around her, Caroline's artwork offered a revelation of the conflicts she was experiencing; for her, it served as catharsis. She worked intensely, and to the extent that she was able to express her conflicts pictorially she appeared to be able to cope with them. When it became more difficult to motivate her I began to be concerned and to feel that therapeutic intervention was needed.

In this case we can see a specific potential of art. To the extent that one can pick up a brush and begin to work actively, one can externalize the depression by producing pictorially the depressed content. For a time there is catharsis and a relief from anxiety. The activity permits one to distance oneself for a little while from the black moods and the anguish.

José

Thirteen-year-old José was still in sixth grade (usually a sixth grader is 11). He was in a special class for hyperactive, disruptive, underachieving children.

His mother and father both worked. They seemed to have no control over José's running loose on the street at night. José was very fond of his mother but seemed to have great ambivalence toward his father, who was reported to be both indulgent and strict; he did not spare the hand. José was reported

Figure 2

always to have been restless and hyperactive, but his parents did not recognize that he had problems.

José's main way of dealing with his world was to blame others for his difficulties and in general to deny his responsibility for anything. He was competitive and impulsive. He was always touching his friends, either in a loving or in a provocative, semi-aggressive manner. José would thrust himself on a friend by wrapping him in a giant bear-hug or he would jut his hands out and playfully punch him in the groin. He was provocative and disruptive in school, all for the purpose of having life in the classroom revolve around him. He did not have a well functioning conscience. He was mad at the world and he was a sore loser.

Alone with an adult, José was extremely likeable, cooperative, and polite. In a group, however, he was constantly bucking authority, was rude and out of control. In the first instance, he was warm, smiling, and sweet, and in the second he behaved as if he were the boss and thought everyone was there to serve him; he defied the world. Once his aggressiveness had provoked a direct confrontation and authority had been reasserted, he became calm, quiet, and obedient.

Figure 3

See also color plate IV.

I had come to know José from seeing him once a week for 45 minutes along with the other members of his class. It was a difficult class to handle, being made up of the so-called disruptive children who were the outcasts from the other sixth-grade classes. Being outside the ordinary routine, the art class became the testing ground for all sorts of behavior.

I very soon discovered José's central role in determining the attitude and mood of the group. He could trigger, or refrain from triggering, the uncooperative spirit. I therefore set about improving my relationship with him. I would invite him to stay on after his class left to help with the chores. I would offer him opportunities to use material when he was alone with me, but he accepted the invitation only once. I would send for him to do errands, talk to him, and in general I showed a genuine interest in him. On these occasions he was always his sweet self—talkative and friendly. He would leave with a skip to his gait.

In his artwork he was notably constricted and uncreative. As soon as he touched a piece of paper or other material he would sense his limitations and immediately want to throw his work away. He would start over again but would eventually give up and refuse to go on. Only with a great deal of attention and encouragement was he able to finish a piece of work, and even then he could not always stay with it to the end. By himself, he could not see the potentialities of his work and it seemed hard for him to face any challenge. He could not commit himself to doing anything. Perhaps this child wanted to appear so big at all times that his sense of inadequacy in art work led him to flee rather than risk failure.

Since I showed a personal interest in him, he spent a lot of time in the art room with me. He would always look in when passing through the hall or would ask for special permission to visit and help me. He seemed hungry for warmth and personal contact but was not himself able to give more than a fleeting smile or a flippant remark. Those rare instances when he was able to produce anything in art came when I gave him my complete attention; even then he needed moment-by-moment encouragement or advice.

I asked him once if he would paint a large person for me. Only gradually did this picture (Figure 4) emerge. At first the figure had no feet, no hands, and was all blue. One could see that he could not differentiate between body parts and clothing. With my encouragement to look at himself and to add more, he was able to complete it to this extent; as we see, by the time it was finished it had a robot-like quality, was quite colorful except for the unpainted face with its empty expression, and it had clothes on. It was quite a feat for José. Looking at this picture one senses its empty, hollow feeling. It is an excellent portrait of a boy whose behavior has itself become the substitute for a solid sense of self.

In another painting that also reached relative completion, José first made a brown line across the paper and immediately protested that he had made a mistake—could he have another piece of paper? After a discussion with me he decided to make some more brown lines; again he was ready to flee and then,

Figure 4

after another consultation with me, he decided the brown lines were tree-branches and he could even see a bird sitting on one of them. He then proceeded to finish a painting that was primitive for his age level but actually the richest thing he had produced all year. The bird was indeed fantastic and brilliantly colored against the green and brown background of trees. José was really pleased but could not quite believe in his success.

By making every effort to mitigate failure I had enabled this hesitant child to risk failure and achieve a limited success. To this extent something good had been experienced and a very shaky ego had achieved some limited mastery. Given a multitude of such experiences, one could envision the possibilities for internal growth.

Benny

Quite different was the case of 6-year-old Benny, a boy full of expressive ability but infantile in his painting. Benny was in second grade when I came to know him. Tall for his age, rather heavy, and a big eater, Benny was gawky and poorly coordinated in both gross and fine motor activity. He lacked muscle tone and was pliable to the touch. His writing was labored and almost illegible, though he was quite intelligent. He had a big smile, a certain charm, and an almost voluptuous warmth for the few who were his friends.

Benny's behavior did much to make one think of him as a great big infant. In order to attract attention he placed himself in the center of the class both physically and verbally. When other methods failed he resorted to buffoonery and aggressive provocations. He wanted very much to be liked, for he was

Figure 5

like a hungry baby. His restlessness and poor behavior were self-defeating, however, since they attracted attention in the form of reproaches from adults and complaints from children.

Benny was a child born of old Puerto Rican parents. His father was punitive and sadistic; he was infantile and demanded his wife's complete attention. He saw Benny as a competitor, a sibling, and resented his wife's indulging the child. The father paid no attention to his son except when he punished him.

Benny's mother was a sickly, asthmatic woman who overprotected her son but could not show her love for him. She kept him an infant and gave him no opportunity for physical activity or play with friends. He sought gratification by demanding more and more things. The family's response fed these demands.

Benny acted in ways that made children call him crazy. He would take a dare even if it required him to lie down in the middle of a busy street. His buffoonery was a defense as well as an attention-getting device—if you make fun of yourself then you prevent others from doing it.

The crowning blow to Benny's poor self-image came when he was in first grade. Benny had been improperly circumcised in infancy and the operation had to be done again. On top of all his other emotional struggles came the threat of castration at the age of 6 when this operation on his penis was performed.

In Benny's pictures one can see his tremendous but not always successful struggle to contain the regressive forces that were at play in him. We also see an expression of fantasy life, as well as moments of synthesis and achievement. He had great difficulty resisting the impulse to play regressively with muddy colors. His tendency to spill paint all over the paper, onto the floor,

Figure 6

and finally all over himself was consistent with his sloppiness, his awkwardness, his inability to contain himself, and his regressive behavior in general.

Unfortunately it was not possible within a large class to give Benny the opportunity to regress for a while, experience some relief and catharsis through uninhibited messing with paint, and then to reorganize at his own speed. Instead his messing brought him shame and humiliation before his peers and the adult. This he denied by clowning and by becoming wildly exhibitionistic of the mess he had made. Thus he spilled all over the place in his behavior as in painting, and one could not help but be aware of his presence at all times. However, even in the large classroom where I could give him only limited attention, it was always possible to somehow control Benny's behavior.

Most apparent in Benny's pictures is development from a regressed product to one more appropriate for a 7-year-old. The first painting he was able to complete was an infantile figure in blue (Figure 5). It was barely distinguishable from the blobs of paint around it. Then he did a figure that was bold and solidly painted with a large, grotesque face without color or boundaries and with sticks for arms (Figure 6). Then came some figures in pairs (Figure 7) that started as blobs or amorphous shapes that Benny then sought to contain and define by painting a black line around them. In the second painting of this same session (Figure 8) his ability to keep control was straining, and we see bulges all over and one figure indeed seems to be already in flight. In the last

Figure 7

painting shown (Figure 9) we see clearly the emergence of Benny himself. He is ice-skating and obviously feeling much better—indeed, on top of the world. One can see the improved self-image and increased competence.

We can speculate as to the reasons for the regression and the ensuing progress. It is likely that before I worked with Benny his opportunities to use art materials were extremely limited or nonexistent and hence the temptation to use them regressively was great. Another factor could have been internal disorganization due to the start of a new school year and to the recent surgery. Opportunity to explore the medium may help to account for his growing competence. Whatever had happened in the past, Benny now was in an environment that permitted some degree of self-expression. Also, he was being seen periodically by a social worker and for the first time he developed and sustained a friendship with another boy.

Benny's progress in painting also depended on my awareness of his difficulties. If left to himself completely, he would start with a blob and then define the shapes as he tried to gain control. Finally, he would lose control, regress, and destroy his work by making a muddy mess of it. As much as possible, I kept an eye on him and took his work away and put it to dry before he went out of control. This gave him the chance for growth. Each successful experience did much to encourage him to retain control on his own. He took pride in his success, as we can see in the delightful, moving, expression of his self-portrait.

Benny's paintings also tell us other things about him. His exhibitionistic tendencies find expression in his large, strong, whole figures placed in the middle of the paper. There is a great deal of movement even at the beginning. Many of his figures seem to dance; when paintings are rigid and static and

Figure 8

empty one has much more cause for concern. Perhaps his dancing figures are somewhat effeminate but what we mainly see in the paintings as well as in the child is a strong personality.

Benny permitted himself to mess and smear and also to paint with a strong feeling of thrust. We see then that art permits expression of aspects of the self that don't get ready expression elsewhere. In Benny's case the relatively mature, competent performance in art makes apparent a potential for growth. Art permits him to practice this competence in a safe area and therefore gradually furthers the process of development.

Figure 9

Art Therapy in a School for Schizophrenic Children

The second school I will discuss is very different from the large public elementary school. It was part of a private residential treatment center for schizophrenic children. This institution housed 24 children whose schooling was provided by the city's Board of Education. Only 20 of the children in residence attended the school; and 20 additional children, who lived at home and came for both education and treatment, were bussed in.

The families of all children are seen regularly by social workers in an approach that is largely pragmatic, with the main emphasis on helping the parent learn to cope with the child's difficult behavior. The children are also seen once a week in therapy by a psychiatrist. But the institution's special approach to the treatment of schizophrenia consists of setting up an environment that is both stimulating to ego development and socially corrective. This is looked upon as the main tool for treatment. There is an attempt to foster in the child the ability to control his reactions to stimuli and to correctly perceive, order, and manipulate his world through the processes of social interaction. The hope is then to increase an individual's capacity for self-regulation by developing in him a self-awareness and a confidence in his ability to act in his own behalf. As the child's pathology comes into confrontation with the environment, the child is forced to modify his behavior in the direction of socially acceptable forms.

The school attempts to reduce the likelihood of problems occurring for the child in order to make it possible for him to pursue achievement and mastery. In so doing, however, it slips into an authoritarian mold and so controls the environment that the very confrontations essential to this treatment approach are too often eliminated. Curiosity and pleasure in learning are seldom in evidence, perhaps because independence and individuality are not encouraged. In fact, the school encourages mainly intellectual competence and literacy in a very narrow sense. I think what we find here is a beautiful marriage between a highly structured therapeutic approach and a public school mentality that fears disruption by sick children and fears innovation. Thus, within this small and exclusive setting many of the ills prevalent in today's schools are perpetuated.

I conceived of my role as therapeutically oriented teaching. I sought to encourage successful use of the medium by many means—exploration, catharsis, sublimation, externalization of some mental image, or expression of fantasy. Sometimes I functioned as an art therapist, sometimes as an art teacher, and at other times as a disciplinarian. Often when one child had difficulty controlling himself, it would spread like wildfire because many had tenuous controls and there was only one adult present. Class sizes ranged from 2 to 9, and since there were only 8 groups that ranged in age from 6 to 14 there was little flexibility in grouping. Most of the children were hyperactive.

Art activities are a threat to children's controls. Color calls forth an affective response, a loosening of controls, encouraging freedom and offering a chance to explore, express, create, and have a cathartic experience. It affords an opportunity for a new experience of oneself, for ego growth, an opportunity to try again for a synthesis of feeling and thought and to take a fresh look at one's ability. Given an adequate ratio of adults to children and taking into account each individual's needs, it should be possible to make this a good experience for all the children and to help them achieve success.

Again, as in the public school, art was fitted into a 45-minute period once a week. Art classes were held in the regular classrooms, which made it necessary to carry supplies from place to place and imposed certain limitations on the program.

For some schizophrenic children, having to make a choice may be too burdensome; an abundance of materials may be distracting and may provoke anxiety. I found it best, therefore, to limit the number of materials. A child still had the chance to decide what color to use or which piece of paper to select or just simply "What shall I make?" Indeed, deciding what to make is extremely difficult for many children.

My strong wish to encourage the use of art for expression and sublimation was a further reason for limiting supplies mainly to drawing materials, paint, and clay. Other materials were introduced only where it was necessary to provide special motivating sparks. In some instances it was impossible to use paint with a group because of its stimulating effect. In those instances clay modeling and drawing were more successful.

Rhonda

Rhonda and Alphonso were the only children in the class. Seven-year-old Rhonda was a black child whose intellectual functioning was retarded. She was extremely fastidious; it seemed that her mother kept her this way. She must sit and look nice and was never allowed to play because she would get dirty.

She was frequently tense and upset. She did a great deal of head-shaking and body-rocking in her seat and would often put her arm down on her desk and bang her head on it over and over again. There was a perseverative quality to everything she did; she would often ask me the same questions time and time again. "Where do I go when I leave here?" "Why?" "After that what do I do?" "Why?" She tried very hard to understand her experiences and put them together into a meaningful whole. She seemed frozen, with affect split off from behavior—she feigned feelings but never really felt them. She seemed to know how one should look and sound when one felt angry or sad and imitated those looks and sounds; she pretended to cry but there were no tears. She was hypersensitive to and aware of people around her and what they were doing. She would copy what Alphonso did and would want whatever he had, to the point of wanting to sit in his seat.

Rhonda never ceased to be jealous of everything and everyone she saw. Alphonso often had chocolate pudding for lunch. Rhonda wanted it. She would refuse to eat any of her own lunch. She would yell, "Leave me alone." and "He bothers me." meaning, I believe, that his having the pudding bothered her. Other times she would sing, "I want pudding and can't get it."

Figure 10

It was sometimes possible to tone down her jealousy by pointing out something that she had that Alphonso didn't have. She might then relax and eat or she might begin to sing, "His lunch is bad."

Rhonda always began her art sessions tense and hyperaware of what Alphonso was doing. She would often stand poised with her brush in the air watching what he did, herself unable to begin. But once she got started, she gradually relaxed and enjoyed her work. She would express her pleasure in working with the art materials by making effortful noises.

Rhonda was inventive in her use of collage materials and was quite a colorist in painting. She loved to mess with the glue and paints and indeed she badly needed the opportunity to make a mess.

Her painting sessions followed a pattern. She would spend most of her time mixing and messing with the paints. A few minutes before the end of the session I would give her a clean piece of paper and she would paint on it. In an attempt to put her more in touch with herself I asked her once if she could make a girl. In her first attempt, she put in a triangular shape in red and then a circle to the left in light green with yellow over the green. She said this was "father." Then above the red Rhonda made another circular shape in purple. She put curly hair on it, eyes, eyebrows, a round mouth, and then legs and arms. It had no body. The resultant picture was fragmented.

Often Rhonda had to put a line around her painting paper to make it safer to go ahead and then she would work within this border. One day one of the brushes had a residue of red paint on it and, knowing Rhonda's fastidiousness, I gave it to Alphonso and gave Rhonda a clean one. Immediately she started saying, "I want a red brush. I want the brush Alphonso has. I want to sit over there. That's the place I was going to sit." I responded with, "I know you're always jealous of Alphonso," and explained why I had given her the clean

Figure 11

brush. I went on to say, "We don't always have the same things; you can make your brush red too." This didn't help so I proceeded to talk about myself and Rhonda's classroom teacher, pointing out that we sometimes have the same things but mostly we each have different things. Then together we put her brush in the red paint. Suddenly, she said, "I have a chocolate pudding for lunch today," and then started to paint. During this same session she put her hands in the red paint, squealed with delight, and then squeezed her hands together. She also made an orange figure (Figure 10) and in the excitement of making it proceeded to encircle it. She cleaned up beautifully that day, ate her entire lunch, and played contentedly in the afternoon.

One day Rhonda was upset and confused because Alphonso had run away from school that morning. I suggested that perhaps she would like to paint Alphonso running away. Rhonda was quite excited by the idea and proceeded to make two paintings. In the first the face had a big mouth with lots of teeth (Figure 11), and in the second one there was Alphonso with a big red school next to him. She was thus able to put into the paintings both her anger at Alphonso for running away and her feeling that school was an exciting place.

Rhonda's painting sessions followed the same pattern and she continued her exploration of body-image at the end of each session. Looking at a drawing basically similar to Figure 11, she exclaimed, "Is this me? Yes, it is!" A painting of the school's principal with whom she had a specially warm relationship followed the same pattern. In a painting of her social worker (Figure 12), for the first time we see a body, but the arms are still coming out of the head. Unfortunately, my service at this institution ended and I never had the opportunity to see what further development might have taken place. It is not unusual for younger children to show arms coming from the head, but if this mode of representation persists it often is an indication of neurological impairment. Since we were in the process of exploring body-image and since

Figure 12

Rhonda functioned on a retarded level I would hesitate to draw diagnostic conclusions on the basis of this drawing.

It is clear that both learning and catharsis took place in Rhonda's art sessions. She worked very hard to achieve a unification of experience with affect and at moments she succeeded. She used the opportunity to play and mess safely and thus to experience a release from her fastidious life, and she also managed to explore who and what she was. I would often suggest that she feel herself—her eyes, nose, mouth, head, body, arms, legs—in an effort to clarify her self-perception. Rhonda's paintings show that at least within art activity growth was possible.

Alphonso

Alphonso was 6 years old and lived about two blocks from the school. His fine motor coordination was very poor. He couldn't hold a pencil properly, and it was difficult for him to squeeze a glue bottle. He had great confusion about how long it took for time to pass. When he was through with an activity anxiety and panic would well up in him and he would be hard to control and very provocative. The panic would often make him dart out the door, out of the building, and down the street towards his home. At times he was so quick that he would reach home before anyone could catch up with him.

Alphonso would jump up at 10 o'clock and say, "Now it's time for lunch." I kept a schedule of the day on the board and, pointing to the clock, I would show him that at 10 we do art, at 11 we do math, and at 12 we eat lunch. This helped keep his anxiety in check.

Alphonso was extremely provocative; he would threaten to bite or to eat you. Twice he did bite me, once just after he had clung to me for a moment and once when I told him I had missed him when he was absent. It seemed to me that this was his way of dealing with feelings for people. Either he wanted to incorporate you or to hurt you. He bit visitors as well as teachers.

Alphonso was extremely bright and was capable of getting thoroughly absorbed in what he was doing. But he had little tolerance for the cleanup that signified the end of the session. Anxiety would rise up in him and he would want to spill and throw things. He would become very wild and want to run. One could get him to do something at such a time only by holding on to him firmly and doing it with him.

He often needed someone to physically restrain him from either running or biting. After I held him for a while, saying nothing that would contribute to his panic and letting him know that he would not be allowed to lose control, he would calm down. All the tension and excitement would be gone and Alphonso, thoroughly relaxed, could be interested again in an activity. One could see that he was tormented continuously by boundless anxiety. His eyes were always crusted and red and swollen. I doubt that he was able to sleep for any extended period of time.

Alphonso had relatives in Portugal and he had been there to visit. When he would quietly threaten to run away and I would ask him where he wanted to go, he would answer "To Portugal." "But," I protested, "there's an ocean between us and Portugal. It's cold and wet and deep." He would answer, "I'll run on top of it." When the family was in Portugal, Alphonso actually had run away.

At times Alphonso thought he was omnipotent and wanted to be the center of attention. He would, when in such a mood, kick, put his feet on the table, lean backward in his chair, turn tables over, bite and hit in order to show me that he was all-powerful. This effort to exercise control over me stood in contrast to the wild panic that was beyond his own control.

During the art sessions Alphonso was able to sublimate very well. He was eager to work and paid close attention to the task at hand. He was not at all interested in Rhonda and he did not need my continuous attention. Once he had the materials he wanted, he set to work with intense concentration. He could, however, accept suggestions or help when it suited his purpose.

Alphonso enjoyed painting most of all. He had an interesting fetish: the color purple. Perhaps for him it had some sort of magical power. When I first gave him my usual palette of primary colors he immediately called out, "I want purple—give me purple." I said, "I will show you how to make purple," and he was quick to say "Red and blue." I showed him how to mix the color and he set right to work. Later, I showed him how to mix other colors but he rarely used them.

Once, at my suggestion, he tried making a person (Figure 13). Using his beloved purple, he depicted the figure sideways, first outlining the head, then filling it in, then proceeding in the same way with the body, and finally adding the legs. I asked him where the boy was and he said, "He's walking outside." The painting is strong, bold and active and at the same time simple and forthright. Another painting (Figure 14) shows a boy running. It also has an interesting, almost geometric quality.

Figure 13

At around this time Alphonso began to take medication so that his behavior in school was more within bounds, especially in the morning. The drug often wore off by lunch time but the art session was always in the morning so he was very subdued, compliant, and quiet. All provocative behavior was suppressed; he was not anxious and had no need to run while under the influence of the drug. As a result there was a very interesting shift in his painting. He still used purple but now he started with the number 1 and in a somewhat circular fashion painted consecutive numbers around his paper (Figure 15). When he finished with one sheet, he would ask for another; once he continued well up into the 20's on three different sheets of paper.

This child illustrates a very different use of art. Alphonso is able to sublimate: he can divert energies away from his conflicts into a constructive and pleasurable experience. He was able to convert the impulse to run into painting a boy walking with outstretched legs and, later, a boy running. However, sublimation did not outlast the moment. The pleasure derived from painting a running boy did not induce a lasting displacement. Far from preventing his flight it excited him so that he then needed to run all the more. But even more interesting is how he was able, when on medication, to convert

Figure 14

his flight-into-action into an action-on-paper accomplished by the succession of consecutive numbers: a direct conversion from gross locomotor action into an obsessive-compulsive symbolic action, drained of the energy needed for a real working through and devoid of heartfelt pleasure. The drugs inhibited everything: the pleasure, the excitement, and the flight.

Five Prima Donnas

I will now describe my work with a group of five 10- to 12-year-old boys, called by their teacher "five prima donnas." A word from any one of them could set the entire group in a turmoil. They had to be strictly disciplined, and in order to maintain control one or another of them was frequently threatened with removal from the room. All five were hyperactive. One of them was mute

Figure 15

for the first 3 months. At home he never spoke to his family, but toward the end of the previous year he had started speaking in school only. Now, in a new class with a new teacher, he again was mute. This, however, didn't prevent him from joining in the fun. Another of the five was extremely slow and obsessive in his artwork. His father was an artist and had taught him many things. The boy was very capable but would always mess up his work, destroy it, or leave it unfinished. He could not tolerate having success in this medium. Yet another of these children was very talented. Everything he did was beautiful. He had exquisite taste and judgment of proportion, design, form, and color.

Every one of these children enjoyed his art session and looked forward to it all week long. Yet in view of the authoritarian structure of the school and the highly vulnerable controls of the five boys, it was an extremely difficult group for a lone adult to contain.

Artwork, with its implicit call for freedom and relaxation, helped weaken the children's self-control. It was impossible for them to paint as a group. Clay, on the other hand, was an excellent medium. It is real and concrete; shaping and molding it demands a certain control.

For quite a while before Thanksgiving the word *turkey* took on highly sexual overtones. If one child said "turkey," the entire group would go into convulsions, as if someone had said a sexy word. "Turkey" may have become so charged because holidays provoke anxiety, particularly in those children who are going to go home for the occasion. On one particularly difficult day I took my usual attitude, saying, "What's so funny about a turkey, and besides I wonder if you can make one?" I succeeded in getting one child interested and helped him to get started. The others immediately began to redirect their energies from convulsive laughter into a contest to see who could make the biggest turkey. They worked at a feverish pitch for the rest of the time and in the end produced five very different but equally large and impressive turkeys. They were extremely proud of this accomplishment for weeks afterwards—proud enough to preserve the turkeys until all of them were completely finished, whereas previously they had broken each other's clay work to pieces in between art sessions.

Long after Thanksgiving a new set of expressions for penis, vagina, buttocks, and breasts turned up, producing the same kind of behavior as had the word *turkey*. I surprised them by being more frank than their classroom teacher. I was quite matter-of-fact about the differences between men and women, and succeeded in getting one child interested in making a clay figure of a woman with breasts and a hole for the vagina. The others became interested too. A more clear-cut example of sublimation through the channeling of libidinal energies into creative work would be hard to find. The entire tone of the room changed from one that was highly charged with anxiety and the threatened breakdown of all controls to one where each was busily at work striving to make his product bigger or better than the next. The result was satisfaction in achievement, in contrast to the frustrating, disintegrative experience the boys were having earlier.

Here it was possible to resolve internal conflicts through art and, at the same time, conflicts between the boys and external authority. The group seemed to be heading for a confrontation with the art therapist, threatening to depose her and preventing her from conducting the art sessions. By allying myself with the boys and accepting their excitement, I succeeded in heading off the confrontation. Thus I was able to help them gain control over their impulses, successfully handling a situation both difficult for those in authority and destructive to the children.

Art Expression in Psychotherapy

The third setting was a community psychiatric clinic where low-cost or medicare-sponsored help was available. The clinic was run by a psychiatric social worker and had on its staff a part-time psychiatrist, psychology interns, social workers, social work students, and educational therapists. Even though I was by title "educational therapist," I functioned as a psychotherapist.

The theoretical orientation was psychoanalytic and the treatment offered was psychoanalytically oriented psychotherapy. Group therapy and other methods of treatment were being tried out on a limited scale. Since I was labelled an educational therapist I saw mainly children who were referred by their schools.

Liza

Liza was referred to the clinic at the age of 7½. Her school complained that she fought constantly, couldn't sit still, didn't get along with her peers and stared at them continuously, and didn't keep up with her school work. At home attempts were made to maintain strict discipline but they met with difficulty. There are no illustrations for this case, for the value of the artwork lies strictly in its usefulness to the child at the time it was made.

Liza lived with her maternal grandparents. Her mother lived in the city but rarely came to see her child, and her visits were not very welcome to her own mother. Liza had always lived with these grandparents except for the second and third years of her life, which were spent in Puerto Rico with an aunt who has a child of about the same age. At that time she called her aunt "Mommy" and her uncle "Daddy." The family is large and close except for Liza's mother. This was never explained to Liza, who remained unsure who her mother was. Not knowing to whom she really belonged, she had a very uneasy, insecure status in the household. At the time I was working with her, she learned by chance that her real father had died. Liza had known him only through photographs but she must have longed for him nonetheless for she seemed to mourn his loss.

Liza weighed only 4 pounds and 3 ounces at birth. She cried a lot during the first 3 months and was fed frequently to improve her sucking reflexes. She is reported to have walked at 8 months and to have demanded a bottle at night until the age of 7. Toilet training, according to the grandmother's report, was harsh. Beginning at 4 months, she was put on a potty chair in the morning and the afternoon for ½ hour, was given a bottle at the same time, and had movements regularly. The grandmother insists that training was completed at 8 months for bowel and bladder. When Liza walked she would go over to the potty and sit down even though she could not take off her diaper. The rest of her development to this point was reportedly normal.

Liza didn't eat very well and there was a battle in the household as her grandparents tried to force her to eat. When she didn't give in, she was beaten with a strap. She ground her teeth at night. Reportedly she was constantly kissing her grandmother, telling her she was the best mother in the world; this only annoyed the grandmother. Liza played the grandfather against the grandmother by telling him things the grandmother told her not to tell and when he threatened to hit her she asked him how he could do this to his "favorite." It appeared that she engaged in a constant battle for control of her world and that she yearned to be an adult and to order everyone else about instead of the inadequate, bad, ugly, unacceptable child she felt herself to be.

Liza made good use of her therapy sessions, responding readily to those adults who gave her constant attention. She established a transference relationship quickly and easily. She played out her need to control by reversing roles: she became the therapist, teacher, or other grown-up lady (never mother) and the therapist became Liza, the child who had to do what she was told.

Apparently many of her problems stemmed from her early and severe toilet training. She established sphincter control but never really accepted and integrated the control of her anal drives, and this is what we see in the forefront of her attempts to control any situation she found herself in. She equated being bad with being anal. Also related to anal problems was her grimacing during sessions and playing that she was a genie; apparently she felt as if she were bottled up and about ready to explode. Her need to mess was just as excessive as her need to control, and her need for constant attention may have had something to do with her fear of not being able to maintain control.

Although Liza usually enjoyed painting, like many children who have a very poor self-image she would avoid putting paint on the paper at first. Putting a mark on the paper is a big commitment and can be very difficult for those who think very little of themselves. For Liza, painting was both an expression of her conflicts and a direct gratification of her anal drives. She would order me to paint and while she had control of my actions she would allow herself to begin to mess with the paints. She would make a mess by mixing colors on the tray, would wipe up the mess, and then make another. While doing this she once said, "My grandmother makes me nervous." When I asked her how, she responded with, "Forget it."

Liza very much enjoyed cleaning up. She liked to pour the excess paint on her hands and squeeze it through her fingers and all around her hands, saying, "I'm having fun." Gradually her interest in cleaning up came to center around this ritual. It was an occasion for sensual pleasure linked to anal play.

After a time, conflicts aroused by the painting process became so intense that Liza began to express them verbally. When she was mixing colors on the tray, she would drip water all around and say anxiously, "Oh! Look what I did." I would reassure her, saying it didn't matter, that it was all right to do that. She would make a grimace and with half-closed eyes and her head in the air say, "It doesn't matter, it doesn't matter," and laugh. Once she said, "I'm bad, like in school." In response to my inquiry as to what bad is, she said, "I do things like this," and then she made grimaces and gestured all around in the air with her arms, saying that she looked like a genie and that she was ugly. She went on, "You're my mother, you hit me and I tell my father, but you said not to tell him and I get in trouble. . . . Bad also means like you do pishy, kissy."

Since the central conflict belonged to the anal phase of development, it seems logical that Liza used painting the way she did. We see here that manipulation of art material can serve not only for expression of conflict but also for gratification of one side of the conflict—the anal infantile urges. Liza used painting for both purposes and at the same time the painting stimulated her to deal verbally with the very same conflicts.

Ken

Ken was 9½ years old when he was referred to the clinic by his school because of often bizarre, disruptive behavior and learning difficulties. His problem gradually emerged as I put together what I knew from his parents and the school with what took place in the sessions.

Ken is the first child of parents who married late in life. Both parents seemed to prefer their second son, 5 years younger. Ken was overweight, wore baggy pants, was poorly coordinated, and lacked self-esteem. All this made him so uncomfortable that he looked odd or foolish and was a natural target for teasing. He presented himself as an ugly duckling, though in fact his features were not unattractive.

In a way Ken was repeating his father's early history. The father was the older of two sons, the younger also being preferred, and the father was now working in a family-owned store with his own younger brother, who bossed him around as if he were a lackey. Ken's father was very infantile in all of his relationships.

Ken's mother struck me as a woman who suffered from very ambivalent feelings toward her family. Insecure in her role as wife and mother, she vacillated between drawing Ken close and being furious with him. During Ken's customary sleepless evenings she would allow him into her bed or would herself lie down in his. At the same time his wakefulness would make her very angry. She was capable of violent outbursts and had been known to inflict severe bruises on Ken's body.

When I first saw Ken he struck me as a gawky, fearful child whose fine motor coordination was also very poor. His anxiety made his hands tremble and although he became quite relaxed in his relationship with me, his movements continued to be fidgety and nervous. He was a stocky child who tended

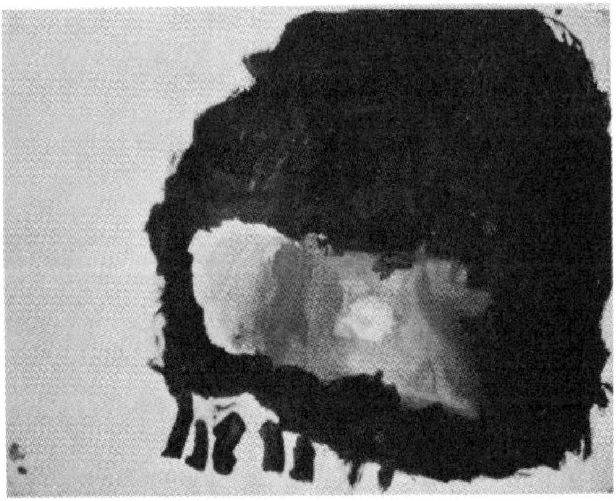

Figure 16

to cling to his mother, touching and stroking her in a somewhat infantile fashion, but he could actually part from her without any difficulty.

Throughout many of our sessions Ken would play with a toy cash register. He would be the storekeeper and I was to have all the money and buy things from him. It was very difficult for him to charge what things were worth.

In the sessions Ken talked about the sun exploding and about exploding volcanoes. Fantasies of playing with his father were associated with ideas about the extinction of dinosaurs. Playing with the cash register stimulated talk about a fire in his father's store, about getting his finger cut off in the cash register, and about finding out about the fire while his mother was in the bathtub. He would open and close the drawer of the cash register, making the motions of putting money in and taking it out but actually leaving the money on the table. He mentioned that his mother walked around naked and made a mistake and walked into his room. "Women do that when boys are asleep." Ken readily acknowledged that little boys sometimes only pretend they're asleep.

We see in Ken a struggle to cope with some very exciting feelings and thoughts. He adopts his parents' ways of coping with internal conflict and low self-esteem and presents himself as incompetent. By his slovenliness and babyish behavior, he sells himself short and exposes himself to derision. The bizarre behavior and aggressive outbursts at school are a desperate attempt to assert an already defeated self. He adapts by denying selfhood on a mature, age-appropriate level and asserts himself as an infant. He unconsciously seeks punishment and humiliation as an affirmation of his essential impotence, at the same time fantasying at a conscious level about playing baseball well enough to join the Little League.

Figure 17

Painting served two main functions for Ken. It facilitated expression, both in pictures and words, of troublesome fantasies, exciting thoughts, and conflicts. Also it gratified him and bolstered his shaky self-esteem. His free-flowing thoughts had a fluidity that enabled him to move freely from their expression through play into their expression in paint.

Ken painted a space ship (Figure 16) so near the sun that it needed a heat shield to keep it from burning up. At the same time it was dangerously near a storm. One day he painted a small mountain (Figure 17), decided it was snowing and put some snow on the peak, then sought to obliterate the whole mountain by piling up the snow higher and higher around its base. While painting this picture he talked of looking in his father's *Playboy* magazine to learn about people's bodies. He spoke of where babies come from and said that men doctors know about ladies and operate on them. I offered to answer his questions but he said he could find out what he wanted to know from books. It pleased him that I helped him paint the extensive background of his mountain picture.

In painting Figure 18 Ken was dealing with such an exciting fantasy that he wet his pants. First he painted a blue sky and a turbulent ocean with swirls and a whirlpool. He said that the two tones of the sky and water were like two people or two nations. I should paint one part and he the other. While painting he talked about being in camp in an old boat that was about to fall apart. The counselor said to abandon it. Ken was wearing a life preserver but could only swim 5 feet. He wanted to paint a boat moving away from the whirlpool. When the painting was finished he started playing with a clock and said that the main

Figure 18

line was broken. He said that the generator was no good and so it couldn't work and nothing was going right.

He seems in this session to humiliate himself by wetting, thus reasserting his impotence in the real world, while in fantasy he seeks to resolve his inner turbulence. He does not paint that boat moving away but instead plasters a boat made of play-dough on top of the turbulent painting.

Occasionally Ken's painting was more self-nurturing and free from conflict, as in Figure 19, which includes a cherry tree with birds, a lake, a deer, and a boy. It is especially interesting that the painting began with the cherries in mid-air. Branches were then added and finally the tree trunk. This way of proceeding seemed to symbolize his struggle to pull together the fragments of himself into a more substantial, positive whole.

Through his painting Ken struggles to cope with the anxiety and fear aroused by his fantasies and conflicts. The paint seems to stimulate the expression of his feelings and at the same time contain them so that he is never completely overwhelmed. Painting provides some gratification and catharsis as well. It gives him an opportunity to seek resolutions as he does when he paints the whirlpool and then says he wants to paint a boat moving away from it. I feel that these fantasies and conflicts are very much rooted in Ken's infantile oedipal sexual wishes as well as in aggressive wishes. These wishes, which should long since have lost their hold on his behavior, instead continually find gratification in fantasy while Ken has a tenuous grasp on reality and an ineffective, ego-alien method of coping with it.

Ken and I used painting for the primary goals of treatment: to build his ego and to reinforce whatever strengths he could summon from within. Competence in painting was secondary. However, painting certainly contributed to his self-esteem; for instance, he once asked if his paintings were worth $100. I

Figure 19

See also color plate V.

never encouraged an unrealistic appraisal of them as he would have liked me to, but I did hang them on the wall as a testimonial to his expression and mastery. We see that painting in psychotherapy can help build ego strengths as it can in education and art therapy, even though it is not used solely for that purpose.

Natasha

Ten-year-old Natasha is the youngest child in a family that has had serious problems with the other children. She has a teen-age brother and a sister in college. The brother ran away from a residential treatment center where he was placed because of delinquency. The sister has had severe depressions. The mother, a very anxious woman with unrealistic expectations and unusually high standards for her children, is always dissatisfied with their performance. She is unable to handle any family situation consistently. Natasha was referred for educational therapy because her mother would only consent to her coming for help if she could rationalize it as a need for help with a learning problem. Natasha does not, however, need help with reading, for she reads a year above grade level. Therefore, I spent as much time on psychotherapy as on reading.

Figure 20

Natasha presents a sophisticated facade, like a primped lady always conscious of her appearance and always dressed in the latest fashion. But behind this facade is a child who thinks everything she does is bad. Her standards for herself are thoroughly unrealistic, a pattern taken on from her mother, who makes demands that Natasha and her siblings cannot possibly meet. Natasha is very constricted and inhibited. She struggles for perfection through rigid control. She is afraid that her inadequacies will show and she doesn't want people to know she isn't perfect. She is afraid of losing control but, like other members of the family, she occasionally resorts to screaming to get her way. On the one hand she told me that she is a conceited snob, and on the other hand she is sure that whatever she does is no good. Her pseudo-sophistication is a poor defense for her.

Natasha was concerned about what it meant to be coming to a mental health clinic. She said she thought she was normal but was afraid she was not. She had many fears and suffered from hypochondriacal symptoms.

She found a certain kind of safety in painting in the sense that entering into this activity provided a cover, the rationalization that permitted her to enter into a therapeutic relationship.

Natasha used art materials at every session. She was eager and enjoyed painting even though she approached it in a gingerly way, knowing that what she did would never meet her expectations. Her paintings were as defensive, hollow, and constricted as herself. It was safer to hide behind a stereotypic facade, just as it was safer to exhibit herself as a pseudosophisticate.

For Natasha painting was sufficiently cathartic to permit her to talk more freely about herself and her feelings about her family. She would tell me defensively, almost before she began to work, that her painting was no good. I would use this opportunity to point out to her how she feels about herself. When she realized that her work could never meet her extreme standards she would become careless, as if to prove that she really was no good because she couldn't keep from messing up her picture.

I tried throughout the sessions to give Natasha an opportunity to express feelings and concerns she had never verbalized before. It is not surprising that she finds life very difficult. When she had become relaxed enough to talk freely, we had the following exchange. "The world is no good and miserable," she said. I replied, "The world is very much the way you make your world. You can make choices and have it the way you want." "I mean the whole world," Natasha answered. I said, "You can't do very much about that, but you can about your own world." Natasha replied, "I don't know if I'll be around long enough for that; I don't think it's worth living." I pointed out to her that she has a world outside her home, where she chooses her friends and increasingly will be able to choose her activities and make a life for herself different and more to her liking than the one she has at home. I sought to build up her self-confidence and to indicate that there are other values than her mother's and other ways of living and that what she did was worthy of her own respect.

As a result, she relaxed greatly and we see a concomitant relaxation in her painting. The first picture of a girl (Figure 20) was much more constricted than the second (Figure 21). The background of Figure 20 is a solid black expanse. In Figure 21 not only did the background change to blue but the girl appeared much more human.

In the sessions with Natasha, painting was first a stereotypic, defensive expression of a highly constricted young person who was struggling to keep control. The process of working with the paints relaxed her defenses sufficiently so that she became able to give verbal expression to some of her concerns. This, in turn, permitted a further relaxation so that the paintings themselves became less stiff and noticeably more alive. After a time Natasha was even able to incorporate into her pictures marks that troubled her because they didn't fit into her idea of perfection. Painting made therapy possible. It became the vehicle that facilitated the verbal expression of conflict.

Concluding Remarks

Art is inherently therapeutic.[2] To what extent it can become therapy depends in large part on the setting in which artwork takes place. Goals

---

[2]For further clarification of the relationship between art and therapy within the field of art therapy see Elinor Ulman, "Art Therapy: Problems of Definition," *Bulletin of Art Therapy*, Vol. 1, No. 2, Winter 1961; and "Therapy Is Not Enough," *Bulletin of Art Therapy*, Vol. 6, No. 1, Oct. 1966.

envisioned for groups and for individuals and conceptions of the teacher's or therapist's role can vary greatly, but limits are set by the larger goals of the institution.

Within a school one's role is clearly educative and one's philosophy of education, of course, has much to do with how one educates. In a classroom conducted by an enlightened, therapeutically oriented teacher, there is an understanding of processes. I do not wish to postulate a dichotomy between process and product, for this division is artificial and misleading. Rather, I wish to emphasize that there can be no genuine product without a dynamic process, although there can be beneficial processes that do not culminate in any finished product. It is through the process that the so-called working through or therapy takes place. In a school as in other settings, the child's needs shape the therapeutic process. As growth and development occur, the nature and function of therapy also evolve.

As educators we want the child to move forward intellectually through opportunities to master the outer world. We want this growth not to be restricted to cognition but to include emotional growth. Therapy can be viewed as a special kind of learning that deals with a person's inner world and his immediate social world.

We can consider art activity in any setting in terms of the function it serves for an individual and in terms of the characteristics on which its growth-inducing potential depends. It can serve similar functions in many different settings, but the sphere in which the growth potential lies differs according to whether the emphasis is on educative goals or psychotherapeutic goals. In both art education and art therapy one seeks growth through developing skill in the expressive use of the medium. One tries to encourage each person's ability to use the medium to the best advantage. In psychotherapy, on the other hand, one seeks to uncover and deal with inner conflicts. Art here serves as a tool subordinated to this process.

Both teachers and therapists are essentially motivators or facilitators of process. As a public school art teacher I tried to inspire autonomy and left the children free to make their own decisions. However, it was not freedom to do nothing or to play. There was a task at hand: the child was to explore a material and give shape to an idea. We expect reasonably healthy children to be open to the world and not so preoccupied by their conflicts that they are deaf to the teacher's attempts to stimulate their awareness of self and world and the relationship between them. In the ordinary school setting a certain amount of first aid can be given the troubled child healthy enough to make use of it.

With comparatively intact children we see that often a little goes a long way. In the case of *Benny* we saw remarkable progress in a short time from primitive, fragmented work to age-appropriate, integrated productions (see Figures 5-9).

An art therapist works with smaller groups and more intensively than does a teacher, so there is a closer relationship between adult and child. This helps

Figure 21

the child learn how to use the art experience to his advantage. As we see in the examples taken from the special school, this relationship between art therapist and child is of paramount importance. It flourishes in an atmosphere that is noncompetitve and nonjudgmental. The accepting attitude of the therapist frees the children to be themselves. Acceptance does not mean that the therapist gives the children permission to act out, but it does mean that she encourages them to be and feel expansive. This attitude fosters the child's trust in the therapist's desire to help him towards success.

This relationship forms a basis for corrective experiences. Disturbed children are preoccupied. They often cannot be motivated by experiences that are brought to a group's attention by a teacher. In order to reach each child one must begin by finding out exactly where he is at the moment. Progress is slow and a great deal of time and individual attention are necessary to bring it about.

In psychotherapy with children (as contrasted with art therapy) art is but one tool. The child may shift from play to art or he may choose to do nothing at all. Art materials may be used for regression, for defense, for the expression of fantasy, or for the somewhat more direct gratification of instinctual drives. One need not necessarily aim at sublimation, nor does one always urge completion of a task begun. The aim is rather to understand and interpret the meaning of behavior.

The relationship between a psychoanalytically oriented psychotherapist and his patient is very different from that between art therapist and child. In psychotherapy the patient is encouraged to transfer onto the therapist past feelings and attitudes by the therapist's remaining as neutral as possible. The therapist wishes to help the patient understand his conflicts and this is done by making interpretations, not by helping the child to achieve. The psychotherapist might interpret how the child uses the art experience and what conflicts are revealed through it.

However the goals may differ in these settings, the basic aim of teacher or therapist is to facilitate individual growth. This is the essential common bond. Despite the distinctions we have pointed out, art can serve the same purposes for children regardless of the varying conditions under which the work takes place. Through the process of doing in art, in the course of psychotherapy as in art education or in art therapy, one communicates with oneself. Viewing each work as an expression of the child who produced it, we can see in it to what extent the child was able to communicate with himself.

Art can be used in a variety of ways. In the public school setting, we saw *Caroline* use it as a cathartic experience that gave temporary relief from a mood, in this instance, overwhelming depression (see Figures 1-3). Art can permit one to take the risk necessary to achieve a genuine success; also in the public school, we saw it serve that function for *José* (see Figure 4). Through art one may find in oneself a strength and ability previously unknown. Early in the course of psychotherapy, *Natasha's* inability to be in touch with her real self was reflected in stereotyped work; her capacity to let go of her rigid controls in art came as a surprise (see Figures 20-21). It enabled her to risk revealing herself to the psychotherapist, and at the same time her performance in art became the prototype of healthier functioning in other aspects of life.

We have also seen that art can be used for displacement and sublimation. The following examples happen to come from the area of art therapy. With *Alphonso*, both occurred when he switched from running away to painting a child running away (Figures 13-14). When he finally turned to painting numbers moving in succession around and around his paper, the wish to run away had been further displaced (Figure 15).

The *five prima donnas* provided an example of sublimation (Figure 16). We saw energies rechanneled from the use of highly charged words into goal-directed work, the production of symbolic clay sculptures.

All children use art for the expression of fantasy. I have illustrated here how in the course of psychotherapy the pictorial expression of conflict-laden fantasy aided in the verbalization of conflicts and at the same time served to gratify wishes. *Ken's* pictures (Figures 16-19) both contained and expressed emotions that would most probably have reduced him to panic if brought into the open without the aid of painting. The process of painting almost always prevented panic by binding the anxiety attached to the fantasies in the very act of expressing them.

Art also weakens controls. This capacity to loosen the repressive forces that control instinctual drives makes it possible for art to serve all the various purposes we have just summarized. It also permits one to use art for instinctual gratification, as we saw in all three settings, in the cases of *Benny*, *Rhonda*, *Liza*, and *Ken*. In *Benny's* case the loosening of controls and the regression in painting encouraged disintegrative tendencies that could only lead to trouble in his particular public school situation. I therefore sought to show him that he could remain in control and permit other aspects of himself to gain expression. This experience fostered the synthesis of emotional and intellectual forces that made his later successes in painting possible. For *Rhonda*, the gratification in art therapy of her impulse to mess never was destructive. It was something she needed to experience and it was therefore therapeutic. After gratifying this impulse in a socially acceptable way she was able to use painting in an effort to explore body-image and discover her real self (see Figures 10-12). Painting used in psychotherapy permitted *Liza*, as well, a direct expression of the central conflict. Through the expression of fantasy in painting *Ken*, also in psychotherapy, permitted himself to gratify phallic wishes. In general, the function such gratification serves and whether it is desirable to allow it to continue depends on the individual and the circumstances.

Art serves yet one more purpose that is not confined to any particular individual or situation. It is a universally pleasurable experience and therefore expansive of the self. It affords this most important and appropriate gratification while at the same time it may be used to serve other functions. Creative experience allows for the loosening of rigid defences, fosters integration, and so provides the opportunity for a restoration of the wholeness of the individual.

Children's Work as Art

JOACHIM H. THEMAL

Sincerity, economy, skill, emotional impact and intelligence are the ingredients of any work of art. The charm of children's work is usually based on sincerity and naïveté; it seldom has the emotional impact of adult work. And it nearly always lacks skill and an intelligent approach. Economy, though present in children's work is, as often as not, meaningless bareness.

Among the children who have produced good, bad, and charming work over the years in our Fine Arts Workshop, a few youngsters have always emerged who have produced paintings and sculptures that seem to transcend the childish approach, and are works of art in their own right. Functioning strictly on their own level, these children manage to create things that are acceptable at any level of criticism. The fact that the scope of contemporary art is practically without limit is (as I hope the illustrations show) not the decisive factor of this acceptability.

Although, in our institution, little use is made of the children's art work for diagnostic purposes, the emotions, repressions, and aggressions that are unconsciously released by the children are a form of therapy which the children administer to themselves. The accent in our art room does not lie in directed therapy, but on art itself. This has developed a kind of ivory tower atmosphere where there is freedom of expression. It is this that attracts the

Figure 1

The artist, a 10-year old boy, is also outstanding in sculpture; but then, most of our good painters are also good sculptors.

Figure 2

By a 12-year old boy. White clay, sprayed with dirty water. 15 inches high.

children to the art room—a climate, a special world, where the uninitiated adult fears to tread. The children have, rightly, come to the conclusion that, with few exceptions, these adults know nothing about art and that their admiration is lip-service.

The children, aged 8 to 16, come mostly from broken homes and all have emotional difficulties. They range from almost normal to quite sick; those found to be markedly delinquent or retarded are transferred as quickly as possible. The children reside at the institution, which is a year-round treatment center. I, as the art instructor, am also resident for part of the week. There is a public school on the grounds, where I teach part time. In addition, I have after-school sessions, at which attendance is voluntary. Since the children are away from home, they are in search of relationships with adults. While they are assigned to their social workers, house parents, etc., they have free choice of activities, of which art is only one. Close friendships with the activity workers often follow and, in fact, nearly all the children who are doing exceptional work in the art room are also personally attached to me.

Although there is a nucleus of children who attend art sessions regularly, these do not form a group, nor do I encourage conversation or a spirit that is anything more than that of a loose fraternity. Art, if it is to mean anything, is no group activity. This was brought home to me forcibly when one of our boys said, with a deprecating gesture, "Oh, art is lonely!" For this particular extrovert child to be confronted with a blank piece of paper, reflecting his own emptiness, was as much of a threat as solitude is to many adults. Although earlier in life this boy had had moments in the art room where the

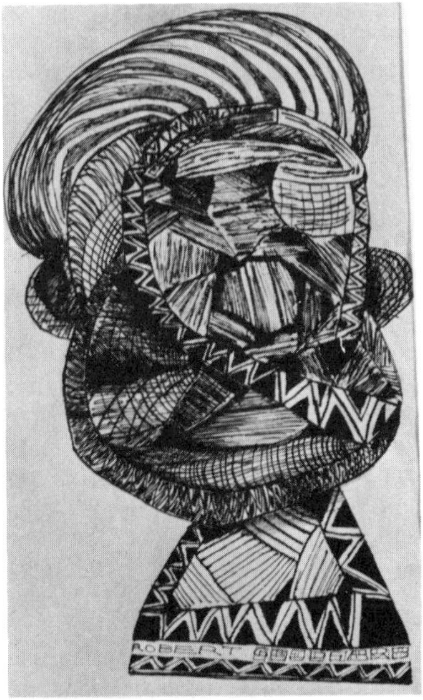

Figure 3

This picture, by a 13-year old boy, was obviously not done in one session. The continuation of interrupted work is facilitated by our good filing system —separate sets of alphabetical shelves for finished and unfinished work.

empty paper was to him, as to other children, a fairy land of potentials, at this particular point of his adjustment he needed competitive sports rather than art.

Solitude is something that has to be achieved and is a necessary condition for any creative act. A group can be mutually stimulating on an intellectual plane—planning a trip, a mural, the plot of a play. But on an emotional plane—which is where art begins— the interaction among children who work in the same room is reduced to perhaps borrowing another child's technique or some especially appealing detail as a point of departure for something entirely new. Apart from such influences, which mature artists undergo too, anything meaningful (be it in painting or sculpture) must and does develop in isolation. The art room, in fact, represents for many children an occasional refuge from all the emphasis that is laid these days on group activities, group spirit, and "leadership." (What does one do with all those leaders?)

"Stimulation," "motivation," and other contemporary clichés, although valid in other areas, are incompatible with meaningful art activity. I never tell children what to paint. In fact, I prefer that they do not paint at all, rather than paint something I suggested. If they sit around bored, not knowing what to do, sooner or later some idea will gestate, something that has meaning to them. Boredom often is the prelude to creation. While artificial stimulation occasionally results in nice little pictures for the art teacher to show, it is in fact a barrier to self-realization and a disrespectful interference with the child's personality. It is part of a cultural pattern that makes originality suspect and is used to level everybody up or down, as the case may be. A "motivated" picture—or, in plain words, a painting suggested or prescribed by the art teacher (and some of them are wonderfully "stimulating" and convincing)—simply drowns out the child's personality, superimposing that of the art teacher. To superimpose one's own supposedly healthy pattern over that of an emotionally disturbed child may be temporarily helpful in a living situation, but is meaningless in the art room.

Not other people's ideas, but firsthand, personal experience is the raw material of art. Such experience having become almost non-existent in an era of mechanized distraction and a push-button existence from cradle to grave, the present-day city child has to rely on his inner experience if he is to produce anything meaningful. Some children will only do one good picture, the story of their life. When the effort is repeated, when they manage to make two good pictures, then a habit of using art can be formed. I know children who come regularly to the art room to translate each new experience, be it the advent of spring or their unhappiness at not receiving mail. They have formed a habit, discovered a safety valve that has become necessary to their mental metabolism. And, of course, the more emotion, the more of themselves they pour into a painting or a lump of clay, the greater both the therapeutic value of their work and its artistic merit. Other children only come when they are disturbed. They come to paint compulsive, repetitive, time-consuming pictures, and they stay away when all is well with them.

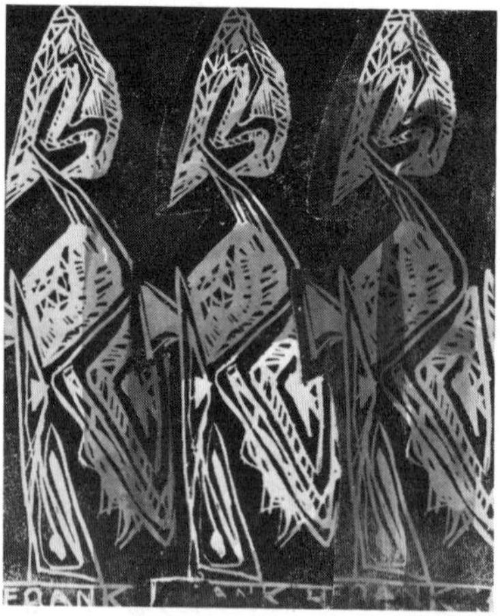

Figure 4

By an 11-year old boy. Linoleum cut, printed three times. The block was cut freely, without a prepared design, by a sort of doodling with the knife on the linoleum. No piece induced by a teacher's planned motivation could convey the emotion of this little masterpiece.

Figure 5

Self-portrait using mirror; charcoal, by an 11-year old.

Within the art room an atmosphere conducive to concentration is preserved by our insistence on good manners and a certain formality of behavior. A child who does not conform to standards is sent out and may be forbidden to attend for a period of time. If he wants to come back and paint, he knows he will have to behave himself. He discovers that it is much easier to exist within limits than to act out his false pride in being a behavior problem. The very eagerness of the children to work—especially with clay—helps to keep them in line. Forced to make a choice, when they fight or argue, they will rather give up their fight than their clay. I sometimes work on my own things and may say to a noisy child, "Be quiet, we are working!" With repetition, this results in a kind of conditioning, so that the child's bubbling energies are directed into channels proper to the art room—just as plugging up a water pipe produces pressure where it is wanted.

Besides basic decorum, we insist on a good clean-up and hard work. I may refuse to look at something done in three minutes with, "Don't try to be a genius." On the other hand, I may pick a discarded doodle from the garbage can when I feel it has potential merit. The ideal situation is for a child to come in with an idea, which he describes to me, sometimes with sketches. He expects suggestions as to the material he should use. I always make a ceremony out of giving out materials and demonstrate their basic use. Based on my knowledge of the child's abilities, I may suggest something he has used before and has not yet fully explored, or something new when I feel he has become stale in the old medium. With some children the medium itself,

Figure 6

By an 11-year old boy. An unconscious caricature of the artist's father. Our knowledge of George Grosz's work no doubt contributes to the charm this drawing has for us.

rather than the idea, becomes the point of departure. Black and colored inks appear to have a particularly stimulating effect. I am well supplied with material, have a great variety of papers, paints, and a few special items which the children consider it an honor to be entrusted with. We use conventional media, but mix these freely. Since the children have freedom of choice in subject matter, it follows that they also have free choice of medium. This means that sometimes 15 different children will work in 15 different media, including a variety of clays.

I have not found many girls to be very creative. They are much more conventional than boys, and cannot use their emotions, which seem, rather, to get in their way. Nearly all our brave little flower and still-life pictures come from the girls (see Figure 13). They don't seem to go through that wonderfully creative period boys experience between the ages of 11 and 13, when they are still sufficiently uninhibited to be direct, still naïve enough to be sincere, not yet ashamed of their feelings. Their awareness and intelligence are awakening, they begin to try to come to terms with reality, without as yet being too critical of what they are doing. Above all, they begin to take pleasure in their manual dexterity: their hands actually do what their eyes tell them to. Girls, on the other hand, seem to pass directly from childhood into the awkward teens, with all their conflicting emotions. They don't believe you when you tell them that what they are doing is good and they resent it if you tell them it is bad or could be better. They compare their work, always unfavorably, with that of others, and seem to have no love for it.

Figure 7

By a 12-year old girl.

Figure 8

This happy picture by a 12-year old boy is an example of the painting game that is part of every picture and is one of the reasons why painting has such appeal to children. Each painting has its own set of rules, and following them creates the inner coherence—or style—of the picture. There are disturbed children who cannot follow their own rules, but there are others, equally disturbed, who can: their sense of harmony prevails. Adult painters, of course, play too. Picasso even cheats at his own game when he juxtaposes realistic and semi-abstract figures.

Figure 9

Pen and ink. This 14-year old boy uses art not just for occasional withdrawal, but practically as a drug.

Figure 10

Life-size head by a 15-year old boy. Fired clay treated with furniture polish and cigarette ashes.

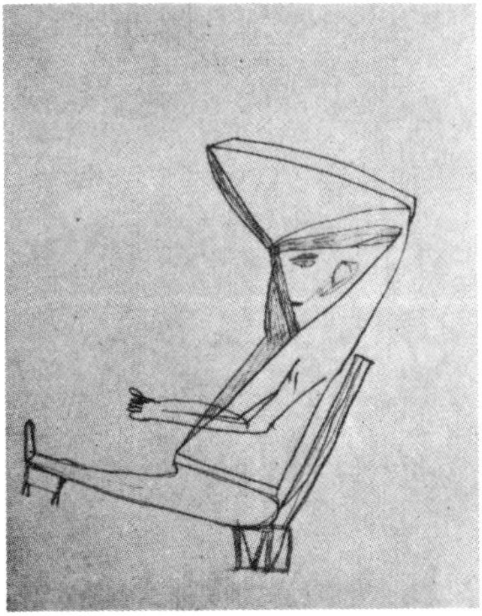

Figure 11

This 12-year old boy obviously loves comfort.

I do not share the current belief that all children should be made to paint large. A large piece of paper is often frightening to a child as too much of a commitment. It can also lead to sloppiness, emptiness, and poverty of content, just as many contemporary paintings are large, empty, and sloppy. Children who like to work small will eventually come round to using bigger areas as they gain self-confidence. It is often the older but still infantile child who does best with large works, as though he wants to create for himself his own sizable reality, or unreality—and more often than not, his pictures are peopled with monsters or dinosaurs. The important thing, of course, is that within the setting of the art room a child feels perfectly free to do whatever he

Figure 12

Same artist as Figure 7. Though the picture appears economical, the figures were scratched into a surface that had first been treated with innumerable layers of white, ochre, and black poster-color, inks, and furniture polish.

Figure 13

A scribble by a 14-year old boy, later developed with care, thus adding impact through hard work while preserving the spontaneity of the scribble.

wants—smear and splatter, if he must, or paint large or compulsively small. He knows his needs best.

Although I discourage copying, sometimes one can do greater harm by preventing children from copying than the copying itself would do them. Carvings made as "copies" from photographs of bold, simple sculptures even helped one boy overcome his rigidity and perfectionism. He was also encouraged to use the flat side of the charcoal stick for his sketches.

An off-beat remark may steer a child away from the pictorial cliché, which is a problem in any art room. The exposure of some conventional attitude, a touch of ridicule, may sometimes shock a child into thinking for himself. It will give him the impetus to find his own language and symbols to express his own emotions. Sometimes the word "obvious" is helpful—it seems to cover a variety of sins, from the cliché to sentimentality, slickness, and bad taste.

No instruction is ever given in the art room that is felt by the child to be instruction, unless it is specifically requested. However, the children do rely on me to find some magic to redeem catastrophes, erase blotches, cover up goofs. They look to me to show them how failures can be turned into successes, and this gives them a sense of security and helps them achieve freedom in their work.

Although we have showcases where the best pictures are exhibited each week and where especially productive children will get one-man shows, the spirit has remained non-competitive. There is a mutual admiration for, and pride in each other's work. Exhibition, besides giving the children a feeling of accomplishment, meets another need, perhaps the greatest need of all—of which creation itself is only the first step—namely: to communicate.

Figure 14

Watercolor by a 12-year old. This is a boy whose talent had for years been exploited by his teachers and parents as a social grace. When he first came to me he made a number of charming little landscapes that were admired by everybody. One day I said: "Aren't you getting tired of those nice little pictures? Anything you know how to do isn't really worth doing!" He responded to this with a glitter in his eyes, as if visualizing experiments to come. He began to paint freely, almost unconsciously. This painting symbolizes his slow progress toward a solution of the problem that brought him to our school. It is remarkable for its economy, the sense of space, the way depth is achieved by a simple cross, the balance between lines and masses.

Art and Craft

EDITH KRAMER

The term "arts and crafts" is in itself a sign that in our culture there is little understanding of either art or craft. "Arts and crafts" is an emasculated hybrid which fulfills the function neither of art nor of craft.

The basic experience of craft is the transformation of raw material (such as lumber, fabric, yarn, leather, etc.) into useful and handsome objects by a logical, comprehensible process.

In art amorphous, malleable material is transformed not into a useful object but into a symbolic one, which conveys and expresses experience.

The decorative arts can be best understood as an overflow of the joy of making objects. Thus a decorated pot expresses the potter's pleasure in his pot; it celebrates the pot and makes it more of a pot.

I will illustrate with an anecdote the relationship between the logical, planned process that belongs to craft and the expressive function of art. I conducted a carpentry class for eight-year-old boys, and at one time they were making footstools. I had planned the stools to be made from 1″ by 4″ lumber by a simple procedure which could be comprehended and executed by eight-year-olds using basic carpentry tools. Procedures were alike for all the children; only their skill and working tempo differed. The demands made on the eight-year-old carpenters were that the footstools had to be sturdy and that they must stand steadily without rocking. Degree of finish differed according to skill and temperament.

After the footstools were completed the children decorated them with tempera paint that later was finished with a coat of clear shellac. No patterns or prescriptions for decorations were given. Suddenly the more or less identical objects began to differ.

The most meticulous worker, a somewhat constricted child, painted his stool brown and could not be induced to add any decoration.

A capable, rather wild boy painted his stool black with a yellow design. It looked as fierce as its maker, somewhat like a wasp.

A Jewish boy painted a menorah on a blue ground.

The most infantile child of the group just mixed paints on the top of his stool and quite lost sight of the idea that he was decorating a piece of furniture.

When all the footstools were finished there were ten radically different objects, each of them looking a great deal like the child who made it.

Naturally the individuality that can be expressed through a footstool is limited. Only when art is freed from its decorative function can it become fully expressive. This is one reason why art and craft should be taught separately, with only occasional overlapping, of which this story is a good example. Art reduced entirely or chiefly to the level of decoration becomes abortive. Indeed, the decoration of the footstools was successful because the boy carpenters also had a good art program and thus could apply their artistic training to this project.

If we keep in mind the lesson contained in this little story, it will be easy to decide in each instance whether a project is valid. We want projects that never contradict but always support the basic experiences of art and of craft.

Truly expressive art is sometimes out of reach for children who are very constricted, or fearful, or empty. Also, expressive, creative work can be sustained only for a limited period of time. Periods of reduced vitality such as illness, evening hours, or times of tension are not always suitable for highly creative work.

There is a need, therefore, for projects which allow a child to succeed in making something with his own hands simply by following a logical procedure that does not tax his limited capacities beyond endurance. But we must be careful to choose projects where the pleasure is indeed one of achievement, however simple, and where this achievement is commensurate with the child's capacities.

For example, if a child makes paper hats, or any of the simple origami figures, he follows a procedure which he could not have invented himself but which he can fully comprehend. The result depends entirely on his actions. Or, if a child makes a boat by sawing up a piece of lumber, the boat will be as simple or as complex as he can make it. Some children are so disorganized or insecure that they cannot perform even on the simplest level, and it may be necessary to give them a lot of help. Still, what is asked of them should be at least theoretically within their reach.

Kit Craft

I am against projects that contain a falsehood. For instance, there are kits which demand no more of the child than to assemble highly intricate parts that are conceived and finished in an adult style which could never be duplicated by the child even if he were functioning at his highest level. He learns how to assemble parts, at best an industrial skill.

Sometimes, with the best of intentions, projects of this kind are used as a bribe to induce reluctant children to spend time with a group-worker. Fairly valuable material may be assembled into such objects as mosaic ashtrays, jewelry, or model boats. The children take home things they have supposedly *made* but actually have only *assembled;* they have been given a gift. When inducements are necessary it is better to offer gifts outright, preferably food and drink, or to offer prizes for games. Something as valuable and serious as craft should never be distorted and corrupted, even to serve a worthy purpose.

While assembly kits give immediate satisfaction, they backfire because they set a standard of commercial perfection which no child could possibly attain. Children get jaded, used to achieving highly finished results with very little effort; they become less and less ready to exert themselves in independent actions where they risk failure. At the same time this commercial perfection discourages children, making them less able to accept what they actually can achieve.

For example, when pouring plaster into commercial molds results in commercially perfect, slick sculpture of an adult style, this will inhibit the child's creative imagination. He will lose courage and ambition to sculpt things in his own simple and childlike style. An added disadvantage is that nearly all available commercial molds are in execrable taste by any standard.

Now, to learn to cast plaster is a fascinating and educational experience, but this experience can be had without producing those commercial atrocities. Any number of simple objects can be cast in plaster. Rubber molds can be made of everyday objects (for instance fruits can be cut in half and children can themselves make relief molds from them). Such an activity is vastly more educational and exciting than the use of commercial molds, and *it separates the craft from the pseudo-art to which it has been linked.* The pleasure of reproducing an object is retained without the destructive side effects which commercial molds introduce into the experience.

Painting by Numbers

Numbered oil paintings are possibly the most destructive of all pseudo-arts. Not only is the finished product in bad taste and the picture conceived in an adult style which no child could (or should) duplicate. The manner whereby the painting is achieved contradicts the process whereby any painting is originally created. In the numbered painting, the artist's skillfully blended colors are artificially divided into many confusing, irregular little areas whose shapes bear no relation to the objects depicted. Colors are chosen by number, which means that even a color-blind person could manufacture the painting successfully; anyone who can read numbers and is sufficiently patient and compulsive can do the job. The child then miraculously achieves a pseudo-art object without having learned anything about the making of such an object. Indeed the methods he has used contradict common sense and the creative process in every respect. He has learned neither about art, nor about craft; he has done simple busy-work and has produced an object that is guaranteed to be ugly.

Numbered paintings are sometimes defended on the ground that simple busy-work, even compulsive work, can be helpful in certain situations. This is true. However, such busy-work should not pretend to be art. There are many activities where a useful, even handsome result can be achieved by mechanical and meticulous application, for example, weaving, darning, embroidery, even jigsaw puzzles. All such activities are preferable to number painting.

Coloring Books

Coloring books should never be used during art sessions but they have a limited usefulness for young children, as an occupation for times when more arduous work cannot be sustained, for instance, during illness, periods of fatigue or of anxious waiting. Recognizing the content of a picture is so different from drawing a picture that no child is led to think he has *produced* the drawing which he has colored in. He knows that he has only decided on the color of the objects in his book. To separate drawing from color is a logical and legitimate procedure in simple illustration; the child does not learn anything that contradicts the art of illustrating. The greatest objection against coloring books is their bad taste, saccharine sweetness, and insipid content.

The Second Wind

Today we have a tendency to underrate people's capacity for sustained effort. True achievement is attained not at the first try but on the second wind. In every creative task there is, after the initial enthusiastic thrust, a moment of letdown when one is ready to give up. If this letdown is overcome, unexpected reserves of strength almost miraculously lead to achievement. The experienced artist (or mountaineer, or scientist) knows about both the despair and about the rewards of overcoming it. The inexperienced child (or adult) has to be helped, even forced, to have this experience.

There was a time when children were cruelly forced to finish every task, even the most tedious. Work begun had to be completed, just as the unfinished lunch was served for dinner and breakfast, getting more disgusting with every meal. Today we do the opposite. We make things too easy. We confuse pleasure and fun. Creative work is not *fun,* like playing games and riding a roller coaster. It is a *pleasure* which makes demands but which repays effort with exquisite satisfaction. It is our responsibility to introduce children to such pleasures.

Part II

PRACTICE OF ART THERAPY

WITH ADULTS

Family Art Therapy: Experiments with a New Technique

HANNA YAXA KWIATKOWSKA

The origin of the term "Family Art Therapy" is closely linked with the recent development of a new trend in psychiatric research—the study of the family as a unit in the search for the genesis of schizophrenia. Such studies have been conducted by several groups of researchers: Nathan Ackerman in New York; Murray Bowen, formerly at the National Institutes of Health, Bethesda, Maryland, presently at Georgetown University; James Framo and Ivan Nagy at the Eastern Pennsylvania Psychiatric Institute; Don Jackson and Gregory Bateson in California; Theodore Lidz and Stephen Fleck at Yale; and Lyman Wynne and his colleagues at the National Institute of Mental Health in Bethesda, Maryland. These groups differ in their approaches, techniques, hypotheses, and findings; but their work is based on a common idea—a psychodynamic interpretation of schizophrenia that takes into conceptual account the social organization of the family as a whole. From this concept emerged in several of these groups a new psychotherapeutic technique called "conjoint family therapy" where the patient, or the one recognized as such by the family, and the parents and siblings are seen together in psychiatric interviews.

My work as art therapist at the National Institute of Mental Health in the Section on Family Studies headed by Dr. Lyman C. Wynne enabled me to explore the use of art as a means of communication and self-expression within the family group. These art therapy sessions with the whole family have also provided an unusual opportunity to observe how the family unit functions in a situation less formal and less subject to their established mechanisms of control than is the purely verbal psychotherapeutic interview.

From another point of view we can consider family art therapy as a new form of group art therapy which, to my knowledge, has not yet been applied elsewhere. Psychologists, psychiatrists, and art therapists have used art with organized groups for spontaneous self-expression or as a projective technique in conjunction with interview group therapy. Art activity is central in some procedures described in the literature, peripheral in others.[1] The art products have been handled in a variety of ways, corresponding to the authors' theoretical orientation to therapy in general.

The difference between family art therapy and the types of group art therapy cited above—indeed the uniqueness of family art therapy—is that in family art therapy we deal with a group which is not merely linked by their general maladjustment or by a common symptom. The family has lived as a group for many years—since birth in the case of the patient and his siblings. These people through the years have developed their own interactional pattern and a whole interlinked system of defenses. They have formed subgroups within the family group, alliances of some members of the family against others, and developed their own patterns of thinking which have produced the special culture or climate of a given family.

Is the schizophrenic patient's family different from other families, and if so, how does it differ? Family art therapy is one of the techniques being used in research to investigate these questions. Its procedures evolved in the following setting: On a small psychiatric unit the patients, young adults or late adolescents (schizophrenics and non-schizophrenics), are hospitalized. The prerequisite for the admission of the patient is that his family take part in whatever therapeutic procedures are recommended by the psychiatrists in charge. These are: Conjoint family psychotherapy sessions twice weekly (patient, parents, and siblings), in certain cases regular weekly sessions of parents with social workers, psychological tests, and family art therapy. Besides this, in most cases, the patient is seen in individual psychotherapy by one of the psychiatrists who also sees him with his family.

---

[1] H. Azima, Fern Cramer and E. D. Wittkower: Group Art Therapy. Allen Memorial Institute of Psychiatry, Montreal.

George R. Bach: *Intensive Group Therapy,* Ronald Press, 1954.

Dorothy W. Baruch and Hyman Miller: "The Use of Spontaneous Drawings in Group Therapy." *American Journal of Psychotherapy,* Vol. 5, No. 1, January 1951.

Michael B. Dunn and Robert A. Semple: *But Still it Grows.* Monograph. The Devereux Foundation, Devon, Pa., 1956.

Margaret Naumburg and Janet Caldwell: "The Use of Spontaneous Art in Analytically Oriented Group Therapy of Obese Women." *International Journal for Psychotherapy, Psychosomatics, Special Education,* 1959.

Lucile Rankin Potts: "The Use of Art in Group Psychotherapy." *International Journal of Group Psychotherapy,* Vol. 6, No. 2, April 1956.

————: "Two Picture Series Showing Emotional Changes During Art Therapy." *International Journal of Group Psychotherapy.* Vol. 8, No. 4, October 1958.

Development of Family Art Therapy

The idea of using art therapy with the families came through accidental participation of family members in individual art therapy sessions with patients. Art therapy was earlier used on the project only individually; it happened occasionally that a family member would visit the patient at this time and the patient would ask to show him his art work or to have him present at the session. This was agreed to under one condition: that the parent or sibling would actively take part in the session. The art productions and interaction of this fraction of the family were so revealing and produced such unexpectedly interesting material that we wondered what would happen if we included the whole family regularly in the art therapy program.

Six family art therapy sessions have proved to be a minimum to decide if the response of the family promises to provide therapeutic possibilities or further research material. Quite often the time element presents a serious difficulty as most of the fathers have full-time jobs, and many of the mothers work. However, despite resistances and the time problem, a large percentage of the families have continued beyond the evaluation period. Out of 17 families seen in evaluation, only four families were discontinued. The others continued to meet; one of them, at the time of writing, for 27 months.

In the later course of the work, because of the complexity of the interaction as well as the extraordinarily demanding character of these sessions, a participant observer joined the group. This was either one of the therapists, a psychiatrist, or a social worker, who was engaged in family psychotherapy with the same family. Like other therapy sessions in our program, the family art therapy sessions are tape-recorded. Abstracts of all sessions are dictated or written immediately after the session.

The families, not surprisingly, initially present great resistance. Again and again we hear the same protestations: "Are we back in kindergarten?"; "I can't draw a straight line"; "You will never make an artist out of me"; etc. But, astonishingly, most of them become so involved in the experience that the separation, when it is time to end our meetings, is quite painful, and the rejection the family feels has to be dealt with as a special therapeutic problem.

As this new procedure developed, many changes of technique were necessary—there was nothing to guide us except our own experience. We experimented with several approaches to the structure of these sessions. At first, the members of the family were seen individually for one or two sessions to establish rapport with the art therapist. The patient, seen previously alone, had already established rapport. The family was then seen with the patient. Different configurations were experimented with, the patient meeting with one or both of the parents, or a sibling, sometimes depending on availability. This way of organizing the sessions was used with the first three families of schizophrenics. They were seen for periods of 6, 11, and 12 months in weekly family art therapy concomitant with individual art therapy sessions with the patient.

Even this provided a valuable field for observation and study of the family's psychodynamics, but the structure had its drawbacks. The difficulty of the switch from separately established individual relationships with the art therapist to the group situation produced an increase of resistance and anxiety. Both the patient and the parents resented the invasion of the relationship which they had managed to establish separately, sometimes with great effort; various members of the group, most frequently the patient, withdrew or became less responsive.

Subsequently, families were seen from the beginning as a group of all the available members including the patient; this was much more successful. Only for particular reasons such as disruptiveness, resistance, or need for support was one of the members of the family seen alone, as described in the examples below.

For instance, in one family the patient became isolated from the rest of the group—a repetition of the habitual family pattern. The parents, very responsive and fascinating, became so involved in expressing their own problems that they practically ignored the presence of their schizophrenic son. The patient tried to focus some attention on himself by attacking the parents verbally and attacking the art therapist through his refusal to take part in the activity of the group. This patient has since been seen separately; art therapist and patient gradually established a relationship with each other. Not only did the patient become able to take part in the family art therapy sessions, but the therapist had developed an interest in him which she could maintain without effort despite the parents' more direct pressure for her attention.

In another family the father kept saying he had no talent in comparison with other members of his family, and used this as an excuse for refusing to continue attending. Special sessions were held with him in order to show him that talent was not crucial in these sessions and to cut through this manifestation of resistance.

One mother refused active participation in the sessions even though she made no objection to being present. This produced a great deal of tension and anger in her husband and son, the patient, who were irritated by her lack of cooperation. The mother was a rigid, domineering person who assumed the role of a defenseless and fragile woman seeking protection from her husband. When an individual session was suggested to her, she said, "Why was I singled out?" "You singled yourself out," she was told. The scribble she had made in her individual session (figure 1) was called by her "A Woman Made of Wire." When asked for comment she said, "What more can one say of a woman made of wire?" She had always been very preoccupied with the physical well-being of her children, but probably unable to give them much more warmth than the surrogate "wire mothers" used by Dr. Harry F. Harlow and Dr. Robert R. Zimmerman in their

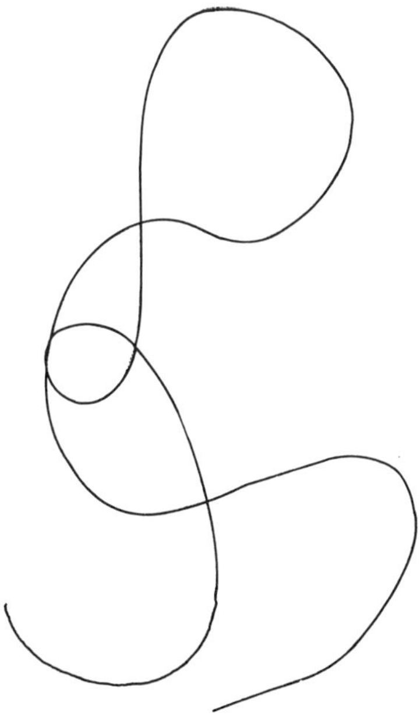

Figure 1

experiments with baby monkeys.[2] This rigid representation was an acknowledgement of a view of herself which she had been afraid to recognize and reveal.

In the following family psychotherapy session the mother's lack of participation in art therapy was discussed; the therapist pointed out how her actions affected the rest of the family, how she really controlled them in this and other situations. This experience was seen by the psychotherapist as a turning point in family psychotherapy; it loosened her defenses to the point where she could fruitfully participate in the group.

Therapeutic Goals

To see each member of a family separately is tempting as a relief from the intensity of family art therapy sessions, where the art therapist herself comes to experience the climate of the schizophrenic family. If individual sessions are too readily used in the face of every difficulty, the goal of understanding and working therapeutically with the family as a whole is impaired. For this reason, techniques have gradually been worked out to help the resistant member of the family tolerate the difficulties of the group situation without taking him away from it. Sometimes a directive approach is helpful, especially when the suggestions are given to the entire group. Although specific instructions are never given, the art therapist may suggest a new medium, or an experiment in which the entire group has to take part. This may prove less threatening to the reluctant member than the simple invitation to spontaneous self-expression.

In family art therapy as in family psychotherapy, the emphasis is always on spontaneous self-expression. Yet some standardized procedures have been developed for more accurate comparisons of different families' responses, particularly during the evaluation period. The same variety of media is offered in the same sequence to the families; certain specially devised procedures are used with all the families. One of these is the well-known scribble technique, used with the families in a special way. After each member has developed a picture from his own scribble, the family is encouraged to make a "joint scribble." One person makes a scribble and all present try to find pictorial suggestions in it. Then each paints on this picture in order to bring it to completion. This procedure has not only encouraged families to venture into a joint activity, but it has also proved to be one of the most helpful ways to permit the family to express,

[2] Harry F. Harlow and Robert R. Zimmerman: "Affectional Responses in the Infant Monkey." *Science*, Vol. 130, No. 3373, August 21, 1959.

Figure 2

recognize and accept feelings which are below the conscious level.

The following examples are illustrative of what transpires from the introduction of the joint family scribble and how it is used therapeutically:

A mother, who usually painted conventional, insipid pictures of flowers, landscapes, and "old-fashioned little girls," persistently denied any feelings of anger. She was, however, the one who implanted this set of ferocious teeth in the mouth of a man which the family developed together out of a scribble (figure 2). When the art therapist commented on the anger and aggression the picture expressed, the mother agreed to it with the others, without trying to deny her own contribution.

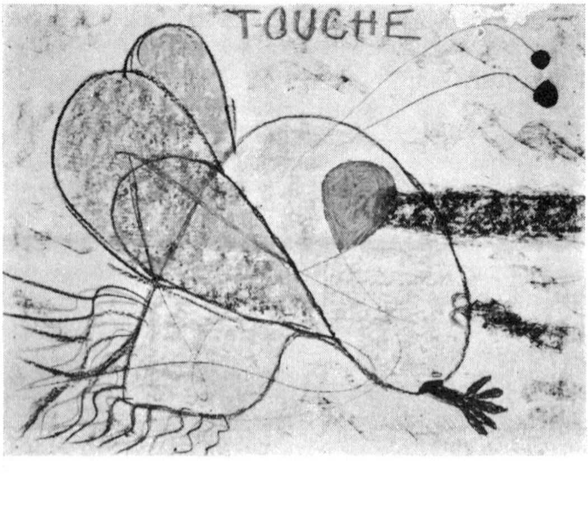

Figure 3

Figure 4

Another family, who was quite resistant to art therapy, and at this session especially apathetic, suddenly came to life when the father quite unexpectedly added a blood-red "forked tongue" to a rather delicate and benign "grasshopper" (figure 3) which they had started to make out of their scribble. This aggressive note was a starting point for a lively interaction. The patient and her brother competed with each other in adding flames and fire coming out of the nostrils and eyes of the so-called "insect." The whole family delighted in the recognition of shared aggression, which earlier had been buried in apathy and depression. The title speaks for itself: "Touche."

Figure 4 is developed from a scribble made by the husband and son of the woman who drew the "Woman Made of Wire." She was present at this session but refused to draw. The father and the son (the patient) joined in this expression of violent, even murderous feelings. The elements of the picture are unrelated, and the effect is bizarre. These features commonly appear when tension in the family increases.

Figure 5, this witch-like portrait of "Mme. Defarge Without Knitting Needles," obviously shows how this same man felt toward his wife at this moment. What the pictures expressed was discussed by the family; the mother was able to recognize how her cool detachment aroused so much rage in her family.

It has not been possible in this article to describe all the methods used, or to give detailed case histories. But I would like to mention briefly some of the therapeutic values peculiar to family art therapy as compared with family psychotherapy, and why it may become an exciting adjunct to research in the study of family dynamics. Psychiatric team members familiar with art therapy found that the inherent nature of this activity makes special contributions possible.

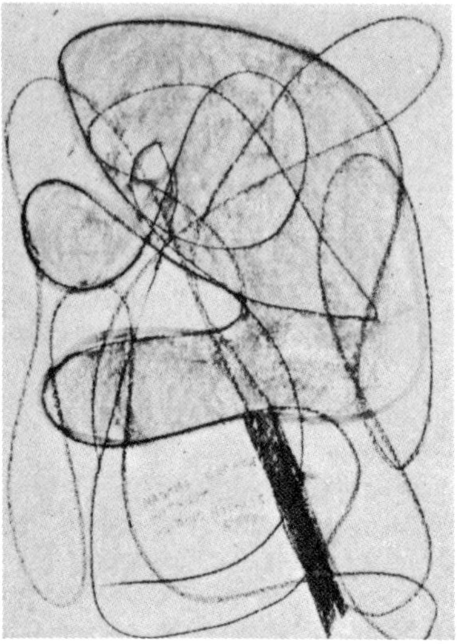

Figure 5

The family is less guarded than in the verbal situation; the groupings, the dependency of one member on another, become obvious in the choice of places, media and subjects. Anger and hostility are expressed without such an intense feeling of guilt; family members are often able to accept their real perception of themselves and perceive the other members of the family through their art projections as different from their habitual stereotyped images of one another.

For example, we noticed that several mothers while attempting to portray their young adult schizophrenic daughters represented them as small girls or infants. One mother, feeling displeased with her drawing, kept begging the art therapist for help. When she was advised to look at her daughter, she said, "I don't have to look at her—I know how my daughter looks . . ." This gave the art therapist a chance to question whether she sees her daughter as she really is today—a young woman, and not the baby she had drawn.

Another mother made a picture (figure 6) of a "baby in bunting." At first she connected it with her grandchild, but then exclaimed "It might be that I never can think of Suzy as a grownup person . . . I always think she is still a baby in bunting . . ." Suzy's response to this some time later was a very impressive abstraction (figure 7), which she explained as follows: The large central form is a "powerful mother," with "eight children (still unformed), all but two cut off from her" (by masses of blue wavy shapes). Suzy is outspoken about her feelings that children should go their own way and be separated from their mothers. The two children not yet separated are herself and her younger brother—the oldest of the siblings is married and has managed to "cut himself off from the powerful mother."

Contributions to Research

Up to this point, this article has dealt, for the most part, with the therapeutic aspect of family art therapy. It has its counterpart in research. In the Family Sudies Section at the National Institute of Mental Health, where the main focus is on studying thought disorder in the families of schizophrenics, family art therapy serves a special purpose. Its findings confirm and strengthen hypotheses concerning family interaction in schizophrenia, as formulated by the researchers. These findings are compared with parallel data from individual and family psychotherapy and from projective tests.

The material obtained in family art therapy has brought into sharp focus:

1. The similarity of the patterns of thought and perception in the schizophrenic patient, his parents and siblings, which were observed repeatedly in different sets of families.
2. The dynamics of the schizophrenic family, their interalliances, identifications and role shifts.

In one area of research, the comparison of the schizophrenic patient with his "well" sibling [3] was studied. The art productions of a number of "well" siblings revealed the following characteristics: Representational pictures are usually fairly well-organized, unified, and show no gross distortions; but if there are no limits set by objective reality, if the picture is to be developed from a scribble, or is intended to express a mood or a feeling, the change is impressive. Only then one realizes how frail is the ego of these siblings. Whenever the defenses which keep them in touch with reality are loosened, their productions become disorganized, fragmented and bizarre.

Figure 6

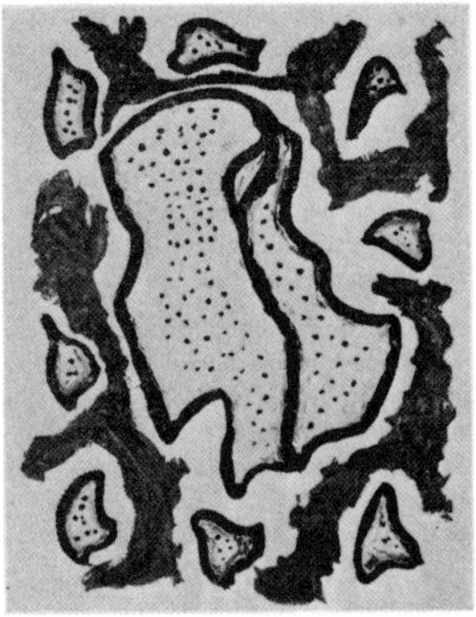

Figure 7

See also color plate VI.

In the families of schizophrenics we have noticed that frequently a parent, whose perception of reality seems quite appropriate, goes along with the bizarre, fragmented productions of the other parent and of the patient. He accepts their pictures and comments quite matter-of-factly without recognizing their pathological aspects. We have obtained clear and permanent records of this particular phenomenon in art productions of certain of our families.

These two illustrations (figures 8 and 9) are pictures by a schizophrenic daughter and her mother. In figure 8 the daughter tried with great effort and concentration to draw from nature a tree and hills. At first glance the picture does not indicate distorted perception. Only

[3] Juliana Day, Hanna Yaxa Kwiatkowska, Lyman Wynne, et al: "The Psychiatric 'Patient' and his 'Well' Sibling." Presented at the Annual Meeting of the American Psychiatric Association, May 9, 1960.

Figure 8

on closer scrutiny do we notice that each new element interrupts the continuation of what was represented earlier: A tree trunk cuts short the blueness of the sky, blank on the other side of this trunk; the other branch interrupts the continuation of the hill. This seems to be a remarkably subtle but clear illustration of this patient's disjointed thinking, which can easily escape us when we converse with her.

Let us now look at the mother's picture (figure 9). It also represents nature, but is done from memory. What are the two dark arcs shooting into the sky? They were explained by the mother as "roads," without the slightest indication that she noticed anything wrong. The father also did not find anything unusual in the picture when he and his wife discussed it together, even though his own pictures were quite well organized. Their daughter's perception of reality is very similar to her mother's. The father appeared not to notice their similarly distorted or fragmented perception. In this family we found many other illustrations of this pattern in their art productions.

Another family consisted of a schizophrenic daughter, a "normal" father and a mother who had had a recognized psychotic episode in her history. The sibling in this family did not take part in the family therapy. He lived in another city, was married and successful in his job. At the family art therapy sessions, after an initial period of resistance manifested by conventional representations painted by both parents, the family became gradually freer, more spontaneous and unguarded as to what happened in their art productions.

The father's pictures revealed a disturbance in his thought processes, practically imperceptible in other transactions with him. His pictures alternated between completely unrelated elements, as in figure 10, to which he gave the most incongruous associations, and stereotyped geometric patterns formed of rectangles, squares or ellipses executed with compulsive exactness, as shown in figure 11. These last pictures, even though they are obsessively organized in a pattern, impress us as being not much more than colored fragments. Associations made by the family to figure 12, another of his pictures, provide a magnificent example of how the whole family is at ease and operates naturally in a context completely alien to other people.

After this particular session the art therapist and the observer could not recall the comments made by the family about the picture. The following verbatim excerpt readily explains why this happened:

Patient: "What on earth is it?"

Father: "Well, it's all on earth, but, you know, scattered around. . ."

Mother: "What's floating around on the sides of the skirt there . . . I want to know. . ."

Patient: "What are these?" (points out center flower shapes)

Father: ". . . these . . . flowers, South Pacific island flowers . . . she has been in Japan . . . a little girl came out of the sea. . ."

Mother: "With a skirt on? . . . I mean, modest!"

Father: "Well, blue skirt . . . it got dyed blue in the sea . . . she is a little surprised with what she sees on earth. . ." (mother laughs, but her laughter has a note of mockery)

Figure 9

Mother: "Does she have green tears or is it a miracle pickle?"

Father: "They are just splashes of water of the spot . . . and that's all . . . and that's a bridal veil, she came out with a bridal veil. . ."

Mother: "What's that, hibiscus or what?" (points out orange spot on the girl's head)

Father: "It's her hair, red hair. . ."

Mother: "Oh, she's red haired. . ."

Father: "Just dabbling. . ."

The art therapist and the participant observer frequently experience such confusion while attempting to discuss a family art therapy session. The session seems to have been full of significant material, but only a blurred memory of it remains. When playing back such a tape one discovers that what is said by the family members about their art productions often has no coherent meaning. This search for non-existent meaning produces in the therapists some temporary anxiety and confusion. Their personal experience of the climate of the schizophrenic family helps them understand why the patient, who was raised in such a family, could not learn to think clearly.

* * * * * *

This paper describes the development of family art therapy and touches on its uses as a new therapeutic and research tool. Working with family groups promises a valuable and exciting new role for art therapy. It is as yet too early to evaluate its future development. However, intensive study of the art productions and recordings of the sessions continues to bring forth new and creative ways of viewing the family of the schizophrenic.

Figure 10

Figure 11

Figure 12

See also color plate VII.

An Art Therapy Program for Geriatric Patients

IRENE DEWDNEY

In February 1970 I was asked to design an art therapy program for some of the geriatric patients at the London, Ontario, Psychiatric Hospital. Although at that time I had had little experience in working with the aged, I was able to develop the program that is described below. I hope that this report suggests methods that may be useful to others dealing with patients of this kind.

The physical facilities available for the program determined the size of the group. The art therapy room contained a table approximately five feet wide and thirteen feet long. I was therefore limited to working with ten patients, the number that could be accommodated in comfort and with sufficient work space.

Members of the group that has participated since the start of the program are diagnosed as follows: presenile and senile dementia, four; cerebral arteriosclerosis, two; depressive neurosis, two; alcoholic, one; manic depressive, manic type, one. The group consists of eight women and two men.

For some time I had been using a modified form of the Denner technique [1] with a small group of chronic schizophrenics, and it seemed a good procedure to use as a starting point with my geriatric patients.

Denner's technique is based on the theory that emotional tensions block perception. It can be described as a total assault on the autism of severely schizoid patients. She has designed drawing exercises that bring into use all of the senses. For example, a typical early exercise is based on the use of a coffee cup as a subject for drawing. Feeling the shape of the cup is followed

[1] See Anne Denner, *L'Expression Plastique, Pathologie, et Rééducation des Schizophrènes*. Paris, Les Editions Sociales Françaises, 1967. (The review of this book that appeared in the *Bulletin of Art Therapy*, Vol. 6, No. 3, April 1969, contains a comprehensive summary.)

by repetitive exercises designed to transfer the rhythm of its curves to paper. Where motor control is severely limited, the therapist may guide the patient's hand with his own. Visual perception may be stimulated, too, by viewing and discussing pictures of cups or patients' attempts at rendering them.

A progression of objects and related exercises moves slowly and systematically towards representations of human beings. As the patient learns to see and draw objects as real and as separate from himself, he becomes capable of treating human subjects the same way. With staff members posing for him, he is finally able to relate to them as persons.

About four months later, when I became more familiar with the needs and behavior of the geriatric group, I began to experiment with other approaches. I was discovering that the geriatric patient, even when senility was evident, reverted from time to time, to the functioning, organized, younger person that he or she had been. Sometimes the remission lasted only a short time but sometimes an improved level of functioning was maintained.

Possibly because of my own need to relate to a better functioning person, I began to search for this younger person, encouraging recall of memories through discussion and questions. This made it possible for us to meet on a more equal basis. I began to see my patients as whole people, not just as they were at this point in time but as they had been, as well. This perspective also enabled me to feel more compassion for the frustrations they were experiencing in their present circumstances and yet at the same time it motivated me to encourage them in maintaining contact with the younger, functioning person I was discovering.

Some Techniques Used in the Program

In my opinion, the assignment itself is less important than is the attitude of the therapist. I say this with several qualifications. The assignment must be rewarding, offer variety, and be within the patient's ability. But most important, it must not add to the confusion he or she may be experiencing. For this reason I am inclined to favor assignments that encourage organized thinking rather than free-flowing abstract expressions.

The three procedures described here are designed for three levels of ability to function. I am well aware that they represent only a few within a wide range of possibilities.

Drawing and coloring an object from observation

This is an exercise in relating to the reality of an object, and therefore it is particularly good for patients who are losing their grasp on reality. Here the patient is encouraged to reproduce the object as closely as possible. Innovation is not encouraged. Each person is given a choice of a simple household object, cup, bowl, pot, and so on, and is supplied with oil pastels in colors that closely match the object selected. The patient is encouraged to make on one sheet of paper two or three drawings of his chosen object. This offers him and the others in the group a chance for critical judgments in the last part of the session.

When I brought flowers and leaves for the group to draw, I discovered that they enjoyed these more than they did the household objects. Possibly the flexibility and the organic quality of these natural objects appealed to them. The plant forms chosen are handled by the patients and very often are arranged on the paper to be used as patterns for drawing. I've made it a practice to intersperse this assignment among the others.

Picture completion

This assignment is suitable for more intact patients who can afford the release of imagination; it demands more originality and skill. Here I use a whole figure of a person, cut out of a magazine and pasted on the sheet of paper. I had learned from experience that most older people find drawing people too threatening. Here the patient is expected to draw in an appropriate background. This assignment should be used discriminatingly because some patients are unable to translate a flat surface into the concept of space and perspective.

Shapes and Colors

This procedure is suitable for those with minimal drawing skill; it is the simplest of the assignments. The patients are expected to arrange dark cardboard shapes (circles, squares, triangles, and rectangles) I have cut out. They then trace their arrangement to make a design and finally this pattern is colored. For some the procedure remains very simple, while for others it becomes quite intricate and complicated. This particular assignment is also good for patients whose eyesight is poor.

The Problem of Memory

The first two assignments call upon the patient to use his critical faculties more than does the third one, and in all three he is encouraged to focus on the work at hand. These exercises are not, however, directed especially to the stimulation of memory, whether of recent or past experiences.

For some time I had been depending upon the discussion to encourage such awareness. Then on one occasion I asked the group to draw the table at which they were sitting and to identify, with written names and positions, the ten people sitting around it. To assist them, I wrote the ten names in large letters where all could see them. I found that not one person was able to identify all ten and most were able to place correctly not more than three or four. Whether this was an indication of withdrawal and separation as a part of the senile process or whether it indicated a deficiency in activities that might bring the group together I cannot decide. Possibly it is a combination of the two. This response suggests the need for activities that not only stimulate older memories but also encourage immediate interaction.

I am now exploring various assignments that might help the patient retain his memories for as long as possible. The following exercises encourage contact with the past when the patient functioned at a better level. I am introducing them slowly, interspersing them among the less threatening assignments. Some patients accept with pleasure the tasks listed below while others complain that they are painful.

A drawing of the family tree
How many relatives can I remember and place on the tree?

A drawing of a house or apartment in which I used to live
Can I remember how it looked from the outside? Can I remember how the rooms were arranged? Can I remember how it looked in relation to neighboring buildings?

Drawings of remembered objects frequently used around the house or on the job

Setting, Materials, and Organization

It is a good thing that the art therapy room is away from the ward so that patients can work in an environment other than the one in which they spend most of their time. Such a change is in itself stimulating.

Space limitations necessarily determine the size of the drawing paper that can be used. However, I have found that for most geriatric patients a very large sheet of paper is uncongenial, particularly when oil pastels, colored nylon pens, or pencils are used. We use sheets of paper that are approximately 12 by 16 inches. This size can be successfully worked with by most patients in the allotted drawing time of 40 minutes.

The large table allows several wheel chairs to be drawn close enough to give their occupants a good working position. I prefer the large table to several smaller ones also because the participants are more likely to function as a group. Their proximity to each other encourages interaction.

The session is limited not only by space but also by time (one hour). Therefore I rely on colored oil pastels that come in a wide range of colors and on brilliantly colored felt and nylon pens. I am sure that tempera paints would open up new forms of expression but as yet we have not used them in this group.

Each session is designed as a unit and each part of it is important. When the patients arrive they are greeted and addressed by their formal names. I feel that this form of address helps them retain their sense of dignity whereas the use of first names suggests an adult-to-child relationship.

They find their places around the table and when they are settled the assignments are offered. Those who have stayed with the least demanding ones are encouraged to try something more complex. To discourage dependency, the therapist helps only those who appear to be in difficulty or those whose level of achievement has remained constantly low. She may merely help locate an appropriate color or may offer suggestions when asked for them.

While the patients are drawing, the therapist encourages discussion about events on the ward, physical complaints, and any other topic that develops. In addition, she almost invariably invites the patients to talk about themselves when they were younger. Often the women enjoy talking about the meals they used to cook and the men about the jobs at which they used to work. These discussions also provide the patients with an opportunity to express their anger and frustration about their present situation.

When the time is up, the patients are expected to sign their drawings. When the group first came to art therapy, at least three of the ten had forgotten how to write their names but now they all are able to. We forget that most geriatric patients in a custodial hospital have little or no need to sign their names. Unless opportunities are made, this important part of the person's identity becomes lost. As they are also expected to date their drawings, the date is always written in large letters and numbers on the blackboard.

The drawings are then collected and the therapist holds up each drawing in turn for discussion. This portion of the program is just as important as the artwork itself, for the following two reasons: First, the attention and concern of the total group is focused on the drawing of each patient, thus giving it an importance it might not otherwise have. Second, the patients' critical faculties are stimulated by their having to articulate spoken judgments.

The person who did the drawing is expected to recognize it as his and has the first opportunity to talk about it. The drawings are discussed from the following viewpoints:

If an object has been used, how closely is it reproduced? If the patient has drawn the object three or four times on the same sheet, then each person in the group is expected to choose the best attempt. The therapist holds up the object as well as the drawing to facilitate the comparison.

If it is a picture completion, has the cut-out figure been given an appropriate setting?

If the design is abstract, how should it be hung? The therapist turns the drawing four ways and the group decides in which position it looks best.

The group is usually supportive in this part of the session. Most criticism is tempered by recognition that each person has done his or her best.

As the patients leave, the therapist shakes hands with each of them, again addressing them formally. The drawings are sent back to the ward with the patients and are displayed there.

Therapeutic Goals

The geriatric patient is very often aware of the deterioration that has taken place in his ability to function, and this inevitably leads to feelings of frustration and to loss of self-esteem. Thus the whole experience in art therapy should be designed to encourage a sense of self-worth through both the activity and the discussion. I continually stress the importance of maintaining self-identity, a conviction of the importance that each one of us has as a unique individual.

One becomes aware of an ambivalence on the part of some patients that expresses itself in a reluctance to expose themselves to these focusing exercises. One also becomes aware that the maintenance of self-identity in these circumstances and under these conditions is sometimes a painful experience. At the same time people are reluctant to accept paternalism and to stagnate.

Most of the time there are a few of the ten who object to the "kindergarten" aspect of the session, but almost invariably all participants leave the session expressing a feeling of achievement. Possibly they have found assurance that they can still function in an organized fashion.

It is very necessary for the geriatric patient to express the anger he or she feels at the frustrations of the life he must lead. Very often I support this expression by agreeing that it would be difficult for me to tolerate the situation in which the patients find themselves. I much prefer an angry patient to one who has lost his identity.

It is important for the therapist to accept the geriatric patient as a person who has functioned well in the past, and for the therapist to expect that younger functioning person still to be available. It took me some months to gain this perspective, to see the patients as they had been. However, when this attitude is achieved, paternalism decreases and the patient's dignity is maintained.

I wonder if it is not a mistake to fail to encourage the geriatric patient to recall the past when he or she functioned at a more satisfying level. It is possible that the past provides a reservoir of identity and strength upon which to draw.

Techniques for Individual and Group Art Therapy

JAMES M. DENNY

Some techniques for the teaching of art therapy [1] and for use in individual and group art therapy are presented in this paper. Our concern is primarily with the instructions given our clients and the attitudes we try to encourage rather than with the techniques of painting, the selection of media, and interpretive principles. The techniques to be described range from the highly exploratory to the specific and concrete, from those which promote inner awareness to those concerned with outer awareness, and from those stressing building controls to those designed to loosen them. In large part, these techniques were developed by the author and his clients, the latter being normal and disturbed university students; thus these approaches were designed to meet particular individual and group needs. The literature on art therapy has also provided invaluable suggestions.

Next to nothing is known about the response to various art therapy techniques on the part of different populations. A survey of past issues of this journal indicates that art therapists have written little about techniques and have found theory, results, interpretation of art products and definitions of the field to be of much greater interest. It appears that the art therapy literature of the past gives the lion's share of attention to catharsis and the release of unconscious material through free expression. Clinical research needs to be conducted on the effects of particular techniques and combinations of techniques on a variety of groups. Meanwhile, therapists must choose techniques in the light of a deep appreciation of their effects and of patients' readiness to make use of them.

Art therapy is related to a variety of theories. The art therapist is well advised to utilize techniques well rooted in a theory which he understands, for which he has a personal affinity, and which seems relevant to the clinical situa-

[1] See James M. Denny, "Case Study: An Art Therapy Workshop for the Staff of a University Counseling Center," *American Journal of Art Therapy*, Vol. 9, No. 1, Oct. 1969.

tion. A flexible application of theory combined with awareness of the client should lead to selection of the most useful techniques. Our own theoretical approach combines elements of existential and humanistic psychology and has been detailed elsewhere.[2] The art therapist is a full participant as well as an observer in the therapeutic process, helping the client to experience *who* he is and might become rather than *what* he has produced.

What occurs in art therapy may be thought of in terms of behavioral processes, e.g., catharsis, increase or decrease in effective communication, self-disclosure, and changes in attitude and behavior. In theoretical research into self-disclosure Culbert[3] and Jourard[4] have made an important contribution applicable to the study and practice of art therapy. Self-disclosure may occur in art therapy not only through words and behavior but also through painting, an important personal record to be confronted and discussed. Culbert differentiates self-disclosures from self-description. Self-description is that "self-data that an individual is likely to feel comfortable in revealing to most others. Additionally, self-description includes information that an individual knows about himself, that is readily perceivable by most others, and by which he agrees to be known." By contrast, "Self-disclosure refers to an individual's explicitly communicating to one or more others some personal information that he believes these others would be unlikely to acquire unless he himself discloses it. Moreover, this information must be personally private; that is, it must be of such a nature that it is not something the individual would disclose to everyone who might inquire about it."[5]

A client's willingness to disclose himself in his art products and a discussion of them is related to the self-data which he holds at the moment. Culbert[6] conceptualizes this in terms of a four-cell matrix in which one is known and unknown to self and known and unknown to others. In cell one art therapy clients would be known to self and known to others through their paintings, behavior, and words. In cell two they would be known to others but not known to self; in cell three they would be known to self but not known to others. Finally, in cell four they would be unknown both to self and others. Jourard[7] hypothesizes that too much or too little self-disclosure may jeopardize the client's psychological well-being. Basically, we come to know ourselves and to grow through experience with others: "It takes two to know one."[8] When the art therapy client engages in much self-description and little self-disclosure

---

[2] James M. Denny, "Art Counseling in Educational Settings," *The Personnel and Guidance Journal,* Washington, D.C., Vol. 40, Oct. 1969.

[3] Samuel A. Culbert, *The Interpersonal Process of Self-Disclosure: It Takes Two to See One,* Washington, D.C., NTL Institute for Applied Behavioral Science, Explorations in Applied Behavioral Science, Renaissance Editions, Inc., New York, No. 3, 1967.

[4] Sidney M. Jourard, *The Transparent Self,* Princeton, N.J., Van Nostrand, 1964.

[5] Samuel A. Culbert, *Op. cit.*

[6] *Ibid.*

[7] Sidney M. Jourard, *Op. cit.*

[8] Samuel A. Culbert, *Op. cit.*

there is minimal opportunity for reality-testing and feedback from others. In the use of the following techniques, therefore, the art therapist is urged to help the client grow from superficial descriptions of himself and his art products to greater intimacy and self-disclosure.

Exploration

Exploratory tasks are liberating. They encourage the client to release conscious controls and to express himself as spontaneously as possible. The tasks should be simple, direct, and nonthreatening. The pictorial results are akin to verbal free associations in psychoanalysis. Exploratory tasks are particularly useful in initial sessions, but they may be repeated with benefit throughout the course of therapy.

Automatic Drawing (Scribble Technique)

The client is encouraged to relax and to make free lines or scribbles on paper. He makes a series of these and stops when each feels complete. In variations of this technique the client closes his eyes while scribbling, draws with his non-dominant hand, or is instructed not to take his hand off the paper until he has finished. The results vary from simple, unbroken lines to developed scribbles composed of lines and masses of colors. Series of scribbles may be examined for sequential development: from simple to complex or constricted to expansive or vice versa. They may be searched for suggestive patterns, shapes, and repeated forms to be developed into deliberate compositions. They may be studied from the point of view of movement, for the number of colors used, and so on.

Scribbling provides an excellent starting point for therapy as defenses are relaxed and a result can be obtained without much talent. Children scribble before they draw recognizable representations of their world; the task may thus be thought of as playful and regressive. Naumburg [9] has noted that this kind of drawing is not primarily diagnostic "but is intended to release spontaneous images from the unconscious of the patient or pupil." Figure 1 shows a quick, springlike scribble which uncoils with abandon across the page. Later scribbles produced by this patient became more complex but still reflect this relaxed and open manner. Figure 2 is a "bug" or "insect" which developed from another patient's more controlled scribble. Although the bug has a humorous quality, the lines remain safely in the center of the paper and are filled in in a compulsive style. The therapist discussed with the client the latter's need to remain safe, protected, and immobile (the bug has no feet).

Free Drawing

The choice of subject, manner of execution, and media are left to the client; he is encouraged to express himself freely and not to plan his picture.

[9] Margaret Naumburg, *Dynamically Oriented Art Therapy: Its Principles and Practice,* New York, Grune and Stratton, 1966.

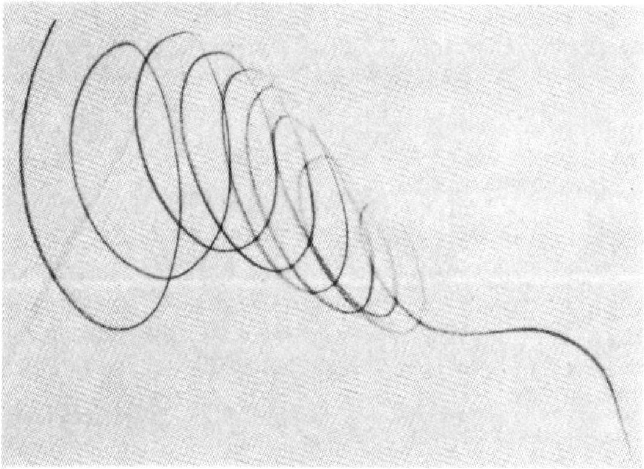

Figure 1

This very basic technique may be used repeatedly throughout the course of therapy. The absence of directives makes the free drawing an excellent diagnostic as well as therapeutic device; the results often mirror the patient's present problems, defenses, and strengths. Patients in groups may be asked to select the free drawings they like best or least, find most interesting or uninteresting, expressive or puzzling, and to tell why.

Blob and Wet Paper Techniques

Blobs and dribbles are made on wet paper with watercolors or inks. These spread to make shapes and can be developed into finished compositions. Wet paper may be crumpled into a ball and spread flat. When paint is dropped on the paper it flows into the wrinkles and patterns emerge which may be developed expressively.[10] Inkblots can be made by dropping colors on paper; the paper is then folded and pressed. The resulting shapes may be deliberately altered and elaborated. Similar inkblots may be given to various group members to develop, with interesting and widely varying results.

Media Exploration

Clients explore what forms and feelings are stimulated by the use of various art media. Choice of subject matter may be left open or a theme may be selected to be completed in a single medium or in mixed media. The selection of medium itself often has considerable meaning. Some may choose the same medium repeatedly to avoid feeling threat, disgust, or loss of control. When the therapist believes that the client can profit from an exploration of additional media, these are introduced with appropriate support.

Color Exploration

The psychology of color forms a vast literature, and the selection, use, and

[10] Miles A. Vich and Janie Rhyne, "Psychological Growth and the Use of Art Materials: Small Group Experiments with Adults," *Journal of Humanistic Psychology*, Palo Alto, California, Fall, 1967.

Figure 2

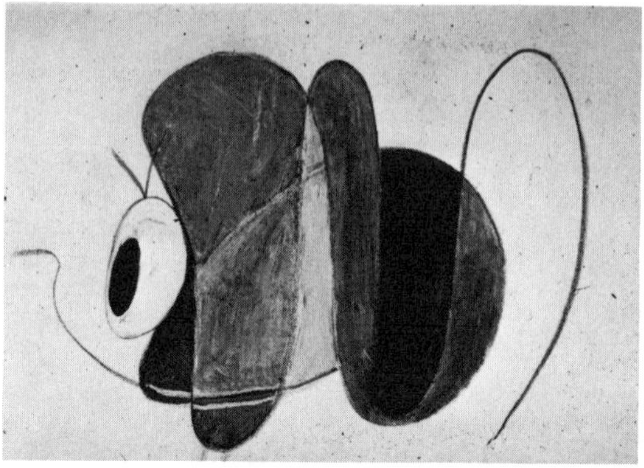

meaning of color are very significant in art therapy. Color exploration is perhaps best exemplified in the exhaustive work of Ernest and Edith Zierer who have developed a system called "Creative Analysis," where paintings are analyzed with the patient in terms of "integration and disintegration" of colors, the hypothesis being that failure to achieve integration of colors reflects personality disorganization.[11]

In our own work the client may select the color he likes most and the one he likes least and work with these in a free composition. Through discussions with the therapist or group members he perceives how his selected colors interact, what personal meaning the colors have for him, and whether they diminish or enhance each other. He may also paint freely with two to three hues which he feels best represent him or his problems and moods. If the view of self is negative or the mood painful, he may be advised to paint with colors which would seem to counterbalance those he has chosen. Finally, clients may be asked to explore one color in depth; the selected color may have either positive or negative associations. Clients may be asked to pay special attention to one color, for example green, in their natural surroundings, to prepare them for painting with a variety of tints and shades of one color.

Drawing Completion

In the drawing completion technique the client is presented with one or more sheets of paper with a few simple lines or shapes. These serve as starting points for his drawings and must be incorporated in the finished picture. This approach was developed for therapeutic purposes from the Drawing Completion Test by Kinget, a projective test of personality consisting of eight simple drawings which the patient must complete. Kinget notes ". . . that the material

[11] Edith Zierer, "Creative Analysis: Color Integration as a Diagnostic and Therapeutic Tool in Individual and Family Treatment," in *Psychiatry and Art,* Irene Jakab, (Ed.), Basel, Switzerland, S. Karger, 1968.

used does not threaten the subject by the strangeness of its appearance or by its emotional implications, but rather appeals to him by its simple and neutral character."[12] One or more of the Kinget figures may be employed in art therapy as initial stimuli. Individual responses to the same stimulus figure vary widely and lead to lively group discussions.

Rapport-Building

Art therapy sessions are frequently divided into a period of painting followed by a period of discussion. Group members often sit quietly painting alone and can feel quite isolated until the discussion begins. In individual sessions, the client may feel alienated from the therapist while painting, or may feel he is being examined with a cold diagnostic eye. Rapport-building techniques encourage exchanges between participants during the creative phase. Attempts are made to reduce psychological distance between clients and therapist, to make a natural transition from production to interpretation of the art products.

Conversational Drawing

Group members work with chosen partners sitting across from one another to communicate with shapes, lines, and colors. For a brief period each pair shares a mutual world (the piece of paper) and is asked to communicate without words within its confines. When the drawn dialogue is complete, the partners discuss what they have produced. Conversational drawing provides a relatively easy opportunity for group members to become well acquainted in early sessions.

For example, in one group an aggressive, sexually provocative Caucasian girl selected a passive and sexually inexperienced male of Japanese ancestry with whom to converse. She began by drawing a hard, straight red arrow towards him. He responded with a weak, faint purple line which curled back towards himself. The more open and insistent her approaches became, the more he evaded her. Much to her surprise, she discovered that he could approach her graphically when she stopped making direct overtures. This led to useful group discussion of traditional sexual roles and how these clients were playing them.

Other Ways of Working in Pairs

Partners draw, paint, make a collage, sculpt, or build something together. Conversation is encouraged, and the manner in which each pair communicates, shares the work load, and develops a finished composition is most revealing. For example, one client may have all the ideas and the other may do most of the painting. Their feelings toward each other and toward the completed work are discussed with the group.

---

[12] C. Marian Kinget, *The Drawing Completion Test: A Projective Technique for the Investigation of Personality,* New York, Grune and Stratton, 1952.

Both conversational drawings and other ways of working in pairs were developed independently by the author, but note is made of earlier references to similar techniques by Horowitz[13] and Boenheim and Stone,[14] who report the positive effects of such methods in building rapport with schizophrenic patients.

Painting Completion by the Group

Each group member names an object, event, or feeling and then depicts it. One or more group members make additions which they consider improvements, e.g., a body is added to a face, a face is given expression, people and a landscape are added to a house. Patients are invited to express their feelings about changes made in their pictures. Rhyne[15] has noted that such experiences "can make you aware of how you feel and what you do when you let others put upon you anything they want to."

Bach[16] introduced a similar technique where each group member in a circle begins a free drawing in any medium. After a short time, all the drawings are passed to the right for additions, possibly in other media. This continues until each member's drawing comes back to him. Individuals may elaborate the original drawing or add unrelated and idiosyncratic details.

Painting with an Observer

One member of a pair says what comes into his mind as he watches another paint.[17] The observer-commentator may respond primarily to form or to content, may serve as critic or as alter ego. The painter is advised to respond to the commentary as he sees fit. Discussions following this procedure are often concerned with feelings of dependency and autonomy, with acceptance of self and others.

Expression of Inner Feelings

These techniques help the client get in touch with inner feelings and fantasies and make visual representations of them. These tasks may increase or decrease the client's anxiety as he becomes increasingly aware of himself. The therapist helps him express and face his feelings and approach the solution of his problems.

Affective Words

Words connoting feelings and psychological states may be used as stim-

[13] Mardi J. Horowitz, "Graphic Communication: A Study of Interaction Painting with Schizophrenics," *American Journal of Psychotherapy,* Vol. 17, No. 2, 1963.

[14] Curt Boenheim and Bernard Stone, "Pictorial Dialogues: Notes on a Technique," *Bulletin of Art Therapy,* Vol. 8, No. 2, Jan. 1969.

[15] Janie Rhyne, "The Gestalt Art Experience," *Gestalt Therapy Now,* Palo Alto, California, Science and Behavior Books, Chapter 22, 1969.

[16] George R. Bach, *Intensive Group Psychotherapy,* New York, The Ronald Press, 1954.

[17] Miles A. Vich and Janie Rhyne, *Op. cit.*

Figure 3

uli for paintings. Jakab[18] has suggested a rapid depiction of the series love, hate, beauty, charity, anxiety, and freedom. Paintings made in response to these words tend to illuminate the client's feelings towards himself and others. Many other words may be chosen, and perhaps it is best to use those volunteered by clients themselves. Word pairs such as strength-weakness, love-hate, dependence-independence, and masculinity-femininity express important internal polarities. When a series is painted, each patient's productions may be discussed as a group or all the paintings of one feeling may be discussed together.

Figures 3 and 4 represent an oriental male student's drawings of love and charity. The red overlapping hearts on a field of blue and the tin cup of charity are extremely conventional. The client's compulsivity may be seen in the careful outlining, shading, and exact central placement; he complained of not being able to draw the figures more perfectly. He was very dependent upon, yet extremely hostile towards, his mother and other females. These two drawings reveal his bland, stereotyped expressions and his inability to get in touch with his own real feelings.

Problems and Feelings

The client paints a recent or recurring problem or feeling or his mood of the moment. A sequence may also be attempted in which he portrays an unpleasant feeling or event, a pleasant or joyful feeling, and a very recent or immediate feeling. This task requires that the client be aware of his feelings, put them on paper, and attempt to solve his problems through painted expression and discussion with the therapist and group.

[18] James M. Denny, "Case Study: An Art Therapy Workshop for the Staff of a University Counseling Center," *American Journal of Art Therapy,* Vol. 9, No. 1, Oct. 1969.

Dreams and Fantasies

Clients may be asked to bring dreams to the art therapy sessions or they may be asked to paint them when they happen to be mentioned. Those who have difficulty telling their dreams may find it less difficult to paint them. Daydreams and fantasies, especially repeated ones, also provide a rich source for paintings. Clients are left free to depict the entire dream, or to select the parts that interest or trouble them most.

Guided inner journeys or fantasy trips can be conducted under conditions of induced relaxation. The familiar Jacobson[19] technique of deep muscle relaxation so frequently employed by behavior therapists is useful. Following these exercises, clients are directed to close their eyes and to paint the images that arise. Clients may also be asked to take inner journeys to various parts of themselves or into feelings and problems. Painted "solutions" of these concerns are then encouraged. Structure may be given to fantasy trips. For example, the individual may be asked to visualize a wall or barrier (unsolvable problem) and then be told that his mind will provide a means of getting around, over, or through. Either the barrier or the means of overcoming it are then painted and discussed.

Three Wishes

Asked to paint three wishes, clients often depict desires for things, personal security, altruism, and so on. Responses to this request seem to reflect breadth of ideas, level of maturity, and degree of egocentricity. When only three wishes are assigned, responses tend to be conventional. It may therefore be advisable to ask for five in order to make room for more highly individual responses. Among matters for discussion are the strength of the wishes, how much the client feels they are obtainable, and to what extent he

[19] E. Jacobson, *Progressive Relaxation,* Chicago, University of Chicago Press, 1938.

Figure 4

expects others to grant them as compared with the notion of working for them himself. One client drew a car, a plane, and a house representing her wish for travel, change, and the security of a home of her own. However, the wishes were faintly drawn in tones of gray. After discussing her drawings with the group, she realized that she felt she would never obtain these things and was afraid to reach out for them. She expressed a new determination to try to get what she wanted on her own.

First Memory

Clients may be asked to draw their earliest memory or the first important event in their lives. Gardner[20] has said that this request elicits "a crystalization and condensation of many psychic processes which have persisted in memory." This procedure is especially useful for revealing the historical antecedents of the client's present situation.

The Road of Life

Patients paint the "road" or "path" which they have been traveling for the past several years. The road one hopes or expects to travel may also be painted. This task requires that the individual place himself in historical perspective and examine his feelings regarding the course of his life.

Figure 5 is by a 25-year-old man on a "path of life" which leads through a "cool, sheltering" forest. Although he thus describes his environment as friendly, the picture was titled "The Infinite Mask." He discussed his need to hide behind a series of masks, three of which are seen in the picture. He felt he could never truly know himself or let others know him "because there is always another mask."

Music, Poetry, and Expressive Movement

Music, poetry, short-story reading, expressive movement, and dance may all stimulate feelings that can be painted. In a reversal of this procedure, we may proceed in the opposite direction by responding to paintings in terms of poetry, song, and movement. Unfamiliar, unconventional music and poetry seem to elicit paintings that are more individual than those made in response to hackneyed verse or obvious program music. Sensory awareness techniques as developed by Gunther[21] are sometimes useful at the start of a painting session.

Self-Perception

The following variations on direct self-portrayal are designed to help the

---

[20] Richard A. Gardner, "Techniques of Child Psychotherapy: Tape One—Introduction and Pre-Treatment Evaluation," Fort Lee, New Jersey, Behavioral Sciences Tape Library, 1970.

[21] Bernard Gunther, *Sense Relaxation Below Your Mind,* New York, Macmillan Co., Collier Books, 1968.

Figure 5

client toward more complete awareness of his body image and his personal needs—in short, of himself as a whole individual.

Immediate States

Clients select one or more of the following phrases to paint and discuss: "I am," "I feel," "I have," and "I do." Another variation is derived from Krippner's suggestion that individuals take nine small cards and respond to the question, "Who am I?" on each.[22] Number one is considered the most important characterization and number nine the least. The client is invited to consider what life would be like without number nine, number eight, and so on. Any of the series might be painted and discussed.

Draw-A-Man and Draw-A-Person

The Goodenough[23] Draw-A-Man test and Machover's[24] Draw-A-Person test are among the most frequently used psychological diagnostic instruments. Goodenough asks the subject to draw the best man possible, and to include the whole figure. Machover simply asks the subject to draw a person. In art therapy either the Goodenough or Machover directions may be used and followed by discussion of the drawings. The figure may be drawn in pastels or paints (only pencil is used in the original procedures). A drawing of a member of the opposite sex is also revealing.

Self-Portraits

Self-portraits vary from the realistic done with or without a mirror to the

---

[22] Stanley Krippner, in *Growth Games,* by Howard R. Lewis and Harold S. Streitfeld, New York, Harcourt, Brace, and Jovanovich, 1970.

[23] Florence L. Goodenough, *Measurement of Intelligence by Drawings,* New York, Harcourt, Brace, and World, 1926.

[24] Karen Machover, *Personality Projection in the Drawing of the Human Figure,* Springfield, Ill., Charles C Thomas, 1941.

Figure 6

abstract. Various media, such as pastels, paint, clay, or collage, will affect the result.

Phenomenal, Ideal, and Real Self-Portraits

Three figures are drawn, the instructions being given for one at a time. First, the client simply draws a person, any person he wishes to draw. This "phenomenal" figure then is the same as the one produced according to Machover's directions. The "ideal self" is produced in response to the request to draw oneself as one would really like to be or to look. Finally, the client draws himself as he believes he really is or appears. The three drawings are looked at together with particular attention to similarity or difference, body image, and clues to opinion of self.

Self-Portrait with Time Limits

Clients are asked to draw a full-length self-portrait in one minute. The time limit forces quick decisions about such important elements as size, placement, pose, proportion, facial expression, and inclusion of body parts and details. Figures 6 and 7 show one-minute self-portraits by a man and a woman. The man's drawing is built around a series of rectangles (even the originally round head is squared off) intended to emphasize strength, solidity, and masculinity. The client was himself dissatisfied; he recognized the weak legs and the generally stolid, cardboard character of the figure. The woman's very different figure is built around a five-pointed star. She had used star shapes to symbolize herself in previous art therapy sessions. Her drawing has the movement which the man's self-portrait lacks. We can see from it that she is an excitable and very active person while the man's picture is that of a person given to deliberation and step-by-step planning.

Draw Yourself as an Animal

Clients may be asked to draw themselves as any kind of animal, or as the kind they feel they are most like. Such drawings stimulate discussions that are both revealing and funny. Patients may also be asked to draw the animal they would most and least like to be.

Interpersonal Relations

The following techniques are calculated to make the client more aware of others and of the way others perceive him.

Portraits of Group Members

Group members are asked to draw each other. Portraits depicting an individual may be grouped together, or the artists may take turns discussing their studies of others. This assignment often helps group members clarify

Figure 7

Figure 8

and bring into the open their feelings towards each other. Therapists may invite group members to portray them, and they in turn may make portraits of their clients, being careful not to exclude anyone.[25]

Four Portraits Technique (Portraits by Pairs)

This is an excellent way to bring group members together, and it almost always stimulates a spirited discussion. People choose partners or the therapist directs the formation of partnerships. Each person draws a self-portrait and a picture of his partner.

A result of this technique is illustrated by Figure 8, a self-portrait, and Figure 9, a startling portrait of the same woman by her male partner. Although the self-portrait is rather faint, the client has captured the gay, fun-loving attitude she displayed in the group. The portrait is drawn in reds, oranges, and yellows, the eyes are shown humorously, and there is a flower in the mouth. The man's portrait of her is also in bright colors, and is similar in its wide-eyed, smiling expression, but it is scathing. It seems like an ex-

---

[25] See James M. Denny and Ann C. Fagen, "Group Art Therapy with University Students: A Comparative Case Analysis," *Psychotherapy: Theory, Research, and Practice,* Vol. 7, No. 3, Fall, 1970.

Figure 9

posure of her insistent superficiality, her ever-smiling facade, and her oral aggression (she habitually interrupted other group members).

Portraits by Combined Effort

Group members sit in a circle, and each member in turn serves as the subject, first making a drawing of himself. This picture is passed along and each group member works to make the portrait more like the subject. The subject sets the basic structure and to this extent controls the actions of the others. He may draw a full figure, a full face, or a profile, or may work abstractly. He may employ one or more colors, give the figure much or little movement, and, perhaps most important, leave the others more or less opportunity to add. When the drawing is completed, the subject is invited to ask the others about their contributions. Finally, he may change the portrait to make it fit his ideas about himself.

Draw Your Family

The family portrait tells much about family dynamics. The client may draw his family of origin, an extended family, a family established through marriage, or a family he dreams of having. He may or may not include himself. Interesting results can be obtained when family members are sculptured in clay as the figures can be moved about.

I have found the family portrait to be particularly useful in the initial session of marriage counseling. Kwiatkowska has written in detail about the use of this and related techniques in both family art therapy and diagnostic evaluation by means of families' art productions.[26]

Kinetic Family Drawings

Burns and Kaufman have introduced an interesting variation in family portraiture; clients are instructed to draw all of the family members "doing something—some kind of action." [27] This tends to eliminate the usual rogues' gallery lineup, and the kind and location of the activity add interest.

Portrait of the Group

Periodic drawings of the therapy group provide valuable information about the group process. They may take the form of individual portraits, often shown in a ring, or of abstract expression about the group experience. Clients may show that they are freed or that they are frustrated by what happens in the group; they may also show feelings about support or rejection from group members and the therapist, and so on.

Group Mural

The group works cooperatively on a large surface. Rolls of wrapping paper may be attached to a wall or laid out on the floor, or the group may draw on a sidewalk with chalk. The choice of subject matter may be left open, to be arrived at in the course of painting, it may be decided upon by the group before they start to paint, or a subject may be assigned by the therapist.

The Individual's Place in His World

The techniques discussed below can increase the client's awareness of his relationship to the world around him, and may help him accept and deal with it.

House-Tree-Person

First introduced in 1948 by Buck,[28] a series of three drawings showing a house, a tree, and a person has been used extensively for personality evaluation. For purposes of art therapy, the house, tree, and person can be

[26] Hanna Kwiatkowska, "Family Art Therapy: Experiments with a New Technique," *Bulletin of Art Therapy,* Vol. 1, No. 3, Spring, 1962.

————, "The Use of Families' Art Productions for Psychiatric Evaluation," *Bulletin of Art Therapy,* Vol. 6, No. 2, Jan. 1967.

[27] Robert C. Burns and S. Harvard Kaufman, *Kinetic Family Drawings (K-F-D): An Introduction to Understanding Children Through Kinetic Drawings,* New York, Brunner/Mazel, 1970.

[28] John N. Buck, "The H-T-P Technique: A Qualitative and Quantitative Scoring Manual," *Journal of Clinical Psychology,* Monograph Supplement No. 5, Oct. 1948.

Figure 10

put into one drawing. The client is thus faced with the task of relating a human figure (usually assumed to be himself or to contain elements of himself) to such common environmental features as tree and house.

Figure 10 was drawn by the man who produced Figure 5. He stated that the person is not really missing but is living "contentedly" inside the castle. He is quite self-sufficient and wants no one to enter his domain. He added that others may come in by chance "but they will not be *invited* in by me." The trees serve to protect the castle and afford a pleasant view "which is desirable when one is locked up inside." Even though the turrets look as if they are about to fall, the client insisted that his house was sturdy and impenetrable.

Elements Picture Series

Wittgenstein [29] obtained drawings of the four ancient elements of Empedocles, air, earth, fire, and water, primarily for diagnostic purposes. In art therapy clients may paint the four elements in rapid sequence. Discussion then often centers upon the client's feelings about these natural forces and his ability to utilize and control them. Talk of possible death by one of these forces often leads to a wider discussion of feelings about dying. This task is illustrated in Figure 11 where the miniscule figure of the client is threatened by the elemental force of water shown as rain, sea, and tidal wave.

Collage and Assemblage

Collage provides the client a specially good opportunity to create a small personal world from an almost unlimited variety of materials. Themes may be decided on in advance or the client may work at random until patterns

[29] Graf Wittgenstein, "Pictures of Prescribed Subjects: The Dynamics of the Unconscious in Paintings of the Four Elements," *Bulletin of Art Therapy,* Vol. 3, No. 4, July 1964.

Figure 11

and meanings emerge. Paper and paints of all sorts may be combined with cuttings from newspapers and magazines, string, buttons, wire, wood, cloth, natural objects, and other odds and ends found on short excursions. Hutton[30] writes that "the term 'collage' is a canopy extending over a wide area which includes assemblage, construction in depth and even possibly 'environmental happenings'. . . ."

Summary

A résumé of techniques for use in art therapy has been presented. These approaches are useful only when the client's particular personality and needs have been considered and when he furnishes us with signs that he is ready to benefit from a certain task. Fascination with a particular technique should never be allowed to dictate its use. It is hoped that these approaches will be used discriminatingly by art therapy students and professional therapists, not as recipes to be tried at random. The choice and timing of an approach should always depend upon the client or group, who themselves will provide the clues.

A predetermined program of techniques is usually to be avoided. Such a series is likely to be appropriate only under special circumstances, e.g. sensitivity training with groups of normal adults, or training sessions for therapists where techniques are presented in an ordered series directed toward a particular goal.

---

[30] Helen Hutton, *The Technique of Collage,* New York, Watson-Guptill, 1968.

Art Therapy for Adolescent Drug Abusers

DIANA WITTENBERG

Veritas is a residential treatment facility in New York City for adolescent drug abusers. It began operation in October 1971. Much of the impetus for setting up such a facility came from community pressure and the staff of Roosevelt Hospital, where, shortly before that time, 24 percent of all adolescent admissions were for drug abuse. It was found that physicians often were either overly suspicious of these patients or were all too easily deceived by them. A gifted former drug abuser, alert to the manipulative behavior of addicts and able to interpret it to the staff, was therefore hired and proved invaluable. It became apparent that a special residential treatment facility was needed, so Veritas was established as an autonomous operation associated with Roosevelt Hospital.

Background

At the time of writing, the 65 residents of Veritas lived full-time in two small converted apartment buildings. The young people, between 11 and 24 years old, come from varied socioeconomic and ethnic backgrounds. Over 50 percent of the residents are female—a very unusual feature in a residence for drug abusers. The residents are referred by Roosevelt Hospital, social agencies, courts and probation departments, police departments, churches, schools, and parents. Apart from a resident nurse, the full-time staff consists mainly of former drug abusers not formally trained in the behavioral sciences but particularly adept at understanding adolescents with drug problems. The part-time staff consists of a consulting psychiatrist, another physician who serves as a medical consultant, visiting school teachers, a psychologist, and a consultant in art therapy. I had worked with the Roosevelt Hospital staff and had achieved a degree of success in reaching some of the very withdrawn and difficult patients. With the creation of the Veritas program I assumed the position of consultant in art therapy for the new therapeutic communities.

Initial Difficulties

Theoretical Questions

I will not go into the staggering problems of containing over 60 very disturbed adolescents in two small buildings, of teaching them the elementary lessons of how to cooperate in order to coexist. I will admit that from the start I had some doubts about using art therapy in Veritas's highly structured and authoritarian setting. My brushes with authority as an adolescent in the fascist capitals of Central Europe left me firmly opposed to the authoritarian approach—especially in the areas of education and therapy. At Veritas constant demands are made on the residents to confront their inadequacies, hostilities, and self-defeating attitudes, both in intensive encounter sessions and in their day-to-day dealings with the staff. To my mind, this could serve only to strengthen the superego at the expense of the ego. However, I recalled Anna Freud's assertion that in adolescence the superego is alienated from the ego and that support of the superego is what is needed most. Perhaps this explains why, to my surprise, the authoritarian approach works for many residents. I saw frightened, hard-core drug abusers—completely unable to deal with either their drug problem or any other life situation—emerge after only a few months as reasonably well functioning individuals. Their manifest symptoms were modified; they looked well, identified with the parental image as represented by the staff, were in accord with the goals of their community, and were mindful of their futures.

In a recent trip I made to the Soviet Union under the aegis of the American Orthopsychiatric Association I found somewhat similar programs for alcohol abuse, whereby the alcoholics are organized into communities of their own, given supplies, and required to pursue "work therapy." (I might add that I visited two hospitals for the mentally disturbed and in both art is used therapeutically in rehabilitation.)

Adding to my misgivings about the art therapist's role in the program was the injunction I received to "stick to art and leave the therapy to us." The view that art therapy is a frill is perhaps understandable in the light of the fundamental difficulties the director and his staff faced. They were responsible for raising the funds that were crucial to the continuance of the Veritas residence and program. In addition they had to resolve myriad questions on every detail of the program. It is to their credit that they did decide to establish and then to continue the art therapy program.

Problems of Communication

I discovered that the residents and staff of Veritas had developed a language of therapy for which I had no frame of reference or background. In order to communicate with the residents and staff (if not actually to speak their language, at least to understand what was meant), I had to learn their vocabulary. (See "A Vocabulary of Therapeutic Terms.")

A VOCABULARY OF THERAPEUTIC TERMS

Haircut
A verbal reprimand followed by feeding of information on how to effect the desired change

Flagging
Unimportant and frequently minor changes in behavior or one's routine manner of doing things, indicating some unexpressed feelings or preoccupation; taken as a signal that attention is needed

Tripping
Concentrating on or daydreaming about something usually not pertinent to the present situation, this being a diversion or way to avoid confronting immediate situations or feelings

Tipping
Grouping together on the basis of some similarity (sex, color, projected-image, etc.) for the purpose of finding security in numbers and avoiding the threat of the one-to-one confrontation

Lug
A pointed remark, slightly sarcastic, for the purpose of making one aware of something through gentle ridicule; a destructive tool if not used carefully

Carom Shot
A form of indirect confrontation where a defensive, nonreceptive person is reached through the medium of another; usually used in the group encounter setting

Negative Contract
A silent understanding between two or more people, whereby one does not tell on the other or at least does not help the other to grow and change; frequently the result of tipping

Stuffing Feelings
Holding on to feelings created by situations or by interactions with others, allowing them to build up, with an eventual release through flagging, displacing, or reacting

Shooting a Curve
Getting what one wants by asking permission from a second person in authority for something refused earlier by another authority; a form of lying by omission

Physical Problems

In addition to the foregoing problems, I encountered great difficulties in setting up a space for the art workshop. The extremely limited physical facilities at the Veritas residence sent us initially to the leaky basement. After many months of trying to work in 2 inches of water every time it rained, with art materials that gradually became more and more waterlogged, we reached the limits of frustration tolerance and sought a more suitable space. Our only alternative was a dark 9′ by 12′ lounge that is also used for counseling, sewing, and teaching. Thus, we have to clear the area after every art session, and since there is no nearby closet available all materials have to be carried up and down a flight of stairs. About one-third of the time alloted for art work is spent in setting up equipment and supplies and getting the restless, overworked young people to settle down to work.

The many problems I faced made the period of adjustment difficult. I had to reevaluate my attitudes and confront my personal bias, learn a new vocabulary of therapeutic terms, and make do with extremely inconvenient facilities—all the while feeling my way toward the direction the art therapy program should take and, in general, finding my role in the overall program. What sustained me was my feeling for the young people and my admiration for the zealous devotion of the staff to an extremely demanding program.

The Art Program

The art program has the overall purpose of introducing Veritas residents to art as a means of expressing and ventilating feelings, both about themselves and the situation in which they find themselves. Initially, we envisioned programs in various arts—graphics, music, film, dance, poetry, pottery, etc.—but we were forced to realize that there is not yet enough money or time to pursue such an ambitious program.

Participants in the art program are divided into two separate groups with separate approaches: a group at the residence and a workshop group meeting outside the residence in my private studio. Those who enter the second group are approaching readiness for return to the community.

Group at Residence

For the most part, the art group at the residence is drawn from newer admissions to the community. A resident must express an interest in participation and must be judged by the staff as ready to benefit from the experience. The turnover is large because some newcomers cannot yet concentrate even for a short span of time or accept the minimum discipline and cooperation necessary in any work group. Since I am not yet able to offer such disturbed residents individual sessions, they are asked to leave the group. Sometimes, after a period of adjustment, they are ready to come back.

The limitations of the physical setting for art therapy at the residence determine the working method to some degree; only short-term projects can be undertaken. Moreover, most of the residents are suspicious of anything new that is offered and they are afraid and insecure, having failed at almost everything they have attempted. They are convinced that anything they do is bound to be of no value. They are afraid to venture out, to draw a line, to use color, to draw the human figure.

The first 15 minutes of each 2-hour session, the young people work in pairs. They are asked to face each other and draw the other's face on a 9″ by 12″ sheet of paper according to a method developed by Nicolaïdes[1] and modified by art therapist Elaine Rapp. Partners face each other, establish eye-to-eye contact, and then begin to draw. The rule is laid down that one move his pencil only while looking at the person he is drawing. While he is looking at his paper he must not draw. The sketch proceeds very slowly.

The purpose of this exercise is to establish contact with the partner by looking very intently and trying to find the most characteristic aspects of the other's face. If a drawing made in this way closely resembles its subject, probably the directions have not been followed. Therefore the participants are freed from the competition to produce a good likeness. This is a game that cannot be won by achieving a conventional goal.

Immediately following the above exercise, the partners make another 15-minute sketch of each other using ordinary methods. Members of the group invariably notice improvement in their drawing abilities. All are encouraged to show the others both drawings. There is much friendly laughter (especially at the first drawings) and many tell about their feelings toward the partner and how this affected the way they drew. The atmosphere becomes less anxious and intense. Most are able to accept their work and allow me to keep their drawings for the purpose of recording improvement. This way of starting a session helps the new resident begin to communicate feelings not only through art but also verbally. He begins to take part in the creative process and to recognize nonrepresentational aspects of art. It also tells me something about his ability and about his way of responding to instruction.

The second half of the session is less structured. Everyone is encouraged to work on his own, choosing from among a variety of materials: crayons, paints, charcoal, collage materials. The young people are usually invited to use these materials freely in a playful manner. The response is varied, as is the subject matter. Some of the work indicates a preoccupation with sex and drugs, particularly the work of the newer participants in the program. As a resident's exposure to the Veritas program grows, he tends to drop such preoccupations. Psychedelic art gives way to more conventional work, as if the psychedelic represented the crazy part of oneself.

Often even the inhibited can respond to the pleasures of using art materials in an unstructured situation. For those young people who have no background in art or are extremely fearful or apathetic I suggest doodling as an expression

[1] Kimon Nicolaïdes, *The Natural Way To Draw: A Working Plan for Art Study.* Boston, Houghton-Mifflin Co., 1969.

Figure 1

of feelings. I may set up a still life as a model for realistic or abstract design. Often the ongoing activities stimulate a resident to talk about his reactions to his early experiences and to his new situation in the residence. By means of the unstructured second part of these art sessions, the new resident begins to gain some insight into his feelings and the art therapist starts to learn about areas that are emotionally charged. A record of the resident's initial feeling state is established and a contribution is made to diagnostic evaluation and treatment planning.

About once a month, if the group climate permits, I set up another kind of game. Everyone does a collage, selecting pictures from magazines and other materials for color, design, and to tell a story. At the outset everyone is told that he will discuss the story of his collage and his feelings about it and that his account will be taped. The young people enjoy the process of making the collage and talking about it. As their tapes are played back, most elaborate further on the feelings connected with their productions. I have found it best not to ask leading questions, but to allow the participants to speak spontaneously and naturally. Because this method of working presents some unusual features, three collages, together with notes on their makers and excerpts from each person's comment on his work, have been selected as illustrations.

Tom is an 18-year-old black who had been in the Veritas program 4 months when he made the collage shown in Figure 1. He came as a court case, convicted of heroin abuse. He is bright and alert and well liked at the residence. He is making good use of group therapy. On his last home-visit his uncle—with whom he used to live—tested the potency of some heroin he was pushing by giving Tom a shot. The young man related the incident in detail after returning to the group and began to work out his mixed feelings about his family. Part of his taped comment about his collage follows:

> My collage consists of many different colors. Colors represent feelings. Dark colors are hurt feelings; light ones are the good feelings a person has.

> . . . You can see that the person at the bottom has a long destination . . . a mountain to climb . . . at the end of it a hole. Two birds are showing him the way to go. There are dark clouds and beyond it a bright sun. The picture is like talking about the surface of things first, walking through sand, and then getting to the hard things. Climbing the mountain is harder.

Maria is a very obese 18-year-old girl of Italian descent. She came to Veritas 3 months ago as a heroin user. She retains a strong attachment to her large family. Her adjustment to Veritas is fair. A high school dropout, she is now using tutorial services to qualify for college entrance. Her comments on her collage shown in Figure 2 follow:

> My collage has four parts. The Hunt's tomato sauce is my heritage, in which food is so important. The next one is a beautiful woman, soft and warm. Then the little boy with baseball cap and dog. He made me feel good. The last part is about an Oriental woman. She made me think of traveling. After I'd put all this down I put a naked baby next to the beautiful woman. She's his mother. Just before I finished I cut out the beautiful face of Elizabeth Taylor. She's my idol. Then I put below some ads for Dole pineapple. I had to throw this in to show what's going on; it's like throwing in a little reality.

Anna is of part American-Indian descent. She is an attractive, outgoing 16-year-old girl who came to Veritas as a serious amphetamine abuser with a record of sexual promiscuity and truancy. Her family was unable to help with any of her problems. In her 3 months at the residence she has been very eager to please, to conform to the difficult routine, and to cooperate.

> My collage [Figure 3] is about children because they're real. They haven't been poisoned by grownups yet. Children show their emotions openly. I

Figure 2

Figure 3

wrote what I saw in their faces next to them. But sometimes there's more than one emotion. The little boy with the dog looks peaceful, and I wrote *serenity*. But I also saw *fear* in the way he hangs on to his dog. The two boys in their swimming trunks seem to have fun but they're not smiling; they look cautious. I entitled the whole picture "Love."

Workshop Studio

The art workshop, which meets weekly at my private studio, is designed for those young people who, having become sufficiently self-reliant to leave the residence and plan their own work, will soon be ready for discharge. They must be willing to give up their free time—workshops meet on weekends—and must be able to work harmoniously in a group with a minimum of supervision. They must have sufficient frustration tolerance to stand failures and the obstacles usual in all creative work.

In many ways the workshop studio is an art class. Each participant is given individual attention at whatever stage of development he finds himself. I stress basic skills in drawing and composition and discuss perceptual and psychological properties of color. Since these young people tend to work mainly in abstractions, I am trying to introduce the idea of real forms as a basis for abstractions, to teach the art of selecting aspects of nature and transforming them into symbolic entities.

The young people in the workshop have been in the Veritas program for some time and have been deeply involved in encounter and confrontation groups; they are extremely verbal. I consider verbal interpretations of their art productions contraindicated for young people already saturated with verbalization. I try to remain a friendly, neutral participant in an individual's project, encouraging him to increase his skill while being realistic about a work's shortcomings. I try to convey my total acceptance of each individual as a person while maintaining high critical standards in my attitude toward his art work. The atmosphere fosters pleasure in creativity, the acquisition of skills, and the attainment of feelings of self-worth.

Since their work can stay put week after week in my studio, the participants embark on fairly ambitious and long-range projects. One young man has begun to carve a 3′ log. He is not only learning about woodcarving but, being of mild manners and upper-middle-class background, is also finding useful the opportunity to discharge a great deal of hostility hammering away at his creation. I do not discuss his feelings or encourage him to put them into words; sometimes it is a relief to abandon the art therapist's usual role. Despite a quite imperfect log and still undeveloped skills, he perseveres and has a definite goal for himself, and I encourage him while pointing out at the same time the limitations imposed by the material and by his own stage of artistic development.

Another participant, a young woman with a background in the arts, did a very large picture, part painting and part collage incorporating almost every conceivable material. At the end she almost destroyed it by spraying wildly with a spray can, seemingly out of control. I did not lead her into a discussion of causes; I merely pointed out that the work had lost a great deal of cohesiveness. The workshop studio provides a place where feelings can be ventilated even if they are not talked about.

The young people appear to enjoy their experiences in the workshop, even more than the end results of their productions. They ask to stay longer and close up shop reluctantly. The workshop sessions begin and end with an informal coffee-and-cake time, where everyone is my guest. They behave in a most responsible manner: brushes are washed, wood shavings swept up, coffee cups washed and dried, tables meticulously wiped—all this without my intervention. Occasionally we visit galleries and museums as a group, and everyone is alert, responsive, and well behaved. Some members of the workshop have gone to museums on their own.

I believe that the workshop studio helps strengthen the ego by improving the artistic quality of each individual's work; by enabling participants to relate to each other in a work situation; and by furthering the development of inner discipline. Participants begin to function autonomously, to become more self-reliant. They take responsibility for themselves and their friends and develop trust as they come to know the art therapist and her family in a social situation. They also learn something important by accepting the role of wanted guests who are accepted for themselves.

Summary

I am still working out the methods that will best suit the particular needs of the Veritas program. I am endeavoring to create an atmosphere that is conducive to productivity, that allows the young people an escape valve for their emotions, and in a simple and direct manner provides a therapeutic art experience that will help to strengthen the ego.

The Practice of Art Therapy with Children

EDITH KRAMER

Art therapists who lecture or lead discussions are often asked, "How do you conduct sessions and how does art therapy differ from art teaching?" Such questions also arise in the supervision of students, most of whom must of necessity do their field work in isolation. Opportunities for apprenticeship in established art therapy programs are rare. Yet advice given in the classroom is not easily translated into action. Detailed prescriptions are apt to block the therapist's intuitions and generalities leave him helpless.

There is no immediate solution to this problem. We can only hope that soon there will be more programs where students in training can receive on-the-job supervision from experienced art therapists. Meanwhile the student still needs help in imagining what he may be called upon to do when he works with patients or special students.

I have found it helpful to present in my courses at least one or two blow-by-blow descriptions of actual art therapy sessions. Naturally such examples cannot be taken as models that ought to or can be imitated. They illustrate, on the contrary, the fluid, unpredictable quality of the therapeutic process. They show how actions evolve out of the interplay between the art therapist's philosophy, his personality, the personalities of the people he works with, and the specific situation as it evolves in the course of a single session. I believe that such detailed presentations will also be of interest to the readers of this magazine.

It will not be possible to satisfy curiosity about the later fate of the children who appear in this paper, but I have tried to give sufficient information on each child to make his or her behavior comprehensible.

The Program

All events described occurred between 1968 and 1970 in the Child Psychiatric Ward of Jacobi Hospital, a city hospital that also functions as a teaching hospital for the Albert Einstein Medical College, New York City. It is a 15-bed ward for children between 3 and 12 years old. Their disturbances vary, and include autism, childhood schizophrenia, delinquency, and severe neurosis. The majority are considered borderline cases, not acutely psychotic but in need of intensive psychiatric care and close supervision.

Some of the children are chosen for long-term treatment and may remain for one or two years or even longer. Others are admitted for diagnosis which may entail residency for six weeks to three months, and there are also those who have been taken in because of psychiatric emergency and may stay according to the exigencies of the situation for a single night or for many months.

As this is a teaching hospital all the children are given a fair amount of attention from the psychiatrists-in-training. Their parents also receive more emotional support and psychiatric help than would be offered in an ordinary city hospital. However, both children and parents are likely to suffer repeated separations as the young professionals' training requires them to spend time in different psychiatric units. Efforts are made to avoid such separations for those children who have been selected for long-term treatment.

The nursing staff, on the other hand, is fairly steady and among the nurses and nurses' aides are highly skilled, dedicated, and experienced persons. The board of education maintains an elementary school on the ward, and a nursery school run by the hospital takes care of the educational needs of the younger or more immature children. The services of recreational workers, social workers, and group workers are also available. Team meetings, rounds, and case conferences maintain communication between the many workers, and the art therapist is included in this teamwork.

Art therapy sessions are conducted in a room exclusively reserved for this activity. It is adequately furnished with tables, closets for art materials, shelves for storing finished and unfinished sculpture, and racks for drying pictures and storing portfolios. There is no shortage of art materials, which are purposely kept simple. Available are excellent ceramic clay mixed with fine grog; gallons of poster paint; charcoal; colored chalks; crayons; a roll of 3′ brown wrapping paper; reams of manila paper, both 18″ x 24″ and 12″ x 18″; and bristle brushes in several sizes. There are muffin tins of 12 cups each for mixing colors.

Work with clay is done on oilcloth pads. Heavy cardboard tubes are used as rolling pins. The necessary assortment of sticks and tools is at hand. There is a wedging board, and a kiln is available on another ward.

I am on the ward twice a week from four to seven in the evening. Thus part of my work is done after supper, at a time when the excitement of school, doctors' and parents' visits, and other pressures has abated. I try to see each child twice a week and to schedule my time so that there is occasion for unwinding and maybe for seeing a child alone at the end of the day if this should be necessary.

Since my time is limited I see only those children who are able to create symbols from art materials. Very young or immature children who tend to use clay and paint only in a primitive experimental (or destructive) manner are not included in the program. For them art materials are available in the nursery school. However, when the nursery school teacher feels that one of her children is ready to take the step to more complex symbolic use of art materials, he will be admitted for a tryout and may stay on.

Children are seen in small groups, the size being determined by the situation. There may be three, four, five, or, at the most, six children present at one time.

Sessions are scheduled to last at least one full hour, and are often extended to an hour and a quarter, or an hour and a half. This differs from the usual expedient in work with children whose attention span seems short and whose frustration tolerance is low, to change activities at the first sign of flagging enthusiasm. This commonly followed policy reduces the likelihood of disturbed or chaotic sessions, but it defeats our educational and therapeutic purpose. We hope to help the children reach the reserves of creative energy which become available when difficulties are *overcome* rather than circumvented. Thus the children's most fruitful work is more often than not done on the second wind.

Sessions tend to present a complex pattern, beginning with initial enthusiasm followed by upset and partial disintegration which, if all goes well, is followed by a second period of integration in which creative work is resumed with renewed intensity. Naturally the policy is flexible. Children who indeed cannot tolerate a whole period are scheduled to attend half a session only, and it is possible to dismiss a child ahead of schedule when his behavior becomes entirely intolerable.

The program having been in effect since 1963, art therapy is well established on the ward, and even though the children change, a certain tradition is transmitted over the years. The art therapist no longer needs to justify her existence and is not exposed to the massive testing by staff and children which the newcomer who introduces a new activity must expect.

Art sessions are not conducted according to any preconceived plan. Rather the simple art materials at hand are available for the child to make what he chooses. I try to convey to each child the feeling that I have no ax to grind, that I am not trying to find out about him or to coerce him into doing something that I have planned for reasons of my own, that I want to know him well in order to be better able to help him make what *he* wants to make. I am there to help him find out what *he* can do when he is able to muster all his energies in the service of a creative task of his own choosing.

However, I do convey the idea that art sessions are periods for work, not for regressive play, and that I prefer personal expression to stereotyped repetition. To put it in theoretical language, I offer myself to the child as his auxiliary ego, ready to support him in an adventure which entails taking risks and of which neither he nor I can predict the ultimate outcome.

Naturally this basic attitude may be modified if the situation demands it. There are times when the art therapist must give more explicit directions, for example, if total freedom frightens a particular child too much. A chaotic situation may require temporary rigid structuring; the task at hand may be so difficult that it is necessary to tell the child exactly what to do.

While making myself the auxiliary ego of the child, I do not of course abdicate my role as adult-in-charge, protector of justice and peace. Also since I usually work with groups each child must share my attention with others. However, if the session goes at all well, each will, in the course of the period, have my undivided attention when he needs it most.

An Illustrative Session

On the afternoon I will now describe, four children are present: Alfred, Emil, Steven, and Raffael.

Alfred, 11 years old, is a schizophrenic child who has developed an elaborate system of obsessive-compulsive defense centered around a fascination with electronic and electrical equipment and with chemistry. His activities in the art room are usually limited to drawings of electrical circuits or scientific equipment and to making clay models or transistor radios and the like. After being on the ward for several months he had been discharged to his mother's care. Now, after six months on the outside, he has been readmitted on an emergency basis. He is deadly pale, profoundly shaken, feels trapped and doomed.

Alfred has come to the art room mainly as a place of refuge. He becomes engaged in making "designs." Carefully he places blobs of poster paint on pieces of paper and folds and reopens them, thus producing colorful bilateral configurations reminiscent of Rorschach cards. He signs and dates each of these products, but he is not ready to elaborate on the designs by working them over, to try to see images in them, or to tell stories about them. The activity remains sterile and repetitious. Feeling that I cannot expect much of Alfred today or that efforts to draw him out would only make him unhappier, I leave him to his devices.

Emil is a depressed little boy of 11. He is well liked by the other children and seems on the whole intact, though burdened with many worries. He has been on the ward for observation only and is due for discharge in the next few days. Emil wants to make a clay horse before he leaves. Horses have become very popular on the ward since one of the oldest boys made a large male horse complete with penis in erection.

Steven, also 11 years old, is a newcomer. His left arm has been amputated 6 inches from the shoulder. I have seen him only once before, in an individual session where I was impressed with his dexterity in working the clay with his only hand. He had, with very little help from me, produced a well integrated horse and rider. I have also been surprised by the other children's ready acceptance of him. As far as I can observe no one is horror-struck or disgusted by the missing arm. Beyond these observations I know nothing of Steven.

Raffael, the youngest of the four, is an 8½-year-old Puerto Rican boy. He has been on the ward for more than a year and we are old friends. He was admitted because of swings between destructive and withdrawn behavior that had reached intolerable intensity after his discharge from the pediatric ward of Jacobi Hospital where he had been treated for burns on his right hand, arm, neck, and cheek. One of six siblings living with their mother on welfare, he had been burnt while alone in the kitchen at breakfast time. Somehow his pajama sleeve caught fire and he was rescued by his mother who herself sustained minor injuries as she doused the flames.

Raffael's mother visited him at the hospital daily, but seemed much shaken by the son's disfigurement and barely able to conceal her physical revulsion. It seemed as if his injuries had compounded for her a previously formed conception of Raffael as the family scapegoat, "a runt, a hunchback, a crazy person." This perception of him is in no way realistic. Raffael is small for his age, but well proportioned, he moves gracefully, is endowed with considerable charm, and is well liked both by children and staff.

Competent and ambitious, Raffael runs with the oldest boys on the ward, all somewhat older and bigger than he is. He succeeds, with considerable effort, in being accepted by them as an equal.

Upon entering the art room Raffael turns to the large clay horse that started the vogue for making horses. It was made by Jesus, the leader of the group, and was too large to be fired in the hospital's kiln. Jesus had given it to Raffael as a present. It had originally been adorned with a large penis, but this had broken off in the course of time. Raffael had tried hard to repair it with glue and masking tape. Now he declares that he will smash up the horse to make new clay. Thereupon Emil intervenes, begging Raffael not to destroy the horse but rather to give it to him. Raffael is not moved. I intervene, using two contradictory lines of argument. While I plead with Raffael to let the horse live and to let Emil have it, I try to persuade Emil that it would be better anyway for him to make his own horse. I am not very successful with either of the two boys.

The matter is taken out of my hands by Steven who organizes and leads a communal, controlled destruction of the horse in which all three boys join with glee (Alfred pays no attention to these goings on but continues making his designs). The horse is reduced to clay which the boys gather into an empty can. Emil then gets ready to construct a clay horse of his own. Steven puts water in the can with the broken-up horse and then starts wedging clay that has been soaking for some time. Raffael declares that now he wants to make designs just like Alfred.

I tell Raffael that I am letting Alfred make designs because he is sad and upset and in no condition to work hard. Of him, Raffael, I expect a lot more. Anyone can make designs, they just happen, even a baby can make them. I want *him* to make a picture where *he* decides what's going to happen, where *he* is the boss. I know that he can do it, for I know all the good work he has done in the art room before.

So encouraged, Raffael agrees to paint a picture where he is the boss. He asks for a large sheet of brown mural paper, charcoal, and a tray of poster paint. I tape a 3′ x 5′ piece of brown paper against the wall and hand him his paint. Then I turn my attention to Emil and his horse. A little later I look in Raffael's direction and see that he is about to tear down his paper. It is empty except for a tiny structure at the bottom of the page painted in gray and subsequently scratched out. (See A, Figure 1) I stop Raffael from tearing down his paper and ask whether he had meant to paint the Empire State Building. (This magnificent structure is such a favorite with New York City children that one learns to recognize it in the most unlikely configurations.) Yes, he admits, but it is too small. We contemplate the size of the paper and decide first to draw a sidewalk and then to try again using the whole height of the paper. Raffael manages to draw a fairly large structure but it is fat and squat rather than thin and tall and he is getting quite desperate.

Having egged Raffael on to the adventure, it would be entirely wrong to abandon him to failure now. I pick up the charcoal and, beginning from the bottom up, I draw the left side of the Empire State Building in the schematic

Figure 1

Figure 2

style in which most of New York's children seem to draw this popular symbol. As I reach the top Raffael suddenly understands, takes the charcoal out of my hand, completes the right side of the building, adds curtained windows and then adds all the other buildings in the picture. He contemplates his work and then declares that now he needs an open manhole on the street such as one can see sometimes when men are working underground. Between the two of us we draw a manhole and a Con Ed sign with two flags.[1]

At this point, Raffael has an audience: both Emil and Steven are watching developments on the mural. Turning to them Raffael explains that now he will make an underground passageway and a monster who lives underground, and he will make a house for him to live in. He draws it (see B on Figure 1, and Figure 2) and seems enormously pleased with his idea. Then he draws above ground on the right side of the paper cars, trees, a playground and a sun (which looks a great deal like him). At this point the art session ends because it is time for supper. In the subsequent session Raffael draws a street, two persons, the tree, and the birds on the left side of the page and embellishes the whole with colored chalks. The Empire State Building is colored a brilliant pink-red and outlined in turquoise. It dominates the picture. (In the black-and-white reproduction the tree on the right, colored green and brown, acquires undue emphasis.)

Raffael is eager to show his work to all children and adults, but he is not ready to tell stories about it. Later the psychotherapist, when Raffael leads him into the art room to admire the work, asks about the story of the monster, but Raffael only repeats what he has already told me: the monster is just there; he has always been there; he will stay there in his underground house; there is no more to tell about him. Subsequently Raffael often speaks about the Empire State Building as a great accomplishment, a "masterpiece," but not as a work needing further explanations.

---

[1] "Consolidated Edison" is the electrical utility company serving New York City.

Discussion of the First Session

We can now try to imagine what the art therapy session might have meant for each of the four boys. We must of course always remember that we are now dealing with conjectures. We may be incorrect in some of our surmises and naturally much may have happened that will never be known to us.

As far as one could tell, the activity had been consolatory for Alfred. For an hour he had been a little less lost and unhappy than during the rest of the day. He remains an outsider throughout the session. The other three boys have a good deal in common. They are absorbed in the phallic aspirations typical for their age, striving for acceptance in their peer group, for leadership, for achievement.

Emil had been distressed at the beginning of the session, disturbed by the violence of Raffael's attack on the horse and anxious lest he would never be able to make a horse of his own. When, under Steven's leadership, he joined in the orderly destruction of Jesus's horse and when subsequently he produced a horse himself (I somehow managed in between helping Raffael to see to it that Emil finished his sculpture), the destructive act was redeemed and Emil's fear of destructiveness was alleviated.

The sculpture was adequate but in no way remarkable. It seemed to me that Emil had no passionate inner need to create a horse, but rather a need to be able to make what everyone else in his group had made. Thus Emil's fears were lessened, his self-esteem heightened, but the session had neither made great demands on him nor had it brought him unusual pain or pleasure.

Steven produced no art, but only exerted leadership of a quality that was (as I later learned) entirely characteristic of him. His actions were tinged with violence yet they were also controlled and sensible. He was in process of establishing a position of leadership which he was to retain throughout his residency on the ward. Subsequently Steven's influence oscillated between organizing well planned delinquent escapades and keeping the group functioning in a constructive, rational manner. We can say that the art session brought forth the benign aspect of his leadership.

Raffael's experiences were more complex and more intense than those of the other three boys. It is not possible to fathom all that went into his initial destructive attack upon Jesus's horse. The passion with which he picked up a hammer to smash the clay figure gave the impression of a theatrical gesture, a make-believe ferocity vented on an expendable object. Yet such threatening acts, which occurred quite frequently and always harmlessly on the ward, were reminiscent of his actions at home where he had threatened his family and the family's possessions with a hammer. In those instances he had acted in dead earnest. Although he had never seriously injured anyone, he had at times wreaked considerable havoc on property.

It is also noteworthy that destruction was directed against the work of the biggest, sexually most mature boy of his group. We can surmise that rage against this often high-handed ruler of the ward was vented in the act. Smashing the horse seemed, however, above all an act of liberation, for as long as Raffael continued scavenging and begging from the older boys he surely would not learn to work independently.

After breaking up the horse Raffael was at first inclined to regress, for he wanted to make Rorschach designs like Alfred. However, energy could readily be mobilized for ambitious constructive work. When I encouraged Raffael and showed my confidence in his powers he was ready to tackle a 3′ x 5′ mural. Having just destroyed a horse adorned with a huge (but broken) penis he sets out to paint a picture of the biggest, most magnificently erect thing in his world, and at first he fails totally. Instead of the desired tall, monumental building a miniature structure appears at the very bottom of his paper. Raffael is confronted with the discrepancy between his high aspirations and his feeling of insignificance. No wonder he wants to destroy his attempt.

Was I mistaken, then, to have encouraged Raffael to try to paint a picture where *he* would be "the boss"? (We must remember that I did *not* suggest the subject matter. The Empire State Building was his own choice.)

Subsequent events prove that my confidence in his abilities was not entirely unrealistic, for when I gave him a little help, Raffael's performance improved very quickly. Had he felt as profoundly insignificant and castrated as his first drawing seemed to indicate, it would not have been possible for me to restore his self-confidence simply by drawing part of the building for him. His picture would have been doomed to failure no matter what I might have done (short of doing the whole job for him).

His quick recovery of enthusiasm and inventive powers once I had proved my readiness to actively help him erect his building shows that he has not entirely internalized his mother's distorted perception of him. Even though mother perceives him as a misshapen, disfigured runt, there must be some core of inner strength, some sanctuary where Raffael feels inviolate. Thus another motherly woman's perception of him as manly, competent, and whole could move him to creative action.

The complete picture constitutes an excellent self-portrait. We see a not particularly gifted, somewhat immature child, his world rather impoverished and disjointed. He is haunted by some underlying, nameless trouble, but he has aspiration and vitality and he seems capable of functioning adequately in many areas of daily life.

Looking only at the formal qualities, how would we rate Raffael's picture? If we apply the categories I have suggested previously,[2] we can say that the work includes elements of pictogram, of stereotyped production, and of formed expression.

The area containing the monster is mainly pictogram. The drawing is

[2] "The Problem of Quality in Art," *Bulletin of Art Therapy*, Vol. 3, No. 1, Oct. 1963.

weak and indistinct. The hidden menace of the monster is not visually expressed; its meaning can be understood only through Raffael's spoken comment. Yet the monster part of the picture is very important psychologically.

The playground, street, trees, people, and cars are presented in a perfunctory, stereotyped manner, with the exception, maybe, of the birds which have a certain power and of the sun-face, which is not stereotyped and indeed constitutes an unconscious but specific self-portrait.

The pleasure of giving expressive form, one of the hallmarks of sublimation, can be felt mainly in the gaily colored skyscrapers. Nevertheless we can say that Raffael has experienced the process of sublimation in the making of his picture. At the beginning there had been some expression of aggressive sexuality in the raw, and this was followed by an inclination to regress to the infantile pleasures of smearing and messing with paint. Then Raffael renounced these pleasures in favor of constructive ego-syntonic action. Primitive concern with the penis was displaced onto a universal phallic symbol. As he thus gratified his phallic aspirations, victoriously overcoming his feelings of insignificance, he gained access to repressed and menacing emotional content. Sublimation faltered as he was unable to give full expression to this material, and he turned to more conventional, emotionally more neutral subject matter.

Thus Raffael's finished work fails to attain the inner consistency and evocative power characteristic of complete sublimation, but he has come close enough to sublimation to experience the special kind of pleasure which belongs to it, and we can hope that this will pave the way to kindred experiences in the future.

A Second Illustrative Session

My next story tells about a very different group of children. They are Jane, Paula, Gregory, and Hal.

Jane, an 11-year-old white child, has suffered much from being shifted back and forth between mother and father. The parents had separated when Jane was two-and-a-half years old, and since this time there had been a pattern of mother forcing father to take charge of Jane and her older brother whenever their behavior became difficult, only to take them back as soon as they had adjusted to life with him. At the time of Jane's admission the father had finally obtained legal custody of his two children, but the ingrained pattern of moving back and forth between the two parents had not changed.

Jane's emotional turmoil is aggravated by minor organic perceptual difficulties which made it impossible for her to learn to read by conventional academic methods and made her a behavior problem in school, but she is very good with her hands. She excels in all crafts and has talent for art.

On the ward we find that Jane can, in her better moments, cope with emotional turbulence by submerging herself totally in some constructive activity, becoming oblivious to the world around her. However she cannot sustain this maneuver when her anxiety reaches a high pitch. She then becomes hyperactive, drowning her troubles in loud gibberish and wild gyrations.

Jane's voice is harsh, staccato, and unmodulated. She is inclined to be extremely bossy and prefers the company of the younger children whom she can easily dominate. She is nevertheless much loved by the little ones, for even though she orders them around and screams at them, she also pays a lot of attention to them, defends them fiercely against the ward bullies, and does not herself mistreat them physically. In the art room Jane is usually quiet, busy, often helpful, but always bossy.

Paula, 12 years old, is a large, overweight black child, who wears thick eyeglasses. She has been admitted because of recurrent states of withdrawal of nearly catatonic quality. These are usually preceded by periods of agitation when she becomes aggressive. In the times between these pathological states she seems amiable and emotionally flat.

Paula is the oldest of the six children of an unwed, 30-year-old mother. She has experienced the advent of several men in the home who have fathered her brothers and sisters. There is an extensive history of mental illness and of violence in the family.

Paula's art oscillates between outright psychotic productions, when she covers sheets of paper with her name or with black or dark purple paint sometimes used to obliterate her name, and noncommittal defensive work, when she covers paper with squares and stripes of pastel shades of pink, blue, or violet, or manufactures clay ashtrays or cups. Between these extremes there are times when her work becomes more communicative. She then makes faces and figures in clay and tells stories about them. These tales usually center around mutilation, blood, sex, and death, and they are all told in a flat, amiable manner.

In spite of her severe disturbance, Paula is well liked by her peers. She can be pleasant, cooperative, and generous. The girls in particular protect her during her periods of acute illness.

Gregory, an 11-year-old Puerto Rican boy, is a schizophrenic with an elaborate system of avoidances, rituals and fantasies. He has been treated as an invalid by his family throughout his life and has obtained considerable secondary gain by tyrannizing everyone with his obsessions and rituals. He moves rigidly and speaks in a low, monotonous voice. He seems helpless in everyday matters, such as buttoning a shirt or tying his shoelaces, but he is intelligent and reads and writes well. When crossed or perturbed he stands rigidly, screaming at the top of his lungs. When this fails to bring results he is apt to become irrationally violent. However, in the course of his residency on the ward he has learned to adopt a diplomatic, conciliatory attitude in most of his dealings with the other children. He therefore gets along well with Jane in spite of her bossiness.

Gregory loves to draw and to work with clay. A recurrent topic of his drawings is magical changes of size, particularly the magical miniaturizing of various imaginary personalities. This preoccupation fits in with his production in clay, which consists mainly of smallish lumps reminiscent of fecal matter and adorned with faces and tiny arms and feet.

Hal is a nine-year-old Puerto Rican boy who on first impression appears to be a bright, attractive, somewhat over-talkative and clinging child. Upon closer acquaintance there emerges an extremely disoriented, confused, and unformed being, beset by paranoid suspicions and fears, who maintains himself mainly by clinging to and attempting to control any adult he comes in contact with.

Information on the history of his illness is scanty. Hal's admission occurred three months after a seizure for which he had been hospitalized in a pediatric ward for 10 days. This attack seemed to have aggravated a disturbance that had manifested itself in various ways at least since his second year when he became severely asthmatic. The general picture is one of the interplay between constitutional factors in the child and the mother's inclination to establish a symbiotic kind of relationship with her disturbed and demanding son.

Up to now Hal has produced next to nothing in art, even though he always comes to his session. His time and attention are exclusively focused on observing everyone in the room and attempting to control me and the other children. He will go to any length to be allowed to hold my keys and if he gains possession his time is taken up in locking and unlocking doors and closets, controlling all comings and goings and accompanying these activities with a stream of talk. His behavior would be entirely intolerable if it were not for the frantic quality of it all, which communicates the underlying anxiety and disorientation he is holding at bay.

Hal has been placed with Jane, Gregory, and Paula because he is too immature and confused to tolerate any group in which there is a phallic type of competition for leadership. The four children are in the main self-absorbed individuals each pursuing his or her own aim. Jane's bossiness does not have the quality of leadership. Thus Hal has somehow managed to survive in this setting.

On the day I am about to describe Hal greets me with the news that this is his last day on the ward. Tomorrow he will be transferred to the Bronx State Children's Hospital. This is no fantasy. Hal is indeed scheduled for admission to a long-term treatment program. He has been prepared for it for quite a while, and we have already spent some time packing his ceramic work into boxes in preparation for the move.

Today his first concern is with his work in progress. Would I deliver to him all the clay sculptures that would still be too soft for packing and the paintings that would still be wet? I assure him that I will deliver all precious objects left behind. This calms him a little.

He is nevertheless quite agitated, his voice very high-pitched, his movements jerky. I foresee a very difficult session.

At first Hal manages to control himself by controlling Paula. He declares that he will teach her how to make a cup out of clay and begins demonstrating each step to her. Paula submits amiably and each child produces a cup.

Jane meanwhile has cut a large piece of brown wrapping paper, tacked it on the wall, and pushed Gregory against it in order to trace his body. She then paints his portrait, using the tracing and working very hard at matching his skin color and the color of his clothes (Figure 3).

I have no idea what prompted her to this action. No such tracing has been done lately and no pictures of this kind are currently displayed in the art room or on the ward.

Gregory, having submitted docilely to Jane's wishes, returns to his usual little clay figures and for the rest of the session remains preoccupied with his own work.

Meanwhile, Paula and Hal have both completed their cups and Paula is

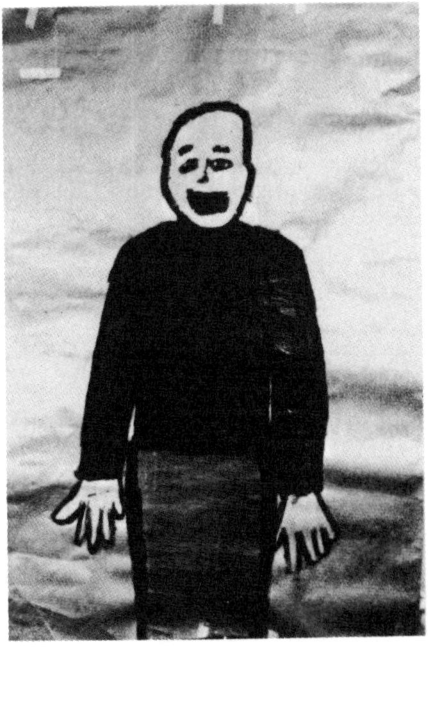

Figure 3

getting tired of being ordered about by him. As he loses control over her, Hal's agitation mounts. He digs up large lumps of clay and bangs them with both fists, declaring that he is killing me. He makes abortive attempts to give the lumps human form (the better to kill me) but seems unable to master his feelings sufficiently to arrive at any recognizable shape.

His hostility infects Paula and both children spend some time symbolically killing me by banging the clay.

Paula subsides after a little while and is inclined to return to the manufacture of more clay cups. When I point out that she has made plenty of them already and that I know that she can make more interesting things, she fashions a little girl's head and torso, but declares that she cannot make a skirt. I help her with this and then suggest that she give the girl a pair of legs. No, says she, in her flat, amiable voice, "the girl got no legs, she was run over by a car and it was so bad they had to cut them off."

Hal meanwhile continues to kill me, rocking the table with his wild drumming, and shouting at the top of his voice. I suggest to him that he may be angry because he is leaving. Maybe he would prefer me to be dead because I am not coming with him, or maybe he would rather see me dead than think of me working with other children.

This attempt at interpretation does not reduce Hal's hostility but his activity becomes more defined. He now rolls out a clay sausage and declares that this is a cobra and that I am this cobra full of poison. He pretends that the cobra is biting him and that he must quickly suck the poison out of the wound and spit it out. The fantasy excited him so much that he begins to spit violently on the floor. I foresee that he will soon spit in my face. Jane is getting quite upset by Hal's behavior and threatens to beat him up. The atmosphere becomes explosive, and it looks as if I might have to evict Hal forcibly from the art room.

At this impasse Hal notices Jane's painting of Gregory, which is nearly finished. It is quite a remarkable piece of portraiture, Jane having succeeded in capturing Gregory's stiff posture and defensive smile (Figure 3). Hal declares that he will now make a tracing of me. His whole manner changes. He purposefully measures out a length of wrapping paper and, climbing on a table, he tacks it against the wall at such a height that he can trace me while I stand on a chair. He places a chair against the paper, orders me to stand on it, and, having thus literally pushed me against a wall, he proceeds to outline my body methodically, taking care to trace my hands, fingers, legs, and feet accurately. This accomplished, he permits me to climb down.

He completes the picture by drawing my face, hair, and blue smock. He looks at his work critically, notices that the left arm is raised higher than the right one, and that the fingers of my right hand are not as evenly spread out as those of my left, but he concludes very reasonably that such irregularities are only natural, for people never stand quite stiff, but move about. He sets

Figure 4

up a tray of paint, and with some assistance from me mixes a skin color. He then proceeds to paint peacefully, and even though his control is to be shaken a few times before the picture is finished he manages in the end to produce a well organized, complete painting (Figure 4).

Now Jane, who has observed Hal's actions, declares that she too will trace me. She quickly tacks up a piece of paper and traces my outline singing at the top of her voice, "I am your father, your mother, your sister, and your brother."

Working very fast, she again achieves a good likeness (Figure 5). At this point Paula declares that she too wants to be traced, and Jane does the tracing for her. Paula, however, does not want Jane to do her portrait. Instead she herself uses the tracing as the basis for a self-portrait (Figure 6).

Figure 5

Paula's performance is much more disorganized than that of the other children. She begins by painting a white blouse, similar to the one she is wearing, but perseverates and also paints the hands white. Then she paints the skirt dark blue. When Jane points out to her that she has painted hands and blouse the same color, she changes the hands to gray and uses the same gray color on the face. She then swiftly paints the face, complete with large eyeglasses. She ends up by attacking the picture with swirling strokes of black paint. However she stops short of entirely destroying her work, and this is, for Paula, quite a victory, for most of her self-representations end up as an unrecognizable black mess.

At this point the session ends. Hal has not finished his picture, and because it is his last day, I promise him that he can come back after supper and finish it.

I explain to the group scheduled for art therapy after supper that Hal has special permission to stay on because it is his last day and he is very anxious to finish his picture. The children accept this and Hal enters on his very best behavior and immediately goes to work.

Among the group now present are two seven-year-old boys, Martin and Alfonso, who are friends and are facing an impending separation, for Alfonso too is scheduled for admission to the Children's Hospital in the near future.

Seeing Hal's portrait of me, Martin decides to make one of Alfonso. Alfonso on the other hand busies himself making a present for Martin, a clay bird sitting on top of a bird house. Thus separation continues as a main theme even in this new group. I will, however, not describe the evening session in detail. It passes without major mishaps or important events. Hal maintains his self-control and manages to finish his picture. I promise that I will deliver it to him very soon.

At the end of the session Hal stays with me to close up and is permitted to hold the keys and unlock and lock doors. When I am about to put on my coat he grabs it, wraps himself in it and rolls on the table like a little baby but then gives it up without a real struggle.

When I deliver his painting to him three weeks later, Hal is pleased but it is evident that his conflicting feelings have by now been transferred to his

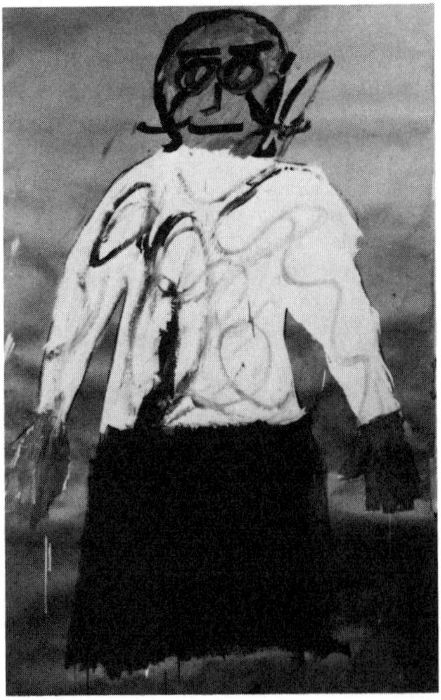

Figure 6

woman counselor at the Children's Hospital. She is greatly impressed with Hal's picture as he had not yet done anything comparable during his residency there.

This does not surprise me, for the painting is unique also among Hal's productions at Jacobi Hospital. Never before had he given any art work his undivided attention. Never had he worked with so little help and prodding. Never before had he painted or modeled a whole human being.

General Discussion

If we compare our second example with the first, we find a few similarities and a great many differences. In each case one child remains an outsider, quite untouched by the session's dramatic events (Alfred and Gregory). Each story has its hero, a child who ultimately gains the most from the session (Raffael and Hal).

The central theme of the first session was the struggle against feelings of insignificance and castration, with its counterpart, the striving toward masculine achievement. When Raffael drew the monster he touched upon more infantile, more deeply repressed material, but it emerged within the context of his phallic strivings.

My role is an active one throughout the session. I discourage regression, encourage independent action, come to the rescue, admire achievement.

Our second session revolved around problems of individuation, of separating the self from the object and of learning to perceive it as a distinct entity.

My role was much more passive. At first it was limited to withstanding the onslaught of Hal's aggression. Later I made myself available for the benign control and possession of my person. The main therapeutic agent of the session was the child Jane, who set an example that helped Hal come to terms with conflicts aroused by impending separation.

The difference in my role stems from the different quality of the relationship which the children had established with me. Raffael perceived me as an old friend, quite distinct from himself and from other people in his life, particularly from his mother. Even though transference phenomena naturally entered the relationship, it was in the main a working alliance geared towards creative work and growth. In a less intimate way, the same attitude also prevailed in my relationship to Emil and to Steven.

Hal's relationship was much more infantile and amorphous. He barely distinguished me from himself and from any of the other adults on the ward. All relationships were as yet cast in the image of the symbiotic tie to his mother. Jane had achieved more individuation, but she was afraid to form ties to anyone whose actions she could not control.

Thus I could not offer myself to these children in any specific role. Rather I had to be available for whatever kind of relationship they would bring forth, only maintaining enough authority to curb excessive destructiveness.

If we look at each child's experiences in turn, we find that Gregory remained quite untouched by the drama. He was probably thankful that Jane, instead of ordering him about as usual, confined herself to tracing his outline on brown paper. The portrait itself made little impression on him. He was above all intent on returning to his habitual preoccupations. He thereby isolated himself successfully against the turmoil around him.

Paula was to some extent drawn into the activities of Hal and Jane. Since she was on an even keel this particular day, her responses were amiable and flat. Her story about the little girl whose legs were amputated, though indicative of her pathology, was in no way unusual for her. When Jane and Hal drew outlines she also wanted to be traced. However, she did not attempt to draw the portrait of *another* person but tried to define *herself*. This is the more primitive and more usual way in which children are apt to use such tracings. Her self-portrait was a little more successful than any of her previous attempts. Although she finally attacked the painting she did not entirely obliterate it. Thus there were some slight gains for Paula.

Both Hal's and Jane's experiences were more intense. In Hal's case the events of the session demonstrated how unusual pressures need not necessarily lead to increased pathology. They can also mobilize hitherto untapped reserves of energy for mastery and integration.

Hal began the session by using habitual defenses, warding off anxiety by controlling Paula and by usurping my role as teacher and disciplinarian. (The mechanism whereby Hal took on my role cannot be termed identification, but rather constitutes a primitive forerunner of it.) As soon as this mechanism failed because Paula no longer complied, his conflicts erupted full force. He perceived me as a deadly power that existed outside himself and that had also invaded and poisoned him. Thus he needed to kill me and simultaneously to rid himself of that part of me which he had incorporated. Hal's behavior becomes floridly psychotic and we perceive, transferred onto my person, all that is most pathological in his relationship to his mother and to all women. The session threatened to end disastrously but then Hal perceived Jane's portrait of Gregory and everything changed.

It is interesting that Jane attained a new level of integrative functioning during a session when Hal's disturbance reached its highest pitch. However, we have no way of ascertaining whether this was coincidence or whether Hal's distress mobilized her to unusually constructive action.

Whatever the reason may have been, Jane, who was in the habit of treating Gregory as a possession she could dominate entirely, chose this moment to perceive him as a person. While her gesture of pushing him against the wall in order to trace him still contained some aggression, her subsequent attempt to create his likeness was serene, without malice, and, within the limitations of her age and talent, quite successful.

Her success was probably crucial for Hal, for it demonstrated to him that a child like himself could do such a thing and do it well. Just like Jane, Hal discharged some aggression in the act of pushing me against the wall to trace me. From then on, however, his perception of my person lost its aggressive and delusional quality. The image of the poisonous cobra was no longer in evidence. Instead Hal produced a painting that could represent his art teacher as he knew her. Noteworthy was his sensible comment that it was quite alright that my arms and hands were not extended in perfect symmetry, because people do move. (Hal was obsessively perfectionistic and as a rule could tolerate no asymmetry.) We see that even while he created my likeness he could concede me some measure of autonomy.

We recall that Hal's example in turn inspired Jane too to do my portrait.

It is interesting to see how the same action can have different meanings to different children. Painting a portrait of me helped Hal to detach my person from fantasies he had transferred onto me. When Jane, on the other hand, traced my outline she brought forth a fantasy, singing, "I am your father, your mother, your sister, and your brother."

The two children's needs were diametrically opposed. Hal was inclined to fuse symbiotically with any woman who became important to him. Being one with her, he could neither perceive her nor establish a relationship with her. He needed to detach himself and to perceive his partner more objectively.

Jane, on the contrary, held herself aloof from all close relationships. She habitually treated me as dispenser of art materials, keeper of peace, and occasional source of information concerning the handling of clay or paint—nothing more. When she drew my portrait I seemed to have become a person, someone close, something like a relative, and so she sang. Her excitement, however, remained within acceptable bounds, and the painting was completed without mishap. We can conjecture that the portrait had made it possible for Jane to allow herself to feel close to me without feeling endangered.

We see that for both children the gain hinged on finding a symbolic object that could contain their feelings and creating an image of it, partly through the primitive method of tracing, partly by more mature observation and action. The ambivalence that had burdened their relationship to the person whose image they created was thereby greatly reduced.

We cannot fathom all the mechanisms that contributed to this change. Finding an acceptable way of possessing another person, indeed obtaining her cooperation in this act, certainly was one factor. Furthermore possessing the person in this symbolic way entailed none of the dangers of actual possession.

Here it occurs to me that for Hal, who was about to leave the ward, a specific problem that arises upon separation might have contributed both to his initial disturbed behavior and to the dramatic change later on. When a loved object is lost, the inclination arises to make up for the loss by internalizing the object. However, since the departure is unconsciously experienced as an aggressive act, hostility against the object is generated. Thus there is danger that the negative cathexis will be internalized along with the object. In such an event the psychic organization is indeed severely burdened.

Although Hal's cobra fantasy was in keeping with his paranoid personality, the impending separation may have helped bring it out so forcefully. Conceivably, painting my portrait rescued him from having to deal with the separation in a more primitive and damaging way, by killing me in fantasy and being forced to take me along with him as a poisonous presence.

I have frequently observed that creating portraits can be helpful in mastering ambivalent relationships. In particular I have found that drawing portraits and having one's portrait made can help mitigate the conflicts and pain of separation.

Just as in our first example, we can observe in this session the dawning of sublimation. At the start, primitive aggressive and sexual impulses are held at bay by various mechanisms of defense. As these give way under the pressure of mounting affect, there is a moment when regression and disorganization threaten to win out. However, as the children find more mature means of gratifying their instinctive needs, aggression and sexual excitement abate, and energy becomes available for objective observation, rational thinking, constructive action, and other ego functions.

We observe that sublimation, or at least behavior that contained elements of sublimation, became possible for Hal at a moment when his habitual mechanisms of defense were inadequate. In my first example, a similar moment of crisis, when ordinary defenses were powerless and disorganization threatened, also occurred. Although this is not an indispensable condition for it, sublimation does frequently develop under just such stress. We may then ask whether the art therapist should actively attempt to lower defenses.

We must remember that the art materials themselves and the invitation to use them freely already invite suspension of obsessive-compulsive defenses. In treating children with such precarious ego organization as those I have described in this paper, it would not be advisable to go beyond an invitation of this kind. Defenses of children like these break down all too easily. Should we show ourselves too eager to dismantle their protective armor, we would risk becoming in the children's eyes suspect allies of the dark powers that threaten them all the time. It suffices if we do not allow the problem of maintaining order and discipline to make us too afraid of turmoil and primitive, affect-laden behavior. We must remember that tolerating just such difficult situations may be necessary to progress.

Concluding Remarks

If therapy consisted mainly of successful, highly revealing sessions, treatment would be infinitely quicker and cheaper. In art therapy as in every form of therapeutic endeavor, much that occurs is inconclusive, much is banal, many sessions are at best moderately successful, some are disastrous. Once in a great while something happens that has the character of a minor miracle, and such sessions are again followed by setbacks, by emptiness, by failures which seem to invalidate the miracle.

When one attempts to demonstrate the workings of a method, however, one necessarily chooses illustrative material that shows some measure of success and contains some drama. Thus I have selected my two examples. The reader should remember that run-of-the-mill sessions are much less interesting. Even in those here chosen the events were memorable only in regard to a few of the children.

As I have stated in the beginning, I am presenting these accounts not as models to be imitated but as samples demonstrating the infinite variety of our work and the surprises that it holds even for the experienced practitioner. This—the element of surprise—I believe to be the hallmark of the exceptional both in art and in art therapy. No matter how carefully it has been planned and prepared for, every good work of art and every memorable art therapy session brings something unexpected.

The theoretical analysis of the events described naturally was undertaken after the sessions were over. Indeed, certain aspects of each event became apparent to me only in the writing of this paper. In the turmoil of the session there is no time for reflection. One must act, hoping that training, experience, intuition, and luck will converge to make one's acts beneficial rather than detrimental to the children in one's charge. In this spirit I try to live through each session.

Montessori and the Compulsive Cleanliness of Severely Retarded Children

LENA L. GITTER

A resurgence of the Montessori Method is sweeping the United States. This educational system was originally based on findings of Séguin and Itard, two French physicians who pioneered in the study of the retarded child. Dr. Maria Montessori, physician-educator teaching in Rome at the turn of the century, modified and implemented their findings. She used concrete materials in a class of severely retarded children to teach abstractions—"materialized abstractions"—with dramatic success.

I used and adapted the Montessori Method in a classroom of 10 children, ages 6 through 16, I.Q. 34 to 52, at the Hillcrest Heights Special Center, a public school in Prince Georges County, Maryland. These children were classified as "trainable."

Though several of the children's fathers were day laborers, more were college graduates and a few were high-ranking military officers; in most families there were siblings of average or high intelligence. My class included mongoloids and seriously brain-damaged children, some of whom had no previous schooling. Nevertheless, the application of Montessori techniques led to noteworthy gains in most instances.

Problems Associated with Toilet Training

A minimum requirement for admission to this special class is mastery of personal hygiene—toilet training. The onus for meeting this requirement is on the parents. Anxiety-ridden parents of a child with severe retardation are apt to pursue this task relentlessly. Toilet training and self-feeding are essential prerequisites for outside help.

In infancy most of these children lie quietly and do not respond to the mother's cuddling and cooing, and so they are inevitably left to their own devices. Safely tucked in a crib, they are cut off from all stimuli. As time goes by, even the attempt at mother-child play ceases because the child does not respond. The child remains inert, staring into space. The mother is grateful that the child makes only the basic physical demands on her.

At the standing and walking stage, toilet training and self-feeding become crucial problems; with all the unescapable stresses and tensions, the "war" begins. Punishments and rewards are introduced even though it is very difficult for the child to meet even the most limited demands. Most severely retarded children do achieve, through trial and error, sweat and tears, toilet training and self-feeding by the age of five or six. Some, however, cannot control sphincters and feed themselves until much later.

The child hates anything that reminds him of the battleground of toilet training. In addition, many parents, concerned about the limitations of their severely retarded child, overemphasize the child's physical appearance. The clean dress, the clean suit are symbols of the perfection the child himself cannot achieve because of his retardation. Cleanliness becomes almost a fetish.

I observed that an exaggerated fear of dirt was common to severely retarded children from widely varying backgrounds; it is hard for despairing parents of any social class to resist using severe measures in trying to inculcate the rudiments of personal hygiene. As people gradually learn from psychiatrists, other staff members of mental health clinics, and visiting public health nurses about the importance of their attitude toward toilet training, some parents of mentally defective children try to be more lenient in handling this problem, but the teacher must still expect such parental restraint to be the exception rather than the rule. In her contacts with the parents she tries, of course, to enlist their sympathy and support.

Entering school will often cause tensions resulting in loss of hard-won gains, which in turn leads to even greater stress. Each child is required to bring a change of clothing to school, to be used as needed. It is a sad picture, the child carrying in one hand his lunch box and in the other a tragic symbol of possible failure concealed in a shoe box or gift box. The understanding teacher discreetly deposits the package in the inner recesses of a closet, until the moment arrives when it is put to necessary use. Even though the teacher maintains a matter-of-fact attitude, the child must return home by school bus with the telltale bag of soiled clothes, a public failure. Often the matron or bus driver has to take charge of this bag of shame, as some of these children are physically unable to carry a parcel. The teacher's best efforts to wrap the bundles inconspicuously are often defeated by the cruel teasing of schoolmates.

The stress is compounded; the child has failed the mother who has worked so hard over the toilet training. New anxieties are created at home where the question, "Will the child be able to stay in school if these accidents recur?" sends the parents into a fever of activity. They try to reduce normal kidney functions by curtailing liquids. All this tends to build even greater tensions in the child.

The teacher has the almost overwhelming responsibility of alleviating the child's fears. Foremost is the fear of dirtying body or extension of self; these children are afraid to handle materials that might leave a residue of soil, and they are afraid to take part in activities that could lead to getting dirty. Smocks and aprons mean little in the face of this all-pervading mania for *cleanliness, clean* clothes, *clean* hands.

This is a major obstacle in trying to reach these children. They resist anything that just might dirty the hands, even picking up a crayon. How difficult, how impossible it is to try to teach without art materials!

The Montessori Solution

It is a Montessori principle to teach preliminary activities that will prepare children to learn what you want them ultimately to learn, avoiding direct steps that would lead to frustration. Therefore, before working with liquid materials, we introduce materials that will not threaten the children with getting themselves dirty. In this way, we side-step their strong fear that any spilling will result in soil.

The children in my classroom learned to pour from a large pitcher into a smaller one, first lima beans, and later rice. The children rake up with all their fingers any beans that spill over. To pick up the stray rice they use only three fingers, making much the same motion that is used in picking up and holding a paintbrush or crayon or pencil. Many of the children in this classroom are sorely underdeveloped in the use of their hands; even the simplest achievement demands persistent effort.

When the children have learned to pour and handle rice, we substitute finer seeds, such as bird seeds. They continue to pick up the spilled seeds with their fingers—the fingers that will some day hold the implements for self-expression.

Next we introduce the use of geometric inserts (Figure 1). The children

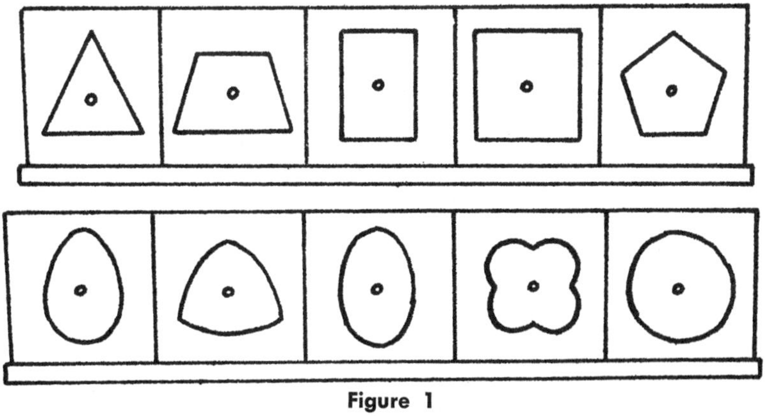

Figure 1

The Montessori metal inserts. The frame is one color, the insert another. The sides of a frame measure 5½ inches, and the insert can be lifted out by a small knob at its center.

Figure 2
"Ice Cream Sundae," by a 14-year-old retarded girl.

learn to combine these shapes; we help them to arrange, superimpose, and trace around the cutouts to form images. They build up new shapes, e.g., the triangle above the square to form a house. Seeing the images materialize tends to stimulate a first interest in drawing and coloring (see Figure 2, which was developed from the inserts).

The Montessori tablets, little painted chips of wood unrelated to objects, provide a useful opportunity to observe children's emotional reactions to colors. Severely retarded girls who have reached puberty are usually repelled by the color red or certain browns, because they just cannot cope with menstruation. In other children, other colors provoke a strong negative reaction. In selecting colors to use in class, the teacher must take these feelings into account.

After all preliminary tactics have been employed successfully, we find there is still not much incentive in these severely retarded children for self-expression. The limits set by their intellectual deficiency have been narrowed even further by lack of early stimulation in home, neighborhood, and school. We must not set our sights unrealistically high, but once some of the children's most severe conflicts have been resolved, they can be led a little way along the slow, difficult road to selfhood.

An Illustrative Example

The story of John and Mary is a case in point. John at the age of 12 was a prime example of the cleanliness cult. His bedridden mother died when he was two. Subsequently he was raised by his maternal grandmother, until at the age of six he came to live with his father, a man of limited means. He dressed

John in the most expensive clothes, surely as compensation for the child's physical and mental limitations.

At school, John at first sat stiffly in his seat after making sure that his chair was spotlessly clean. He would not run and play with the other children for fear of getting dirty. Handed a clothes brush as insurance that he could clean up if he did play, John almost brushed holes in his clothes trying to remove a minute spot accidentally made by a ball tossed by another child. John wouldn't pick up a "dirty" ball. He wouldn't attempt anything at all, for fear of dirtying his clothes or hands. He just sat.

A conference with the father resulted in John's bringing to class special clothes to change into for work and play. This brought him a measure of relief during the time he wore the work clothes. He began to take part in activities that called for freedom of movement to the limited extent that he could master them.

In John's first attempts at painting, he used small pieces of board left over from the building of bookcases in the classrooms. With very thick paint on a ¾″ long-handled paintbrush, John used blue and green paint, blue for the sky and green for grass. He moved the brush over the outlines of the grain in the wood. Following this pattern resulted in an effect that pleased him. He made trays out of his painted boards and was delighted with the results of his labors and with the admiration they aroused in others. Despite this success, John would not do any freehand painting, but would only paint when he could follow a pattern.

Free painting came much later for John. The catalyst was Mary, a mongoloid 16-year-old, whom John liked very much. Mary was dwarfed, about the size of an eight-year-old, and as is often the case with severely retarded children, she was grossly overweight. She had no schooling before coming to this special class.

With no incentive to get up in the morning, Mary had been permitted to sleep as late as she chose; getting to school at a certain time was a real problem. When she arrived in the classroom, she was very disturbed and angry. She stooped down near her desk and would not move from this cramped position. Only lunch time could move her. The teacher had to build from this alone.

Two weeks after school started, a milk program was instituted. Promptly at milk-and-cookies time, Mary would get up and hang up her coat. She then drank her milk, and devoured all available cookies, those served and those in her lunch box. Once unwound from her stooping position, she slowly mastered the pouring and handling of the beans and rice. From there, she took to tracing the Montessori geometric forms.

Birthdays are celebrated in our classroom, with cakes supplied by the families. For Mary's special day a huge, fancy, birthday cake appeared. There was a great celebration, and Mary was very much the center of all the excitement; it was her day. When the cake was all eaten, she got very upset because there was nothing left.

Figure 3
"My Happy Birthday Cake"

A new easel had been set up in the room just a few days before. I suggested that Mary paint a picture of the cake, so that we could look at it even though it had all been eaten. Mary seized the brush and painted away furiously. All that resulted was a glob of streaks without shape or form. Her anger finally abated and she left the paper on the easel with the record of her rage—a wild scramble of emotion.

The next morning, she approached her amorphous underpainting. Quietly she took the brush, and over this background painted an easily recognizable birthday cake, replete with lit candles (Figure 3). The other children were enthusiastic about this work of art and love. John especially reacted with warm admiration for the artistic endeavor of a favorite classmate. He decided he, too, wanted to paint a cake, and so he was at last able to paint without following set forms.

John's art continued to be linked with his basic need for love. While he shied away from any physical contact with the male physical education teacher, he was very fond of the aide who spent the lunch hour with my class, a large woman whose apron pockets often contained a cookie or an apple for John. They played a game where he would have to reach into her pocket to get his special treat. He made a tablecloth from a large piece of canvas and decorated it with big applies and cookies, again using food as his artistic theme and again inspired by association with a beloved female figure. In good weather he spread the cloth out under the trees where the class went for lunch. John quickly wiped up anything that spilled on it, and carefully folded it a certain way and stored it in a special place.

His interest in food and his enthusiasm for cleaning up combined to make John a good helper in the cafeteria; he learned to scrape, rinse, and stack the dishes for the dishwasher. He also helped with classroom emergencies when children wet themselves or vomited. John not only ran for the mop but tried to reassure his embarrassed classmates: "It's all right, it's all cleaned up." His need for neatness and cleanliness had been redirected into satisfying activities which not only gave him a place in the school community but helped prepare him for the future. The staff felt that these activities could eventually be developed into a marketable skill.

Ways of Encouraging Art Activity

There were still 6 of the 10 children who, for fear of dirtying themselves, made only the feeblest attempts to paint. Even the slightest drop of color on their clothes brought on a tantrum. It was a catastrophe; their entire day was ruined.

I tried placing a large sheet of paper on the floor, with different sizes of hoops on it. In these I tossed heaps of large and small pick-up sticks. The children who could not paint first fingered the sticks, and, comfortable with their hardness, arranged them in patterns within the hoop. They drew around the patterns, and when we removed the hoops and sticks, and they saw the designs they had made, they were surprised and happy.

At the next session, some of them discovered that by putting sticks together they could form already familiar Montessori geometric forms, such as the pentagon, the square, and the triangle. These were larger than the geometric forms they had traced. This was another new discovery: seeing the relation between larger and smaller forms. The children began to outline all of the hoops, and to bring the Montessori circle form over to their drawings to compare the size and shape. They made designs of circles with the geometric form and the hoops. These children still couldn't use paint, but they had a medium that allowed some measure of expression through design without danger of getting dirty.

Mary loved music and had taken charge of the record player. She painted blotches of different color, and named her art work "music." Then the music teacher invited the children to move to music and draw freely with crayon on a large sheet of paper as they passed a table. They enjoyed this so much that I tried to copy it in the classroom, this time with paint in place of the crayon. I fixed paper on two tables and placed the paint between the tables. The children used long-handled ¾″ brushes. Most of them enjoyed this but a few were horrified when the paints ran into each other and the paper began to take on a gray-brownish look. Some of them dropped out and rushed to wash their hands.

After this "art work" dried, the 72″ x 36″ paper was pinned up on the bulletin board. It really didn't look too forbidding, though it was indeed messy.

We were cutting out pictures of food from magazines, as an exercise in cutting and labeling. Mary, who had developed into the leader of the art movement, suggested that we paste these pictures on the bulletin board painting. This created an attractive collage. For the psychological needs of the children, it hit the spct. Guessing games followed. We guessed the names of the foods in the display, we guessed the contents of the lunch box, we guessed what foods would be served for lunch at the cafeteria. This inspired some of the children to paint pictures of fruits and other foods.

By this time, we were using six, not just three colors. The teacher has to remember that the paint must be kept thick and creamy. The children were very distressed when they diluted the thick paints with water and the colors ran to spoil their efforts.

Dexterity with brush and crayon carried over to the use of sewing materials. A large needle, burlap, and thick yarn were introduced for simple stitching. The children made place mats and pillow covers, and added felt cutouts which they glued on to the fabric. These made attractive gifts to take home, winning much admiration from their parents. This helped greatly to build up the self-esteem which depends on the approval of others.

At this point, I introduced clay—gray clay. Most children were able to handle this medium and enjoyed manipulating it. Again, edible objects, especially fruits, were the most favored subjects for clay modeling.

The Hazards of Finger Paint

In schools of special education, there is a widespread belief that finger painting is somehow therapeutic, and a considerable portion of the money allotted for art supplies is often spent for finger paints and the special paper which is required. Those teachers who shy away from it feel guilty every time they go to the supply room, and the principal will often say, "You haven't done anything with finger painting this year." Under these circumstances, one day I worked up enough courage to cope with the mess, and made all the involved preparations.

The pans of water were made ready, the children were covered with aprons, sleeves were rolled up, and the classroom was rearranged for the big event. In the Montessori tradition, I presented the lesson by demonstration, dipping the paper into the pan and following the proper technique for finger painting.

As the children watched, many of them held their hands behind them, and I could see by their expressions and gestures that the whole business was repulsive to them. A few did try reluctantly, and eventually took pleasure in the process; even these children rejected red, and black was the most popular color. One of the little girls, who comes from a povery-stricken home and whose father is an alcoholic, made certain gestures while she painted, which to another child, a little boy at the same economic level, had sexual connotations. Most of the children giggled.

Though they may not talk about it, these children are often preoccupied with sex. Their intellectual development is very retarded but their physical development is not. Because they were often left alone as infants, they tend more than other children to seek emotional satisfaction from their own bodies. Some of them resort to thumb-sucking in time of stress and others masturbate openly in class. Finger painting brought out these tension-reducing symptoms.

This experience convinced me that finger paint is unsuitable for classroom use with trainable children. I tried it one more time, using finger paint in combination with music, but even then the children obviously were not happy. Finger painting aroused too much primitive feeling, and they again became very preoccupied with sex. After this second attempt, I stood firm in my conviction that poster paint and clay are sufficient for the expressive needs of these children without entailing the risks inherent in the introduction of finger paint.

Summary

Slowly, most of the children overcame their deep-seated fear of getting dirty, and by the end of the year they painted happily. Even when paint jars occasionally tipped over, they were able to repair the damage quickly and quietly without the devastation such happenings had originally caused. Cleaning up after painting became a very natural pursuit; a reproduction of Rembrandt's "Little Girl with Broom" hung in a corner of our room, and the children began to relate this great painting to their own lives.

Reports from home indicated a carry-over; when the children spilled something, instead of throwing a tantrum, they ran for the mop and put it to good use. They had become free to experience the joy of new accomplishments; in their free time away from school they could write, even if only their own name, and they could make pictures. Their parents shared their justified pride in their art work.

Success in art can lead directly to success in learning to write, and by illustrating the simple rhymes they love, these severely retarded "trainable" children are helped to increase their vocabularies. But they get much more than these practical benefits from their painting. In spite of all the limitations set by their intellectual deficiency, they can use their art not only for self-expression, but, in a true sense, for self-preservation.

Discussion

The relatively rigid structure of the Montessori Method builds confidence. It enables the child to control his environment. Once he has achieved this control, he can engage in freer forms of personal expression. Fluid materials such as paint and clay are no longer a threat when approached by carefully designed stages. After mastering his anxieties, the retarded child can learn to the full extent of his limited ability.

Montessori teachers are trained to pay careful attention to environmental factors that impinge on the child, for they have an important bearing on the learning process. The problem of compulsive cleanliness originating in difficulty with toilet training can be mitigated by a few practical measures based on such objective study and experience.

Classroom accidents occur less frequently if the teacher has been careful to introduce each pupil to toilet facilities on the first day of school, preferably in company with the child's parents. When toilet rooms do not open directly off the classroom, it is always best to send an older or more capable child along if the teacher cannot manage to go with the severely retarded child. As with very small children, it is important to provide easily accessible light switches, to eliminate locks that might accidentally shut a child in, and to see that toilet paper and towels are within easy reach. Parents should be advised to avoid clothes that are hard to remove quickly; pants with elasticized waists are easier to manage than are those that have buttons or zippers.

The careful, step-by-step procedures of the Montessori Method, and the special Montessori materials such as the geometric inserts might be paralleled by other techniques and materials similar in purpose and effect. I believe that the uniqueness of the Montessori contribution depends rather on the special role assigned to the Montessori teacher.

Teaching abstractions by means of concrete materials demands much demonstration on the teacher's part, with relatively little need for spoken explanations. Experience has shown that both retarded children and very young children of normal intelligence understand much more easily when they have seen how something is done than when a procedure has merely been talked about. Since the children understand what they are expected to do, the atmosphere of the Montessori classroom is a relaxed one, where intense interplay of emotion between teacher and child is unlikely to develop.

In essence, the Montessori teacher's approach is more objective than that of most other teachers; she aims to become neither a mother surrogate nor the authority upon whose dictum success or failure depends. She regards herhelf primarily as a mediator between the child and his environment.

Art and the Slow Learner*

MYER SITE

As an art teacher of poor children in a downtown junior high school in Baltimore, Maryland, I believe that a big wrong has been done to them. In most of the current discussion on the learning difficulties of the disadvantaged inner-city child, it is assumed that massive changes must be made in the family environment before these children can grow or be creative. This neatly shifts the blame from the school system to the children and their families. Of course, nobody doubts that we need more resources both for the family and the school. I am, however, convinced that the will, the desire, and the humanity of the teacher are the crucial elements in stimulating and encouraging the potential creative imagination of the children.

The Neighborhood, the School, and the Pupils

The school I teach in is located in downtown Baltimore in a depressed area which once was a middle class residential section of fine, large town houses. A few of these are still occupied by single families, but most have been converted into apartments and places of business. There is a great deal of urban renewal going on, and many families are constantly on the move. All around the school lie blighted neighborhoods or "gray" areas.

A document published in 1962 describes the inner-city neighborhood where most of our pupils live as "the place where the crime rates are highest, where people are poorest; the area where 75 percent or 80 percent of the children don't finish high school, where many babies die before reaching their first birthday, where wretched housing is the rule and the police are your enemy more often than not. It is the Baltimore of the high T.B. and venereal

---

* This article is based on material presented at the Syracuse University Summer Session Symposium on "Creativity for the Exceptional Individual," Syracuse, N. Y., July 1964.

disease rate, of the welfare and unemployment check, the asphalt jungle, thc unwed mother, and the unwanted child . . . the Baltimore of the hard core, multi-problem, culturally deprived persons and families. Some of their characteristics are:

"1. Many do not understand modern urban living.

2. Many are participants in sub-cultures, the values and customs of which are different from those of the urban middle class.

3. Many, particularly children and youth, suffer from the disorganizing effects of transiency and minority group status.

4. Many have educational and cultural handicaps.

5. Many families have such problems as divorce, desertion, unemployment, physical and mental illness, and delinquency.

6. Most young people lack motivation or opportunities to become responsible citizens." [1]

The school building is 64 years old and well maintained. It has a certain homelike charm, but the two art rooms are not properly equipped because they were not designed to be art rooms. For water supply and washing up, my room has only a small kitchen sink in an out-of-the-way alcove. Storage space and bulletin board space are inadequate. We work with large classes on a small budget.

There is no parental participation in a P.T.A. When the school's May Festival was held, hardly anybody showed up from the families of the 400 pupils. Every subject in the curriculum was on display. The few parents who attended showed very little interest in the 60 pictures I exhibited. The art supervisor approved of the pictures but wondered why no 3-dimensional work was shown. Those who know such schools intimately are well aware that art activities are limited not only by the physical setting and insufficient funds for materials, but by the problem children who make it necessary for us to keep under lock and key those supplies we are able to get.

The disordered environment, of course, shapes the children. I get all types in my art classes, and I must teach them as they come. The office does try to make our classes as homogeneous as possible on the basis of academic performance and potential ability, as measured by I.Q. and reading and arithmetic levels. The pupils are divided into regular, low regular, basic, and special groups. The basics are children whose I.Q.'s are between 80 and 90 and whose achievement is more than two years below grade in reading and arithmetic. In the special classes are those whose I.Q.'s fall between 55 and 79, and who have severe school retardation.

Actually so many of the children suffer from combinations of intellectual, emotional, and social handicaps that sometimes I find it very difficult to distinguish between my regular and slow-learning classes. Their general patterns of behavior are pretty much the same.

---

[1] *A Letter to Ourselves: A Master Plan for Human Redevelopment;* Health and Welfare Council of the Baltimore Area, Inc.

Each illustration is labeled with the grade, age, I.Q., and the reading and arithmetic level of the child who made the picture. The pictures, I believe, prove that academic retardation and even limited intelligence do not always mean that the children can't draw, have no images to call on, or that they don't feel. Sometimes, too, a high I.Q. can go with retardation in art.

Approaches to Picture-Making

When I greet my classes at the beginning of the school year, I say, "When you enter my room, you are a person, not just a 7th, 8th or 9th grade pupil. You know a great deal. You've learned in school and out of school. Each one of you has the power to visualize, to see images in your mind, for an image can be a mental picture as well as a reflection or likeness. We all call up images when we hear or read a story, hear music, when we daydream, when we wonder what is going on somewhere, and when we think about the movie we saw last night. We can also use images which seem to come to our mind without intention on our part, images which have been stored in the unconscious part of our mind and which a cue from the conscious mind has brought out of storage all of a sudden."

At first, some of the pupils say defensively, "I can't draw." They usually mean that they can't draw people. I tell them that the word to draw means "to drag" and that since they are not crippled they can draw, they can drag chalk or pencil or brush on the paper and draw lines and shapes and images, to give some idea of their mental pictures. I encourage the children to draw and paint spontaneously, of their own free will and in their own personal style, the things they see and know, wish for, love, daydream about, dream about and have nightmares about, and the things they do not love or like, too.

Whenever possible I invite my pupils to talk about their pictures, *if they want to.* Often I say something like this: "Maybe you'd like to tell me a story in pictures and words—like the comic strips. I know you are at the age where you have secrets with each other, secrets which you don't tell your father and mother. There was a time when you were little children when you couldn't wait to get home after school to tell your mother what had happened to you during the day. But now you don't do that any more. You have friends to whom you tell your stories—maybe you do, and maybe you don't. I am inviting you to tell me some stories, good, bad, anything you like."

If children don't want to talk about what is happening in their pictures, they should not be pushed; their desire for privacy should be respected. The captions on the illustrations, which are the children's own words, show that some told me a good deal about what their pictures meant, what they thought and how they felt about them, while others had little they wanted to say. It seems to me that by asking them to tell me (is there a story?) I give them the idea that I care. It should hardly be necessary to point out that I am not probing with any notion of playing the amateur psychiatrist, and I make no interpretations of their pictures to the children.

Figure 1

"I dreamt that I went to the graveyard and I saw some ghosts coming after me with knives and they caught me and tried to kill me, and then I woke up."

Constance, 7th grade.
Age 12, I.Q. 93.
Reading level 5.6;
Arithmetic level 5.9.

Constance's nightmare picture (Figure 1) is on a theme that recurs often, I find, in the dreams of girls from the slums. Carl's daydream (Figure 2) is of a happy memory from the past, and Alice's (Figure 3) combines well-visualized recollections into an image of future hopes.

Of course, the approaches I have just described don't work with all the pupils all the time. Some of them move slowly toward spontaneity, and especially among the retarded, the withdrawn, and the emotionally disturbed there are children who need special help and attention before they can loosen up. Sometimes it helps the ones who come in empty of ideas and in a bad humor if I invite them to do a "mood picture." I suggest that they choose the colored chalks best suited to express a happy, sad, lonely, angry, or any other kind of mood. This relieves them of the necessity of thinking about images,

Figure 2

"I was daydreaming about some birds out in the woods near Charleston, S. C. where I used to live before I came to Baltimore."

Carl, 7th grade,
Age 13, I.Q. 84.
Reading level 5.6;
Arithmetic level 5.8.

unless they want to, and often they are stimulated to an original, symbolic use of both color and form (Figure 4). Many of their mood pictures look like modern, abstract art, even though most of them know very little about it.

Often, instead of asking the children what they think about or care about, I ask them to recall scenes of action they have observed. I have come to believe that the more a child is slum-shocked, the less introspective he is apt to be. Many of them are essentially nonverbal (even though they can be noisy), and they are full of action and energy, so I can best reach them by asking what they and others *do*. Rodney's picture (Figure 5) is an example.

Figure 3

"I was daydreaming about when I would get married and have a little girl."

Alice, 9th grade.
Age 16, I.Q. 86.
Reading level 7.5;
Arithmetic level 6.9.

Figure 4

"A Sad Mood."

Harry, 7th grade. Age 13, I.Q. 76. Reading level 5.4; Arithmetic level 5.3.

While most of the time the pupils want to draw from images in their minds (Figures 6, 7, 8), occasionally we have a pupil pose in front of the class. In drawing Figure 9, Tyrone observed the model keenly and added his own imaginative interpretation.

A common problem for the junior high school teacher is that the children are at an age when they are shifting from spontaneous expression to concern about their final product in drawing. They begin to judge their productions by adult standards, placing value on accurate representation rather than on subjectively satisfying expression. Unable to meet the demands they put on themselves, they often give up drawing altogether. I try to help the pupils

Figure 5

"One night I saw a man rob an afflicted man."

Rodney, 8th grade. Age 14, I.Q. 91. Reading level 5.9; Arithmetic level 6.8.

I. " 'It's the first thing I've ever done in my life that's not *neat*.' " (see p. 23)

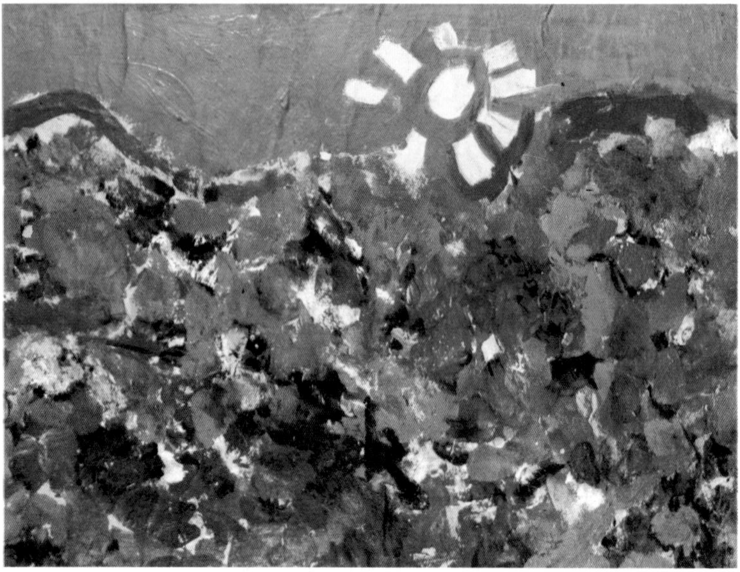

II. ". . . chaotic, aggressive energy . . . channeled into constructive action." (see p. 47)

III. ". . . not the actual storm but a much more destructive and violent fantasy. . . ." (see p. 49)

IV. "To the adults . . . Caroline's artwork [revealed] the conflicts she was experiencing; for her, it served as catharsis." (see p. 64)

V. ". . . the painting began with the cherries in mid-air. Branches [and the trunk] were then added. . . . This . . . seemed to symbolize [Ken's] struggle to pull himself together. . . ." (see p. 87)

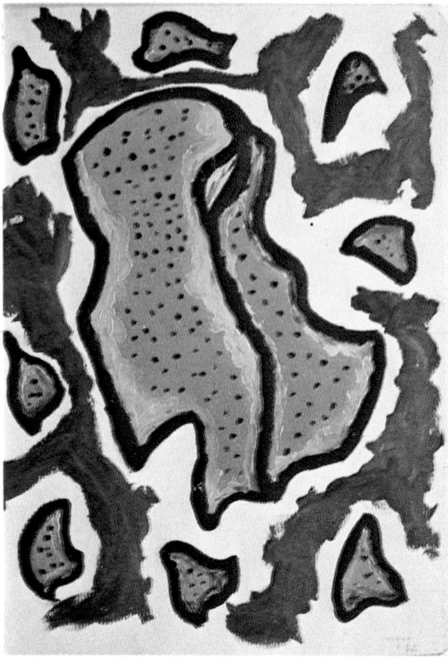

VI. "The large central form is a 'powerful mother,' with 'eight children. . . .' The two not yet [cut off from her are the patient] and her younger brother. . . ." (see p. 120)

VII. "[The parents' discussion of this painting provided us with a] personal experience of the climate of the schizophrenic family. . . ." (see p. 124)

VIII. ". . . if the teacher touches real feeling he can stimulate memory and imagination. . . ." (see p. 197)

IX. "'. . . my mother and father fight . . . and . . . these horror pictures . . . make me feel good inside because if I draw happy pictures, they make me feel real, real sad inside. . . .' " (see p. 202)

X. ". . . the child is both creator and craftsman, for he selects his own motifs and selects material for their execution." (see p. 209)

XI. ". . .drawing corresponds to [the mentally defective child's] way of thinking, which rarely develops beyond the pictorial stage." (see p. 209)

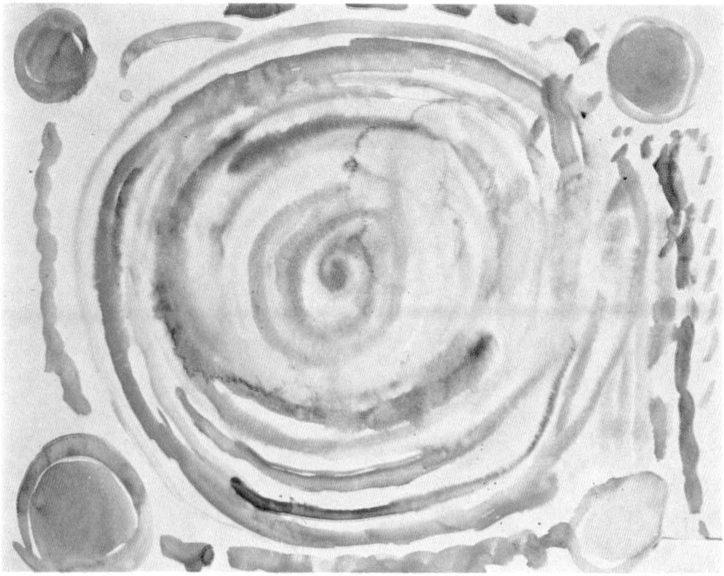

XII. "The spiral, . . . symbol of movement, growth, or expansion takes on a . . . dynamic, self-confident form." (see p. 305)

XIII. ". . . in this coherent portrait [of a fellow patient] he had come a long way from . . . utter fragmentation." (see p. 307)

XIV. "The brush strokes . . . are frenzied. . . . The patient was . . . in [an] anxious state . . . because disturbing thoughts were emerging." (see p. 332)

XV. ". . . she can relax when she momentarily relinquishes the need to keep up the correct, lady-like, grown-up front." (see p. 370)

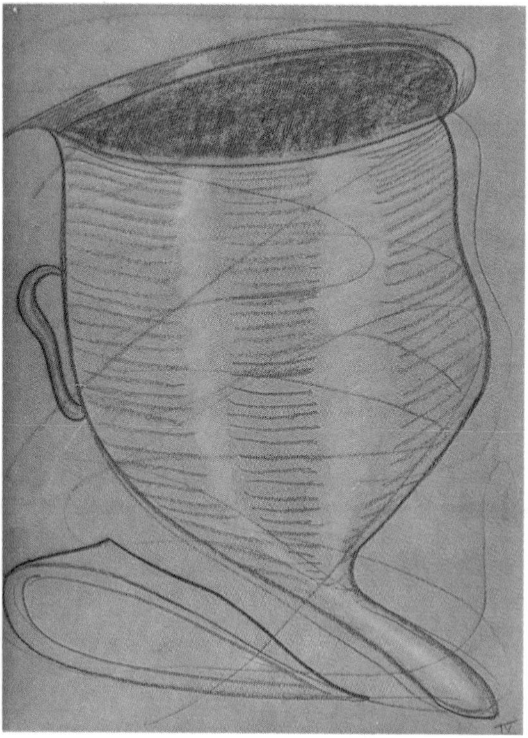

XVI. " 'It's some kind of a giant cup . . . a loving cup.' " (see p. 377)

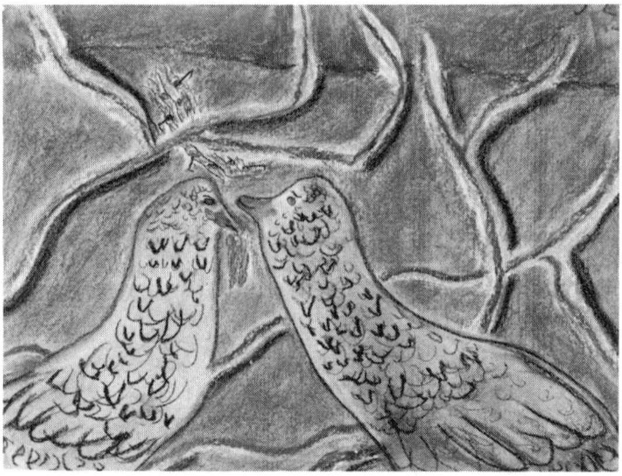

Figure 6

"I was thinking about two happy birds in love."

Charles, 9th grade. Age 15, I.Q. 97. Reading level 7.1; Arithmetic level 6.1.

bridge this gap by making sure that the subject matter of their pictures or the feeling behind their designs means something not just to the thinking self but to the whole person. For if the teacher touches real feeling he can stimulate memory and imagination, the two great tools of the artist, and enable the pupil to generate energy without measure.

Figure 7

"I was thinking about a bum who was daydreaming about a real pretty girl. The man in red is a genie. He is going to give the bum a better start in life."

Geneva, 8th grade. Age 15, I.Q. 82. Reading level 6.7; Arithmetic level 7.5.

Figure 8

"The Spy."

See also color plate VIII.

Willie, 7th grade.
Age 13, I.Q. 87.
Reading level 4.5;
Arithmetic level 3.8.

Figure 9

"James posed in front of the class. This is the way he looked to me. I made out that James just got done fighting, and I put the boys fighting in the background in the alley."

Tyrone, 8th grade.
Age 14, I.Q. 70.
Reading level 4.0;
Arithmetic level 5.0.

Teachers often ask me whether I go in for correlation of art work with what the children are learning in other school subjects. I answer that any time a child feels so strongly about what he is studying in history, geography, science, or English that he chooses to make a picture about it, I am delighted to have him do so. I could count on my fingers, however, the number of times this has happened in my 38 years of teaching.

Obviously I am concerned with opening up the inner emotional life of the children in some form that satisfies *them,* not with obtaining carefully finished products to meet adult approval. Yet when I have exhibited my pupils' work, sensitive artists and art educators have been struck with its artistic quality.

I do not talk much to the children about art principles, beyond calling their attention to the filling of space and to good contrast of light and dark. Color I consider a personal expression, so I do not give advice about it. And I sometimes have a class look at pictures by every individual in the group, and by pupils from other classes, pointing out the different ways that people of their age draw. I do this to help them feel their way to their own personal style of expression, but perhaps this is incidentally a lesson in drawing technique.

Children's Responses

Recently I asked some members of a regular 8th grade class to write down for me how they feel about our way of making pictures. Evelyn wrote: "I enjoy very much drawing and expressing my own ideas on paper. I prefer doing it this way than for you to tell us what we have to do. This is the only period that we have that a teacher doesn't command us to do something whether you are in the mood or not. Lots of times when I come to art I like to just sit and study the other person's picture. Or sometimes when I am mad, to go around the room and straighten things up. This seems to calm me down."

Barbara said: "I like the way you tell us to draw what we want because we may have things on our minds that we can't talk about to other people. And if we can put them down on paper then we can think them out. I know this is a fact, because sometimes when I come to art I have things on my mind that I can't talk about to my friends or to anyone so I put it on paper. And sometimes it helps a lot just to get it off my mind for a while."

Damon wrote: "I think it's nice the way you let us draw what's on our mind because we might have something on our mind and by drawing we can put it on paper. Some of the things we draw doesn't mean we have them on our mind it could be a cover up so they won't have to think about whats on their minds."

I have noticed that many children draw the same ideas or themes again and again over a period of weeks and months. Some of them seem to be consolidating a sense of their own identity by repeating designs or representations in their own special way. Leonard explained his many drawings of ships by

Figure 10

"I made up this picture of a girl. I like to draw pictures of girls."

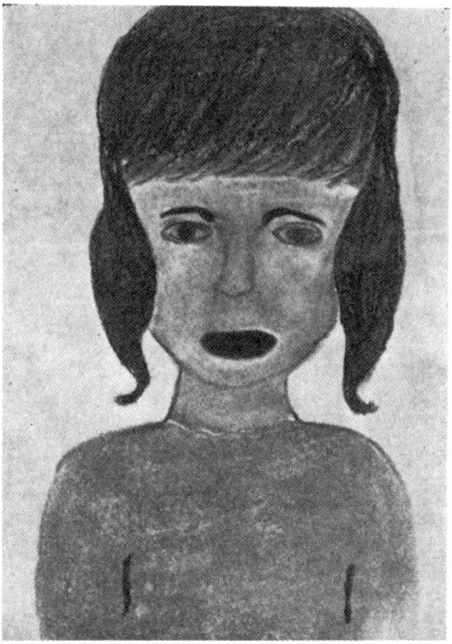

Shirley, 9th grade. Age 15, I.Q. 82. Reading level 4.6; Arithmetic level 5.1.

saying, "Ships are a hobby for me, also, when I am 17 I'm going to join the Naval reserve submarine division. There is something about ships that make me like them. . . Maybe it is the way they look or the way they move." Jimmy wrote, "I have a great interest in war, you was right I am going to serve in the armed forces," and Donovan stated that "Flowers are the most beautiful things in the world." Jane told me, "I like to draw girls because I am a girl and I'm also interested in myself," and Shirley (Figure 10) apparently had the same idea.

Gloria wrote, "My thoughts are sometimes sad and sometimes gay. . . I try to color things gay that are gay and things that are sad, sad color." Rodney (recall his down-to-earth picture, Figure 5) answered more systematically. "I like art class because

a. He teaches us in the right manner.
b. Our teacher asks us about the pictures we draw.
c. He explains how to make certain things.
d. He also lets us use his materials.
e. He lets us draw what we want.
f. He tells us sometimes what to draw.
g. He tells us what colors to put in sometimes."

Rodney is quite right. I invite the children to draw from their own ideas in their own way, but I do not follow a hands-off or laissez-faire policy.

There are occasions when I sit down alongside a child and talk with him, but there is seldom enough time for this, and that is another of our big problems. But none of the children continues to lean on me; they gain their own sense of freedom. I believe that if an art teacher has the touch, he will know which way to go, when to direct, when to suggest, when to elicit. When I get the children to the stage where *they* feel able and willing to express their own feelings and images, their own esthetic sensitivity, *then* they work freely and with some confidence, whether they make representational statements or symbolic designs.

Victoria felt she spoke for others besides herself: "I like drawing what I want to and I know the other students do too, or how could we get some of the hurt feelings we feel inside out without expressing it some other way or telling someone about it." Jasper, an 8th grade pupil, drew so many horror pictures (for example, Figure 11) that I asked him to write down for me why he made them. This is what he said:

"I like to draw these horror pictures. They give me a happy feeling because sometimes my mother and father fight and argue about things and I just go upstairs and get some paper and pencil and draw these horror pictures and they make me feel good inside because if I draw happy pictures, they make me feel real, real sad inside; but when I draw horror pictures, they make me feel happy inside."

Figure 11

"I saw this monster in a nightmare I had. He was killing people.

See also color plate IX.

Jasper, 7th Grade.
Age 14, I.Q. 84.
Reading level 4.4;
Arithmetic level 4.5.

Figure 12

"These are two people I know who fuss at me all the time. I am the little string doll in the middle."

Jasper, 8th grade. Age 15.

Figure 12 came a year later than the nameless monster of Figure 11; it portrays Jasper's problem more directly, and with something approaching a very grim kind of humor. And by this time he was able to see himself at times not as a string doll but as a human being (Figure 13), lonely and troubled but manly.

For Jasper and Victoria and many others free art expression provides an outlet that helps them to maintain their emotional balance. I recall the prophetic words of Lawrence K. Frank, written 16 years ago:

> ". . . we cannot glibly . . . repeat the conviction that the individual personality is important. We must . . . provide what is necessary . . . to assist personalities to emerge as unique personalities capable of achieving inner order. . . For this the arts offer the major resource available today . . . [when] children are growing up in a world that is . . . full of confusion and conflict. . . If the child is able freely to translate his perplexities . . . into art productions, he can get them out of himself, where he can better manage them. . . The expression of emotions . . . like resentment and anxiety, through drawing, painting, and working with clay . . . allows the child to express what he 'cannot or will not say,' usually because expressing his real feelings is not allowed by parents or because he does not know what he feels until he has translated it into . . . symbolic expression. . . There is increasing evidence . . . that the arts may become the most important activity in schools for fostering mental health. . ." [2]

A Teacher's Convictions

Like most cities, Baltimore has a standard junior high school art program outlined in a guide that teachers are supposed to follow. Among its aims are the development in the pupils of an appreciation for art forms, a knowledge of art history, and an understanding of basic design. Esthetic education of this kind has an important place in my program, but in this paper I have concen-

[2] "The Developmental Role of the Arts in Education" in *Art Education Today;* New York, Columbia University Teachers College, 1948.

Figure 13

"This is me walking in Druid Hill Park in the summertime."

Jasper, 8th grade.
Age 15.

trated on what the children make with art materials. And here I depart from the curriculum guide, which calls for the learning of numerous skills and techniques the children are supposed to acquire by making various two- and three-dimensional art products. In my classes art activity consists almost entirely of picture-making with chalk, charcoal, and pencil.

I have already indicated some of the problems that stand in the way of more elaborate productions—the physical limitations of my classroom, the large size of my classes, the many disturbed and delinquent children. Clay, for example, is a wonderfully expressive material, but under our conditions of working, if we used it a teacher could spend the whole art period cleaning up.

Besides the objective difficulties, there is my own belief that every child should be encouraged to express something uniquely personal. This requires that in a 50-minute period, I, as a teacher, must pay attention to *individuals,* as I elicit, suggest, direct, and look at productions. Every child in each class is on a different cloud or wave-length, and I must hop from cloud to cloud and wave-length to wave-length. I would not have it any other way.

We concentrate on picture-making because I have found that in our circumstances, it is the best way to get these children to use not just their hands, but their minds and hearts. We do so much of our work with chalk because the pupils can handle it quickly and easily while they are emotionally involved with what they want to portray and express. They become deeply absorbed in carrying out their ideas and need little technical help, so I am relieved from wasting my energy and theirs on discipline problems and mechanical problems.

I feel great humility as I work with my pupils, as I try to understand them and their purposes, and the significance of creative education for them. I know that each and every group of slow learners and also regular learners that I teach is composed of individuals with varying emotional, mental, and cultural equipment. Art behavior is not always what is expected at a given developmental stage. Past experience, environment, and many other factors do not follow an age pattern. Some of these children need release from inhibitions and others need help in organizing their thinking and feeling and some need both.

The teacher has to respect not only a person's ability to create, but also his inability. I think, for example, of Gregory, who wrote to me: "I know what you are thinking about my drawing. You're thinking that I can't draw. That is the same way I feel. My mind is always empty. There is nothing never on my mind." A pupil like Gregory will sometimes be surprised when he finds that after all he has something to say if I see his emptiness as a feeling of inadequacy which can be cured by the right treatment and not as innate stupidity.

I am not the kind of teacher who pulls strings while puppets move. I look upon my classroom as a place where my pupils can experience some taste of dignity for being who they are and what they are. This is denied them in most of their lives. The way I teach is shaped by my conviction that art is a mode of expressing the uniqueness—the humanness—of the individual. It follows that no formula, no method, is possible apart from the painstaking encouragement of each child to express what he experiences either in his response to the physical world or to that less palpable world of the imagination. I treat their productions with respect, so that they have a chance to communicate graphically much that they cannot put clearly in words but that they feel vividly and honestly.

Underlying the rapport I try to develop with my pupils is one major, human attribute, the quality of empathy, that is, the act of imagining oneself in the place of another to the point of feeling that what has happened to the other person has also happened to oneself. The attitude is one of acceptance and understanding, of an implicit, "I see how you feel. This is the way you see it, this is the way you draw it, it is your way."

I have observed that empathy, one of the components of *love,* can give comfort and support to the child, or adolescent, or adult student. Empathy enables me as an art teacher to stimulate or elicit picture-making. Dr. Daniel A. Prescott, in his book *The Child in the Educative Process,*[3] has this to say about empathy and love and children's needs: "A person who loves actually enters into the feelings of, and shares intimately the experiences of the loved one, and the effects of these experiences upon the loved one. Fundamentally, to love a person is to value him, feel deep concern for his welfare, happiness, and development, and be ready to help him. . . . Fundamentally, insecurity is the inability to value oneself. . . . A child can never value and believe in himself until he has had the experience of being valued and believed in by another. Consequently, if parents . . . do not make the child feel deeply valued, simply because he is their child, the child will not be able to value himself. . . . This is one of the most enduring and persistently disturbing of maladjustments. Overcoming it requires great *patience.*"

Do I think of these things only when I work with slow learners? Not at all. I think of them as I work with all kinds of people, regardless of their I. Q., their reading and arithmetic level, or emotional state. All of them are people with feelings and ideas and images which I attempt to elicit as a springboard for free expression. But I think of these things with slow learners especially, for they need more individual attention and slower teaching procedures than the fast learners do.

Conclusion

Some readers may wonder why I lay so much emphasis on mood and first-hand personal experience, on love and empathy and respect and spontaneity. I can only say that art is the story of man's life, that it reflects his needs and helps toward their realization; that art is an organic process in-

[3] New York, McGraw Hill, 1957.

tegrating body, mind, and spirit; that art without a capacity for feeling is inconceivable. If this is not sufficiently clear an answer, I can only appeal to you to search your own hearts and ask yourselves what original longings brought you to be so concerned with creative art as a way of life.

I have presented the results of spontaneous picture-making by inner-city school children. My work is based on respect for people, and belief in their ability to feel and to experience free expression in an art form. It is done within the limited resources available to me. I believe I have presented evidence that the failure of school systems has been to an extent pushed off on the children and their families.

I leave it to the reader to decide whether the children's pictures and their words do support the idea that slum children have a rich inner life waiting to be developed in a classroom setting of love and approval.

Therapeutic Art Programs Around the World

Art and Applied Art by Mentally Defective Children

François-Michelle School in Montreal is a private day school for mentally defective children which is subsidized by Quebec's Provincial Department of Family and Social Welfare. An art program was started eight years ago when the total enrollment was 14; today, 105 children attend the school, which provides transportation for them in its own buses. The pupils are from 7 to 18 years old, with I.Q.'s ranging from 35 to 75. There are four all-day classes of 10 to 12 children and six half-day kindergarten classes of 8 to 10 children.

See also color plates X and XI.

Embroidery by Suzanne at the age of 13, IQ 76, mental age 10.

Applique by Suzanne at the age of 15, IQ 76, mental age 11.

The principal and seven full-time teachers are assisted by three part-time specialists: a psychologist who directs the psycho-pedagogical and research programs, evaluates the children, and offers psychotherapy when appropriate; a teacher of rhythmic movement; and an art teacher. Louise Cimon, who founded the art program, is equipped by training not only in art but also in the fields of psychology and education to meet the special needs of the retarded child. As a member of the psycho-pedagogical team the art teacher has the opportunity to contribute observations both on the children's behavior in the art room and on their artistic productions, providing valuable clues to each child's intellectual and emotional development. Further, in the course of the program's evolution, close collaboration between art teacher and classroom teachers has been established. During the years of her work at the school, Miss Cimon gave all teachers courses in art expression and craft techniques, so that they could take part in conducting a program that now includes such applied arts as knitting, weaving, appliqué, and embroidery.

Miss Cimon points out that the child is both creator and craftsman, for he creates his own motifs and selects materials for their execution. In embroidery, for example, he makes his own design, transfers drawing to cloth, and then decides on the colors and picks out the yarns to develop his ideas. For the first aim of the art program at François-Michelle is to encourage the child to express himself freely and fully. The mentally defective child often uses words with difficulty, but drawing is his natural language. It corresponds to his way of thinking, which rarely develops beyond the pictorial stage.

The art room is bright and gay. It contains low tables, a special wall for displaying drawings and murals, and wide shelves for storing finished work. The children come in groups of four for two half-hour periods each week. This makes possible the individual attention essential if the retarded child is to do his best. While he needs more affection and active encouragement than does the normal child, when he has been helped to feel secure he responds with gratitude and earnest effort.

The art teacher's attitude is non-directive; she seldom suggests motifs. Collective projects are sometimes undertaken, but more often each child works individually. When he has completed a piece of work, the teacher questions him about it. Miss Cimon notes that as the child talks he often will draw details he had not thought of before, or he will go on to speak of many things that have nothing to do with the drawing, as if his artistic effort had opened up the door to his fantasy world. These exchanges with the art teacher become something like free association; they not only give the staff some insight into the child's personality and problems, but seem to help expand his awareness of himself.

Although the artistic style of the mentally defective child never matures in the same way as that of the normal child, Miss Cimon has observed that the work of retarded children whose I.Q. is above 50 often reveals remarkable individuality and shows a fine sense of color and rhythm. Normal children are apt to lose this kind of imagination and freshness around the

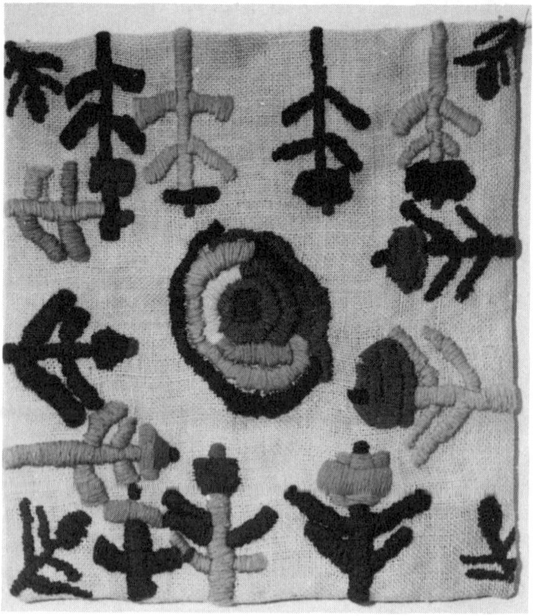

Embroidery by Pauline, 17 years old, IQ 50, mental age 8½.

Applique by Jeannine, 11 years old, IQ 50, mental age 5½.

age of eight or nine, and here the very handicap of the mentally defective child may prove to be a paradoxical advantage. If he is given the opportunity to make use of his natural gifts, his taste is less open to early corruption, because, as compared with the normal child, he is far less aware of social demands and is more exclusively centered on trying to exercise his own capacities. This relative isolation also helps account for his powerful response to the least possibility of expression and makes expressive opportunities especially important to him.

"Our experiments with crafts proved so successful that we began to receive inquiries about the purchase of finished items, especially embroideries," Miss Cimon reports. "This gave us the idea of holding a public exhibition in order to put to the test the artistic and commercial value of the children's craft products, without regard to the age or intelligence of the craftsmen.

"Our first exhibition was well attended and everything on display was sold. The event was featured in radio and television interviews; newspaper reports stressed its social value, and art critics approved of the esthetic quality of the exhibits. Four craft shops asked for the chance to buy future work, and professional craftsmen offered to hire some of our adolescents as apprentices.

"Therefore this exhibition marked the beginning of a new venture. It

Embroidery by Claire, 18 years old, IQ 65, mental age 12.

taught us that our art program may help some children, upon leaving our school to make a contribution to society, to earn social status, and, finally, to achieve at least partial economic independence."

Embroidery by Marie-Marthe, 13 years old, IQ 68, mental age 8.

THIS Is Therapy?

JOACHIM H. THEMAL

You again? Oh no!
"Oh yes!"
You didn't clean up your mess yesterday.
"That must have been someone else. And the table was filthy to begin with. Anyway, what do you have your clean-up girl for?"
She's fired.
"You fire her every day."
She keeps coming back. What can I do? Tell you what: if you stay away the whole season, I'll give you a merit award at the end of it.
"Promise?"
I promise. I gave Jack one last year.
"Nah—I think I rather stay and annoy you."

"Can I use ink?"
How old are you?
"Eleven."
You have to be twelve for ink.
"Can I use watercolor then?"
How old did you say you were?

"Twelve."
You have to be thirteen for watercolor.
"So, give me some charcoal."
You are a ten-year-old liar. Take what you want, but treat it properly.

"What shall I paint? I know: a-picture-of-my-grandmother-riding-a-bicycle. She doesn't know how."
She ought to at her age.

"Can you mix me some flesh-
color?"
There is a jar of instant flesh on
the second shelf. Can't you read?
It says "instant flesh."
"How did you make it?"
White, orange and green.
"Green?"
Green is the secret ingredient.

"How do you like my picture?"
"Your picture stinks."
You leave him alone. As a matter of fact, it is rather nice. Just throw it in the sink and wash it off a little and it will be even better.
"Yeah! And then throw it in the garbage can and it will be great!"

"How do you make a turtle?"
If you don't know how to make a turtle, don't make a turtle.
"I think I remember what they look like."
"Whyn't you take a he-turtle and a she-turtle and leave them alone for a while. *That's* the way to make a turtle!"

Stephen! I didn't give you permission to use clay. What's that blob anyway?
"It's George."
It doesn't look like anything.
"It's goin' to."
I think you have to give it a longer chin. Let me show you, like so. Take this tool and get the hair—
that's better. Put the hair over one eye. Don't even bother to make the eye. That's *good!*

You know? It's beginning to look like George.
"That looks like George!"
See? I told you. What are you doing? You are ruining it!
"He's sticking pins into it."
"Here, take the rolling pin and bang it! I hate George!"
"We all hate George."
You can't do that! This is a Jewish school! You can't make Voodoo in a Jewish school. Oh Christ! And I helped him with it, too. Suppose the Rabbi hears about this?
"He eats bacon."
"That was Pastrami."
"He looks nice with a halo."
Who?
"The Rabbi."
When did you see him with a halo?
"He always wears it."
Now that you mention it . . .

What's that supposed to be?
"You are looking at it upside down."
And what is it right side up?
"A retarded amoeba."
It does look rather retarded, doesn't it? Why don't you add some blue here, let me show you . . .
"You loused it up. Some art teacher!"
They pay me five bucks extra every time I louse up a kid's painting.
"I let you louse up some more if you give me a kick-back?"

"Can I have a compass?"
Here you are.
"Not that one. One of the good ones."
Sorry, I don't have any of those left.
"Yes, you do."
Did I ever lie to you before?
"Yes."
The fact is, you are really too young for those expensive compasses. You don't have the necessary coordination. Do you know what coordination means?

"When you have control with your hands."
I give up. Here's your compass.

Yes?
"Mr. K. wants to know can he borrow some paint?"
Ask not what the art room can do for Mr. K. . . .
"Ask-what-Mr.-K.-can-do-for-the-art-room, I know. So can I have some paints?"
We are out of paints, so sorry.
"You are always out of everything."
"Especially when it comes to chiselers."
"Mr. K. has three children and is too cheap to buy his own paint."

Marlene and Diane, will you stop fighting. No, I don't want to hear anything. Just stop fighting.
"She's too lazy to get her own water."
We provide separate but equal facilities for children who can't get on with each other. Sit over there.
"I sat here first."
So, *you* move, Diane.
"She's the one who started."
So, you both move to different places.

"Oh, God!"
"Not now. See me later."
What happened?
"I upset the water."
So, clean it up.
"I won't. It wasn't my fault. It was an accident."
So what, just clean it up.
"What if I don't?"
I won't let you come and paint any more.
"That's blackmail."
Of course, our whole educational system is based on blackmail.

"Can I have some paper?"
You've had three pieces already.
"I goofed."
"He got angry and ripped it up."
You didn't have to take it out on the paper.
"Yeah, take it out on people!"

"I am sick of this
painting. Can I leave now?"
O.K.
"I'll be back tomorrow."
"He's threatening."

And who are you?
"I'm new. Is this Arts and Crafts?"
Certainly not!
"This is f i n e arts!"
"Yeah? What's so fine about it?"
"Why'nt you shut up!"
Come right in. What's your name?
"Larry . . .
. . . is this a place where
I can paint a picture?"

Part III

CASE STUDIES

Spontaneous Art in Education and Psychotherapy*

MARGARET NAUMBURG

Introduction

Before I illustrate the way in which spontaneous art can be employed both in education and psychotherapy as a means of orientation and deeper self-knowledge, let me begin by disarming those who fear that this would reduce creative art expression to a mere tool of psychotherapy. For these unplumbed possibilities of spontaneous art expression can in no way diminish the supreme satisfaction that original creative art offers us. On the contrary, this new technique simply adds another dimension to artistic expression. Remember also that the creating of images has been a basic mode of communication for man since primeval times. And because such symbolic visual power is universal and is still alive today, we are able to encourage the release of spontaneous expression in new ways, in order to develop fresh forms of human adjustment.

It is frequently asked, why consider what is done in art therapy through the release of spontaneous imagery from the unconscious as though it were art? To meet this doubt, let me remind you that the unconscious is the constant vital reservoir from which all forms of creative expression draw their energies—whether the product becomes great or insignificant art. When pupil or patient has been encouraged to express his unconscious thoughts and feelings through imaged projections, this sometimes leads to achievements which have been recognized by a number of art critics and artists as having genuine artistic merit.

In relation to this problem of what is or is not art, the well-known Swiss art critic and architect Sigfried Giedion has discussed the similarities that he discovered between the cave paintings of Southern France and Spain and the work of such modern artists as Klee, Arp, and Braque. In the expression

---

* Presented at the Syracuse University Summer Session Symposium on "Creativity for the Exceptional Individual," Syracuse, N. Y., July 1964.

of primeval artists and artists of today, Giedion has uncovered similar techniques. He found that neither group was concerned with perspective; both emphasized symbolic expression and avoided naturalism; and both made use of transparency, showing configurations of different overlapping forms and making bodies transparent in order to portray their inner and outer nature simultaneously.[1] Such techniques are also often employed by mental patients in their spontaneous art projections in the course of art therapy.

Characteristics of Art Therapy

I am concerned here with the specific techniques of analytically oriented art therapy, a therapeutic approach which emphasizes the projection of spontaneous images as a direct communication from the unconscious. It is distinguished from psychoanalysis and other well-known forms of psychotherapy by its emphasis on the use of spontaneous art productions as a non-verbal form of communication between pupil and art teacher or patient and art therapist. While psychoanalysis reduces the symbolic images of dream, fantasy, and daydream to words, art therapy encourages their projection in drawing, painting, and sculpture. Freud wrote: "A part of the difficulty of dream telling comes from the fact that we have to transpose these [dream] pictures into words. 'I could draw it,' the dreamer says frequently, 'but I don't know how to say it.' "[2] Freud did not encourage his patients to make pictures of their dreams, but that is exactly what art therapy does do.

While art therapy acknowledges its indebtedness to Freud, it encourages a more active role than does lying on a couch. The pupil or patient must of necessity stand at an easel or sit at a table to paint or model. He is encouraged to cultivate the use of "free association" in order to discover for himself the symbolic significance of his spontaneous art productions. This technique, originally developed by Freud, means the spontaneous reporting of every thought or feeling as it arises from the unconscious, without rejection or criticism.

Since spontaneous images of dream or fantasy are experienced as pictures, it is not surprising that their immediate expression with pastels and paints is more direct than words. Not only are art therapists convinced of this, but growing numbers of psychoanalysts have also come to recognize that techniques of art therapy are useful as an adjunct to psychoanalytic procedures.

Training in Art Therapy Techniques

In the Department of Art Education at New York University for the past six years I have been giving courses that emphasize the new psychological approach to creativity. While planned originally for art educators, they also attract students from such other disciplines as psychology, occupational

---

[1] *The Beginnings of Art. Part I, The Eternal Present.* New York, Pantheon, 1963.

[2] *A General Introduction to Psychoanalysis.* New York, Boni & Liveright, 1920.

therapy, social work, and special education. In the first year I give two courses, "Art Education and Personality" and "Case Studies of Pupils or Patients with Emotional Blocks in Creativity." Then follows an advanced Case Study course in the next year. These courses were made possible by the sympathetic support of Professor Howard Conant, Chairman of the Department of Art Education.

Regardless of their professional background, students are expected to have had creative art experience. Those who have had no previous training in dynamic psychology are expected to supplement what I am able to offer them with additional reading in dynamic and abnormal psychology. Invariably I find that the special techniques required for making a competent case study have not been included in their previous training. Only psychiatric interns and psychologists receive such training and therefore I have had to condense and modify the form of the psychiatric interview so as to include data in our interview technique relating to spontaneous art productions.

The case study methods course requires, first, that the students learn how to obtain a family and personal history; second, they must learn to develop insight into the subtlety of interviewing. In this special type of case study, the interview technique must include ways of obtaining from the pupil or patient his free associations to his art productions, as well as verbal responses concerning his personal life and problems.

Students inexperienced in the art of interviewing soon discover that it is not as simple as it seems. Educators especially find it difficult to break their long-standing habit of actively imparting information to passively receptive pupils, rather than drawing the pupil out.

Another new experience to students is the necessity of training themselves to recall verbatim all that took place in a session. Frequently, even though they do recall what pupil or patient did and said, they forget to record the part that they played in the interview. Many students do not at first recognize that a therapeutic relation is a two-way street, and what the educator or art therapist says and does is an active influence in the therapeutic process.

Sometimes students who found it difficult to recall the substance of an interview experimented with the use of a tape-recorder, but the results were far from satisfactory. A jumble of unimportant data interfered with following the essential points; the students got bogged down in irrelevant details and so failed to deal with the most crucial elements.

There are, of course, always problems of emotional relationship between teachers and pupils. Much of a teacher's success depends on how he handles his relation to a class. In psychotherapy there is an analogous relation between the therapist and his patient; there it is called "transference." This process, as experienced in analytically oriented art therapy as well as in psychoanalysis, means that the educator or art therapist is temporarily projected into the role of various significant people in the life of either pupil or patient.

When the educators in my courses began to understand the importance of dynamic psychology as applied not only to their pupils but also to themselves, they recognized the limitations of the required psychology courses, which usually omitted any understanding of unconscious motivation. As they became more aware of its universality and importance, they began to realize how much this new educational approach might accomplish in the future. As their insight increased, teachers came to understand how the release of spontaneous art from the unconscious could have a therapeutic effect on their pupils. This realization helped many of them to overcome their original anxieties concerning the application and use of art therapy.

In order to give you an understanding of how the release of unconscious conflicts is assisted by spontaneous art expression, I shall present condensed reports of case histories developed by two of my graduate students at New York University; the first case history was developed by a student in the Introductory Case Study course, the second by a student in the Advanced Case Study course. These will illustrate how the techniques of art therapy can be applied.

Case Study of a Nine-year-old Child

This case study of a nine-year-old girl was made by her teacher, a young woman in one of my Introductory Case Study courses. She was a regular classroom teacher in a fourth grade class in a Queens Public School. During the second term she selected Lee for her first case study because the girl was extremely depressed and withdrawn.

At the beginning of the school year this pale and sickly child cried incessantly and often asked to go home. She claimed that she missed her mother and father and would sit alone in the back of the room during the period when all the children were allowed to choose any activity that they preferred.

The teacher realized from her training in the case study course that she needed the child's family background and early school history in order to get some clues to the reasons for Lee's lack of adjustment in school. But the school files had nothing. Teachers in earlier grades told her that Lee had cried a great deal, was frequently late, and acted strangely in class. When this teacher reported to the principal that the child needed help, he agreed; but he said that the only available agency, the Bureau of Child Guidance, would not accept anyone from the school with an IQ over 90. (When children *are* referred to the New York Child Guidance Bureau it takes at least two years before they can be treated. One might well ask how New York City can ever begin to deal with the problems of delinquency and other types of childhood maladjustment when the City refuses to spend money for the much-needed preventive therapy for school children.)

Lee's teacher next tried to reach the parents. The father, who was the manager of a fashionable apartment building, assured her teacher that Lee would soon outgrow her difficulties. The teacher found the mother taciturn, stolid, and uncooperative. She believed, she said, that her child was dull. When the teacher suggested that the child needed to have more play and companionship with other children, the mother said that she did not have much time to take her out to play in the park.

In order to see Lee alone, the teacher invited her to come to her for special drawing lessons during half of the lunch hour. It was only after gaining the child's confidence in these individual sessions that her teacher finally found out, as will be told later, the real reason why the mother would not allow her daughter to see other children after school. Gradually the teacher began to see how Lee's isolation was related to the way she was treated at home; her whining, crying, and withdrawn behavior then became understandable.

Lee responded with delight to her teacher's interest in her. She produced a series of pictures of whatever she wished, which helped her to talk about herself and her home situation. From the very beginning she made pictures eagerly and began to explain quite freely what they meant to her.

The Art Sessions

Lee called Figure 1, which was made in the first art session, "My Mother,

Figure 1

My Father, My Sister and Me on Horses." Realizing that she had made the horses all the same size, she said, "I guess I made them too big."

"Tell me about your horse," the teacher said. "Oh, you know," explained Lee, "Fury from television. He's like Fury. I tamed him myself. That's why he doesn't need a bridle. He was wild but I tamed him."

Here we have immediate responses that show growing ego assertion by this previously timid and withdrawn child. The teacher's written comment was that "Lee looks like the farthest thing imaginable from a tamer of wild horses."

When her drawing was approved by the teacher, the child said, "Anna draws better." The teacher assured her that "Anna draws *differently,* but not better." But Lee emphasized her insecurity by continuing to insist, "But Anna draws better. She can make a scrawl and it looks good. When I make a scrawl it doesn't look good."

"I can show you," said the child's teacher, "how to make a scrawl, if you like, but you may want to have a different style of picture from Anna."

Lee became so interested in her picture that when it was class time she would not stop, but worked in the back of the room to finish it.

Several weeks later she produced another horse picture. She had been unable to think of anything to draw and her teacher said, "Lee, if you were the greatest artist in the world, what would you draw?" "A fox hunt," Lee replied immediately, and made a lively picture where the running movement of the horses is clearly shown (similar to the horse in Figure 4). After some time, she was able to give details about her early interest in horses; this is told later, in proper sequence.

Figure 2 shows Lee holding the hand of her favorite Beatle, Paul. Like so many youngsters, Lee, too, fell for the Beatles. As in some earlier pictures, she depicts herself in a red dress—a dress she says she does not have, but it must be one that she longs to possess.

Figure 2

Figure 3

A picture of the Four Beatles (Figure 3) was drawn some weeks later from a scribble and shows considerable development of Lee's sense of design. "They don't look exactly like the Beatles," she said, "but they look like the Beatles as I see them. You can tell who they are." Here were signs that the child's powers of creative expression were opening up. For she recognized that she had said something meaningful to her in this picture.

Figure 4 was drawn several weeks later. When she could not think what

Figure 4

Figure 5

to draw, the teacher asked her, because she had now become articulate about her personal feelings, whether she could make a picture of what she loved on one side and what she hated on the other. This appealed to Lee and she quickly drew this picture, placing "The Things I Hate" on the left side and "The Things I Like" on the right.

When it was finished, she said, pointing to the hate side, "At the bottom—that's the baby throwing blocks at me." The hate side also includes a woman in black with her arm raised. "This," Lee explained, "is Mother. I hate her when she hits me with a stick." By this time Lee was able to talk more freely about her difficulties at home, as for instance how she felt when the mother would hit her for teasing the baby. There is also an artichoke and a blue dress on the "hate" side.

On the "like" side are "asparagus, my doll, fur (that's a bear rug), my bicycle (I'm an expert rider), and a horse." (The doll is labeled "troll" for a type of doll that was the rage among the girls in Lee's class.)

When asked by her teacher how she became interested in horses, Lee replied, "I asked my parents that the other day. They said that twice they took me for a pony ride when I was a little girl and I liked it and they showed me pictures of horses and said, 'See the nice horsey.' " Asked if she had ever gone horseback riding, she said, "No. We can't afford for me to go horseback riding, but almost every Sunday I have about six rides on the Carousel in the park. I always ride a black horse." (In her first picture she had drawn herself on a black horse which she had tamed.)

Lee spent an entire period drawing the handsome green dragon shown in Figure 5. She said, "The dragon will be my pet and will protect me with its tail." (Note that five pointed spikes were attached to the tail, and spikes project from the dragon's horns and feet. Its toenails are strong, curving black claws. Clearly Lee was seeking protection from a hostile world through creating this mythical creature. Note also the strength, beauty, and originality of this design.)

Changes were now beginning to be observed in Lee's classroom behavior. Although she still retreated to the back of the room at story time, she began to listen with interest to the stories. During the period when other children told about what they were doing she now paid attention, responding sometimes with a smile or a look of longing. Some of her classmates remarked to their teacher on how much Lee's behavior had changed since the lower grades.

The horse in Figure 6 Lee called "Brownie, a magic rocking horse" who was "swimming around in the water just like people." She said she wished that she could learn to swim but her parents had never taught her. When it was explained to her that the YWCA or the Red Cross would tell her where to go for free swimming lessons, she thought a moment and then said, "Oh, I see. The Red Cross doesn't want anyone to drown."

Lee's Relationship With Her Mother

Now Lee was able to tell her teacher that she was always late for school because she was so tired when her mother woke her up; the whole story of Lee's tardiness came out at last. When asked whether she went to bed early enough to get rested, she answered hesitatingly at first, "Yes," and then changed to, "No, I don't really go to bed early. My mother always makes me do my homework over and over until it's perfect. But I'm beginning not to let her help me with my homework any more. I ask her if she wants my teacher to give *her* a grade and I tell her that my teacher says it doesn't have to be perfect because she checks it anyway."

In the next session more about Lee's home situation was revealed. When asked by her teacher, "Who do you go to the park with? Your friends?" Lee answered, "No, my parents. My mother says I can't have friends over and I'm not allowed to go over to their houses either."

"How come?" asked the teacher.

"No reason!" answered Lee.

"No reason?" pressed the teacher.

"My mother says I must come straight home and do my school work." said the child.

"But, Lee, I don't give you much homework," insisted the teacher.

Figure 6

The child was silent for a moment. Then she said, "My mother says that the other children live in nice houses and our apartment is small. She says if they see where I live they'll laugh at me and won't ever want to play with me again."

"Do you think that she's right?" asked her teacher.

"Yes," said Lee.

"Why?" asked her teacher.

"Don't you?" countered Lee.

"No," the teacher answered. "I believe that the people who make good friends will want to be friends with you because they really like you and want to play with you. They'll be coming to see you and not your house."

"You mean it?" asked Lee, surprised.

"I do," her teacher assured her.

The teacher pressed her to decide whether her best friends in the class would rather play with her in her home or with a boy all the class disliked. Lee grinned at this question and said emphatically, "With me." During the afternoon whenever she caught her teacher's eye she smiled happily, and would sometimes sympathetically squeeze the teacher's arm.

The teacher then had a talk with Lee's mother about allowing Lee to play after school with her schoolmates. Finally the mother admitted that she was afraid the other families would look down upon an apartment manager's child. In vain the teacher tried to assure her that this was not so. But it was Lee herself who with new-found confidence now took the initiative and began to invite her school friends to come over to her home. She explained that without telling her mother she would bring a child home to play, and she added gleefully, "Now I invite friends over without asking Mama because once they are there she gets too embarrassed to say anything."

Further liberation of the child from the mother's domination took place after her teacher heard from Lee about the mother's early life. The mother had been the oldest of a large family and had been responsible for the care of all the younger children. There had never been anyone, said Lee to help the mother with her school work when she was young. The mother had gone to high school but not to college.

When the teacher heard this she asked Lee what she thought her mother was trying to do by giving her all this extra help. Lee thought for a while and said, "Giving me what she didn't get when she was little?" "Is that what you think?" inquired the teacher pointedly. "Yes," answered the child. "But she also says she wants me to be ahead of everybody in the class and know more than they do. That's how come she gives me extra work." "Why do you think she wants you to be ahead of everyone else?" continued the teacher. "So I can be intelligent and well educated like she is," answered Lee.

"Like she is, or like she wishes she were?" the teacher asked. Lee pondered a moment. "Like she wishes she were." Then Lee began to laugh wildly as the point of this talk hit home. "Does knowing this," asked her teacher, "frighten you?" "No," she answered quietly. "Do you think that your mother has a right to make you do what she wants for herself?" "No," said Lee. "Do you think that perhaps you can tell her that you would rather not do this extra work?" asked the teacher. "I tell her that I won't do that extra work already," Lee answered, "but she always hits me then."

Lee was very quiet for a while, but then she began to smile at her teacher. It seemed as though the child began from that time to gain even greater courage to face up to her mother. She now knew that she had the support and approval of her teacher in asserting herself.

Comment on the First Case Study

This case study is an unusual example of how a sympathetic teacher was able, by her perceptive approach to a child's repressed conflicts, to build up the child's ego strength. In spite of the rigidity and hostility of the home environment Lee was herself able to develop a more nearly normal life with her classmates in school and also, in spite of maternal prohibitions, to find friends among other children. Although this teacher's efforts to change the mother's attitude had not been successful, the fundamental change and active independence in Lee's behavior enabled the little girl to function actively and happily both in school and after school hours.

But rarely is a grade teacher able through such insight and sensitivity to help a withdrawn child like Lee to find her own center. This I regard as true psychotherapy, developed by a teacher within the limitations of a large fourth-grade class in a Queens public school.

Case Study of a Four-and-a-half-year-old Child

This case study was made by the child's mother, a student in my advanced case study class. She is an artist and a psychologist, engaged professionally in advertising. Like several students of both sexes in my classes, she was not teaching and therefore undertook a study of her own daughter. As you will see, only a young woman of courage and integrity could have met and dealt successfully with her particular problems, both personal and financial, in caring for her fatherless child while she held a demanding daily job.

As Polly's mother reports quite objectively, "Polly is a sturdy and strong four-and-a-half-year-old child, often pretty-looking. Her nursery school teachers, her mother, and adult friends consider her to be bright and imaginative, with above average intelligence." I know the child, and this is a modest statement about this charming little girl.

Forced to support herself and her child from the time of her pregnancy, Polly's mother has had to employ nurse baby-sitter companions five days a week while she was away on her advertising job. During the year when this case study was made two older women who were fond of the child took care of her until the mother returned from work each evening. Polly's mother notes that since she and the child share an apartment with her sister, "Polly's short life has been lived entirely with four women. This further complicated the child's daily life." The males in her life, as her mother explains, have been limited to her pediatrician and the husbands of some of the mother's friends, seen only occasionally. The mother is fully aware of this imbalance in the child's life and the consequent over-emphasis on the child's attachment to her.

Polly's poignant, daily struggle to keep her mother from going to work was reported very objectively by Polly's mother. While we feel the pain and struggle of the little girl to keep hold of her mother, the mother says not a word about her own anguish and conflict as she was forced each day to leave her child in the care of others.

The mother simply stated that "Polly's sadness at seeing her mother leave every workday morning was suffered wordlessly during her babyhood. Several times she cried, for she was not absolutely sure that 'Mama' would come back. By the time Polly started nursery school, however, and had to be taken there promptly so that her mother could get to work on time, Polly found a way to strike back at her mother for deserting her. She thought of all sorts of ways to hold up her own departure for nursery school. If she dressed herself, she would deliberately slow down her movements. If her mother dressed her so as to get her off in time, she would behave as awkwardly as possible in order to block her mother's efforts. Or she would invent various demands to delay her mother. This situation became more acute each morning until both Polly and her mother would argue loudly as the child resisted all efforts to hurry her up; finally the mother would literally have to drag Polly out of the apartment to get her to nursery school. A helpful solution of this impasse was offered by one of the nursery school mothers who suggested a plan for her own little daughter to meet Polly, so that the children went to nursery school together each morning. This became a happy solution of the difficulty, as Polly liked going to school." Nevertheless Polly naturally continued, her mother reports, to resent her mama's daily absences at work.

The Introduction of Picture-Making

It was early in Polly's nursery school days that her mother first introduced the child to the idea of making pictures, in the hope that Polly would be able to use this as a means of releasing her pent-up anger and frustration. She had become able to express herself in both action and words, and her mother notes that now "Polly was able to admit her anger. . . She resented a new baby-sitter at this time and her behavior was very naughty."

The child responded eagerly and always loved to make pictures. The mother therefore encouraged her to draw in the mornings when she herself was busy dressing or preparing breakfast.

Polly soon also used the making of pictures to help overcome a night terror of some creatures that she called the "moochies." The mother wrote that Polly "had nightmares about snakes which threatened to come into her bed and bite her. After two nights of trying to quiet her fears by explaining that shadows can appear to be frightening, Polly's mother tried another tack. She went into Polly's room, kissed her to stop her tears, and said, 'Can't we tell the moochies to go away? I'm sure they'll be nice about it and go if we tell them to.'

" 'No, they're bad,' insisted Polly. 'They're bad! They won't go away! I've asked them to.'

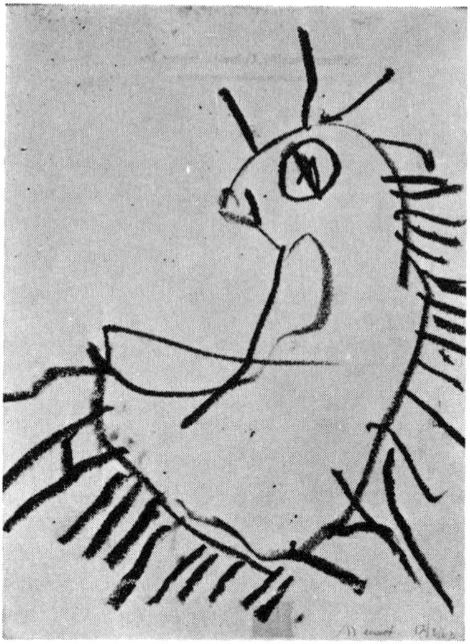

Figure 7

" 'Well, then,' said Polly's mother, 'let's get a piece of paper and a pencil and you can draw a new house for them and then they'll go away.' "

The mother gave the pencil and paper to Polly and this is what happened. "Polly drew squiggly creatures all over it. Each squiggly creature was surrounded with a circle as a house. After Polly had drawn the 'moochie' snakes and given them all new homes, she got rid of her fear of them at night for good, and they were never mentioned again."

This, it seems to me, is an unusually interesting use of spontaneous art expression. The mother suggested a positive use of the child's own drawings, thereby enabling Polly to control and master a fear by expressive action.

A large black and green drawing of an "Insect" (Figure 7) was made spontaneously about six months after Polly had disposed of the "moochies" by giving them new houses. It seemed evident to the mother that this picture was similarly related to some unverbalized fear of bugs, but the child made no further comment about insects and has since then collected many live insects in warm weather and made them homes in boxes in her room.

Figure 8 was produced as a result of the mother's efforts to get Polly to express her unverbalized feelings against the mother's daily departure for work. Her mother said, "We're going to start doing some special pictures about you and school and Mama."

The mother then asked, "Will you do a picture with some of these colors, of you going to school and Mama going to work?" "All right," said Polly,

Figure 8

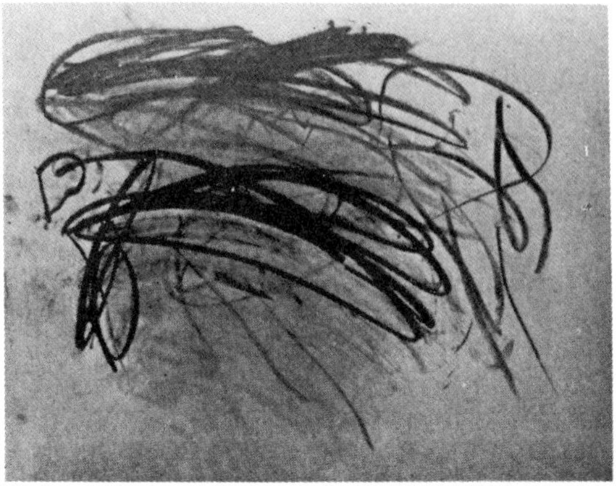

and made this picture of a lion and a snake in blue and black. "When Mama goes to work, I feel like a blue lion," she said. The fierce animals she named and the forceful lines she drew seemed to indicate how angry Polly really felt about her mother's departure each morning.

Figure 9 is a drawing of a doctor and a nurse, and Figure 10 shows patients in a hospital. Polly made five other hospital drawings at about this time, and asked many questions about doctors and hospitals. She knew about doctors from her visits to the pediatrician and at three had said that she wanted to be a doctor when she grew up. Later she began to inquire about what people did in hospitals and her mother told her how she had been born in one, and that she herself had once gone to a hospital to have a sore finger fixed. Polly explained that one of the patients in Figure 10 was bleeding (the darkened area is red) and the doctor and nurse would help. "Apparently," the mother said, "Polly's anxiety about being hurt and possibly having to go

Figure 9

Figure 10

Figure 11

to a hospital was resolved for the time being, after she had made these hospital pictures. But Polly still insisted that she wanted to be a doctor when she grew up."

Perhaps it was because of the sympathetic pediatrician she went to and liked that she fantasied herself becoming a doctor.

As Polly drew Figure 11 she exclaimed, "That's a witch mama!" "Oh" the mother said, "is the child her daughter? She looks different." Polly was

Figure 12

Figure 13

Figure 14

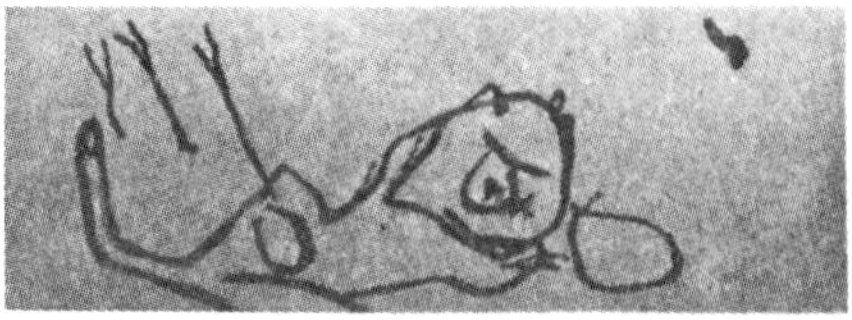

silent for a long moment and then she said slowly, "That isn't really a witch mama; that's really a regular mama like you with her child like me." By calling her mother a witch the child released her anger against her mother for deserting her every day to go to work. Even though Polly was trying to cover up her resentment by finally denying that the mother in the picture was a witch, she had in this drawing been able to express her true feelings.

Two months later, in two pictures, made in quick succession one morning while the mother was dressing, Polly released again her anger against her mother for not staying at home with her every day (Figures 12 and 13). In speaking about these drawings, the child tried to cover up any specific reference to her own mother, but her resentment was clearly revealed. The mother said, "Those are interesting pictures. What are the people doing?" The little girl answered, "This Mommy," pointing to Figure 12, "is sad because she has lost her child. That's why she looks so bad." (Note the interesting reversal between the child's own role in life and that of her mother; Polly really feels that she has lost her mother every day when the mother leaves for work.) The child expressed further resentment against her mother by a slip of the tongue. She identified the second figure first as "the other little girl," which she quickly corrected to "the other Mommy," saying "This Mommy is happy because she hasn't lost her child." (Again this exposed Polly's fear of losing her mother.)

A drawing of a cat, Figure 14, is included because it illustrates Polly's growing powers of observation. Her mother noted that it was "an expression of her liking of animals," and that "the animal form suggests the exact movement of a cat playing."

Comment on the Second Case Study

By quoting the mother's words directly, it has been possible to follow her effective handling of her child's conflicts about the mother's departure for work every morning. She was able to help the little girl by encouraging her to project her hostile feelings into these revealing, symbolic pictures. The clarity and truthfulness of Polly's drawings was made possible by the understanding and insight of her mother. Only a woman with great self-awareness could have dealt so wisely and skilfully with the deep needs of her anxious daughter as did this young psychologist and painter.

Conclusion

These two case studies show how two children were assisted by two of my students to express their problems in both pictures and words. The roles of the two students were quite dissimilar.

In the first case a classroom teacher singled out a maladjusted child in her large class for an intensive case study. In the second, a mother undertook to deal with the serious separation anxiety of her own child, caused by the mother's daily departure for her job. In both cases these students were able to help the children express personal problems which were serious and too overwhelming for such little children to cope with alone.

In neither case were these young women dealing with children merely as competent educators. They were helping the two little girls by means of their own psychological insight, which had been developed in the case study courses and also through personal psychotherapy. In order to reinforce the point that the psychotherapeutic approach can be an asset to all educators, I quote Professor Jersild of Teachers College, Columbia University: "There is much in the professional work of a good therapist that can also be made part of the work of a good teacher." [3] These two case studies are a strong confirmation of Jersild's statement. For the one student as a class teacher and the other as a psychologist have applied their self-knowledge to assisting the emotional adjustment of these two children.

I have illustrated only two of many ways in which fundamental case-study techniques can be employed to resolve personality problems. A number of my students' case studies are longer and more complex; some deal with adolescents, others with adults. To give an idea of the range and variety of the problems that may be dealt with, I cite a few other cases handled by my students. A young boy who has lost an eye in some wild play was able, with the help of a sensitive art educator, to work through his conflicts about this disability in a series of symbolic drawings. A young clinical psychologist who has learned the use of art therapy was able to help an institutionalized delinquent boy to revise his approach to both his family and girl friends through expressive release in words and pictures. There is also a fascinating study, by one of the advanced students, of the bizarre emotional problems of a hunch-backed man of fifty, who had never married and still lived with his dominating and sadistic old mother. The working through of his problems by means of a series of striking pictures and increasing articulateness revealed how his strange conflicts were related to his malformation. Eventually, art therapy made it possible for this man to develop, even though middle-aged, a viable relation in marriage.

---

[3] *When Teachers Face Themselves.* New York, Teachers College, Columbia University, 1955.

There are many other interesting case studies which show the growth and development of my students themselves and also illustrate the various ways in which the personal adjustment of their pupils, patients, and clients was helped through the techniques of art therapy. In the not too distant future, a number of these cases will appear in a book which will explain and illustrate more completely how and why the principles of dynamic psychology are the foundation on which analytically oriented art therapy has been developed.

Elda's Art Therapy in the Context of a Quarter Century of Psychiatric Treatment

SELWYN DEWDNEY

PART I

One of the most frustrating aspects of the treatment of mental and emotional disorders is the rarity with which it is possible to follow a discharged patient's history over any extended length of time. The history of Elda (a pseudonym) is unusual inasmuch as it is well documented over the greater part of 25 years. Throughout this period, whether in or out of the hospital,[1] she never completely lost contact with the staff.

Elda's physical and psychological symptoms ranged so widely over this quarter century that their description and the records of attempts to deal with them fill six thick volumes of case history.

Psychiatrically she went through courses of ECT, insulin coma therapy, a prefrontal leucotomy, chemotherapy, and art therapy. Medically she was examined and treated for obesity, shortness of breath, headache, gas on the stomach, nausea, acute abdominal pain, chronic constipation, burning on micturation, and blood in her urine and stools. Surgically she had four minor

[1] Westminster (DVA) Hospital, London, Ontario

operations: three for ingrown toenails and one to repair severed palmar tendons. In addition, she underwent a leucotomy and a gall bladder removal. Tube feeding was required at three stages in her illness. She was treated at various times for wrist lacerations, plugged ears, and overdoses of Seconal. By 1950 she was fitted with a full lower denture and a partial upper one; she lost the rest of her teeth over the next 5 years. At intervals, too, she claimed to be pregnant, naming a staff member or fellow patient as the father, but tests were invariably negative.

Physically, Elda was short and broadwaisted. She had a dark complexion, frequently marred with rashes. Usually she was careless of her appearance and often went without her dentures. Yet there was a kind of vitality about her, allied with great manipulative skill. These combined to create a childlike quality that pervaded even her most objectionable behavior. Consequently, throughout her hospital sojourns there was almost always a staff member—whether physician, psychiatrist, nursing supervisor, or psychologist, to say nothing of those at less expert levels—who took Elda's current symptoms seriously, treating them with an optimism that seems to have been undaunted by the growing bulk of her record.

The art therapists were no exception. My own acquaintance with Elda began in the summer of 1949, three years after her first commitment to a mental hospital and a bare 6 months after her leucotomy. In those days this operation was felt to be an awesome procedure of which great things were expected, including substantial rehabilitation. As a member of a small women's group that had been formed to "re-educate" lobotomized patients, Elda joined our weekly outdoor sketching excursions. At this stage, however, her attention span was too short for her to achieve anything more than the most shallow involvement. Indeed, 6 years were to pass before Elda came to me for serious sessions in art therapy.

These later sessions, extending over a 2-year period, were remarkably productive. However, it is not my purpose in this paper to prove the efficacy of art therapy. Rather, I shall attempt to detail the art therapy treatment (as practised at Westminster Hospital)[2] in the context of an unusually great amount of information about an individual patient, thereby offering a perspective not normally available.

Background

Elda's mother was unmarried when Elda was born in 1917, but she did marry a man who was not Elda's father a year or two later. This man, steadfastly believed by Elda to be her real father, died when she was three, to be

[2] See Selwyn H. Dewdney, E. V. Metcalf, and F. N. Burd, "Art Therapy at Westminster Hospital." *Canadian Psychiatric Association Journal,* Vol. 1, No. 1, 1956; and Selwyn Dewdney, Irene M. Dewdney, and E. V. Metcalf, "The Art-Oriented Interview as a Tool in Psychotherapy." *Bulletin of Art Therapy,* Vol. 7, No. 1, October 1967.

replaced by her mother's second legal husband. Two half brothers arrived in due course, Elda remaining the only daughter.

The mother, when interviewed by a social worker before Elda's admission to Westminster Hospital, was highly defensive. She declared that "Our daughter was . . . one of the finest girls any mother or father ever had." However, there is a strong hint of early autism in her description of Elda as a quiet girl who preferred being by herself and out of the house most of the time.

The sole success story of Elda's life began when she left school at age 15 with an eighth grade education and found employment in a doctor's home, first as a baby sitter, then living in as the children's nurse. There is no record of why she enlisted in the Canadian Women's Army Corps 8 years later. Her unit went overseas in 1941, and for the rest of the war Elda worked as a laundress. It was during this period that her first recorded symptoms surfaced, in the form of two overdoses of Seconal. She returned to Canada depressed and suicidal. First she was referred to a general hospital; a few months later to the psychiatric unit of a veteran's hospital. In spite of a gloomy prognosis Elda's former employer expressed his interest in re-employing her. In an interview he described Elda as having been "a very loyal person and excellent with the children." He maintained his loyalty and interest in her welfare for at least 2 years after her return from England.

Physical Treatment: 1947 to 1954

After her transfer to the veterans' hospital Elda refused to eat for 3 weeks, during which she received tube feeding and a course of ECT. At this point she had been diagnosed as suffering from hysterical anorexia. Symptoms included throwing objects through closed windows, rubbing dirt into wrist lacerations, and plugging her ears. Further courses in ECT produced no response. Neither did insulin coma therapy—then very much in fashion.

In January 1948 Elda was transferred to the unit of Westminster Hospital that was later to become its Psychiatric Institute. In the new setting she again refused to eat and was force-fed for 9 weeks. During this period the diagnosis was obsessive-compulsive psychoneurosis. She was described as "introspective, irritable, unstable . . . the most difficult person in the hospital . . . with an obsessive desire to injure herself," the result, her psychiatrist felt, of being "caught up in a maelstrom of anxiety, emotional confusion, and conflicting impulses."

At that time the search for physical solutions to mental disorders was uppermost. In Elda's case ECT and insulin coma had been tried and found wanting. Chemotherapy had yet to be born. The hope now seemed to lie in the dramatic new surgical procedure that was coming into favor across the country: prefrontal leucotomy. Elda's negative response to every form of treatment she had been exposed to led to the decision that she was an appropriate candidate for this radical surgery. In February 1949 she underwent a lobotomy.

The following spring and summer there was a noticeable improvement, but by autumn her preoperational pattern was back in full swing. Now she was described as "completely uncooperative and nasty . . . a broody, mildly depressed individual with a hostile attitude towards the world in general." The following year it was noted that she varied "from an attitude of sullenness to one of self-righteousness and euphoria . . . with . . . occasional obscene and profane outbursts."

Over the next 4 years Elda's medical file grew to massive proportions. Exhaustive tests delving into every complaint listed earlier were conducted, almost invariably with negative results. A measure of her physicians' and surgeons' bafflement is reflected in the report of a plastic surgeon, who wrote "I fail to see that any therapy, other than psychotherapy, will be of any value to this girl."

In September 1953, after nearly 8 years in the hospital and exhaustive examinations for her innumerable complaints, the staff apparently decided that nothing more could be done for her and that her behavioral symptoms had subsided to a tolerable level. Inasmuch as she had made one visit home with no harmful effects, she was discharged.

Intensive Treatment: 1954 to November 1956

Within 4 months of this first discharge Elda was back in the hospital with all her former symptoms in full bloom. On discussing her prolonged visit home she not only reiterated the story of a hostile, quarrelsome household, but claimed—with supporting evidence—that her mother wanted to get hold of her pension payments and savings.

Figure 1 represents schematically the main features of the intensive treatment phase. In January 1955, Elda began a course in chemotherapy and shortly afterwards became involved, on her own initiative, in serious art therapy.

Chemotherapy Begins

Elda's readmission was based on her "usual multiple psychosomatic symptoms of conversion type coupled with restlessness, irritability, and some insomnia." Chemotherapy was just coming into use as a psychiatric treatment tool, and the failure of earlier techniques, plus Elda's long history of hospitalization, made her a logical subject. In January 1955 her phenobarbital dosage, begun on admission, was increased to 48 mgm. daily for her continuing insomnia. At the same time experimental doses of Reserpine were prescribed, beginning at 0.25 mgm. daily. The dosage was doubled the following month.

During this period Elda's doctor noted that "She does not sleep well, is emotionally unstable, depressed, has horrible nightmares about snakes who lurk in the cellar and crawl up to her ward, etc. She is quite naive and child-

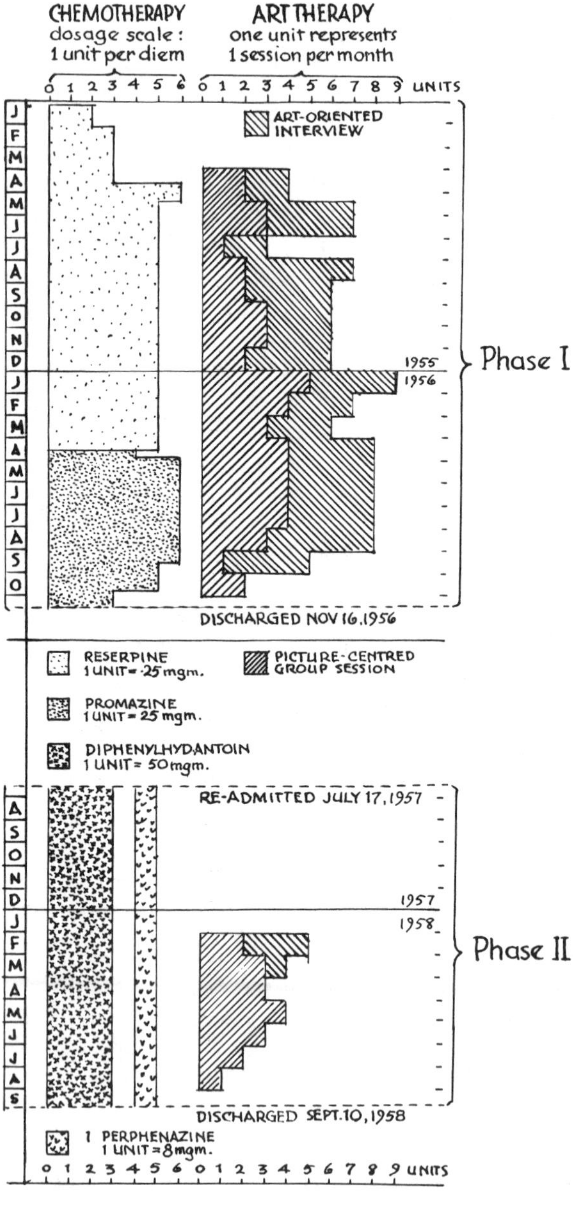
CHEMOTHERAPY
dosage scale:
1 unit per diem
ART THERAPY
one unit represents
1 session per month
0 1 2 3 4 5 6 0 1 2 3 4 5 6 7 8 9 UNITS
ART-ORIENTED INTERVIEW
J F M A M J J A S O N D J F M A M J J A S O
1955
1956
Phase I
DISCHARGED NOV 16, 1956
RESERPINE 1 UNIT = ·25 mgm.
PICTURE-CENTRED GROUP SESSION
PROMAZINE 1 UNIT = 25 mgm.
DIPHENYLHYDANTOIN 1 UNIT = 50 mgm.
RE-ADMITTED JULY 17, 1957
A S O N D J F M A M J J A S
1957
1958
Phase II
DISCHARGED SEPT. 10, 1958
1 PERPHENAZINE 1 UNIT = 8 mgm.
0 1 2 3 4 5 6 0 1 2 3 4 5 6 7 8 9 UNITS

Figure 1

ish . . . reads a large number of the comic book type of mysteries, fascinated by the horror."

Art Therapy Begins

All through the years—by this time approaching a decade—casual corridor encounters had kept Elda's and my acquaintance alive. Nevertheless, it was a great surprise when she turned up at art therapy, unannounced, on her own initiative. She had a definite project in mind. A monster had been giving her a great deal of anxiety. Might it help if she made a drawing of it?

Two things impressed me: first, that she wanted to "draw out" her fear and, second, her earnestness. Instead of the usual loud-mouthed, boisterous kidding with which she normally met me, she was in a quiet, intense mood that convinced me she was not trying to manipulate; rather she had reached a point of desperation that demanded some kind of confrontation.

The following notes were made following her first drawing, shown here as Figure 2:

> Originally the round object with the lightning symbol represented herself being devoured by the serpentine shape. The spiral represented "a tightening process"; the lightning the speed with which she was being devoured. She was concerned about the "tentacle" (as she called it) of the serpent. Shouldn't it be attached to something? I suggested that she express her question by making the end of the tentacle obscure. Later she removed the barrier between the spiral and the form that had originally represented herself, enlarging the lightning. The latter was now menacing the spiral, and any identification of herself with any parts of the drawing had become vague.

After her first self-initiated appearance she was referred to art therapy by her psychiatrist without any particular hope on anyone's part that positive

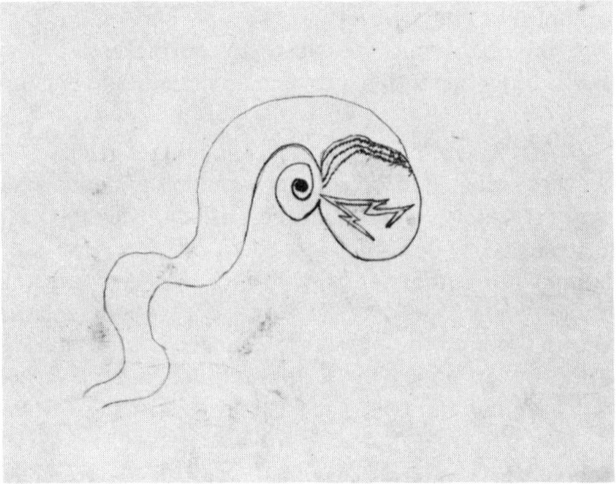

Figure 2

results would ensue. However, Elda's efforts to confront her "monster" for a full 10 weeks were so strongly suggestive of therapeutic progress that a reassessment was made of her treatment program. It was decided, in consultation with her doctor and a staff psychologist, that in addition to her art-oriented interviews with me she would attend the picture-centered group sessions conducted by Irene Dewdney and me. Since a description of this technique and the results obtained therefrom has not been published, a word of explanation is necessary.

As early as 1956, we developed the picture-centered group treatment structure. This grew out of our observation that groups of patients, although working individually in art therapy sessions, often gathered around a single painting at the end of the session and spontaneously discussed its content.

The number of patients attending a picture-centered group session averaged around six, but since a staff psychologist, a nursing orderly, and one or two observers (medical students, psychiatric nurses, occupational therapy interns, etc.) also attended, total attendance ran as high as 10. Participants sat in a semicircle around a well-lit display panel on which were pinned either drawings by a patient who wished to have his work discussed or reproductions of classical or contemporary art. We found that the works producing the greatest discussion were those with a recognizably human content. We also learned that display of two or more pictures, by stimulating comparison and offering a variety of style and content, was far more productive than display of a single picture.

The object of the session was the frankest possible personal response to the pictures, without reference to painting techniques, period, or any other intellectual consideration. It was the art therapist's task to create an atmosphere in which all were equal—patients, staff, and visitors—before the pictures; and the only criterion for judging the validity of a response to a picture was the viewer's emotional honesty. The success of a session and of the pictures used was judged by the extent to which reactions to the pictures led to the airing and sharing of disturbing memories, current anxieties, and wishes and fears for the future.

Normally Elda would not have qualified for inclusion in the group sessions, candidates for which were selected from among younger patients with reasonable prospects for early recovery. Although her attendance at these group sessions was at first regarded with some apprehension, we were surprised to find that her bombastic outbursts, which were largely ignored, subsided as the sessions progressed. Moreover, her frank reactions to the paintings galvanized the group. When the therapist remained unperturbed by Elda's unrestrained attacks on paintings by Rembrandt or other "Great Masters," the group realized that in relation to the pictures, no holds were barred.

Not only did Elda enliven the group sessions, she gained from them.

Even as early as her second group session, it was noted in the art therapy records that "Elda showed none of her usual front of boisterous, rollicking comment and repartee; [she] was serious, intent, and made intelligent—often sensitive—comments throughout." When a weekly picnic schedule clashed with the art therapy group sessions, she was bitterly resentful. "If they make a rule," she complained, "they should keep it. I come down here for a reason."

Over the months that followed, Elda's drawings grouped around four themes, which I designate as (1) the Monster series, (2) the Bottle series, (3) the Human series, and (4) the Staring Eye series. Only 6 out of 43 drawings lie outside one or another of these four categories, while as many more might be termed composites of two or more of them.

1. *The Monster Series:* The weeks that followed Elda's first appearance in art therapy saw an extraordinary sequence of drawings, each defining a little more clearly the feelings she had about those closest to her in her family. My notes on Figure 3 (May 26, 1955) follow:

> Elda again drew the subject she had had on her mind for a long time. The Threat was there, and then she had difficulty drawing "something beautiful." The little, lightly drawn cross on the right was to represent her father who died in the First World War. But she wanted it to look more beautiful and pleasant and didn't know how to go about it. Then she wanted to connect the Threat and thing or person she hated with her father because "it began there." She then drew a snake and it expressed for her the most horrible thing: "the devil." She even colored it with purple chalk, the color she hated more than any other [she said].

In regard to Figure 4 (June 23, 1955), I noted:

> Elda started out drawing her "significant" drawing, essentially the same one she had done on previous occasions, but with new variations. She

Figure 3

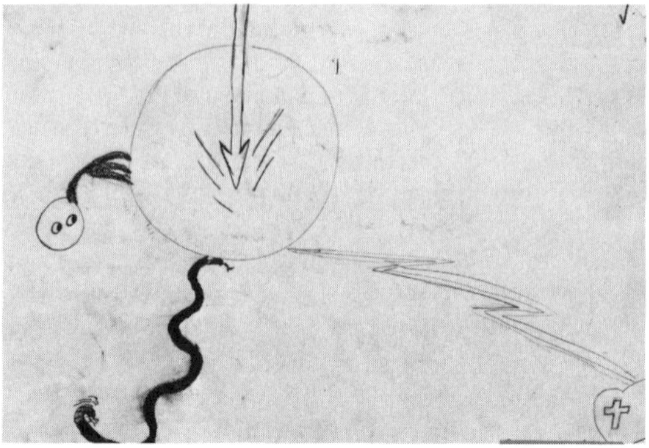

Figure 4

is very subdued and introspective while working on this drawing, in contrast to her usual explosive behavior.

After Elda drew Figure 5 (June 30, 1955), I noted, "She is on the verge of interpreting the hammer-spear symbol that penetrates the circle in each instance." This comment proved to be overoptimistic. There can be little doubt about the symbolism that dominates this drawing, but throughout her therapy Elda was never to face the sexual anxiety so expressively rendered here. Figure 5 was rendered in strong color and with far more definition than any previous drawing. Significantly, as will appear later, she used purple for both the body of the crablike figure and the snake. The central, circular figure is rendered in shades of red; the penetrating spear is black. The part of the crab's claws that touch the edge of the circle change from red to a delicate pink. Note, too, how the snake's head is bent against, or averted from, the circle.

Figure 5

Figure 6

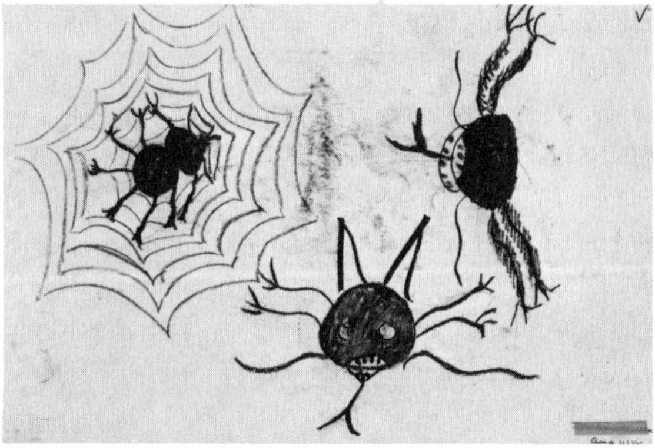

In the July 12 picture-centered session the group discussed a series of drawings done by one of their number who challenged Elda to put hers up at the next meeting. She agreed, but offered no comments of her own when they were displayed, stating that only two persons knew what they were about. "One won't talk, and if the other one [the therapist] does he'll get shot in the head."

After a private session at the end of the month, reviewing the drawings she had done to date, I noted, "Elda suggested that she narrow her field down to one subject out of the four contained in her series to date. She unhesitatingly chose the mother theme."

By this time she had made six drawings, consistently identifying three of the four figures as mother, stepfather, and real father—while evading any interpretation of the central monster form with equal consistency.

At a group session early in August, during discussion of a fellow-patient's drawings, Elda revealed how strongly she projected her feelings into her work.

> For some weeks Elda has been asking whether T.F. could be present to explain his paintings. This was arranged . . . and proved to be exceedingly productive. Elda showed a most remarkable interest in the session ("as if," the psychologist remarked, "she was personally responsible for its success") and went out of her way to express her interest in T.F.'s work and admiration for it. . . . Interestingly, she expressed—as she has done before—her inability to work at a fantasy level, apparently regarding her own symbolic drawings as directly dealing with reality. She even forgot, when the discussion turned to the frequency of snakes in drawings, that she had used a snake herself. Apparently the snake in her drawings is not *really* a snake, but her stepfather, most literally.

Concentrating now on renderings of her mother, Elda went through the transition noted in the following excerpt from my notes of August 11, 1955:

Elda came into the art therapy room and settled down to her drawing very quickly. She described her drawing of the previous week to me. The flower was her mother when she was younger (i.e., *good*). The flower fading was her mother changing. The purple flower was the original mother dead. Then came a transition into poison ivy and poison. Here Elda stopped. She couldn't put into her drawing the feeling of horror towards her mother; nothing she drew had enough of a threat. I suggested then that she might choose another symbol and concentrate on it. She turned over the page and drew three spiders [Figure 6]. She felt dissatisfied with the first because it didn't look "awful" enough and because she had put a web around it (which made the spider appear innocuous). Then she drew the mouth of the spider. The last two attempts came closer to Elda's concept.

2. *The Bottle Series:* Only a week later Elda produced a drawing, Figure 7, that set my therapeutic hopes soaring. Here she was not only able to show how bottled up her feelings were, but was also able to integrate within an enclosed space sources of anxiety that she had always represented separately. Equally hopeful was the first appearance—bizarre and rudimentary though it was—of a human face. On August 25, I noted: "Elda discussed her drawing of last week. The bottles, she disclosed, represented herself. She pointed out that one was closed off at the top and rooted at the bottom; that was she, so to speak, stuck where she was." Then on August 30:

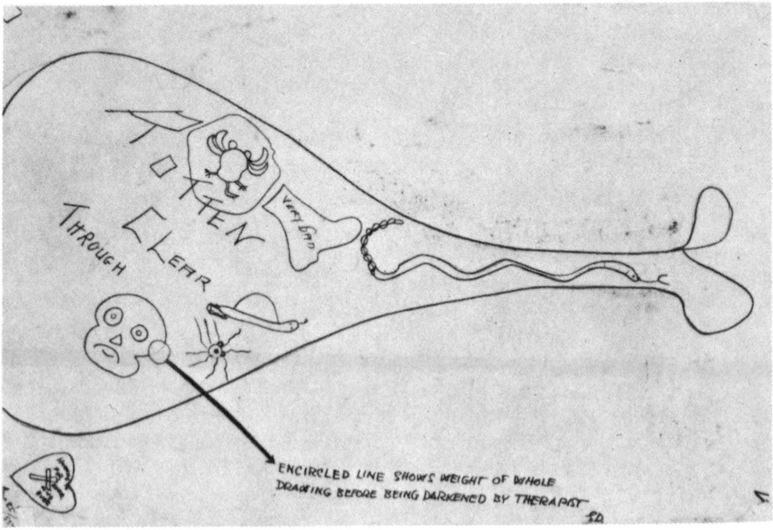

Figure 7

> Elda had a private session with me and discussed the bottle symbol at some length, at first in terms that suggested strong sexual associations. Later she related it to—almost identified it with—her stepfather. For the first time she had something good to say about him. On her last Christmas visit he was the only one who was kind to her. When she was drunk (he told her afterwards) she sat on his knee. In fact, whenever she was drunk she made for the nearest man.

Elda successfully evaded any further exploration of sexual associations with her drawings. Two days later I noted:

> She wants to draw a larger bottle next week so the details within can be dealt with more fully. I suggested that she might soon begin to relate the larger periods of her life to each other by showing aspects of the bottle and its contents at various stages of her life.

Coincidentally with Elda's increasingly serious involvement in the private sessions she was making progress in her group relationships, as can be seen in the notes for this period.

> [September 13] Elda for the first time made a successful effort to be serious and socially sympathetic throughout a session. She afterwards told me it had required a great deal of control to repress her hostility to P.B. (the newcomer) when he tended to monopolize discussion towards the session's end.

> [September 20] Again Elda was quiet, thoughtful, and contributing rather than boisterous, superficial, and disturbing. It seemed to require less effort than a week ago, for she allowed herself witticisms and humorously hostile remarks but so much more quietly that she *fitted* the group activity rather than fractured it.

> [October 11] This has been Elda's best day. There was not the slightest

Figure 8

Figure 9

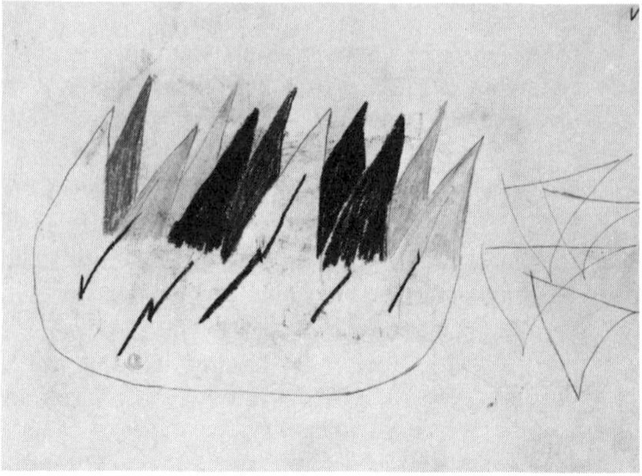

> manifestation of her boisterous attitude. She now seems to feel completely secure in the group, with a status of her own, and all necessity for putting on an act seems to have dropped away. She did see a menacing face in P.B.'s drawing that seemed of real concern to her, but only during the first half hour. The discussion began with reactions to the prints but quickly shifted to a discussion of mother love. Does a mother love her sickly child more than her healthy one? A "bad" child more than a "good" one? I recall now that the first shift from pictures to life came out of my asking whether a certain Picasso nude would be a "good" woman or a "loose" one. They were unanimous in rejecting the idea of looseness. Elda, too. A month ago she would have seen nothing but the woman's nudity and have made a big display of how shocked she was.

Meanwhile, in her individual drawing sessions, Elda had continued to explore the bottle theme. At the end of September she made the drawing reproduced in Figure 8. She interpreted it only as an expression of her negative feelings about some staff members and patients on her ward. However, her next drawing, Figure 9, revealed the link between this drawing and the bottle theme:

> Elda expressed difficulty in drawing the vase so it would look broken. We discussed whether her difficulty wasn't due to a deeper feeling that it wasn't really broken. She then noticed that the base was whole and speculated: "Maybe it's impossible to break."

Thereafter, the bottle theme disappeared, except for a hint of it some months later which will be discussed in context. It seemed to me at the time that Elda's failure to break the vase completely was symbolic of a basic "togetherness" and justified some optimism about her future. Indeed, this

Figure 10

optimism was shared by the staff generally, leading me to place a more difficult goal before Elda.

3. *The Human Series:* I discussed with Elda my belief that she was approaching a state of health that would warrant her discharge and suggested that she was ready to deal with the persons in her life in terms of direct representation. She demurred but was finally persuaded. Her first drawing amazed us both because it was drawn so much better than either of us had dared to hope and because it represented "a little girl." This drawing is not reproduced here, but during the next two sessions she made even more significant drawings. My notes on Figure 10 (November 3, 1955) follow:

> Drawing a baby according to a formula she had picked up, Elda was having trouble. After a technical hint or two she gave up this stereotype and drew her baby spontaneously. This, she realized, was herself. ("Getting down to brass tacks," as she put it.) Elda was dissatisfied with the expression—as she saw it—of "horror" on the baby's face. She was led to accept this at its face value and so discovered the source of the horror: her stepfather. When I suggested that she add a drawing of him she said it was quite impossible. We discussed him as a "monster." Elda readily agreed that the monster had a human form but was able only after considerable difficulty to accept the possibility of *representing* him as human and allowing the monstrosity of his nature to be expressed in the *child's reaction* to him.

The best she could do during this session was to add the head in the lower right corner of the sheet, significantly the same position occupied by the heart and cross that represented her "real" father in the Monster series.

She was unable to recognize the ambivalence in the baby's stare, which seems more expressive of pleased surprise than of the "horror" she saw in it.

A week later Elda added the drawings in the center and to the left. In the center she rendered, for the first time, a childhood memory—an incident in which a window sash fell on her arms, pinioning them to the sill. Therapeutically this drawing opened no doors but it showed a surprising advance toward naturalism, even when compared with the baby rendering of the previous week. In fact, the drawing is a fair self-portrait. The head in the upper left corner was not interpreted.

The following month revealed the greatest progress yet, evident in her group sessions as well as in the privately conducted drawing sessions.

> [December 13] Elda made a surprising remark toward the end of the session when we were comparing P.B.'s early drawings with his later ones: that he was now working at the same level that she had been working at earlier, and that the kind of drawing he had been doing formerly was a diversion that had absolutely no effect and was comfortable to make or look at because it avoided any real self-expression.
>
> [December 15] Elda came in all set to go. She had something on her mind and wanted to draw it. [See Figure 11.] Her first attempt was her recurring symbol: a spider. . . . Her second attempt, on a larger scale, also discouraged her until I showed what a big step she had taken.

This was, indeed, a most encouraging development, an attempt to relate her delusional monster figure to what was obviously a drawing of herself. Note the child's expression of desperate resignation, while the mother-monster's humanized face portrays pleasant indifference.

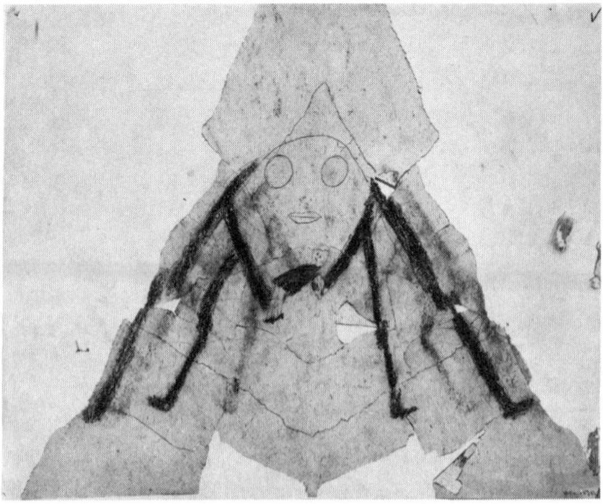

Figure 11

During a group session the following week a Fra Lippo madonna was discussed. Elda noted "tenderness" in the mother's expression. When one of the group asked, "What mother doesn't love her child?", another answered, "The mother who resents her child." Elda supported the answer vigorously.

> Towards the end of the session where we had concentrated on one person's work I mentioned the possibility of other people's putting up their work for discussion. Elda first denounced the whole idea, then brought over her drawing of last Thursday [Figure 11] and began discussing it in the group's hearing. I pointed out that it was not as menacing as she had meant it to be; there was a very human mouth to her spider. This made her quite furious—even more so when I said that there was almost a smile on the mouth. She tore up her drawing and generally enjoyed the whole outburst.

Two days later, she dropped in to art therapy to say goodbye before Christmas leave. Bubbling over with good spirits, she planned to spend the holiday with a fellow-patient at the latter's home. This visit, free of the tensions that arose when Elda went to her own home, was a great success.

> [December 29] Elda exuberant over her Christmas with F.B., which seems to have done her good. She forgot that she had torn up her spider drawing, and wanted to know what had happened to it. Finally she stated that she hadn't torn it up, though no one had accused her of it.

In this session she redrew the spider and victim, using the sketch I had made at her request of an insect's mouth parts and various graphic devices to express menace (Figure 12). Compared with Figure 11, however, it turned out to be far less expressive of the contradictory undercurrents of feeling the earlier work so subtly conveys.

January brought changes and some confusion. Elda became increasingly concerned about an elderly woman on her ward, hereafter referred to as E.M., who apparently was trying to make friends with her. The identity of the spider symbol now began to shift from mother to stepfather. During a third session in which she ventilated her hostility towards E.M. it began to appear that she was using E.M. as a focus for angry feelings about her mother.

Nevertheless, Elda's gross symptoms were subsiding. In February her psychiatrist reported that she was "less contentious, negativistic, and irritable than formerly. She appears to be attempting to gain some insight. . . . She is also attending art therapy and producing a series of drawings by which she attempts to express her feelings. . . . She expressed considerable hostility towards her mother and stepfather. At the same time she is rather depressed, hurt, and feels quite lonely and insecure, as she feels they exploit her."

Later that month he wrote that Elda "still has difficulty in expressing freely her conflicts although she has some insight into these. It is felt that

Figure 12

art therapy constitutes a medium to express her conflicts and identify these. It is hoped that this may serve as some measure of stabilizing therapy."

Through February Elda appeared to get more value out of the group sessions than the private ones. Her drawings were made in a desultory way, more a touching up of earlier ones than the tackling of new themes. Her most recent spider drawing (Figure 12) continued to interest her. The building at the bottom, she explained, was drawn to emphasize the scale of the spider, an idea no doubt derived from the horror comics and movies with which she had formerly saturated herself.

In a group session she revealed a second traumatic childhood experience. An Austrian print showing a flaxen-haired young girl in a field of flowers launched the group into reminiscences about being lost as children. This prompted Elda to recount—

> . . . a grim experience she had had as an eight-year-old. She threw a shoe at her brother; it missed him and went through the window. She ran out of the house and tried to sleep under a newspaper in the woods all night. She was picked up by the police the next morning and was walloped when she got home. Later she brought out her drawing of the spider for the group to see and discuss. She explained what she had

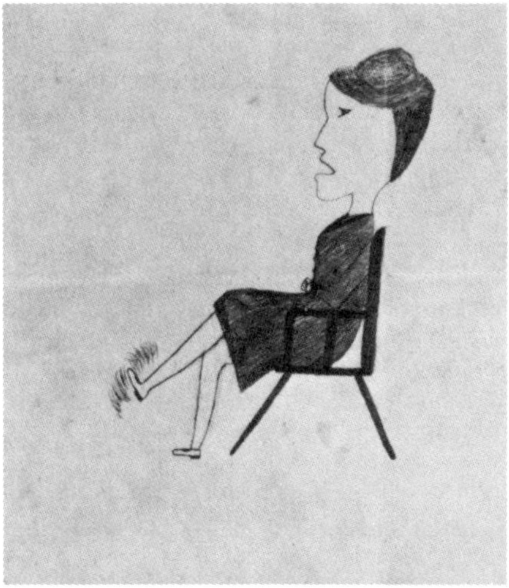

Figure 13

tried to do and went into the personalities behind the drawing, treating it seriously and expecting the group to do the same thing. They did respond. . . . It was suggested to her that next week the group might discuss the whole series of drawings that led up to this one.

[February 16] Elda chose paintings to show the group next Tuesday. We discovered the drawing she had torn up (preserved in an envelope) and pieced it together. Elda did little work this morning apart from this.

[February 21] Elda was quite agreeable to having her drawings pinned up. But soon after they were put up she took down the last one [pieced together] because it threatened her too much. I agreed because I did not want her anxiety to dominate a good group discussion. Elda commented quite freely on her drawings but was somewhat hostile when nobody asked the questions she felt should be asked.

Essentially, Elda was merely going over old ground in her comments—reinforcing it, perhaps—but not making any therapeutic advances.

Figure 13, a picture of E.M., absorbed two full sessions. On close observation it will be noted that the outline of the whole body was drawn first; clothing was added later. Note, too, the emphasis placed on the tossing foot, a mannerism that particularly irritated Elda. She insisted that E.M. was smiling, and claimed that she found it impossible to give the face the disagreeable expression she intended, a hint of ambivalence that recalls her reaction to the first of the two monster-with-girl drawings.

Concurrently, Elda's psychiatrist commented that "she shows her usual conflict in regard to her feelings and vacillates between her dependence and her sense of rejection and being exploited by her parents. . . . This patient has shown considerable improvement in the past few months."

Elda's mother had requested that her daughter be allowed to come home, and it was decided that she had progressed sufficiently for a trial visit. Elda herself had mixed feelings about this. She wondered "whether the 'nice' letter she got from her mother reflects a real change . . . or was only written at the suggestion of someone in the hospital."

I noted after a group session on March 20 that—

> Elda returned from her visit with little or no display of hostility (towards her family). She brought up incidents of her childhood, and W.M. made the point that it was necessary to be loved in childhood to be able to love later on. She agreed wholeheartedly. As far as she was concerned she had received *no* love as a child.

PART II

4. *The Staring Eye Series:* Through most of April 1956, Elda's attendance at group and private sessions was steady and productive. During the first week she undertook, for the first time, a drawing of her brother (not shown). She had great difficulty with this and was not able either to complete or to discuss it. Significantly, perhaps, she left out the face, the arms, and the upper legs. Since she had already successfully completed the drawing of E.M. (shown in Part 1, Figure 13) in the same sitting posture in which she tried to represent her brother, her difficulty could not have been due to lack of skill. Rather, the subject seems to have involved a level of anxiety that blocked off full execution.

At the month's end Elda's mother telephoned her long distance to announce that Elda had won a car in a raffle she had participated in while at home. Apparently a number of people, including her stepfather and brother, had shared in the cost of the ticket, and both of them were driving the car. The car appears to have provided a bridge of association with either or both since thereafter both the car itself and a detached tail fin of the exaggerated type then fashionable frequently appeared in her drawings.

During interviews Elda was never better. In mid-May, for example, "We discussed how disturbing change is and how we like to ignore it, even preferring a consistently bad person to an occasionally but unpredictably good one. We went on to consider Elda's own attitude towards change. She felt that on her last visit home her mother and stepfather had changed. 'Have *you* changed?' I asked."

An awareness that her changing attitudes towards others might reflect changes within herself emerged from this interview. My notes end with the observation that "in manner this was Elda's quietest—but also most intense interview. This woman is improving, undeniably."

Yet, with the very next drawing session my optimism collapsed.

> When Elda came in I asked her if she would prefer to talk or draw. She wanted to draw but was up a "blind alley" (my phrase, of which she approved—particularly the word *blind*). The eye in Figure 14 bothered her. I told her she could cover up the eye and proceed with other items inside the circle. She worked by herself for the next 20 minutes, adding the material concerning her brother (church, McGill, and man).

Because it served as a sort of therapeutic watershed, Figure 14 deserves special attention. It is instructive to compare the content of this picture with that of Figures 3, 4, 5, and 7 (see Part 1), in all four of which the stepfather-rattlesnake was prominent. In Figure 7 one might interpret its position in the neck of the bottle as the snake on the point of *escaping*. Its absence in Figure 14 might signify that the stepfather was no longer a problem. It may be recalled that the spider motif, originally associated with Elda's mother, became attached in Elda's mind to her stepfather. This motif, too, is absent from

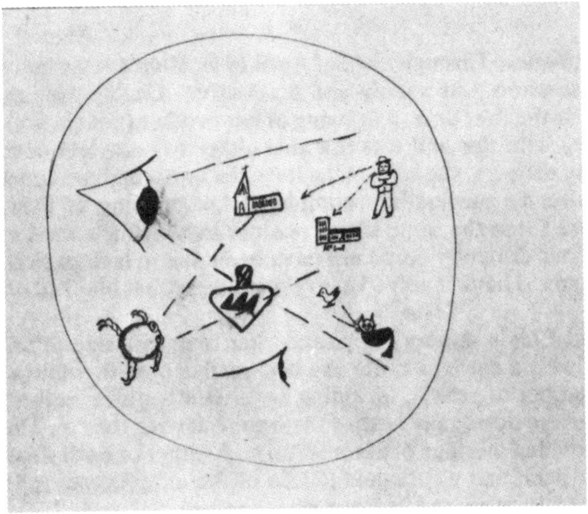

Figure 14

Figure 14. The spider appears only once more and in a very different perspective.

The crab motif, on the other hand, is prominent in Figure 14. (It disappeared in subsequent drawings.) It is of interest to note the striking difference in style of representation between the crab and all the other figures in the drawing—the sensitive lines and shadings, as contrasted with the hard-edged, stiff treatment of the other figures. On June 21 after a private session I noted:

> I spent some time showing Elda how her present and past crab drawings all contained something "cute," almost endearing. I suggested that this indicated a double standard in her thinking about her mother. This was particularly evident in the way Elda had drawn the crab's claws. Her reaction to this: "You're not supposed to see so much!"

Actually, Elda's interest had begun to shift away from the Monster motif. There followed a series of five drawings (not shown), each consisting of a group of figures enclosed within a circle, as in Figure 14. In the last three of these drawings all direct human associations disappeared. An automobile appears in two of them and may have been an unconscious reference to the brother who actually drove it. In four of the five, abstractions appear within a circle, increasingly dominant. In the third drawing a large sharp triangle is attached to the rim of the circle and is edged on one side with triangular teeth, which Elda began to obliterate by filling both the teeth and the spaces between with a linear texture. There could be no doubt that the trend was now seriously regressive. Elda's interest in the drawing sessions had visibly subsided, and in the group sessions her tirades against ward patients and staff flared up again. On June 26 after a group session I noted, "Elda came down in a great fury against someone on the ward, and the session was well on the way before she could express anything but hostility." And again on June 28 after a private session, "Elda not feeling very productive. She was cooperative, however, when I asked permission to show B. J. (a fellow patient) some of her early drawings."

Figure 15, an undated drawing made some time during June, appears to have been an attempt to integrate the Staring Eye and Monster themes. As if drawing away from direct confrontation with the spider-monster, Elda drew it in profile. Two other features of this drawing demand comment: the overall shading in black and grey and the placing of the eyes, in profile, one above the other, in the same relationship as the eye-like protrusions, one above the other, of the lights on the automobile tail fin at the bottom of Figure 14.

In all the drawings Elda had made since entering Westminster Hospital there were few hints of what was now to emerge, and at the point where it seemed that the door of art as a medium of meaningful self-expression had finally closed. Any hints became apparent only in retrospect. My notes of July 5 read:

> Elda brought down a *Look* article on Picasso, which we discussed. She settled in quickly without any prodding. Ten minutes later she was show-

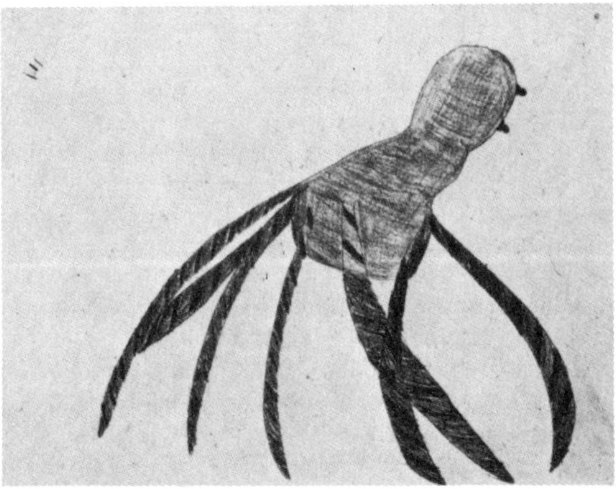

Figure 15

ing her drawing, "Guess Who?" (Figure 16). It was a self-portrait. Elda was happy as a king; this was the way she felt, she said. . . . She went back to the table to draw another figure and was singing, "All the nice girls love a sailor." This she has never done before; nor has she ever seemed so absorbed, let alone happy. She followed this up with a third caricature. . . . She swears she has never done anything of this kind before.

Picasso's art was not unfamiliar to Elda; prints of his paintings had frequently been used in the picture-centered group sessions. Yet her caricatures are her own and not direct imitations of Picasso. One has only to compare Figure 16 with any other illustrations in this paper to be struck with the extraordinary—and solitary—emergence of an impressive flare for carica-

Figure 16

Figure 17

ture. The drawings did not come out of nowhere. Each had a definite subject. The egg-shaped figure is a representation of her favorite female orderly. The self-portrait is uncannily like her as she appeared in her sulky moods. The third figure, which she labeled "The Innocent," may have been herself in a mischievous mood, but she never identified it one way or another.

No less curious than the sudden appearance of these clever caricatures, and despite considerable interest on the part of both patient and staff, was the rapidity with which Elda's interest in the drawing sessions faded thereafter.

Elda began to use small sheets of paper and oil pastels to make the sort of drawings that appear as Figures 17 and 18. These took only a minute or two to dash off, following which she would chatter inconsequentially with any one who happened to be around.

Any impulse to regard Figures 17 and 18 as a continuation of the caricaturing impulse cannot survive even the most cursory examination. In the baby face of Figure 17 the crease on top of the head (suggestive of Elda's lobotomy?) and the curlicue ear can only be described as schizoid. The crease in the center of the nose tip and the detached tongue (?), colored green against red lips in the original, also suggest disordered thought processes. The intended humor of Figure 18, "Just an Old Wood-Chewer," is obscure to say the least. The saw-toothed pattern that first appears in the broken bottle of Figures 8 and 9 (see Part 1) and that recurs in various minor contexts thereafter is now associated with the mouth of a monster. Although Figure 18 is perhaps the most powerful expression of Elda's anger, all control is gone. Reproduction in black and white fails to show that the "wood," painted red, is so ambiguously related to the mouth that some of the teeth, painted purple, come in front of and others behind the wood. For the last time the eye in

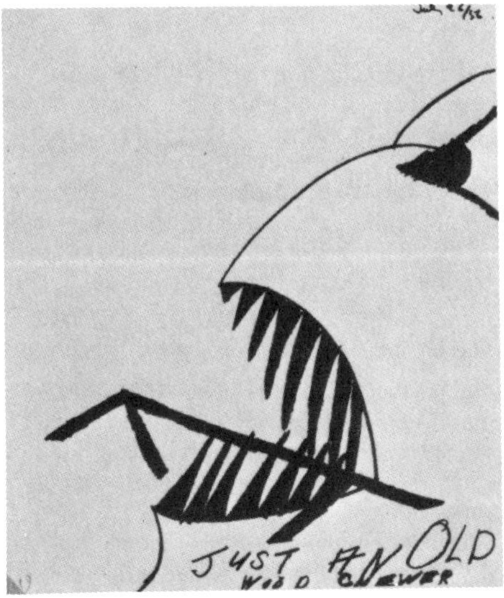

Figure 18

profile appears, but backwards, indicative of confused thinking at the least and surely symbolic of Elda's growing inability to look purposefully into herself and her problems.

By mid-September of 1956 it had become quite clear that Elda's interest in the art-oriented interview had come to an end.

> Elda drew a tree this morning which expressed very little of anything. I suggested to her that she had "graduated"—i.e., had got everything out of art therapy that she could. Whereas formerly she had come to the drawing sessions bursting with things to do, she is now drawing only to be cooperative. She will, however, continue the picture-centered group sessions. I made it clear to her that she was still making important contributions there. [September 20]

Such was indeed the case. In scanning my notes from August to the end of October I find such comments as "made one statement that was used extensively in the discussion," "looking very well—vivacious but sensible," "in a particularly receptive mood." In only two instances out of more than a dozen sessions did I note that she had been disruptive or confused. Even her occasional and brief negative outbursts were accepted as "playful hostility," or "happily hostile," their phatic quality being such that no one took them at face value.

> Apart from some "hostility" towards the psychologist (in the form of playful testing) at the beginning of the session, Elda was very subdued and related well to the discussion about childhood experiences. . . . She

showed some moderating of her feeling towards parental figures, particularly her stepfather. [October 2]

Elda's psychiatrist, too, felt that significant changes had taken place, especially in her attitude towards her mother. Now she was "very desirous of obtaining support and affection from her mother who, she feels, up until recently, tended to exploit her."

By the beginning of November the staff decided by concensus that although Elda was still too impulsive and erratic to be successfully employed, her negative symptoms had subsided to the point where she no longer needed hospital care. In mid-November she was discharged and went home.

Final Phase of Intensive Treatment: July 1957 to September 1958

Seven months elapsed between Elda's November discharge and her readmission in July 1957. During most of her home visit Elda coped adequately with a rather difficult family situation. In June, however, in an unseasonable trip to Florida with her mother, she experienced what she described as "sun-poisoning." Returning home, she voluntarily entered the provincial mental hospital where she was described in old, familiar terms: "very irritable and unpredictable," "prone to extreme tension," "very suspicious," "ideas of persecution," "creating disturbances on the ward." The whole panoply of psychosomatic symptoms was displayed again. (At this time Elda underwent her third operation for ingrown toenails.)

Over the last four months prior to her discharge, Elda's Promazine dosage had been tapered off from 150 mgm. to 75 mgm. daily. On readmission to Westminster Hospital the somatic symptoms persisted, and daily dosages of 150 mgm. of Dilantin (diphenylhydantorin) and 8 mgm. of Trilafon (perphenazene) were prescribed, the dosage remaining constant thereafter.

Meanwhile Elda's mother had developed severe circulatory problems and was scheduled for an amputation. The stepfather wanted Elda to come home for the operation, but she was reluctant. Her psychiatrist noted that "She feels all the old disagreements would arise as her mother is quite unreasonable, selfish, and domineering." Then came news of her mother's death on the operating table, only two weeks before Christmas. Elda was given home leave, but—stopping off en route to change trains—she took a heavy dose of barbiturate and found herself back at Westminster Hospital.

Although her observable reactions to her mother's death were minimal, the psychiatric notes early in 1958 enumerated the old, familiar symptoms: ". . . boisterous, euphoric, hyperactive . . . voluble . . . deliberately provocative . . . seeking attention and support . . . demanding and verbally aggressive toward female staff . . . rude, tactless, and uninhibited in her remarks . . . morose . . . hypochondriacal complaints . . . marked insecurity and dependence . . . capricious and erratic . . . ."

Elda did not resume art therapy until a month after her mother's death. Her preference for the art-centered group sessions over the private sessions now became pronounced. Even when she turned up for a private session she rarely drew, preferring to discuss her current concerns.

> This is the first sustained interview I have had with Elda since her return. . . . She spent the first month or more with her older brother . . . then was with her mother for the duration. As always she got along very well with her brother and his wife; with her parents it was another matter. Her mother irritated her with a number of petty mannerisms; her stepfather was as impossible as ever. . . . It was almost more than she could bear to be cooped up all day with her mother.
>
> Although her stepfather is living on pensions from three sources, Elda is convinced that he is still trying to exploit her. He is currently . . . trying to sell the house and all its contents, including Elda's furniture. . . . She is afraid he is pulling a fast one. [March 20, 1958]

In both the group and private sessions Elda continued to show a concern with areas she had been exploring before her discharge. Her strong feelings towards E.M., the fellow-patient she had drawn in Figure 13 (see Part 1), persisted. A further excerpt from my March 20 notes touch on the basis for Elda's aversion to E.M.

> What bothers her most is E. M. standing nearby staring at her. Elda asked me if I knew that sometimes men were attracted to men and women to women. Well, it was like that with E.M. E.M. was strongly attracted to her and it made Elda very uneasy. So she would tell E.M. not to be so damn stupid, and E.M. would tell her not to be so rude.

A week later Elda surprised me during our private session by saying she had something on her mind that she wanted to draw (Figure 19). In my notes of April 3 I made the following comment: "This drawing is of her mother on the day of the funeral. Elda's first difficulty was with the smile. She felt it inappropriate that her mother should look happy, yet described at some length how young and relaxed she looked."

The drawing, of course, was pure fantasy. Elda had not attended her mother's funeral. She had not seen her, in fact, since the previous summer. During this same interview she went into a detailed description of her mother's "growth" (arterial clot), the gangrene that had set in, and what she had learned about the operation itself. However, "my suggestion that she make a second drawing of her mother . . . was emphatically rejected. Thus, while she could describe verbally what her mother . . . had gone through, when it came to a visual rendering she could only deal with the subject at a wishful level"(hence the smile).

Elda appeared to see nothing peculiar about the construction of the coffin—the lid attached to the lower, closed half, instead of the open section. Nor did she remark on the falling pot of five flowers, which might be taken to symbolize the whole family (of five) doomed with the death of the mother.

Figure 19 was the last drawing Elda made in art therapy. She continued,

Figure 19

however, to attend the picture-centered group sessions. Notes from this period reflect a gradual recession of her more severe symptoms.

> Elda was hostile at first, but became friendly as time passed. She spoke of her worst dream: "An Egyptian mummy grabbed me and I was dead-—just like that." She said this dream had recurred frequently over the past 20 years. [May 6,1958]

A week later in the picture-centered group session a reproduction of Van Gogh's "Old Peasant" prompted a discussion about death.

> Elda made no attempt to evade the question either by the outbursts of hostility or the major digressions with which she usually defends herself against threatening topics. She simply answered that she would be very frightened.

By this time Elda was regularly employed in the hospital reception center, combining some clerical work with service at the counter, cleaning, etc. By summer she was reported to be "carrying on quite well." This, for a woman who had been repeatedly diagnosed as unemployable over a period of many years, was an impressive change. Comments by staff in subsequent weeks confirmed her improvement: "Elda was much milder and more affectionate," "Elda was very mild and pleasant," "more sociable and quiet than usual," "has continued to conduct herself in an exemplary fashion."

In a September group session she was described as "very friendly and excited about leaving the hospital." Even her hostility towards her stepfather was expressed in more moderate terms. E.M. had died early in the year, and Elda was openly relieved that this source of stress on her ward had been removed.

Period of Limited Recovery, September 1958 to the Present

Early in the fall of 1958 Elda was discharged and remained out of the hospital for nearly 4 years, by far the longest period she had been able to cope outside of the hospital since her first admission.

At first she went to live with her mother's surviving sister. Then, she apparently began to transfer to her aunt the same suspicions she had had about her mother: that she was taking too great an interest in Elda's money, a considerable sum having accrued from unused pension funds during her hospital sojourns. Sensibly enough, she left her aunt's home and moved to London, Ontario, where she boarded with a woman to whom the hospital frequently referred discharged patients.

At this stage she visited the art therapists' home and tried to manipulate them into endorsing an application for a visa to enter the United States, where she had relatives. To this end she misrepresented the facts, but not skillfully enough to get what she wanted.

Through most of 1961 she lived with her stepfather. When psychosomatic complaints recurred, she moved back to London, where she lived alone in an apartment but could keep in touch with the hospital and with fellow patients also discharged and living in the city. Soon she was complaining that her friends wouldn't leave her alone, and in June 1962 her paranoid and hypochondriacal symptoms prompted her to return to the hospital on a voluntary basis.

Over the succeeding weeks she attended three art-centered group sessions and one drawing session. In the group sessions she focused feelings of apprehension on her impending gall bladder operation. In the drawing session she wished to draw a staff member who irritated her, but gave up after a few unsuccessful sketches.

A mounting series of symptoms culminated in a temper tantrum in which she smashed the glass window of the ward door and severed a palmar tendon. A report just before this incident noted "an increased emotional reaction of a hysteroid type much resembling the state seen in her pre-leucotomy period . . . a highly dramatized hysterical acting out."

A successful operation restored the function of her tendon, but post-operative swelling of her hand and wrist persisted to the point where her surgeon reported that "There is nothing we can do from a surgical point of view; in fact, I doubt if physiotherapy can offer this girl much until her mental status has cleared."

Nevertheless, Elda was considered well enough to go to her aunt's for a week's trial visit. Immediately after her return the psychiatrist who had been the person most consistently interested and involved in her case for more than a decade died of lung cancer. Elda's reaction revealed how strong a capacity for affection had been retained over the years, for she "became very upset emotionally and behaved in a grossly hysterical manner. She wept frequently and very loudly for several days."

That fall the physical symptoms intensified. Her thinking, too, became confused. For example, she developed the delusion that she was about to inherit a handsome legacy, generous portions of which she declared would be conferred upon her favorite staff members. Elda soon abandoned this novel attention-getter when she found no one took her seriously. Through most of 1965 she exhibited the whole spectrum of her psychosomatic symptoms. After a formidable battery of physical tests—none of which produced positive results—Elda's status was changed from "voluntary" to "certified."

Although my wife and I had frequent friendly encounters with Elda in the hospital corridors, she made no move to attend art therapy until late that autumn, and then came only once to the group and once to a private session. My note on the latter occasion was brief, ending with the observation that "essentially she remains the same old Elda."

Over the next 2 years her symptoms subsided once more. The psychiatrist's evaluation changed from "no appreciable change" to "quiet, but impaired judgment." In mid-1968, under a change in provincial mental health regulations, her case was reviewed and her status altered to "informal" (i.e., voluntary) and "incompetent" (unemployable).

Elda was discharged but maintained regular contact with the hospital for medication. She took an apartment in the city, supported by her veteran's disability pension and the interest on accumulated funds. Since that time she has displayed no symptoms demanding further hospital treatment. Her record was marred only once when, apparently in a fit of absent-mindedness, she carried her purchases out of a store without paying for them. She was charged with theft until the hospital intervened and the charges were dropped.

As of this writing, Elda is in her fifth year since her last discharge and appears to have achieved sufficient stability to cope with the limited responsibilities of a pensioner.

Discussion

In reading the concluding sections of this paper, it may be easier to follow the discussion of earlier events by referring to the sequence presented in the Chronological Summary on pages 134-35.

Our information about Elda's life prior to her first hospitalization in 1946 remains sketchy. Although a few fleeting glimpses of her childhood emerged in art therapy and Elda's mother was interviewed by a social worker at the beginning of treatment, background information is too scanty to provide more than the bare outline presented in Part 1.

Nor do we have much information of any significance about Elda's feelings during the physical treatment stage (1947-54). There can be no doubt about Elda's desperate wish to end her life at this period; but we can only

CHRONOLOGICAL SUMMARY

(I) Period of Physical Treatment, 1947 through 1954

(A) Time spent in and out of hospital

In hospital throughout the period except for a brief home visit at the end of 1950; and at home after discharge, September 1953 (apparently because unresponsive to the treatment available) until readmitted early in 1954.

(B) Symptoms and major events

Severe self-destructive symptoms persisting throughout most of the period. Overdose of Seconal in 1950. Hypochondria and a wide range of psychosomatic symptoms become prominent 1950-53. After return from approximately 4 months at home, hypochondria and depression noted; these symptoms persist throughout 1954.

(C) Major features of treatment

Tube feeding, ECT, insulin coma, preceding prefrontal leucotomy (lobotomy) in February 1949. 1949-54: exhaustive examinations and tests, with treatment of a variety of minor physical

(II) Initial Phase of Intensive Treatment, January 1955 to November 1956

(A) Time spent in and out of hospital

In hospital throughout the period except for brief home visits. Discharged as improved but unemployable, November 1956.

(B) Symptoms and major events

Anxiety and insomnia, in addition to all former symptoms, noted at the start of this period. Towards its end, all symptoms gradually subside.

(C) Major features of treatment

Chemotherapy started January 1955 and continued throughout the period.

Art therapy, both art-oriented interviews (individual drawing sessions, see Figures 1-18) and picture-centered group (discussion) sessions started March 1955. Group sessions continue throughout the period. Individual sessions show increasing promise (high point in July 1956, see Figure 16) but taper off and end several weeks before discharge.

(III) Final Phase of Intensive Treatment, July 1957 to September 1958

(A) Time spent in and out of hospital

In hospital from readmission July 1957 (after 8 months at

home) except for abortive home visit at the time of mother's death, December 1957. Discharged September 1958 as improved.

(B) Symptoms and major events

Had performed adequately at home but returned with hypochondriacal and paranoid symptoms. July-December 1957: symptoms gradually subsided; mother's death precipitated brief flare-up. This is followed by marked improvement, leading to discharge 9 months later.

(C) Major features of treatment

Chemotherapy resumed on admission and continued throughout the period.

Art therapy resumed January 1958. Group discussion sessions take precedence over individual drawing sessions (see Figure 19) which taper off (last drawing April 19) and end several months before discharge. Attendance at picture-centered group sessions continues until discharge.

(IV) Period of Limited Recovery, September 1958 to Present

(A) Time spent in and out of hospital

Out of hospital from September 1958 until voluntary readmission June 1962. Remains in hospital until discharge in 1968 except for a one-week trial visit with aunt in 1964. From 1968 to present, out of hospital except for brief stay in 1970 after being charged with shoplifting.

(B) Symptoms and major events

September 1958 to June 1962: lives with aunt, then in London (Ontario) boarding house, then with stepfather (1961), then alone in apartment (London). Paranoid symptoms and hypochondria gradually increase, leading to return to hospital. 1962-64: hospital stay marked by hysterical acting out and reappearance of prelobotomy symptoms. Death of her psychiatrist soon after her 1964 visit to aunt leads to demonstrations of genuine grief. Gradual decrease of symptoms, 1965-68. 1968 to present: living alone in apartment in London, Ontario.

(C) Major features of treatment

Chemotherapy throughout hospital stay 1962-68.

Art therapy: brief attendance at both group and individual sessions (no drawings made) soon after admission (1962) and again late in 1965.

Surgery (removal of gall bladder) 1962; other minor surgery to repair self-injury, 1964.

speculate on what was going through her mind. Had she talked, for instance, to her former employer? Had he told her personally (as he had told her doctor) that he would rehire her as soon as she was out of the hospital? What we do know is that Elda was treated by every physical therapy then known, including the last desperate expedient of brain surgery.

The Role of Chemotherapy

The first substantial break in Elda's illness followed the introduction in 1955 of a psychotropic drug, Reserpine. Whether or not chemotherapy can be given credit for the changes that ensued in Elda, there can be no doubt about the general impact of the introduction of chemotherapy in the mid-fifties. The largely unpredictable outbreaks of physical violence that had typified "disturbed" wards subsided with magical speed. It is not surprising that high hopes of a total cure were entertained in those early years.

Gradually, however, it became clear that the role of chemotherapy was mainly social: that is, patients who formerly had been unable to tolerate group or person-to-person relationships—or were too unpredictable to be trusted with this kind of involvement—were now far more frequently accessible. This most certainly had an impact on the attitudes of staff towards psychotherapy as a form of treatment. Formerly, for example, at the very point in art therapy at which a patient began to confront himself at the drawing table with images of his underlying fears, the ward staff would complain that art therapy was "too upsetting." The referral would be suspended until the patient had "settled down." With the use of tranquilizers ward tensions relaxed, and staff apprehensions about sending patients to art therapy faded substantially.

A few years ago, prompted and supervised by a staff psychiatrist, we launched an ambitious study aimed at comparing the art of patients on a course of a given drug with that of a matched group taking a placebo. What seemed to be a straightforward—even simple—research plan turned out to be so complex that the project was drowned in a sea of variables and proved to be merely an exercise in frustration. Yet we are firmly convinced that chemotherapy and art therapy together offer far more promise of therapeutic progress than either alone.

The Role of Art Therapy

It should be noted here that during the intensive treatment stage art therapy was the only form of psychotherapy to which Elda had access. It must be emphasized, however, that the psychiatrist then in charge of Elda's case took a strong personal interest in her, and although he undertook no formal psychotherapy with her, his interest was a positive therapeutic factor.

The change from a purely pragmatic sequence of physical therapies to a broader and more personally directed program was reflected in Elda's therapeutic progress. Her work in art therapy added a special dimension to her treatment and pointed clearly to the storm center of her dilemma. The early drawings, Figures 1 through 13, appear in Part 1. Figures 3, 4, and 5 define the major foci of her anxiety: mother and stepfather as monsters contrasting with the "real" father, whose love (the heart, see Figure 7) lies remote and buried (the cross). Although the loving father has died, the wish for one is still alive, as indicated by the scribbled lines of communication in Figures 3 and 5 that are converted into a shaft of lightning in Figure 4.

By the time Elda made Figure 7, the circular figure, previously surrounded by menacing symbols, has been converted into a bottle that *contains* them. Only the buried, loving father remains outside bearing the label (too small to read in the reproduction) "Happiness for Ever and Ever."

Thereafter, the love theme disappears, to reappear only once and then ambiguously. Discussing the baby in Figure 10, Elda identified it as herself. She was staring at her stepfather in "horror," she said, although he was not drawn. When I urged her to add him to the drawing as a human being rather than as a monster, she drew in the back of a man's head in the same position on the paper (the lower right corner) as that in which the symbol of the loved father had been placed in the Monster series. Elda was unable to resolve the ambiguity of this head; one may speculate that she was unconsciously merging the two subjects into a single "love-hate" relationship with her stepfather.

Elda's struggle to sort out impulses of affection that she seemed only half aware of from the anger she so obviously needed to express was likewise exemplified in the confusion associated with her attempts to symbolize her feelings about her mother and stepfather. We have already noted the ambivalence, in the form of "cuteness," that appeared in her crab-spider forms, which were renderings of feelings about her mother. Just as it seemed she was getting close to recognizing this incongruity, the spider image became associated with her stepfather.

A Freudian analyst would undoubtedly point to the evidence in Elda's drawings of a deeper problem, frequently expressed graphically but never spoken of: her anxiety about the whole sexual area. Even my skepticism about the validity of diagnostic conclusions based on the evidence of a drawing in the absence of the patient's reaction to it must yield to the unmistakable symbolism of the central drawing in Figure 5. Here the simple circle of previous drawings is elaborated into an almost blatant vaginal motif (appropriately *red* in the original), and the theme is reinforced—even though it hardly needs to be—by the penetrating black arrow (corresponding to the hammer of Figure 3).

One need not seek far for other evidence of Elda's sexual concern. In Figure 7 we see the highly suggestive placing of a rattlesnake in the neck of a bottle. In Figure 12 the female victim is being visibly raped. It is significant, in my opinion, that the vagina-cum-penis theme emerges with new strength in Figures 17 and 18. In the former the detached green tongue (or banana?) placed between red lips inescapably conjures up sexual associations. Figure 18, with its profile view of the monster's mouth and the ambiguously placed stick, is perhaps the most powerful expression of sexual anxiety that Elda was able to achieve. Even in her final drawing (Figure 19) the displaced coffin lid is ready to clamp over her mother's (and by inference Elda's) already covered lower parts should the slightest threat of insight emerge. Any skepticism one might feel about Elda's identity with her mother smiling in death must yield to the strength of Elda's own death wish during the early period of her illness, as well as to evidence provided by her only self-portrait beyond babyhood (Figure 10) where Elda found another excuse to hide the lower part of the body. There was also her abortive effort at drawing her brother, referred to on page 123.

Therapeutic Perspectives

Elda's illness, observed and treated at various times in the course of two-and-a-half decades, had many aspects, not all of which can be dealt with here. Even her art therapy—whether or not it contributed to her partial recovery—offers no more than an inconclusive perspective on her whole history.

The limited record of Elda's background at least establishes that she was unable to satisfy her affectional needs and hints at an emerging autism. It would appear, however, that her talent as a babysitter, then as a children's aide in a doctor's family, arrested what might otherwise have developed into a full-blown psychosis. It is clear that she functioned adequately—indeed exceptionally well—since her employer was still eager to take her back even after her nearly 5 years of absence overseas and in the face of an already severe illness. One wonders why Elda enlisted in the army, exchanging a seemingly secure milieu where she was wanted and functioned well for an unknown future in a military setting in which there was clearly no scope for her proven talent with children. The records tell us nothing. We can, however, scarcely doubt that as a children's aide she must have found and given affection at a depth she had never experienced as a child and would never find again.

Inevitably, the symptoms that first emerged in her army life would be exacerbated and would multiply in a mental hospital at a time when more rigid standards of ward routine and discipline prevailed than are now in vogue. At that time the majority of psychiatrists had no training and little interest in any therapeutic horizons beyond the physical alternatives. Each desperate effort that Elda made to impress the staff with her emotional needs was met with a negative—frequently punitive—response: electric shock, forced feeding, and finally a lobotomy. Gradually, Elda learned the futility of direct rebellion and—consciously or not—developed the psychosomatic symptoms that were to bloom and proliferate as she learned that here was the means of commanding the serious personal attention she craved.

It was logical, therefore, that during the intensive treatment phase, relieved of her more desperate impulses by the moderating effects of the psychotropic drugs and receiving personal, empathetic attention from her psychiatrist and art therapists, Elda's more severe symptoms should subside. Why, then, the final therapeutic impasse? Perhaps—and most probably—her childhood deprivation of parental love left Elda permanently impaired. Had she never learned—or learned (as a child-care worker) too little and too late—to earn and accept affection?

One way of accounting for Elda's venture into the military life is to assume that her emotional needs had been satisfied to the point where she felt ready to explore the larger world. It seems likely, too, that she was beginning to experience an attraction to the opposite sex and was lured into the army, as were many other women, by the fantasy of being surrounded by male admirers. In any case, she made two attempts to commit suicide while overseas, and was never again successfully employed in civilian life.

During the physical treatment phase of her hospital life Elda's affectional needs, if recognized at all, found no therapeutic response. By contrast, she did respond to intensive treatment that gave her a more personal kind of attention and offered—through art therapy—a channel of communication and a means of self-exploration.

Elda's drawings unequivocally point to a deep anxiety about her sexual inadequacy, and she was never able to identify this anxiety. As long as she could cite, and graphically express, her negative feelings about mother, stepfather, or E.M., the main issue could be evaded. Only after these had been dealt with, one by one, did it become necessary for Elda to make a major therapeutic decision. There were four broad alternatives.

The first and most promising alternative appeared only once in the extraordinarily clever caricatures that captured and extended into an integrated expression Elda's capacity for "playful hostility"—her most frequent and successful mode of bringing herself into relationship with persons she liked. A second choice was to retreat into thought disorder and delusion, a course that she followed briefly for a few weeks. (This course is graphically expressed in Figures 17 and 18.) The third possibility was to face her deepest fears through graphic imagery. Here her partial success seems to account for her choice of the fourth option: to cease exposing herself, first to the more demanding private sessions and then to the picture-centered group sessions.

After Elda's return to the hospital following nearly 4 years of coping within limits in the outside world, it seemed that any therapeutic advances she had made during the intensive treatment phase were lost. Presumably, too, her capacity for affection had atrophied. Yet this was a voluntary readmission. What brought her back? Probably it was her strong attachment—evidenced by the depth and duration of her grief at his death—to the psychiatrist who had for so long and so consistently shown an interest in her case. Few who witnessed her mourning could doubt its authenticity. To shrug it off as merely another attention-getting device is to forget that when her mother's death gave her the perfect excuse for such a display of grief there was only a mild reaction. Furthermore, although her extreme symptoms, culminating in the glass-smashing tantrum, occurred some months before her doctor's death, it was common knowledge throughout the hospital that he was suffering from a terminal illness. Soon after his death, Elda made her only self-critical comment on record, asking the unanswerable question, "Why was such a useless person as myself allowed to live and Dr. A. had to die?"

Over the next 4 years, although Elda's hypochondria continued, the grosser symptoms subsided to the point where she was able to carry on with part-time employment in the visitors' lodge until her final discharge.

Conclusion

Elda's history illustrates the complex influences to which a long-term patient is exposed: the changes in hospital personnel, administrative attitudes, and treatment techniques; the shifting patterns of family contacts and concern; and the repercussions of the patient's own varying symptoms in response to changing stresses. Yet, even in the face of many immeasurable factors, I dare to make five concluding assertions with firm conviction:

1. With the inception of chemotherapy Elda received more attention of a positive sort than she had experienced at any earlier phase of her illness.
2. Chemotherapy was a major factor in relieving Elda of her most antisocial impulses to the point where she was able to seek help through art therapy.
3. Through participation in the art-oriented private sessions and picture-centered groups Elda arrived at insights into aspects of her feelings and actions of which she had formerly been unaware.
4. During the period of intensive treatment there was a marked subsidence of her grosser symptoms.
5. Whatever form of treatment, or combination of therapies, was responsible, she stayed out of the hospital for nearly 4 years following this intensive phase.

In my opinion, Elda's severe regression after readmission at the end of her longest discharge was triggered, if not caused, by her psychiatrist's illness and death. And I suspect that without his steady support over the years neither her exposure to art therapy nor the modifications of behavior produced by chemotherapy would fully account for the progress Elda did make.

At the same time, I believe that art therapy gave Elda a unique means of self-exploration and of forming social relations with staff and patients that made it possible for her to survive the trauma of her doctor's death. Moreover, it laid the foundation for her present ability to cope with life outside of the hospital within the limits imposed on this ability by an emotionally deprived childhood.

A Marital Crisis Precipitated by Art Therapy

HARRIET T. VOEGELI, MIRIAM GOLDBERG, and IRVING SCHNEIDER

Art therapy is still in the position of having to demonstrate its effectiveness in producing changes in behavior rather than merely documenting them. This paper deals with a married couple whose lives were seriously affected by art therapy, with results which were unfortunate and might have been disastrous. A marital equilibrium which had persisted unchanged through three years of psychotherapy was dramatically altered within a few short weeks of art therapy. In addition to indicating the effectiveness of such therapy in altering behavior, their case should serve as a cautionary tale for those in clinical practice who are eager to experiment with family therapy and family art therapy. It may also shed some light on the question of who should and who should not be referred to art therapy.

Mr. and Mrs. Baker came to a community mental hygiene clinic because of difficulties with one of their five children. Mrs. Baker is 34 years old. Her appearance is bedraggled and forlorn: one eye is crossed, her hair is unkempt, she seldom wears any makeup and usually appears in a soiled, sack-like dress. One of the clinic staff members described her as "a walking state hospital." Her strikingly drab appearance is out of keeping with her background and position in life. After a lonely and isolated childhood, she went to a local college to study biology, but after two years decided to become a nun. At the end of her first year in a convent she was asked to leave, and a few years later she married Mr. Baker. Her one sister is a nightclub entertainer.

Mr. Baker, 36 years old, is a pleasant-looking, owl-faced man who speaks in a controlled, over-intellectual manner. He has held jobs as an editorial assistant on several important publications. After an itinerant childhood, he went to a Catholic seminary where he remained for five years but was told to leave before he had completed his training. He then began work toward a Master's degree in English literature but again was dismissed before finishing. He describes some of his many siblings as near geniuses who have never realized themselves, blaming their undistinguished performance on his mother's interference in their lives.

The Bakers' marriage has been troubled from the start. When they first came to the clinic three years ago Mr. Baker complained that his wife was given to emotional outbursts, and she complained that he was a procrastinator who failed to complete household tasks and was unwilling to discipline the children.

Treatment History

The Bakers attended weekly psychotherapy sessions with the same therapist, who saw each of them separately, for a period of three years. Mrs. Baker was consistently hopeless and helpless, seeing herself as the cause of the family's difficulties. Nevertheless she was perpetually angry at her husband.

Mr. Baker shared his wife's belief that he had no serious emotional difficulties. His main hope from therapy was to see some improvement in his wife. He undertook literary projects such as poetry and children's stories; though none was ever completed, he dreamed of having them published. He blamed his inability to realize himself as a writer on his having to divert his energies to cope with Mrs. Baker's tantrums.

The psychotherapist found it difficult to help this couple sustain even a marginal adjustment. Neither was able to accept responsibility for contributing to the other's difficulties. They seemed to maintain a tacit agreement that Mr. Baker was well, Mrs. Baker sick; that Mr. Baker was a highly intelligent and literate person, Mrs. Baker a drab and inadequate housewife.

Art therapy was recently added to the services of the clinic. The psychotherapist was finding her work with the Bakers tedious and unrewarding, and proposed art therapy to them in hopes that it would yield fresh material for their sessions with her. Mrs. Baker accepted the idea with a mixture of apprehension and hope. Mr. Baker said he could not attend because he was teaching a writing course on the same night as the art therapy sessions.

At her first art therapy session, Mrs. Baker produced a landscape which showed some sense of depth and color, asking for advice from the art therapist and readily using it. She criticized her picture for being "all split up," and added some elements which did in fact unify the composition. Saying that she had never "done faces," she copied a photograph of a smiling peasant woman. The result was like a grimacing death-mask, but it showed that her perception of the visual world was not very distorted, perhaps even excessively

Figure 1

literal. At the end of the session she expressed pleasure in "getting something down on paper" and said that drawing made her feel better. She repeated this appraisal in her next regular therapy hour.

In her second art therapy session, Mrs. Baker's first picture took her through a gamut of strong feelings. The picture began as a sunset scene with a tree, which she said (very sweetly) reminded her of the view from her back steps. She added a rose bed, then a statue, as though it were an idyllic back yard. Then she introduced a tire-swing, and started violently sketching in overturned bikes, complaining about how her husband never helped "pick up" the back yard. The last and climactic item was a rusty mattress spring; she ended with an angry slash of chalk across the paper. "I guess you just can't have a nice back yard when you have children . . . I know I shouldn't feel that way."

Seeming somewhat relieved, she started another picture, the skyline of Miami Beach at night as seen from a causeway (Figure 1). It was on this causeway that her husband had introduced her to the poetry of Yeats. She talked of their romantic courtship in Miami, and seemed very grateful to have a poetry-reading husband. She was delighted with this bright, warm picture, and the art therapist was delighted too. Mrs. Baker took the picture home to show to her husband.

During the following week Mr. Baker told his therapist that he had quit his Tuesday night teaching job and would like to come to art therapy with his wife. The therapist told him she would check with the art therapist and let him know, but Mr. Baker did not wait for the reply and showed up at the art therapy session the following Tuesday evening.

The First Joint Session

From the moment Mr. Baker entered the room, he directed a steady barrage of flattery and engaging commentary at the art therapist. Invited to choose among the materials available, he selected a Japanese water-color brush. Mrs. Baker followed suit, chose a similar brush and began a graceful oriental scene. While Mrs. Baker worked steadily and seriously on her picture, Mr. Baker turned out seven paintings and quite a few thousand words. Some of his pictures were caricatures, others were probably familiar doodles from adolescence, and others were like illustrated puns. He gave much emphasis to titles, and calling himself a "word smith" began a bizarre page of "symbolic calligraphy," a "system" he had been working on for some time (Figure 2). Another picture was an interpretation of a poem by Yeats which "no critic had ever dared to interpret." Much of this frenetic activity seemed to be directed at drawing the art therapist's attention away from his wife, in the style of one two-year-old competing with another. His attempt was somewhat successful.

The pictures he painted that evening look like the work of a schizophrenic, but somehow they convey the flavor of someone playing at being mad, trying to delineate his madness in a self-consciously intellectual style. In the original diagnostic report three years previously, the psychiatrist had written:

Figure 2

"One of Mr. Baker's central problems apparently is that of determining whether he is a rather misunderstood genius or a screwball, and I suspect that he vacillates between the two beliefs. He uses his intellect to control and eliminate impulses or feelings and to avoid facing up to his life situation."

Mr. Baker was patronizing to his wife: "Remember that Yeats poem I taught you, dear?" Mrs. Baker responded as if pleased that her husband would share with her the fruits of western civilization. Though suspicious of the art therapist, Mr. Baker appeared anxious for her good opinion, and his general attitude toward her was seductive.

During the following week the psychotherapist reported that Mr. Baker denied that he found the art session threatening, while Mrs. Baker acknowledged feelings of jealousy for the first time.

The Second Joint Session

The next art therapy session was a more intense version of the first one. The art therapist made an attempt to dilute the competition between husband and wife by suggesting that Mr. Baker work in clay, but Mrs. Baker then also decided to use clay. She worked carefully to model a child's hand, while Mr. Baker made a number of flippant productions: for example, a perfect clay cube which he titled "Statue of a Gold Brick at Fort Knox." The art therapist was trying very hard not to get sucked up into Mr. Baker's cyclone, and as he began to realize that his attempts to monopolize her attention were not as successful as before, his punning grew more unrelenting and corny. He was even more of a buffoon than before, making and destroying several caricatures of animals, pretending to be a magician or prestidigitator as he made them disappear. Irritated by his frivolity, the art therapist suggested that he would get more satisfaction from finishing one of his promising starts than from making her laugh.

Mrs. Baker mumbled that it was a relief to see someone besides herself get annoyed with him.

On the way home from the session, Mrs. Baker chided Mr. Baker for not being serious about art and not finishing anything, and Mr. Baker replied that she was always ruining everything, saying she didn't understand that he was just "getting the feel of the materials." In her next regular therapy hour Mrs. Baker, as usual, expressed great anger at her husband. She said that the clinic and especially art therapy had brought home to her with new force that her husband's procrastination really amounted to incompetence—he was incapable of finishing *anything*. Then she went back to her old theme, that she herself was worthless, always "ruining everything." She concluded that since neither of them could meet the other's needs, neither was any good, the family would be better off without her and there was nothing left to do but end it all. But Mrs. Baker had been saying that to her therapist for years.

Mr. Baker told his therapist that he was upset by his second art therapy

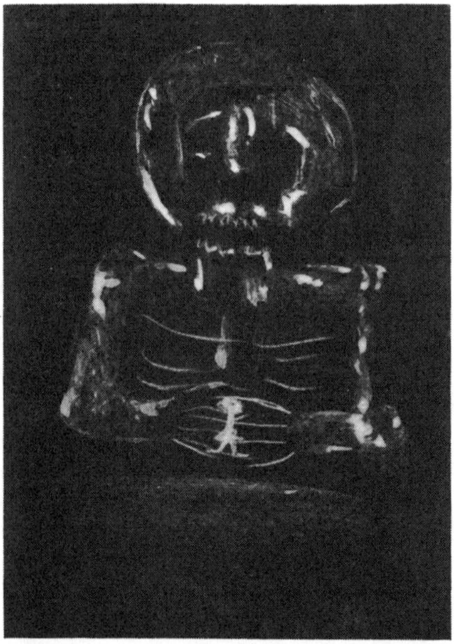

Figure 3

session, and she surmised that the art therapist must have "tweaked his nose a bit."

Six days later Mr. Baker called his therapist to say that they would not attend the art therapy session that night. Mrs. Baker had tried to kill herself by taking an overdose of Seconal tablets and he had already completed arrangements to send her to a mental hospital on the following morning. He said he could not trust her to take care of the family when she was so unstable, and the best thing to do was to get her out of the house and into professional hands so that he wouldn't have to worry about a repeat performance. The suicide gesture had been made late in the day; he had arrived home to find Mrs. Baker groggy from the pills, and had called a doctor who advised lots of strong coffee. The overdose was not reported by the physician, and Mr. Baker's decision to send his wife to the hospital was made without consulting the physician or the clinic.

At the last minute the Bakers decided to come to art therapy anyway. Mr. Baker thought his wife should have a "pleasant evening out" on the eve of going to the hospital.

The Third Joint Session

The mood of this session was a dramatic reversal of the previous two. Mr. Baker was more guarded, less given to displays, and worked more seriously on his pictures. Mrs. Baker was shaky and close to tears. She began with a vague and childish picture of a white skeleton on black paper (Figure 3). Through this rather overstated picture of her depression, she seemed to be testing to see whether the art therapist knew of the suicide gesture and the impending hospitalization. The therapist responded to the picture by saying that she understood it had been a very bad week. Mrs. Baker began to talk freely about going to the hospital.

Meanwhile Mr. Baker had this time followed his wife's lead by also selecting black paper. He did not show any depression but seemed to be caught up in pleasant childhood memories. He drew a turbaned Sikh (from Kipling) which he titled "Rilly Singh." The last of his four paintings was a reasonably serious effort to fill the page with pleasing forms (Figure 4). It still had a rather calligraphic flavor, but it was the least literary and calculated of his efforts. The art therapist praised the picture and Mrs. Baker said very admiringly that it looked "like music."

Then Mrs. Baker painted a big, beautiful but stereotyped rose, and printed under it a sentimental religious poem about God turning a rose into gold. The poem could not have been further beneath the level of Mr. Baker's literary pretensions, but he praised it in a rather condescending way. The evening ended with some amiable chitchat about art in general. The pleasant atmosphere, so wildly inappropriate in view of what was happening to the Bakers, seemed grotesque.

Figure 4

The next morning Mrs. Baker quietly drove off with Mr. Baker to the hospital where she remained for four weeks and received 17 electric shock treatments.

After three years of almost static treatment, the psychotherapist and the art therapist were taken by surprise. It was a painful experience for them and for other members of the clinic staff who shared in the knowledge of these events.

Discussion

How had the Bakers maintained this state of pathological balance for so long, and why had these three weeks been so eventful and potentially destructive?

For three years there had been an unhappy equilibrium between Mrs. Baker as the helpless, unstable female and Mr. Baker as the articulate, long-suffering male. This is the kind of pairing that has been variously described as the "sado-masochistic," the "obsessional-hysterical," or "analytical-emotional" married relationship. The sado-obsessional-analytical partner, usually the husband, functions best in situations calling for logic and syntax. In the verbal therapies his defenses are likely to be more effective than his wife's, his problems harder to get to, and for a long time he may appear to be the better put together of the two despite equivalent or greater pathology. Art therapy can enable the less articulate partner to reveal her underlying strength and organization and thus shift the balance between the two.

Mrs. Baker's two sessions without her husband had revealed some artistic facility, and success had slipped up on her unawares. It was probably her first independent venture in a long time. It is likely that Mr. Baker found her scene of Miami Beach disquieting when she brought it home, and he may have quit his teaching job to come to the art sessions and see what he could do about this uncomfortable situation. (Both of them now say that Mr. Baker quit his Tuesday night teaching job at Mrs. Baker's request.)

In the first joint session, Mrs. Baker appears adequate and talented, Mr. Baker childish and immature, if not downright crazy. Figures 1 and 2 illustrate how their art productions contradicted the basic terms of their relationship. Mrs. Baker is far more comfortable than Mr. Baker in this non-verbal performance. For once his highly developed ability to use words in the service of his strong need to control was of no avail. He told his therapist that he felt very inadequate in art, that writing was really his forte. He probably found the difficulty of exercising habitual controls in art more frightening than do many other kinds of patients.

Comparing this pair of pictures with Figures 3 and 4 we can see the restoration of the original relationship. Mrs. Baker's effort is childish, immature, suggests instability. Mr. Baker's picture is by comparison sophisticated and pleasing.

Figure 5

It seems that the breaking point must have come during and after the second joint session. We can look at Mrs. Baker's every act from that point (the return to lavish self-castigation, the suicide attempt, the willingness to let her husband punish her by putting her in the hospital) as attempts to restore the relationship to its original state.

In retrospect, a picture (Figure 5) made by Mr. Baker during the first joint session when he was so talkative and anxious provides a key to the situation. The art therapist suggested that he project pictorial ideas into a scribble. Though he accused her of trying "to Rorschach" him, he went ahead to make a scribble, and saw in it a theatrical mask with the tying-strings unfurled. As he finished the picture, he put a female face on the mask, making the face behind the loosening mask a male. Nothing could have been a better statement of what was happening to him at that moment. Mr. Baker had been hiding behind the mask of Mrs. Baker's illness for a number of years, and her relative adequacy in painting was threatening to expose him, at the same time that the art therapist was prying at his mask by encouraging him to draw freely.

Mrs. Baker found the exposure unbearable too, because it contradicted the only body of experience she understood. Rather than face her husband's illness, face her anger at him and herself for her self-deprecating way of life, she chose restitution of the uneasy truce by making a suicidal gesture and by allowing her husband to hospitalize her without questioning his decision.

While it is not likely that in other cases art therapy would have such extreme and unfortunate results, in this particular kind of relationship it can be an especially powerful tool. For the Bakers, without adequate therapeutic preparation, the experience of art therapy became too disruptive too suddenly. With the advantage of hindsight we see that it would have been far better to encourage Mrs. Baker to develop her artistic potential in private, to continue avoiding any insight-directed interpretations until she became accustomed to the pleasure she found in painting. If Mr. Baker should have been referred to art therapy at all, he should have been assigned another hour when he would not have had to face the anxiety of a competitive struggle with his wife.

Correlation Between Clinical Course and Pictorial Expression of a Schizophrenic Patient

ERIKA LEHNSEN

This paper deals with observation of a schizophrenic patient over a period of seven months in psychiatric sessions and in art therapy.

The setting is a ward in the psychiatric division of an urban general hospital. It has 25 beds and a total capacity of 35 patients, including those who are in a partial hospitalization program.

All patients are seen in individual sessions by a psychiatrist and receive group treatment four times a week. For the latter, each of two groups or teams of patients meets with a psychiatrist and two other staff members from various disciplines. Others concerned with treatment, including the art therapist, observe group meetings. Afterward, these staff members join in exchanging observations and information which necessarily reflect the discipline in which each staff member works. They jointly make decisions about changes in treatment plans.

The art therapist draws from the entire patient population for art groups of 10 to 15 patients three times a week. On this small unit, occupational therapy shares the shop with art therapy, the former suspending its activities during art sessions. There is limited time available for the art therapist to see patients in individual sessions.

From this sharing of information and exchange of views among the staff, there may emerge close collaboration between two disciplines. In this instance such a relationship between psychiatry and art therapy gives the structure for this paper. The art therapist, representing the younger discipline, stated her wish to give her findings before listening to the psychiatrist's report and he agreed to this sequence. Frequency of exchange between the two varied according to the time available and urgency for the sake of treatment. Sometimes conferences were held twice a week, occasionally at intervals of two weeks. Combined findings were reported periodically to the team staff and later a complete report was presented to the entire psychiatric department.

The psychiatrist's and the art therapist's reports will be presented in this paper alternately, more or less as they evolved during the months of treatment.

Theoretical Considerations

Two kinds of communication from the patient become available: words and visual imagery. It will become apparent that these two forms of expression are very intimately related. The temporal relationship of the two kinds of imagery varies. The visual image frequently precedes the verbal one (reasons for this sequence at a given time will be discussed below). However, as we shall see, some pictorial features are repeated over and over again, almost like an antidotal measure, still used when acute danger has passed and is no longer talked about.

Freud, whose genius led him to the use of words in his treatment method, nevertheless was aware of the propensity of some people to think in pictures.

> We must not be led . . . into forgetting the importance of optical memory residues—those of things (as opposed to words)—or to deny that it is possible for thought processes to become conscious through a reversion to visual residues, and that in many people this seems to be a favorite method. The study of dreams and preconscious fantasies . . . gives us an idea of the special character of visual thinking. We learn that what becomes conscious is as a rule only the concrete subject matter of the thought, and that the relations between these various elements of this subject matter, which is what specially characterizes thought, cannot be given visual expression. Thinking in pictures is, therefore, only a very incomplete form of becoming conscious. In some way, too, it approximates more closely to unconscious processes than does thinking in words, and it is unquestionably older than the latter, both ontogenetically and phylogenetically.[1]

Freud's statement points towards the position of art therapy in this case. John paints concrete subject matter that stands for his hopes, wishes, and fears. Most choices of objects to paint are made unwittingly. When I asked about the meaning, he stayed with the identification of the concrete subject matter ("This is a god, that is a rainbow," and so on). The connecting thoughts were left out. My first responsibility was to receive those images respectfully and safeguard them.

John brings up a series of pictures like those produced by a dreamer thinking in visual images. His pictures give us a narration of a rare conti-

---

[1] Sigmund Freud, *The Ego and the Id*. London, The Hogarth Press, 1927.

nuity. But single images at first glance are baffling. Most of them become understandable only in the wider context. This again they share with dream imagery.[2] We shall be able to observe in the content of the following picture series many parallels with dreams and dream-work, especially condensation and displacement, as described by Freud.[3] Perhaps a considerable part of the painted imagery has a psychic origin similar to that of dreams.

In his chapter on "The Psychology of Dreams," Freud speaks of the probability that we meet in dreams with the transformation of thoughts into visual images. He is here considering thoughts that have been severed from consciousness and are struggling for expression. The image, then, may result from the visually represented memory striving for resuscitation.[4] In other words Freud assumes in dream pictures a regression to the visual image, which then presses towards consciousness again.

Freud deals here with the mutual relationship and interdependency of the repressed thought that cannot be verbalized and the visual image in dreams. We shall meet in our twofold case presentation with a very similar process. The exchange between repressed thought and visual image is demonstrated when a picture is brought up in art therapy and followed by the corresponding thought in the psychiatric session.

Freud gives ample dream material demonstrating this give-and-take, relating dream elements to the personal everyday experience of the dreamer, which he uses as a lead to reach earlier, unassimilated psychic experiences. He briefly hints at phylogenetic contents in dreams when he refers to Nietzsche's assertion that in dreams "some primeval relic of humanity is at work which we can now scarcely reach any longer by a direct path."[5] Jung focused on this primordial part of humanity, manifest in myth and folklore, in developing his archetypal system, one of the cornerstones of his school of thought. After Jung, Erich Neumann equated the growth of ego-consciousness in the individual with the evolution of consciousness in mankind. "The individual has in his own life to follow the road that humanity has trod before him."[6]

We shall meet frequently in John's imagery with regression to earlier, less differentiated forms of consciousness as an attempt to reach solutions. Hartmann tells us that we find also in the healthy organism regressive moves

---

[2] A publication not available in major libraries when this paper was written may contain similar ideas ("Dreams and Art," by Laurine Collins, *The Forum of Mental Health Science,* Hahnemann Medical College and Hospital (Philadelphia), Vol. 1, No. 1, 1971).

[3] Sigmund Freud, *The Interpretation of Dreams.* London, The Hogarth Press, Standard Edition, Vols. IV and V, 1953.

[4] *Ibid., Vol V,* 1953.

[5] *Ibid.*

[6] Erich Neumann, *The Origins and History of Consciousness.* Bollingen Series XLII, Princeton University Press, 1954.

in the service of successful adaptation.[7] John's imagery, seen as such a move, was received, respected, and when possible reinforced.

I tried to create in the art therapy session a place where the patient would feel free to depict visual images that occurred to him, fragmentary or poignant as they might be. I was satisfied with the verbal description of the concrete subject matter that he gave me readily and I did not ask for connecting thoughts. I refrained from verbal interference in order to keep the way open for more pictorial images.

Also, I knew there was a psychiatrist who would take care of the connecting thoughts sooner or later, and I told him my own evolving interpretative ideas. In turn, in my groping ahead for the understanding of John's imagery, I was greatly assisted by the psychiatrist's reports.

I had a double trust: in the organizing function of the visual images themselves on the way to awareness and in the psychiatrist who would use this material in due time for the patient's good.

The Patient's History

The psychiatrist summarizes background information as follows:

John, 22 years old, was admitted to the psychiatric inpatient service because of mutism and withdrawn behavior. Throughout his life he had sporadically become withdrawn at times of object loss or separation—for example at the death of a beloved aunt or on first going to school. But those earlier episodes had been short-lived and self-limited.

Most of the time he behaved in exactly the opposite manner. He was the family clown and court jester, a lively, joking kidder—a boy his parents claimed to find annoying but about whom they told me stories with chuckles and tongue-clucking.

He did fairly well in social and academic performance until the end of his senior year in high school. At that time his grandmother died, and he became extremely depressed and seclusive. He sat motionless in his room for hours on end, not speaking and hardly eating. This went on for several weeks after which he was able to return to school and finish the year. After graduation he stole a family car and drove to Wisconsin where he spent the summer wandering aimlessly but happily. He returned home to begin college in the fall, but immediately upon matriculation became withdrawn and began drinking heavily. His behavior grew more and more bizarre. He spent his days rocking back and forth on his bed or wandering alone through the college buildings. Eventually he was sent home for psychiatric treatment.

During the ensuing four years he fluctuated dramatically between mute withdrawal and wild running around the countryside. Generally he would

[7] Heinz Hartmann, *Essays on Ego Psychology*. New York, International Universities Press, 1964.

become withdrawn in response to a specific event or circumstance. His withdrawn behavior would elicit increased attention and closeness from his parents which would, in turn, elicit an increasingly active, aggressive response from him. When the closeness and consequent aggressive feeling became unbearable, he would flee to Vermont or the Virgin Islands or New Mexico, trips that were marked by euphoric excitement and antisocial acting out. He experimented freely with hallucinogenic drugs and had three hospitalizations of a few days each with what appeared to be drug-induced psychoses.

Finally he was hospitalized for six months at a private psychiatric hospital and then, after a trip to the Virgin Islands, was hospitalized at this center.

On admission he was catatonic and quite regressed and had to be tube-fed for many days. With the help of medication he gradually improved, first eating, then walking, and finally speaking a few words. After six weeks of painfully slow progress, it became possible to take him to the art therapy session, where Miss Lehnsen persuaded him to take brush in hand.

Alternating Progress Reports

Art therapist's report:

Over the first two weeks I met with John in four individual sessions. Initially I asked him to put down on paper whatever came to his mind. I made sure that the paper, 12 by 18 inches, suited him and was conveniently placed. From a variety of paints he chose a plain set of poster colors. He silently outlined the shapes seen in Figure 1, starting with the figure at the center. When he did not want to add anything more, I asked him what had been on his mind when he painted the picture. He readily explained, in a subdued voice, starting again from the middle: "That is a tornado." And to the left? "That is a judge reading a paper." To the right? "Maybe a mountain."

Figure 1

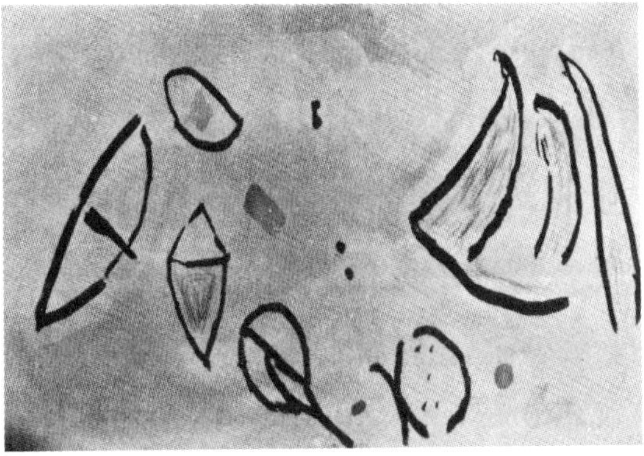

Figure 2

I left it at that and expressed my satisfaction with the painting. I asked him to come back in two days, and he agreed.

We are confronted here with utter fragmentation. The "tornado" suggests sexual activity; the line around it, seclusion. The "judge" indicates feelings of guilt.

At the start of our second session I confronted him with his first picture. I made no reference to his explanation of the painting but showed him how to fill the outlined shapes with color, so that he and I could see them better. Thus I made it clear to him that I had no objection to or question about the picture's content; I was just concerned about its clarity. Besides, by pointing at "our" interest in seeing it better, I emphasized my participation. It was his task to paint as clearly as he could whatever came to his mind, so that he and I could see it readily. He then painted two pictures.

The first was Figure 2, "Arrow, ocean waves." Fragmentation continues in this picture and becomes even worse. Bow and arrow (at the left) suggest tension; the shape next to these is possibly a phallic symbol. But what is the meaning of the waves at the right? The answer is given by the next picture, "Unicorn" (Figure 3). We see a single whole object at the center, isolated in empty space. In mythology the unicorn stands for chastity. The function of the waves in Figure 2 becomes clear. They were needed to wash away guilt, so that the symbol of chastity could appear. However, the unicorn is black, not white as we know it from traditional representations in medieval tapestries.

Of all his pictures, the unicorn remained John's favorite to the end of his treatment. Later on, when from time to time I reviewed the whole series of paintings with him, he always showed pleased surprise and a certain pride when he saw this picture again.

In Figure 4, "Animal," we are confronted with a whole object conceived of in its surroundings. It is the first time that attention is paid to environ-

Figure 3

ment. The animal is at ease. It has found a place to live—grass to eat, water to drink. There are many pictures to come, but none conveys the same degree of relaxation and integration. Light green and pink tones contribute to the picture's peaceful mood.

To sum up: in Figure 1 he states the problem. Figure 2 depicts the tensions arising from conflict, and the resolution of the conflict. Figure 3 shows the changed self-image that results. Finally, in Figure 4, he asserts his right to live. The process has been painted with an economy and condensation worthy of dream work.

Psychiatrist's report:

On the day after the first art therapy session, a Friday, we talked about John's need to masturbate and his guilt over doing so. He recalls that one of his biggest worries after beginning college was that having a roommate would either prevent his masturbation or expose it. Here in the hospital his thoughts were likewise full of masturbation fantasies. He felt that he

Figure 4

finally would be exposed, and deservedly punished. I tried to convince him that masturbation was acceptable, not evil and not abnormal. When we talked again on Monday, he told me that the weekend had been the most relaxed he had had in many months. The next day he drew the unicorn (Figure 3), and a few days later the animal grazing (Figure 4).

Art therapist's report:

I myself started to relax and felt that John was ready to join the group sessions for painting. He remained in the art therapy group until his discharge.

In group sessions the patients sit around a large table or take part in group projects outside the shop. They share art material for use in individual projects. There is mutual interest in productions, and advice, criticism, and help are asked for and given among group members. This occasionally leads to group discussion, sometimes amiable, sometimes angry. Some patients cannot tolerate the group setting and instead find opportunities to paint or sculpt outside the art sessions. Still others decline to take part altogether.

John got along in the group from the very beginning, but I still made a point of meeting with him after group sessions, even if for only a few minutes. I listened to his explanations of his pictures, repeated them back to him, and in his presence wrote them on the back of his paintings.

In his first group session he painted a picture he called "Turning sun with small blue sun." To my question, "Why two suns?" he answered, "Well, when the sun goes down in the west, another one comes up in the east." We shall observe his adherence to the two-sun system in his further work.

John at that time was quite obviously becoming attached to his psychiatrist and started to imitate him. He got the same haircut, acquired a similar cigarette holder, and started using it in his doctor's style. Since the sun is so often a father symbol, the big sun may be taken to represent the real father while the small dark blue sun can be understood as symbolizing John's attempt to identify with the father-psychiatrist.

After this father-son relationship has been established, he ventures on relating to his environment although in a paranoid fashion. He paints four heads—an Indian, a white man and a black one, and a child between them—all looking over a bare hill. A rather large apple appears at eye level. For the first time he gives a more extensive explanation: "Three races and a child who is the only one who stays out of trouble. The earth is fallow. It is harvested, nothing is left. That is an apple from the Garden of Eden."

John at that time felt that people were degenerating (the earth is fallow). He also suspected homicidal tendencies in the group and likened his stay in the hospital to life in a concentration camp. He identifies here and in the next picture (Figure 5) with the child. The apple from the Garden of Eden also appears later on as a symbol of temptation.

John remarked of Figure 5, "Spirits and a child. They all have some-

Figure 5

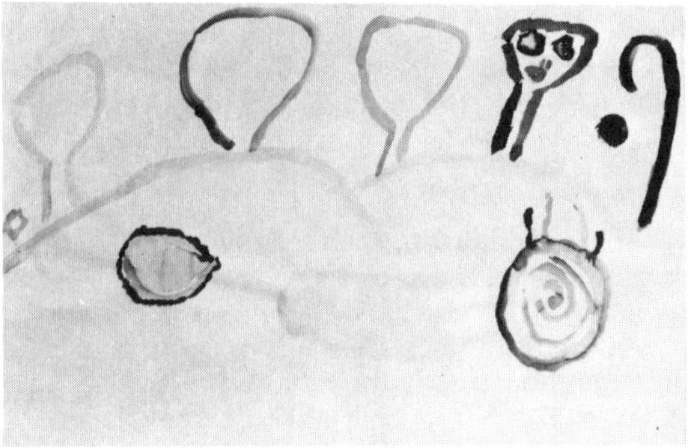

thing. This is something precious" (pointing at the eye shape, lower left). Note that he deals here, and only here, with spirits. They are beings bound to house and home. It is interesting that he chooses spirits at a time when he feels haunted by those close to him. He identifies with a child, the only one who has a face he can see.

At the lower right he paints a spiral, usually a symbol for becoming and growing. Later, in connection with Figure 15, he identified a similar configuration as a "pinwheel or an embryo." Here, the spiral within a closed circle is associated with the child toward whom the ascending lines point, and it is connected by a very fine line with the eye shape. Thus it seems reasonable to assume that the eye shape ("something precious") stands for the womb and that the whole constellation represents his ever-recurrent wish for return to the womb, for protection, not knowing, unconsciousness.

There follows "A Christmas tree. A thing that holds the present. A canopy. The sun." The gift-holding object looks more like a clamp. The canopy points here and later to the need for protection.

Psychiatrist's report:

At this point John was alternating between hyperactivity and withdrawal. He had twice run away from the hospital around Thanksgiving time to be with his family, but at the same time said he was afraid they might really not want him to come home or might be angry with him. I feel that we can see in the blank faces of the spirits the difficulty John has in reading the faces and the minds of his parents.

This conflict between the desire to receive from his parents and his fear of the consequences of receiving had become focused around gift-giving holidays, such as Christmas and his birthday. He said that he desperately wants gifts and attention on these occasions, but once given them he becomes depressed. He feels empty, unworthy, and unable to repay the giver adequately. He suspects that he has been exposed and made to look foolish.

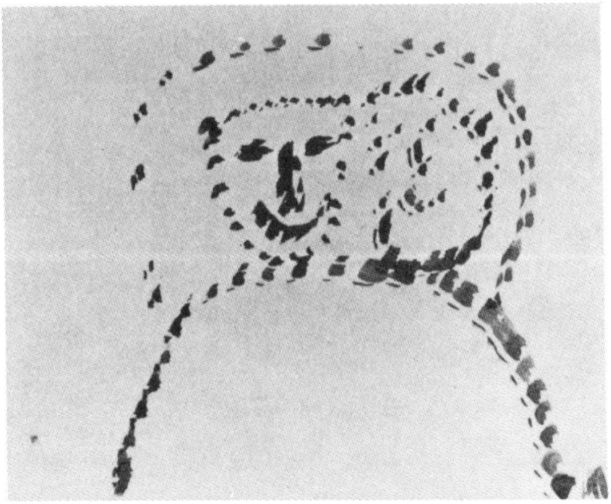

Figure 6

In his Christmas drawing, the gift held in a pincer seems to reflect these feelings.

Art therapist's report:

Next, during a weekend, he painted two pictures with religious content. I found these much later by chance. Both were timid in execution, and when I asked him for their meaning he was hesitant, as if it troubled him to talk about them. The first, painted in lightest watercolor, he named "Satan in heaven"; the second (Figure 6), "The two faces of God." We see two faces side by side over one body, the whole painted in tentative dotted lines. The nurses reported that at the time the pictures were painted he was hallucinating good and bad voices.

He paints the developing conflict quite concretely with dreamlike condensation. First Satan enters (or is in) heaven. The topographical separation of the opposites, elaborated in the history of religion as the concept of heaven and hell, is done away with. God and the Devil (good and bad voices) came together again in space. God has two faces. And with the intolerance of a psychotic for ambivalence, John suffers from the lack of clear separation of the opposites.[8]

These paintings give us insight into John's regressive feelings which he could not put into words. Interestingly enough, he now takes to painting at his own initiative without the presence and knowledge of the art therapist.

---

[8] Erich Neumann *(op. cit.)* devotes a brilliant chapter to the psychological act of the separation of the opposites in early mankind as the beginning of ego-consciousness. The eating from the tree of knowledge (ego-consciousness) is experienced with guilt by early man because it terminates the paradisaical situation of not knowing (unconsciousness). We frequently see in the sick the attempt to regress to that earlier stage of not knowing.

Figure 7

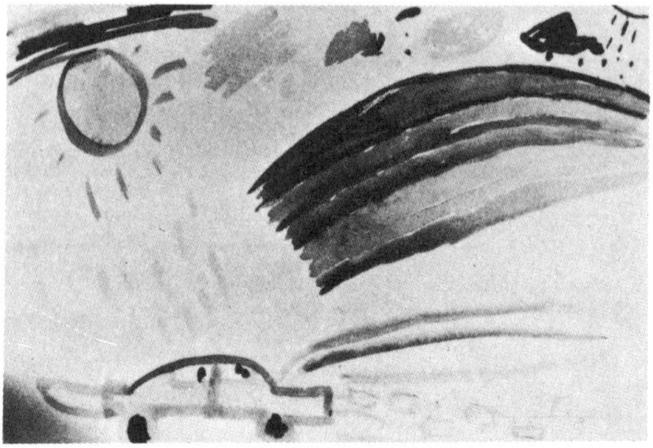

He uses painting to express or exorcise his emotions when he feels the need for it (he later describes this process in connection with Figure 11).

In the next art group he paints Figure 7, "Wedding car and rainbow. Rice, cans tied to the car." He wants to live like other people. He wants to be married. The attention he gives to such detail as the strewn rice and the tied-on cans points to an attachment to formal tradition. This he abandons when he later identifies with the hippies. Here he obviously wishes for the legally accepted sexual relationship. The sexual drive is not only symbolized by the motor car, but also is almost directly represented in the form of a penis as the front part of the car. Again there are two suns. The rainbow, particularly rich in color, suggests a positive mood.

In Figure 8, John pointed out "A boy, a batter, a bat, a baseball, a baseball field." And the arch to the upper left? "That is to protect Johnny" (note the infantile form used by a 22-year-old). And [the arch forming the top of the head at] the upper right? "That is a sea horse." The big face? "That is you, the teacher."

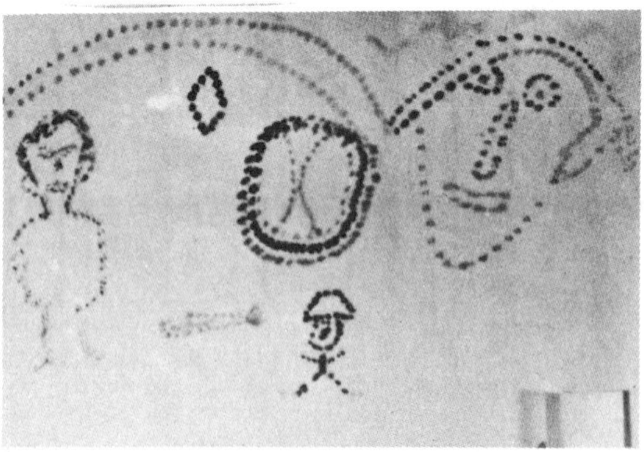

Figure 8

As in Figure 6, we see the dotted line suggesting utter insecurity and fear. The batter runs to hand Johnny the bat, but he has no arms to receive it. I tended to ascribe the role of the batter to the psychiatrist, but the nurses saw rather the father who always tried to push John into sports.

I think here it does not matter whether the batter stands for the father or the psychiatrist. We rather must concentrate on reading the male influence from the lower part, the female influence from the upper part of the picture. The male figure urges him to be a man, to act, to will, "to play the game." We see the upper part of the picture as standing for the protective female. The upper left arch is "to protect Johnny," and the sea horse follows in the same rhythm. My head merges into the sea horse.

The latter reminded me of the story of Jonah and the whale. Jonah had refused to take on responsibility (here Johnny felt unable "to play the game"). Jonah is swallowed by a whale in a moment of peril. He pays for the regressive protection against drowning with an inability to act, caught in utter darkness (unconsciousness) until he is vomited up by the whale and takes up his responsibilities willingly.

Erich Neumann [9] equates this and many other stories in mythology with the growth of the ego in the individual, which he sees as a precarious process in all men and, in the sick, seriously interfered with.

In John this admitted search for protection, together with the refusal to act like a man, gives a similar picture. The struggle for ego-consciousness is quite clearly depicted, only here the victorious outcome is not assured. The regressive elements are quite overwhelming. Even the blurring of animal and human, which occurs frequently in earlier stages of human consciousness, is exemplified by the sea horse joining the teacher's head. However, the large face, identified verbally as the teacher and actually a fairly good caricature of me, also is the first direct rather than symbolic painted reference to a person in his environment. It shows, in spite of all distortions, his awareness of the alliance between him and me. Later, with progress under treatment, he gives us a clearer, more direct portrayal of his relationship to people.

Still, the association of me in my protective, female role with the sea horse challenged me to revise my attitude toward John. Whether or not he knew the story of Jonah and the devouring whale, he appeared to connect me closely with a creature living in the ocean (world womb). This made me vividly aware of his dependence on me. I concluded that I had to stress firmness and emphasize the need for him to depend on me less. For example, the workshop is near the patients' rooms, so when it is desirable I can easily call for patients in person. From this time on I went to John's room 15 minutes before the start of the session, compared time on our watches, and asked him to be in the shop punctually. For some weeks he came on the dot.

---

[9] *Ibid.*

The same struggle to grow up becomes apparent in a painting in connection with which John said: "Christmas and Easter. The child is protected by a canopy. Rainbow and the galaxy. Easter egg basket. The child has a bottle and an egg. A twig of a Christmas tree."

He has named all the objects. The rainbow here is a half circle that almost touches the canopy. I strongly feel that rainbow and canopy are merging in their function as one of the antidotal, protective measures. The egg in one of the child's hands suggests the wish to grow, the beginning of something new, while the bottle in his other hand stands for the ongoing regressive process. The symbol of Easter as the beginning of new life and that of Christmas with an infant as its central figure gave vent to his ambiguous feelings with dreamlike condensation.

Freud points out the economy with which the dream-work thus enhances our understanding of complex relationships. "In the process of condensation, . . . every psychical interconnection is transformed into an intensification of its ideational content." [10] Here we are shown most vividly the interplay between conflicting trends.

Psychiatrist's report:

John appeared depressed during the week when the five drawings discussed above were made. He complained of feeling sad, and there was a marked decrease in motor activity. However, we have observed at many such times a repeated and somewhat unexpected occurrence, namely, that despite these symptoms of depression he is nevertheless very optimistic and hopeful. He speaks of his desire to return to college, to find a girl, to settle down, and so on. His ruminations have a bitter quality at these times which is perhaps best suggested by the drawing of the armless boy struggling for the baseball bat (Figure 8), but they remain hopeful for all that, so that the gay wedding car (Figure 7) drawn during a period of depression is no surprise.

Art therapist's report:

There followed three sketchy drawings, the first described by John as "Animal eating from the tree of life." The same animal that in Figure 4 had earlier expressed John's right to live and to satisfy his sexual needs appears here again, but the peaceful environment is omitted.

Next came "People tearing down the flag." *Two* people under *two* suns next to *two* hills (note the persistent duality) are bending down a pole bearing the United States flag.

The third picture he called "Hippies trying to resurrect the flag." Two people are standing next to the upright flagpole; the stars, however, are painted at the bottom of the flag instead of the top. Again we meet with the

---

[10] *The Interpretation of Dreams,* Vol. V.

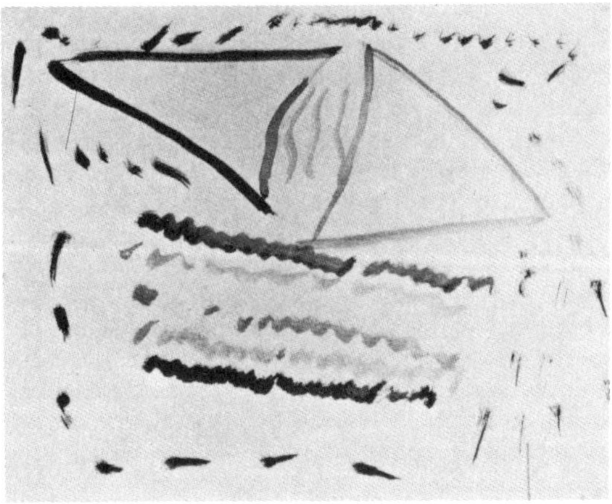

Figure 9

representation of dissent and disunity—and an attempt at reconciliation. He obviously identifies here with the hippies.

On Christmas Eve, on his own, he took a much smaller paper and sketched Figure 9, "Two cells splitting." The little ripples even show the splitting process. After bringing up many images that suggest friction and conflict, he paints this picture. Apparently here he nears awareness that all the preceding images have one origin, stem from one source: his own inner disunity.

With his constant search for reconciliation, he paints the same day "The resurrection of Jesus with stardust, cloud, two suns, God's hand." The last is represented by a green stretch of land with a bare cross standing on it. The identification with the crucified sufferer is obvious and indicates a flight into megalomania.

Psychiatrist's report:

These last five pictures were painted during the two weeks before Christmas. We have already mentioned John's feelings about such holidays in years past: the dual threat of being neglected on one hand or being exposed as worthless and empty on the other.

John was in a state of high excitement at this time, constantly running around the ward, teasing the nurses, and cracking jokes. We have seen that this hyperactive joking has overtones of friendliness but at the same time is unmistakeably aggressive. In any case, the drawings of tearing down and resurrecting the flag were made two days before Christmas and are, perhaps, an expression of his mixed feelings. On the following day he painted the two cells splitting and the resurrection. On the day after that he plummeted again into sadness and withdrawal.

Art therapist's report:

Christmas vacation had passed. John's mood had changed again, and he painted "Four gods, Mercury, Venus, God, Big Brother." The gods were four sloppily painted, smiling faces of equal size, all lined up at the lower edge of the paper. The rainbow, a sun, and a little bird completed the picture. Big Brother evidently stands for his nurse and Venus for a very pretty young nurse's aide. He used to call them by these nicknames. God's face is the same size as the rest of them. Mercury, as god of commerce, might represent the beginning of an interest in money. Altogether these are amiable rather than frightening gods.

There followed "The beetles swimming toward a rainbow." For the first time he chooses a large piece of paper, 18 by 24 inches, and uses more dramatic color. He had grown into a jolly, rather unbearable good-for-nothing, so I first thought that he had identified here with the Beatles. But trouble was approaching, and in retrospect I noticed that the beetles were getting very close to the rainbow, his established symbol for a protector.

Our working relationship had changed. When he came to art group, he was always in a hurry and wanted to finish his painting quickly. He behaved like a teen-ager who wants to get his homework out of the way as fast as possible. Still, in one respect his willingness to cooperate remained the same. He responded promptly when I invited him to an individual session to hear his explanation of his pictures. I once tried to test the consistency of his statements by repeating a question after an interval of some days. He gave me a surprised look and said, "I told you already," putting me in my place.

The next picture "A butterfly," for all its daintiness, was a warning. I have noticed with a number of patients that butterflies often creep out when things are rough or are beginning to get rough. This one is flying over very dark waters.

For the next picture, Figure 10, he returned to his early smaller format (12 by 18 inches), but again used brilliant colors: orange, yellow, and purple for the insect on the right, and brown, red, and navy for the one on the left. The explanation was given in a timid voice. "The brown bug [left] wants to kill the orange bug [right]. The orange bug takes the venom from the brown bug. Infinity sign. The rainbow signifies that it is a beautiful day." This time the bugs are interacting. I strongly felt that the left one represents the devouring mother. The one on the right, although threatened by the fangs, nevertheless attempts some form of intercourse. With the infinity sign he suggests a continuing process.

Psychiatrist's report:

It happens that the patient has a persistent delusion, not about beetles but about spiders. These are related to incestuous wishes and to fears of being engulfed by the mother.

During the year before admission, his wish for intercourse with his

Figure 10

mother's near look-alike cousin became overt and was freely expressed. Also during a family interview with the patient, his parents, and this cousin, he directly told her what he wanted. During this preadmission period, he continuously resisted his mother's wishes.

The spider delusion first occurred on his birthday last year. The mother insisted on having a birthday party, and he protested. She became adamant and arranged the party anyhow.

Powerless to resist but frightened at the prospect of giving in, he ran from the house and fled to a nearby woods where he spent the night cowering in terror. He believed that during that night spiders invaded him and crawled into his tongue. From there they made their way into his internal organs and began to eat him. He is convinced that they are still there.

Art therapist's report:

Recalling the pictures of the beetles, we can now understand how he uses a dreamlike disguise, turning spiders into beetles, and how he is able to lay out the very core of the problem with a few strokes. The next picture, Figure 11, is definitely connected with the problem of incest previously laid bare. John's comment: "Three gods and the sun. The lord, Krishna, another god, the Lord of the Flies. A bug. The gods try to kill me. That's why I'm painting them all the time. I am a god too. Do you think I am God? Do you think other people think they are God?"

Feelings of guilt about incestuous wishes here produce the punishing gods. They are bigger than the ones depicted earlier when he was in a jolly mood. The current gods have bodies and arms for action, while the others had been bodiless and limbless. Now they are hostile; he told about their murderous intent in a rather low, meek voice.

Here he tells us directly that painting is an antidotal measure. Before, we had observed certain features in his paintings, the canopy and the rainbow to which he ascribed protective qualities. He had also confirmed that he used pictorial work for relief from tension when he took up painting at his own initiative in moments of conflict. But here he tells us for the first time in words that painting the aggressor becomes a defense against his hostile power, a form of exorcism.

Psychiatrist's report:

"The Lord of the Flies" no doubt refers to Golding's novel which describes a society of children bereft of controlling adults. Left to their own devices, the children quickly turn to violence, sadism, murder, and cannibalism. John had read the novel.

Art therapist's report:

After the struggle with the threatening gods he paints "The ocean." The sea is often painted when a return to the mother, to oblivion (the unconscious) is desired.

Next came "Fish swimming in the pond." Here the regressive wish for a return to the womb is more specifically expressed, but the whole representation becomes formless. Marked disorganization sets in together with bad behavior on the ward. He becomes sloppy and careless of his appearance, is loud and unmannerly, a teen-ager at his worst. Later, when John and I were reviewing the whole series of pictures, he said, "That shows confusion."

A countermovement sets in as we see in Figure 12, of which he remarked, "Rainbow after a rain storm. That is a lamb." This was painted after John was told that his psychiatrist was leaving for a time. He is willing to accept the departure so he paints himself as a lamb, but the lamb has only two legs and this does not make its gait more secure. Still it is trotting off the scene. The previous storm is openly admitted.

Psychiatrist's report:

The patient had been discharged to day clinic a few days earlier and made straight for the nearest dealer in marijuana and other illicit drugs.

Figure 11

Figure 12

Art therapist's report:

This time the doctor's complementary report is missing. In his psychiatrist's temporary absence, John is taken care of by another doctor and continues attending art sessions as a day patient. After repeated intake of various hallucinogens, easily obtainable outside the hospital, he is readmitted and remains a few weeks as an inpatient. A whole series of changes are clearly sensed in his paintings.

He does a number of portraits of Carlos, a fellow patient whom he likes. Now the relationship is getting closer and has homosexual overtones, but this does not prevent John from flirting with the girls. Often John labels his pictures "Carlos the Lord." Since Carlos is as insecure as John he feels flattered by being called "Lord." The nickname is used half jokingly but it reflects John's groping at this time for a strong authority to lean on. The homosexual interest probably serves to ward off the incestuous wishes discussed above in connection with Figure 10.

In "Mirror face and lizard" the disorganization proceeds and phallic activity is suggested.

Then he paints "Three faces of God. Jesus, Joseph, Mary, apple in the Garden of Eden. Freedom bell." Three faces come out of one large torso with long arms and hands with three fingers each. The middle face, Joseph, resembles Carlos. The freedom bell is drawn only faintly, but to judge from John's behavior it is ringing rather loudly. He becomes very hard to handle and the whole staff works together to find adequate means of control. He had grown fat and strong, and stress was put on physical work as an important part of his program.

The next picture he names "The devil, Miss Lehnsen smiling, myself." There are three faces, quickly outlined with magic markers, the devil considerably larger than the other two, which are the same size as each other. I don't know whether I served as a buffer between him and the devil, or

Figure 13

whether he felt that his own behavior was devilish. The psychiatrist who was temporarily working with him tended to believe the latter. I was inclined toward the former interpretation. Certainly I would dispute John's ascribing a smile to me; a stern, somehow worried look would certainly have been closer to reality at the time.

He had to be hospitalized again to get control over the intake of hallucinogens and to carry him through his psychiatrist's absence.

As an inpatient he again paints Carlos and again labels the portrait "THE LORD" (Figure 13). The picture shows little resemblance to Carlos, who was rather slow and passive. John makes him look like the authoritarian figure implied by the title lettered on the picture. The color of the eyes, hazel, he borrows from his psychiatrist, who is still on vacation.

Two pictures follow in quick succession. In them disorganization, confusion, and violence reach their peak.

Figure 14 was described as "The good lord in psychedelics and mental

Figure 14

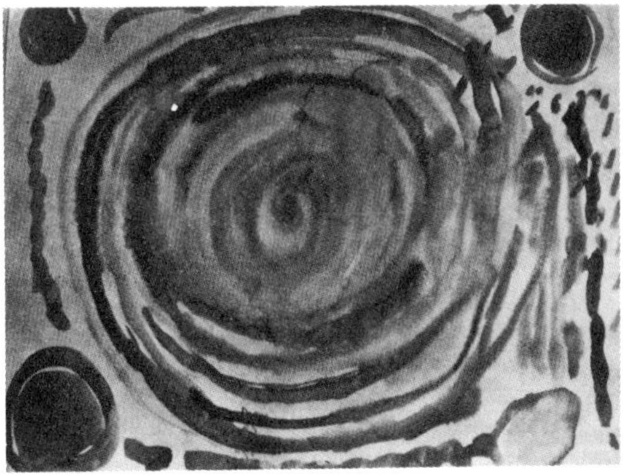

Figure 15

See also color plate XII.

hallucination. On the left just a person." And two days later came "Sprinkling of blood. High mood. Sea. Tree. Lawn." He splashes brush strokes around, using more and brighter color than ever before. Phallic shapes, for example in the good lord's body, and the introduction of lightning speak for sexual excitement, the sprinkling of blood even for violence. The whole staff finds him hard to control, but few complaints come from the patients. Once when I asked my art group how they felt about his behavior, two members said they found him "cute." He plays the part of the "clown and court jester" with the patients just as he had with his family. The patients are not afraid of him. At least in the hospital, violence remains on the fantasy level (and on paper). John's pictures apparently served as "safety valves to the mind," one of the functions that Freud attributes to dreams.[11] At this particular time and place, painting provided a socially accepted means for the expression of destructive wishes.

The effects of the hallucinogenic drugs wear off and John begins to calm down. His temporary psychiatrist told us that John said, "If I can only hold out until my doctor comes back he will make me better." The improvement comes even before his psychiatrist's return.

John explains Figure 15 as "Pinwheel, or an embryo with four suns." The picture immediately shows his return to a better state of organization. The attention given to the four corners convinced me that his orientation was improving. The spiral almost covers the whole large sheet. We have met with the spiral before in Figure 5, but here this symbol of movement, growth, or expansion takes on a much more dynamic, self-confident form. The continuity of the snakelike, swirling line is not perfectly maintained but this may be due to technical limitations. In any case there is no surrounding

[11] *Ibid.*

closed circle as there was in Figure 5. There is room for further expansion and this fits in with John's optimistic mood following the recent crisis.

There follow "A pond with grass and the rainbow," in a mood of subsiding excitement; "A boat, comet, sun," still more peaceful; and "Angel with wings and halo" which brought out John's question and his answer too: "Do you believe in angels? I do." He now has good feelings about himself and is convinced that his behavior is angelic.

Next he painted two more portraits of Carlos, who had been discharged. In the first picture he places him between two infinity signs, but curiously enough, one of the signs is pierced by an arrow which points a way out of the paper. Perhaps John refers here to Carlos's discharge from the hospital, or perhaps he unwittingly tells us that his feeling of eternal bondage to Carlos is fading away.

John had been talking about Quasimodo, the hunchback of Notre Dame. He had built up a clay head of the hunchback about two fists big, artistically the strongest work he had ever done with us. It seemed to me that his feeling for the outsider derives from his own insecurity in society, accentuated now when plans were under way for his own discharge. This makes him identify with the hunchback and makes him want to use weapons aggressively. In one afternoon he painted three small pictures, first, "Pot with glowing metal which will be poured on the nonbelievers. Like Quasimodo." The hostile idea expressed in the picture produces immediate guilt feelings, as we see in what followed.

The next picture was "Candid camera that watches what you are doing. This is a stand or a computerizing robot. Little rocks or suns, sun." He immediately feels observed and judged. There is a camera that watches him, and the computerizing robot will be able to report on his aggressive wishes.

The third picture in the same session he called "House that I would build in the Virgin Islands on my property of three acres." The house is a rather dark little shack without windows, but it does have a door. Next to the house, a lonely little flower grows under a green sky. If John gets into any kind of trouble, he thinks of the Virgin Islands as a retreat.

These three little pictures, painted in less than an hour, lay out the sequential pattern of his behavior. He feels basically incompatible with life on the outside. To defend himself he adopts aggressive measures, and this makes him feel guilty. And his guilt feelings can be dealt with only by flight.

There follows a huge "Heart" covering a third of an 18- by 24-inch sheet of paper. It was fiery red, with some purple in a frame around the edge of the picture. At first I did not know what to make of this immense heart, but then I understood that he had really become attached to the unit, to his fellow patients, and to the staff. As his final discharge was approaching, he became aware of this attachment.

Figure 16 is a portrait of "Theresa," a young Puerto Rican patient he was fond of even though he sometimes moved her to tears by making hor-

Figure 16

See also color plate XIII.

rible faces at her. I felt that in this coherent portrait he had come a long way from the utter fragmentation of Figures 1 and 2. Also, this face was neither connected with a sea horse like the one in Figure 8, nor with the gods and a lord like the ones in Figures 11 and 13. It represented a real person in his environment.

There follows a sketch of the psychiatrist who took care of him during his therapist's vacation. A huge peace sign and a good-bye picture for me followed. In the latter he depicts under a big sun "Fire and rain. A shack. Overturned canoe in St. Thomas." He advised me that if ever I should retire I should go to the Virgin Islands because that was the best place to live.

His last picture was Figure 17, "A bird." His doctor was expected back shortly. The sun dominates and a little sunbeam strikes the bird, hinting at the continuing care he was going to receive as an outpatient. The miniature edition of the sun is almost crowded out and sends his beams towards heaven. Three little flowers on purple earth stretch rather gaily towards the sun. The eye shape next to the flower we know from Figure 5; presumably it is a female symbol.

Discharge from the unit was no easy matter for him. So the bird, instead of leaving the scene, turns towards the middle of the paper. The spiralling arrow at last heading to the right was needed to show the way out.

Summary

I summarize briefly John's pictorial narrative.

We have followed him first through a period of concern with sexual problems, in particular with masturbation (Figures 1 and 2) and the marked relaxation that followed in response to treatment (Figures 3 and 4).

After the relationship with his psychiatrist is established, symbolized in his paintings by the paired suns, social contents begin to appear. They take the form of race problems, disturbing spirits (Figure 5), and of holiday feasts that are not joyous. Still he soon lets us know about his desire to live like other people (Figure 7). Meantime a religious conflict has become evident (Figure 6). We watch him in his struggle to mature, to gain ego strength (Figure 8). His ambivalence toward maturation is further expressed in the juxtaposition of Christmas and Easter.

He sides with rebellious youth, making the hippies the saviors of national pride. John nears awareness of his own disunity in Figure 9, and finds refuge in religious megalomania, still monotheistic. A switch to polytheism takes place in a gayer mood.

He reveals an old delusion about spiders that appear in the disguised form of beetles and that are connected with incestuous wishes (Figure 10). The formerly jolly gods become threatening and vindictive (Figure 11) in reaction to his incestuous fantasy.

There follows the wish for oblivion and for return to the womb. His willingness to accept the temporary absence of his psychiatrist is depicted in Figure 12. The effect of hallucinogenic drugs, taken on the outside and followed by loosening of behavior on the ward, sexual excitement, and violence on the fantasy level, find strongest expression in Figure 14 and in "Sprinkling of blood." During the same period a relationship to a male patient becomes more intimate and has homosexual overtones (Figure 13).

Figure 15 marks the return to organization and order. There follow pictures that show ebbing excitement and his notion that he is angelic.

When plans for his final discharge are made, he admits through his preoccupation with the hunchback of Notre Dame his own feeling of social inadequacy. He defends himself by means of aggressive fantasy. Then his

Figure 17

paintings immediately tell first about his guilt feelings, and next about his constant readiness for flight when difficulties arise.

Nevertheless he had formed relations with people, as a "big heart," a portrait of a female patient (Figure 16), and a good-bye picture to the art therapist reveal. In his last picture (Figure 17) he gives a rather moving account of his relationship with his psychiatrist and discloses that leaving the unit is not easy for him.

Conclusion

Over a period of six months John paints his story spontaneously and with dreamlike condensation. He proceeds with a fairly low ability for graphic representation; artistic qualities in the formal sense are almost absent. Pictorial integration improved during treatment but if we use Henry Moore's criterion for what constitutes art, none of John's works achieves the required level. The sculpture of Quasimodo, which could not be illustrated in this paper, is the only possible exception. The work of art, Moore says, must have a "life of its own, independent of the object it represents." Nevertheless John's paintings share with dreams their peculiar power "to recast their ideational content into sensory images."[12] They give us vivid messages, particularly when we are able to see the pictures in sequence and consider them in their wider context.

What do the paintings mean to the patient? First, I repeat that he painted this series of images spontaneously. This spontaneity establishes their right to exist, tells that there was a need for them. John himself explains their function. "This is to protect Johnny" (Figure 8). "The gods try to kill me, that's why I'm painting them all the time" (Figure 11).

In both instances he tells us in words that the picture and the act of painting have a concrete value for him. In Figure 8 the painted arch offers protection and painting it also serves as an antidotal measure. By painting the vindictive gods in Figure 11 he puts them outside of himself, he exorcises them. The boundary between the object and making the image of the object is blurred.

In these two instances we have the verbal formulation of the relationship between the image, the act of painting it, and the function of the image. In Freud's terminology, John has become aware of painting as a tool for self-expression, self-defense, and adaptation. Needless to say, he also uses this tool unwittingly to assimilate psychic contents in the whole series of images.

I mentioned at the start Freud's explanation of "The Psychology of Dreams." He speaks of the transformation of thoughts severed from consciousness into visual images which press towards consciousness again. It is evident that we deal here with a similar process. The absence of organized thought together with the tendency towards concreteness foster the series of

---

[12] *Ibid.*

visual images, ingenious in their poignancy, brevity, and potency. Potent, that is, as a relieving agent and in their capacity to push again towards awareness. As Harold Kelman says of symbols, they are not the thing itself; they are vehicles which can carry us to the psychic event.[13]

This helps explain the task of the art therapist in the treatment of a patient with relatively low ability for graphic representation in the formal sense but high capacity for producing significant imagery. Her job was to relieve immediate pressure by establishing a nonthreatening therapeutic situation. She had to do what she could do to assist creation of a "vehicle" that could carry the patient towards awareness, or to accept the image as the only expression possible at a given time. It became clear that John's images were not illustrations *of* thoughts, but represented rather the struggle *for* the thought, the effort to achieve conscious realization of a psychic event. To reach such consciousness on the verbal level was the psychiatrist's complex, dangerous, intricate task.

In the course of their joint work, the psychiatrist and the art therapist became aware of the need for more systematic collaboration. But a beginning had been made. They received help from each other on their different levels of functioning. They were aware of working on the same task, the same process. The visual expression closer to the unconscious and the more conscious verbal expression both referred to the same psychic event.

[13] "Life History as Therapy: Part III." *The American Journal of Psychoanalysis,* Vol. 16, No. 2, 1956.

The Use of Painting to Resolve An Artist's Identity Conflicts

JOSEF E. GARAI

Ken entered psychotherapy at the age of 21 because he was unable to deal with the severe anxiety aroused when he used marijuana. He was a tall, well built young art student whose deep-seated, penetrating eyes usually had a suspicious expression. He was unable to complete his artwork for graduation, had broken up with his girl friend, had quarreled with his mother, and was afraid of "going crazy."

Ken was the only child of parents who divorced when he was 5 years old. He was still greatly attached to his overprotective, seductive, rejecting mother. In childhood he had sought to gain her love and approval by exhibitionistic clowning before relatives and visitors and by feats of precocious intelligence. He continued to nurse deep feelings of resentment against his father, who had long since remarried, and only toward the end of treatment was he able to establish any positive relationship with him. Ken's tremendous vitality and physical strength contrasted strangely with his feelings of inadequacy and with his frequently withdrawn attitude.

In addition to the severe anxiety states, Ken suffered from depression and feelings of guilt. There were paranoid projections, hysterical symptoms, and various psychosomatic complaints. He vacillated between impulsive acting out and withdrawal into dreamlike states. He was diagnosed as an inadequate personality with passive-aggressive dependency strivings and sexual confusion.

During the time he underwent psychotherapy Ken was able to utilize his ability as a painter to explore problems of personal and sexual identity and to seek integration of opposing aspects of his personality. He underwent 4 years of individual analytic psychotherapy with my wife, Selma Garai, C.S.W., with regular sessions once a week and additional sessions scheduled to work through special crises. During the final 2 years of individual analysis he also participated in a therapy group led by my wife and me together. It was composed of eight members who met once a week for a one-and-a-half-hour session.

Figure 1

Ken executed all the paintings alone in his studio because he felt he worked best in isolation. He brought in a self-portrait one evening and from then on the members of the group encouraged him to bring in other paintings. During the group sessions Ken was asked to interpret his drawings first and then the members of the group were asked to make their comments. The therapists also volunteered interpretations at crucial times in order to provide a theoretical framework by offering dynamic understanding of unconscious motives and examples of the primary process. All the group members felt that they as well as the therapists were involved in an exciting journey of discovery that promoted their own growth.

Symbolic Self-Portrayal

In a series of self-portraits Ken reflects his struggle for identity, autonomy, and self-actualization. The first painting that he brought before the group (Figure 1) shows him with an expression of defiance. Ken said "This is me as the 'monkey' performing to please my mother. . . . I act like a helpless clown. . . . "

He brought two more self-portraits to the next session. In the first of them, Figure 2, a steel-blue color predominates, covering the uniform and the upper two-thirds of the face. Group members remarked that the facial expression was hostile and cold as well as pouting and dependent. Ken said, "This is me as the Cossack general. I am proud, angry, and firm . . . . "

The third self-portrait (Figure 3) forms a strong contrast. It shows him as a fiery, passionate, yet melancholic young man. The top of the head and the ear are painted a luminescent red, as is the right cheek, while the left cheek appears yellowish green. The group pointed out to him that he seemed to be torn between anger and passion. Ken said that he liked this portrait most of all because it expressed his real self at that time. The fourth self-portrait (Figure 4) was interpreted by Ken and most of the group members as reflecting his serious, introspective, and somewhat melancholic side.

The last self-portrait (Figure 5) was painted about 4 months later. Ken and the group agreed that it looked more as he did in actuality, although he seemed to have idealized himself. He said, "It looks like the person I would like to be some day, . . . sensitive, tender, and full of wisdom . . . . " One group member saw it as "Christlike," and Ken admitted that he had at times envisioned himself as Jesus Christ.

Figures 6, 7, and 8 were made during the same period as were the five self-portraits. Ken remembered their sequence, not the exact time of execution with reference to the self-portraits. All three paintings reflect his struggle for the attainment of integration.

The red-faced clown with fragmented facial features and kite-like wings

Figure 2

Figure 3

Figure 4

(Figure 6) was painted while Ken was under the influence of LSD. The group thought that it reflected his concept of himself as "grotesque, angry, and flying off the handle." Ken refused to comment on it. The next painting (Figure 7) he interpreted as a self-portrait symbolizing his artistic identification. He commented on it as follows: "This is me . . . a mixture of sadness and joy, like Gauguin, connected with nature, very primitive, but blind, . . . no eyeballs . . . . I must always add some little self-defeating thing to torment myself . . . . " This contrast between self-destruction and self-actualization recurs in other paintings.

After 3 months of inactivity, Ken brought the painting shown in Figure 8. At first he seemed to have no idea what it might mean. When one member of the group said it looked to her like a person on a playing card, Ken responded as follows: "Life is a game of chance for me. Here I am the King sitting on the throne. I am wearing a sailor's jacket. I always liked sailors' jackets because they are a symbol of being able to roam around freely and do what comes to one's mind. I have the wings of a bumblebee which permit me to gather the honey and sweetness of life in free flight. Yet my hands and feet are like heavy solid stones holding me down . . . . I am always held back by some pool of water from flying into the open air . . . . " Ken further remarked that he frequently depicts himself as a person emerging from some pond, lake, or

Figure 5

Figure 6

pool. He said that he had read that this reflects a desire to emerge from the mother's womb to experience rebirth. He explained that he felt as if his old self were dying and that this painting symbolized his desire for rebirth. The group was skeptical, and one member pointed out that he seemed to be unable to take off.

In the next painting, however, Ken does appear to be flying or rolling off (Figure 9). He said he was dancing on the ball, like a circus performer. He liked the fast, energetic, and rhythmical movement but was afraid of losing control over it. The members of the group pointed out that his facelessness indicated a lack of self-definition and that the person was balancing precariously and seemed to be rolling off into a pool of water. Two members also noted that the posture revealed a strong feminine trend. Ken admitted that he was passing through a stage of sexual confusion and insecurity and said he felt at times the urge to experience the unfettered freedom of movement of a "gypsy dancer." The members of the group pointed out that the ball appeared to follow its own direction and that he seemed again to be at the mercy of uncontrollable forces like the "sailor on the playing card."

In his attempt to interpret the next painting (Figure 10) Ken was unable to make up his mind whether the two swaying persons symbolized his mother and father or his own *animus* and *anima*, i.e. male and female complementary traits. He finally said they looked too young to be his parents and admitted that he was still trying to establish his sexual identity. Both persons are

Figure 7

emerging from the body of a fish in the water. Ken identified the fish as his mother's womb.

Figure 8

Figure 9

Figure 10

Paintings Concerned with the Father

Ken was held back not only by his mother's rejection and his dependency on her but also by his fear of men and his anger at their refusal to lend him support.

His hostility to men had been brought out by a recent accident. Ken was a very skilled member of his school's fencing team and had challenged one of the Olympic fencing champions to a contest that he almost won. But his opponent's rapier went astray and Ken suffered a neckwound. He bled profusely and was afraid he might bleed to death. The wound was sewn together at the hospital.

Ken needed several extra sessions to work through his fear of sudden violent death. The next painting, Figure 11, depicts a dream that was evidently influenced by that threat. The black figure, himself, is prevented by hostile men from protecting his "hare" and attacking the intruder who is killing it. Ken said that the hare, or sensitive rabbit, symbolized his tender and warm feelings. The intruder who puts the knife to the hare's throat reminds him of his father who wants him to be a "real man" by being tough and unemotional. He also felt that the man might resemble the fencing opponent who attempted, as he put it, to draw his very lifeblood from him. This appears

Figure 11

Figure 12

to be a transferential reaction to all men, as seeming, like his father, to be bent upon his destruction.

Soon after this session Ken tried to get his father to come to his studio to see his artwork. After several invitations that came to nothing, his father actually did visit him and expressed admiration for his son's progress in his artistic career. Ken felt ambivalent about his father's words of praise, which he felt "came too late and were too few. . . ." Nevertheless, he had gained a feeling that his father might yet one day become his model and ideal. This was expressed in the next drawing (Figure 12) that Ken brought to the group 2 weeks later. He said, "This looks like my father. In this painting he looks very strong and noble, like a wise man, really put together, like a 50-year old Greek man . . . . But my father is weak and flighty . . . I really hate him. . . ." The group pointed out that Ken was at least beginning to envisage the possibility of positive feelings toward a strong and supportive father figure.

The Oedipal Conflict

Ken's relationship with his mother at the beginning of his analysis is vividly illustrated in a painting executed about a year before he entered therapy (Figure 13). He brought it out of storage and took it to a group session. But he kept it hidden during the session and only after the other group members had left did he feel free to show it to the two therapists. He was evidently reluctant to expose to the group his most intimate fantasies about his mother. He described the painting as follows: "I am the black man in a crowd in the city, with the Guggenheim Museum and the waterfront in the back. I am the gorilla in the red shirt. . . I'm really a 'dumb fuck' taking care of the queen. She is my mother with a crown on her head and an anxious look on her face, . . . worried about being raped by the brute. On my head is a figure, half a bird and half a woman . . . the bird is clawing my head. It's a symbol of my mother not letting go of me . . . ."

In the following session he showed the painting to the group and repeated the explanation. After a searching discussion among the group members it became clear that this painting was a graphic description of his Oedipal conflict and the resulting ambivalence toward women. He sees them at the same time as alluring seductresses, devouring and oppressive mothers, and demanding queens. His black face and white arm reflect inner conflict between "goodness" and "badness," purity and sin, pleasure and pain, virginity and promiscuity, and depression and joy, themes that emerge in various guises in his painting as in the works of many creative artists.

The discussion of this early painting stirred up further deep feelings associated with his mother. For the next 4 weeks Ken worked feverishly on a huge canvas (Figure 14) that he could hardly get through the door of our office when it was completed. It stunned the group into several minutes of surprised silence by its graphic depiction of sexual intercourse between two very different persons. Several members of the group said that they thought the painting depicted the realization of Ken's Oedipal fantasy. Ken first objected violently to this interpretation and said defensively that he had in mind "intercourse between two lovers." But almost in the same breath he admitted that the man seemed to be much younger than the woman and that the woman's face was like his mother's. He listened attentively to the group's further interpretation and volunteered his own opinion only toward the end of the session, saying, "I guess I still want to get even with my mother. . . . I don't know whether I should love her or hate her."

The interpretations made by the group and the therapists were based mainly on the following impressions of the painting: Ken has intercourse with

Figure 13

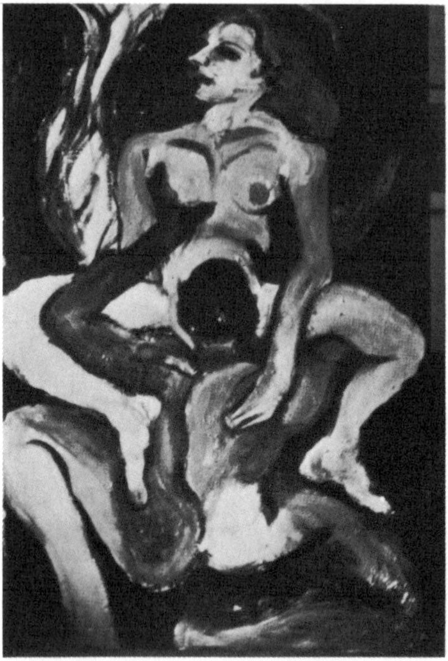

Figure 14

his mother. Her flaming red hair and sensuous lips entice him but she looks haughtily rejecting, diverting her gaze from him and closing her lips tightly, adopting the superior position. Instead of her nipples feeding him, he must support her right breast with his palm. Both dependency and sexual needs remain unfulfilled, since his position compels him to engage in cunnilingus rather than in actual sexual intercourse. Different parts of his back are black, red, and white, reiterating the conflict between good and evil or passion and abstention earlier expressed in the drawing of the "gorilla" man surrounded by the archetypes of women. One member of the group pointed out that she could distinguish the figure of a little monkey emerging as part of the man's left leg. Ken could also see this image and explained it as symbolizing his father who was "sucking semen," trying to castrate him. This would in part explain Ken's castration anxiety expressed as fear of impotence and resulting in premature ejaculation.

Three weeks after showing the intercourse painting to the group, Ken brought in a painting (Figure 15) of a dream from which he remembered awakening in a state of joyful relief. This time he did not wait for the group to volunteer interpretations but went right ahead to explain it, as follows: "My mother is finally dead, buried in the rock-tomb. Her head is cut off and she breathes her last gasp . . . . The monkeys are glad and dancing around the grave. The green guy [bottom left] is me getting rid of my anger, and laughing. The blue fellow [bottom right] represents my more serious self that grieves about her death and wants to contemplate the newly won freedom." Two members of the group pointed to a yellowish penis on the "serious self," which showed a strong erection. After first refusing to recognize this erection, Ken eventually acknowledged it and then explained that his mother's death permitted him to enjoy his sexual potency without further guilt feelings.

Conclusion

Ken brought in several more paintings that revealed his continuing struggle for further self-definition. He learned to express his anger and despair more openly, and this made him able to establish clearer long-range vocational and personal goals. He has held a job as an innovative art teacher for the last 3 years and has established an intimate, enduring relationship with a young woman. His artwork has become freer and more expressive as a result of his having recognized and worked through deep-seated identity conflicts.

His artistic ability came to his aid at critical periods of his therapy. He translated dreams and fantasies into images on the canvas and was assisted by the therapists and by members of the group toward an increasingly deep understanding of his own complex personality and intrapsychic conflicts.

Figure 15

Polar conflicts constitute a rich source of productivity in the creative expression of many artists. I believe that such conflicts are not in themselves neurotic but are rather the very essence of human existence. Ken's paintings are not merely a weapon in his struggle to deal with his neurotic problems. They also demonstrate the artist's ability to probe into the depths of the primary process and to emerge with ever-new perspectives.

The Self-Portraits of a Schizophrenic Patient

AL. MARINOW

The paranoid schizophrenic woman whose painting and modeling were previously discussed in the BULLETIN OF ART THERAPY [1] died in October 1962 as the result of a perforated gastric ulcer. At the time of her death she was 58 years old, and had lived for more than 20 years in the mental hospital of Bela.

Her illness was precipitated in 1939 by an unhappy love affair and the loss of her office job. Despite attempted treatment she had auditory hallucinations from then on. Throughout her years in the hospital she suffered as well from constipation and had an eczema of the hands, conditions which failed to respond to a prescribed diet. She attributed her bodily ills to the malice of her doctor and the nurses, maintaining that they put lice in her hair and on her body, and that these crawling, biting insects constantly troubled her sleep. The human heads on the big insect figures she drew and painted may have symbolized this delusion.

Her vision was poor, and she also blamed the hospital staff for her nearsightedness, believing it was caused by "blacking" which they put into her eyes. The eyes in her many self-portraits were purposely pervaded with black (Figure 1), and light colors, especially white and yellow, usually predominated in the faces, the better to bring out the contrasting darkness of the eyes. On the other hand, she always showed her own eyes as wide-open, and they frequently appeared to protrude (Figure 2). While the blackness suggests her handicap and its delusional cause, the exophthalmic effect appeared to be an attempt at compensation. This treatment of the eyes, as well as a special way of handling nostrils, hair, mouth, and neck, was characteristic of her self-portrayal but never appeared in the other faces she drew.

She not only always represented herself as the young woman she had been before her illness, but frequently asserted that she was a child of five, and indeed her behavior was often childlike. In painting she gave herself the body and dress of a child (Figure 3), yet the head and the face always appeared to be those of an adult.

[1] "Painting in the Treatment of a Schizophrenic Patient," Vol. 1, No. 4, 1962
"Modeling in the Treatment of a Schizophrenic Patient," Vol. 2, No. 3, 1963

Figure 1

Charcoal drawing.

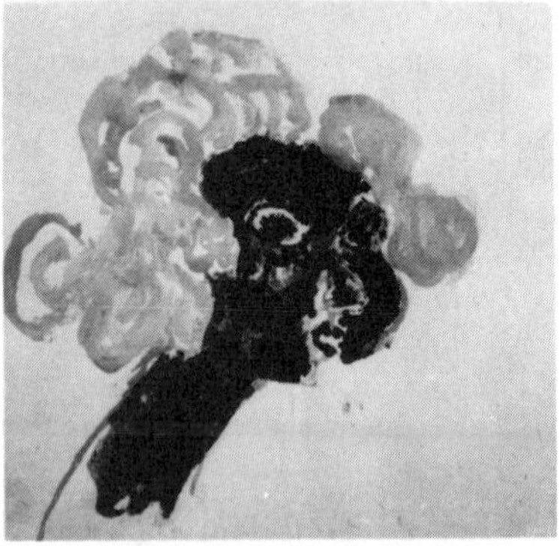

Figure 2

Water color.

Figure 3

Oil painting.

Figure 4

Photograph of the patient at age 57.

Some months before her death the patient looked at herself in a mirror for the first time since she had entered the hospital over 20 years earlier. Seeing her wrinkled face, white hair, and toothless mouth (Figure 4), she burst into tears and declared emphatically that the doctors and nurses had purposely brought about this terrible change by giving her so much medicine. After that she portrayed herself unwillingly and in an unaccustomed fashion, for the first time showing the teeth whose actual loss she had been made aware of (Figure 5). After the unfortunate experience with the mirror she also refused to take the tranquilizers which, along with art and occupational therapies, had been part of her regimen.

As previously reported, painting and modeling led to clinical improvement in this patient, which in turn increased the quantity and raised the quality of her art productions. For a time her new activity and interest also helped her physical condition. As with her other paintings and sculptures, the staff gained some understanding of her psychopathology by studying the form and content of this patient's long series of self-portraits.

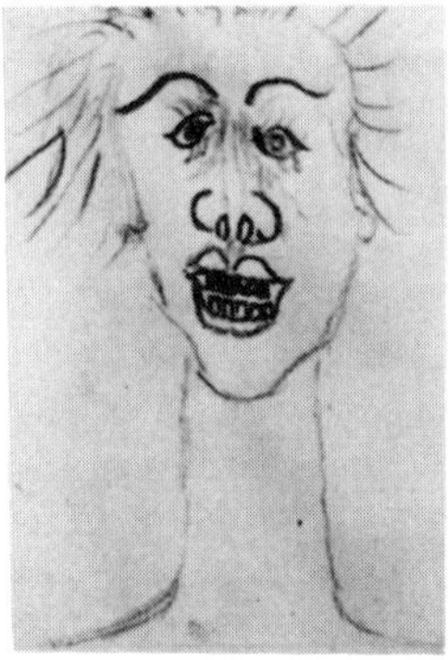

Figure 5

Charcoal drawing.

An Analysis of the Art Productions of a Psychiatric Patient Who Was Preoccupied with His Nose*

JOHN BIRTCHNELL

This article will explore the drawings and paintings produced by a psychiatric patient during a period of six months in the Ross Clinic, Aberdeen, Scotland. It will discuss these pictures as they relate to selected aspects of the patient's case history.

The drawings and paintings represent a sort of psychic excretion which, fortunately for us, the patient has unquestioningly committed to paper. Thus they remain a permanent record of his mental state during his time in the clinic. They are irrational in the way that dreams are and are more or less equivalent to daytime dreams. As do dreams, they have a manifest content in which actual objects and people are depicted and within which is partially hidden, or hinted at, a latent content—the representation of the patient's personal problems and conflicts. The patient himself would be fully aware of only the more superficial manifest content and would probably describe the pictures in only these terms. Such pictures afford a person the opportunity of half-saying things, of camouflaging what he says, of creating ambiguities such that he has a way of denying that he ever meant to say such things.

Is it sufficient merely to have got so far as half-expressing these ideas? Remembering the similarity between the world of dreams and the world of psychotic patients, can we say that psychiatric paintings are a sort of externali-

* I am indebted to Miss Joyce Laing, Art Therapist at the Ross Clinic, Aberdeen, Scotland, for encouraging the production of this valuable set of pictures, for preserving them, and for bringing them to my notice. I also am indebted to the patient who painted them and regret that he must remain anonymous. I would like to thank the Department of Medical Illustration of the University of Aberdeen for the excellent photographic reproduction of the pictures.

zation of psychotic material, a safe way of going mad? Does this kind of painting-out of psychotic material prevent the onset of a frank psychosis?

It is the author's view that a thorough analysis of the content of such pictures provides a valuable indication of underlying psychopathology. It is obviously unwise to compel a patient to recognize prematurely the disturbing thoughts he is hinting at in his pictures; over time, and within the security of a therapeutic relationship, it is desirable to gradually encourage him to become aware of these thoughts and to discuss them. The author was not the patient's therapist; it is perhaps unfortunate that treatment followed the more conventional lines of tranquilizers and supportive therapy.

The present study is an attempt to reveal the psychopathology expressed in the pictures and to show the relationship between this psychopathology and the patient's symptoms, current circumstances, and preceding history. How, then, can the author be sure that his interpretations of these pictures were in fact the ideas the patient was trying to express? There is the very real danger that the author may have read into them some of his own personal fantasies.

The method of analysis adopted, insofar as the author was aware of it, was first to attempt to establish connections between the situations within the pictures and those within the patient's real life. Details of his past life, present situation, and clinical state were available from the case record. Second, the author tried to discover within the pictures internal consistencies in terms of recurrence of themes, motifs, shapes, and so on. An object in a particular place on one sheet of paper became transformed into a different, though related, object on another. A hypothesis suggested by one picture could be supported or refuted by other pictures in the series. The interpretations finally arrived at were those that best fitted the content of the majority of the pictures and that were most meaningful in terms of the patient's history and present life-situation.

During the course of his stay the patient produced approximately 60 pictures. It is not possible to discuss here the content of all of them; instead an analysis of seven of the most significant ones will be undertaken.

Clinical Background and Diagnostic Formulation

The patient was a 19-year-old apprentice quantity surveyor. He had two younger brothers aged 15 and 12 and confessed to having been jealous of the tallness and scholastic success of the 15-year-old. He mentioned that when he was young he was deprived of love; he thought his childhood had been an unhappy one. He considered himself to have always been exceptionally shy, especially with girls. At school he was a poor mixer and he could never keep friends. He feared that he might be homosexual because he felt no attraction towards women. Though he had no girl friend, he was sure that he could get one if he tried and maintained that girls had always run after him. He described an urge to exhibitionism and once, when in the psychiatric clinic, he had hopped out of bed naked in front of a female nurse. At times he felt he was more woman than man. He felt secure with women but not with men.

He described his father as temperamental, tyrannical, and very strict over religion—a man who believed his son had inherited a rebellious temperament and who insisted that his son submit to parental authority. There were frequent rows between father and son, particularly over religion, and during his stay in the clinic the patient thought that he should start a new religion and change his name. His father had worked as a farmer until, when the patient was aged five, the father had had a below-the-knee amputation of his leg, and was forced to seek lighter work. Thereafter he became the warden of a schoolboys' hostel. His mother was a nervous woman who constantly failed to stand up to her husband.

He believed his problem began at the age of 13 when a girl told him he was ugly. From that time he became increasingly preoccupied with his nose. When in a public place he worried about how his nose was looking. He could no longer concentrate on his work and shunned social contact. He considered that it is the face you have that molds your character and not the other way round: people trust each other because of their faces. He said, "My character would be completely different if I wasn't worrying about this nose." He spent a lot of time looking in the mirror sideways and pulling his nose down with his fingers to make it look shorter. He believed that if it were cut off at the tip it would give him a surge of confidence. He persistently asked his general practitioner to arrange for him to have plastic surgery. His nose was, in fact, perfectly normal in appearance.

It might be easiest to see this patient's difficulties in terms of the oedipal situation. He has challenged both his two brothers and his father for his mother's affection, and his father in turn needs to repel his challenge. His jealousy of his next younger brother and the frequent quarrels with his father are evidence of this. Psychoanalysts believe that the young boy's intense desire for his mother is coupled with a wish for the annihilation or disappearance of his father and brothers. These murderous wishes give rise to feelings of guilt and the dread of retaliation. Analysts further believe that the most-feared form of retaliation is the loss of his penis by castration. In this boy's case, at the height of his childhood oedipal phase, his father's leg was amputated. At the time, or subsequently, he might have associated this with his own murderous wishes towards his father and may have felt that he himself so deserved punishment for these wishes as to have attempted to symbolically castrate himself by requesting surgery to his nose. His shyness towards women may be a reflection of his oedipal guilt. The emotions of the oedipal situation are particularly powerful ones and are understandably associated with much shame and guilt. It is highiy probable, therefore, that the patient would be capable of only limited expression of these emotions and would find it necessary to conceal them within apparently innocent pictures.

Analysis of the Pictures

The oedipal situation is the theme of Figure 1. The patient is represented by the crouching young man on the left. His dominating father is placed centrally and his acquiescent mother is fused to his father's side. The boy is feebly trying to gain possession of the central rock, upon which his father's foot is firmly placed. The father stands prohibitively between the boy and his mother and also creates a barrier between them by the pillar produced by his own and the boy's arms and legs. This barrier obviously symbolizes the incest taboo; it is significant that it is contributed to by both father and son. The interlocking of the boy's arm and the father's leg suggests that though they are in conflict, they also have a harmonious relationship. The boy is perhaps glad that his father imposes restrictions upon him. There is the suggestion that the father's leg is both a barrier against and a shield from his naked, seductive mother. Though she is naked, she is half covered by a long curtain of hair reaching from head to foot.

Arching over the father's head like a rainbow is the vapor trail of a spacecraft. This implies that, despite the father's intervention, the mother can take off and fly to her son in a secret but forbidden relationship. The son then is confident that his mother will come to him even though his father does not approve.

His attitude towards the relationship between the parents is clearly ambiva-

Figure 1

lent. Though the mother is fused to his father's side, the curtain of hair also serves as a barrier between herself and her husband. To complete this barrier the father has been given long hair as well. There are streaks of black paint separating the two bodies interrupted only by the father's left hand. The thumb of this hand has a distinctly phallic appearance, though the father's own phallus has been covered by lines resembling the mother's hair, which also covers her genitals. The boy's left hand also has a phallic thumb and is placed on top of the rock for which the two men are competing. The rock in a sense, therefore, represents the mother whom they each wish to possess. Perhaps it is not too fanciful even to suggest that it bars the entrance to her vaginal cave.

The relationships between these three people are hinted at in a number of ways. In the original, the mother is painted bright yellow, and the light, upper part of the boy is painted the same color. The left half of the father's chest is light brown and so is the boy's. This indicates an affinity with both parents. Though the father and mother are standing together they are looking away from each other in a symmetrical manner. The father is looking disapprovingly at the boy, and it is almost as though the mother is making believe that the boy is at *her* side. The boy, if anything, is looking at the rock that represents his mother, but his gaze is obstructed by his father's leg.

An important feature of the picture is the obscuring of all legs—apart from the lower part of one of the father's and one of the son's. It is significant that this is the part of the father's leg which was amputated when the boy was five. It is as though the son is reminding himself of this by placing the leg in such a central position. By putting his own leg directly beneath it he suggests that the same thing might happen to him. The message is, perhaps, that he willed his father to be castrated and that one day his father will retaliate by castrating him.

Figure 2 is structurally very similar to Figure 1. Though it is painted in oils, the brush strokes are more frenzied and the content is more difficult to discern. The patient was clearly in a less controlled and more anxious state when he painted this picture, presumably because disturbing thoughts were emerging. The dominating central figure is probably once more his father. In contrast to Figure 1, he is now facing into the picture, and his buttocks, painted red, occupy a prominent central position. Within the complete series of pictures the rear view of the male, usually depicted as a cowboy in tight trousers and sometimes riding a horse, is a recurrent theme, and suggests an inclination towards homosexuality. The mother, fused to the father's side like a revolver in its holster, is very much less distinct but still discernible. She is still faced outwards, but instead of having a goddess-like appearance, as in Figure 1, she is now depicted as ugly and frightening, like a witch. The elegant spacecraft of Figure 1, the vehicle of the mother's love, is now black and jagged. (See top right corner.) It does not appear to be directed towards the boy.

The central man's legs are separated as though he were a cowboy on horse-

Figure 2

See also color plate XIV.

back. (In two other pictures the male subject is pictured as a mounted cowboy.) His legs now surround what was the rock of Figure 1. The boy has been pushed almost out of the picture and has been transformed into a devilish serpent rising up and peering nervously over his father's leg. There is probably here an association with the seductive serpent in the Garden of Eden. It is as if the rock barring the entrance of the vaginal cave has now been rolled aside to reveal a bright red interior resembling an inferno. Emerging from the inferno is a fearsome face with large eyes and tusks.

This grotesque face within the vaginal cavity bears some resemblance both to the serpentine face of the boy and the witch-like face of the mother. It may imply that their sexual union might produce a monster. It also brings to mind the Gorgon, Medusa of Greek mythology. Medusa was once a beautiful woman, but because one night she lay with Poseidon in one of Athena's temples, she was changed by Athena into a winged monster with glaring eyes, huge teeth, protruding tongue, brazen claws, and serpent locks. Her gaze turned men to stone; perhaps she represents the fearful aspect of woman. She was finally slain by Perseus, a young man who succeeded in avoiding her destructive gaze by watching her reflection in his shield. The petrifying look of Medusa is reminiscent of the moment when the patient was thirteen and a girl told him he was ugly. Since that time he became progressively more apprehensive of having people look at his face.

Figure 3 is calmer; the patient's thoughts and emotions here obviously are more under control. There is once again a dominating central man; the position of his legs is strikingly similar to that of the father's legs in Figure 1. His controlling foot is now placed, not upon the rock, but upon the dangerous Medusa-eye of the strange animal, the face of which corresponds in position to that of the serpent of Figure 2 and the crouching boy of Figure 1. Whereas in Figure 1 the boy was hiding meekly behind his father's legs with his father clearly in control of the rock, the boy here is in the shape of a powerful monster and appears to be ascendant—almost about to overthrow the man precariously placed on his back. The man, who is probably still the father, looks weaker than the monster. He has a fatuous face and a feeble bow and arrow that he does not know how to handle; this is in complete contrast to the powerful and dominant man of Figure 2. It is significant that the monster has an enormous nose that presumably represents the potency that the boy wishes he had and at the same time fears he might have.

He clearly does see the nose as having phallic associations; his wish to cut short his nose is therefore a wish to diminish his potency. The father's feeble bow and arrow, on the other hand, indicate how impotent he wishes his father to be and perhaps even suspects he might be. It is interesting that the father's quiver, fused to his side in this picture, corresponds in position to the mother in Figure 1. An arrow taken from the quiver is being fired in the direction of the path of the spacecraft. It is as though the father is acting as Cupid to the son and his mother. One suspects from these three pictures, and there is some evidence for this in the case history, that the father is in conflict as to whether to relinquish to his son the role of sexual partner to the mother or to assert his claim on her and punish the boy for desiring her.

Under the rider's legs there is once more a cavity that presumably again represents the vaginal tunnel. This time, however, the lower border of the

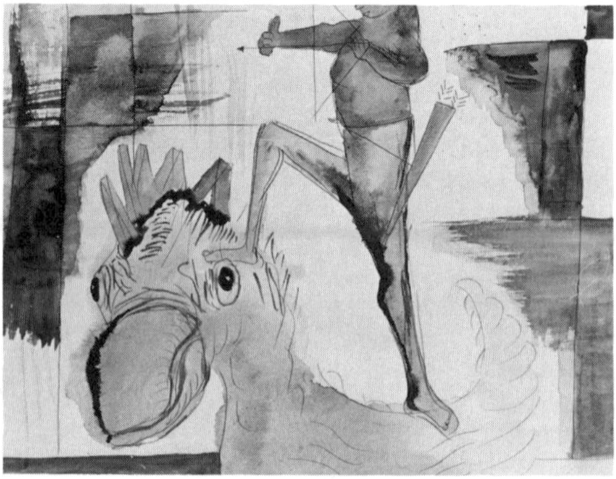

Figure 3

cavity is formed by the animal's back. This is reminiscent of Figure 1, in which the space under the father's knee is bounded on one side by the father and on the other by the boy. The space is vulval in shape and is for the first time wide open. One feels, however, that the animal's large prominent eyes are repelling and that they guard the entrance to the tunnel. They have the quality of Medusa's petrifying gaze. This is perhaps the first indication that the patient associates the eye and the vagina.

An interesting feature of this picture is that the rider of the animal is not sitting astride it. It has already been remarked upon that, within the series, there are a number of rear views of cowboys on horseback and that these seem to be allusions to homosexuality. Standing on the animal's back and facing out of the picture may suggest a turning towards a normal sexual orientation. In this picture, as sometimes in dreams, the man on the animal appears to be both the patient and his father. Presumably this is somehow related to identification.

In Figure 4 there has been an interesting rearrangement of the family trio. The patient's father is represented by the towering figure in the foreground and the patient himself appears to be the smaller distant man on horseback. The figure on the right of the picture probably represents his mother, for into the butt of her revolver has been painted an orifice to represent the vulva. This ties in with the mother's being fused, in Figures 1 and 2, like a revolver, to the father's thigh. The hand cupping over the revolver and the long graceful arm

Figure 4

Figure 5

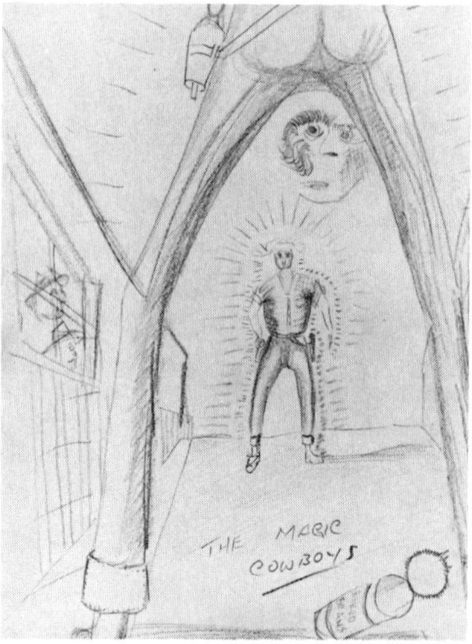

above it bear some resemblance to the mother's flowing hair in Figure 1. The painted-in vulva is not unlike the streaking lines of the woman on the right of Figure 2. Thus the strange animal of Figure 3 appears to have been transformed into the horse and rider of Figure 4. The horse has a long neck merging into a pointed nose that, emerging from between the rider's legs, looks like a huge penis. This is further evidence for concluding that the patient has come to see his own nose as a penis. The rider then is provocatively exposing his penis in front of his father, who is about to shoot at it and castrate him. One wonders whether the figure on the right, representing the mother, is reaching for her gun to shoot the father and save her son.

The drinking horse has created an archway through which the river is flowing. This archway is in alignment with the arched legs of the man on the bank, forming a tunnel. It is also in alignment with the vulva painted into the revolver of the figure on the right, suggesting that again the archway represents the vaginal tunnel. The long grass completes the circular cavity and creates the impression of pubic hair. The correspondence between Figures 4 and 2 now seems to be very close. The mother figure is in a similar position on the right of both pictures. The area under the horse coincides with the cavity containing the monstrous face. The standing central man has shifted to the left to become the man on the bank—again with his back to the viewer. Figure 4 implies that, under threat of attack from his father, the patient voluntarily has relinquished his male role by fashioning his penis into a vagina. This perhaps is related to his assertion that he felt he was more woman than man.

Figure 5 contains a similar alignment of arches, and it seems that the man

Figure 6

on the horse has become the distant man in a gun duel. This could be a duel either between the patient and his father or between the masculine and feminine sides of himself, which in a sense amounts to the same thing. The mysterious floating face clearly is related to the monstrous face between the arched legs in Figure 2, but presumably it is related also to the vaginal revolver of picture 4, which looks as though it could easily be interposed between the two aligned men. The face might be seen as the mother, over whom the duel is being fought and who is protecting the distant man by her presence.

An enlargement of this face is shown in Figure 6. Even though it occupies a relatively small portion of the drawing, it is of considerable importance and has been drawn with great care. It is dominated by a disproportionately large right eye surrounded by an almost complete loop composed of a displaced nose that is continuous with a huge arching eyebrow. This loop is similar to the arch produced by the horse's nose in continuity with the rest of its body seen in Figure 4. Placed, as it is, immediately under the man's pubis, the arch very likely represents a vagina surrounded by pubic hair. In this respect it bears some resemblance to the eye of Figure 3 that is surrounded by the animal's mane in continuity with its nose.

The distant man of Figure 5 appears rooted to the spot with fear, almost as though petrified by the Medusa-eye of the floating face. His own arching legs also have a vulval appearance, implying that the duel is also a sexual relationship.

Figure 7 has much in common with Figures 4 and 5 and helps to clarify the underlying theme. For the first time the gun is actually drawn and is about to be fired. There is no doubt that it is aimed straight at the genitals. This confirms that what is to be shot at in Figure 4 is the horse's phallic nose. Here the young man's legs are separated invitingly, though his large feet appear to stand

Figure 7

out in protest. He is proffering the butt of his own gun and the man in the foreground is reaching for it. The butt, like the one in Figure 4, has been drawn ambiguously so as to represent a vulva; this fits neatly between his legs as if it were a replacement for his own genitals. This then is the most definite representation of the theme that under threat of castration he has voluntarily relinquished his own masculinity and assumed the feminine role. He is perhaps identifying with his mother so that his father may love him.

In Figure 8, as in Figure 2, he has adopted a more abstract style that seems to enable him to bring together a number of related ideas. The sun, in the top right-hand corner, contains a staring face that bears a striking resemblance to the disapproving face of his father in Figure 1. A diagonal barrier has been drawn right across the picture to keep out the sun's penetrating gaze. On the left side of the barrier, at the bottom of the picture, a mass of whirling lines

Figure 8

forms a vortex. This corresponds in position to the central rock of Figure 1 and the red cavity of Figure 2; thus, it is presumably another vaginal symbol. Shooting upwards from the area of the whirling lines is a rocket-like structure terminating in a nozzle. It has a vapor trail and is reminiscent of the spacecraft in Figure 1. It is surrounded by spiky lines as is the distant man of Figure 5. The rocket-like symbol presumably represents the patient under scrutiny from both his father and the world in general. It is ambiguously drawn to represent either a penis rising above testicles or a nose rising above eyes. There is a suggestion of a mouth beneath it. Its nozzle-like termination gives the impression that the penis has been cut across, thus feminizing it. At the same time, the phallic object is in flight from the terrifying whirlpool of the vagina and the stern glare of the father. At a more superficial level the picture suggests the patient's nose escaping from the gaze of other people.

Discussion

It is clear from the analysis of the pictures that this young patient was not preoccupied just with the nose but also with the eye. He saw his nose as that part of himself that penetrates into the world around him—like the prow of a ship—the eye as the hostile stare of other people reflected back at him. This model can be extended in a variety of ways. It can be seen as his aggressiveness and defiance of adults countered by the disapproval and restraint of authority. At the same time the nose can easily be seen to represent the erect phallus directed towards the vaginal eye of the woman. His desire for women is matched by an equally strong fear of them and by a feeling of shame. This is reminiscent of his assertion that his preoccupation began when he was 13 and a girl told him he was ugly. His defiance of authority and his desire for women can, of course, be combined in his oedipal conflict; in order to attain the desired goal of his mother's vagina he must first overcome the insuperable barrier of his father's paternal domination. Thus he saw the staring eye as both male and female.

The sexualization of the face has been referred to by a number of psychoanalysts, notably Fliess, Freud, and Ferenczi. The face, when viewed as a sexual symbol, is always bisexual even though males and females use facial features in slightly different ways. It is not surprising that the most frequently uncovered area of the body should be invested with some of the emotion more correctly belonging to the most frequently covered area, the genitals. The head is roughly similar to the torso in shape and is separated from it by the narrow neck, making it a sort of twin. The shape and position of the facial organs facilitate the drawing of parallels between them and the hidden torso and genitalia.

Figure 8 affords an example of this: the nose, with the eyes on either side of it, can readily be seen as the penis and the testicles. The eyes can be seen either as the paired breasts or as the vulva—they are moist with lids that open and close and are surrounded by the hairy eyelashes and eyebrows.

It is highly probable that the mouth in particular, and also on occasion the orifices of the nostrils and the ears, takes on the qualities of the vagina. The adornment of the female face by cosmetics and even jewelry is further evidence of its significance as a sexual object. It is pertinent here to outline in more detail some of the ideas and emotions that appear to have become associated with the nose and with the eyes.

The nose is the same size in boys and girls; at puberty it grows proportionately larger in boys, so that men have larger noses than women. The genitals also grow larger at puberty and the growth of the nose becomes a reflection of that of the penis. A large nose has therefore come to represent masculinity, just as a large chin has. Women with large noses or large chins tend to be seen as masculine and unattractive. In most quadrupeds the nose is large and pointed and is the part of the body that leads. Many animals keep their noses close to the ground as they move and are acutely aware of the smells they encounter. Smell for them has an important sexual significance; some animals have a stronger smell during the mating season.

Because for most animals the nose is used for exploring and probing, it has come to represent curiosity and inquisitiveness. It is said of an over-inquisitive person that he pokes his nose in where it's not wanted. Related to inquisitiveness is the concept of penetration. It is only a small step from this to intercourse. Children are often warned of the dangers of having their noses pecked off, and parents play a game of pretending to do so, presenting the thumb, protruding between the fingers, to represent the plucked off nose. Clearly these are lightly masked allusions to castration. It is not too difficult, therefore, to conceive of the young man in this study associating his oedipal desire and hostility with his nose, and of expressing his oedipal guilt as a desire for surgical assault upon it.

To man the eyes are much more important than the nose, due probably to his arboreal ancestors. Vision is more important than smell to animals living in trees. Because of the value of binocular vision in judging distances, the eyes in man have become frontal. It is perhaps for all these reasons that sexual interaction is mediated by the eyes.

In contrast to the nose, the eyes appear to be larger in women than in men. This may be because they actually are proportionately larger, because women habitually open their eyes more widely, or because they are made to look larger by cosmetics. Women with large eyes and long curling eyelashes are considered attractive. The position of the eyes in the head corresponds to that of the breasts in the torso. It is likely therefore that parallels come to be drawn between the exposed eyes and the hidden breasts. The association between the eye and the vagina has already been referred to. Thus there are a number of reasons why the eye is readily seen as female.

The eye is a mobile organ; it can be closed tightly or opened wide. When open, it can be directed at, or averted from, other people. A special kind of looking is looking into the eyes of someone else. Because it is usually a sign that one wishes to communicate, it is called making eye-contact. When accompanied by a smile it becomes a friendly gesture. When directed toward someone of the opposite sex it amounts to a sexual advance. Staring at someone without smiling is hostile and disapproving. The object of such an expression is likely to turn down his eyes in submission or shame. Thus the eyes are associated with judgment and accusation.

In the case of the patient, the sexual and accusatory aspects of the eye appear to have become confused. There is evidence that he sees the eye not just as female, but also as vaginal. Possibly it is even his mother's vagina. Yet at the same time he misinterprets the staring of other people as the gaze of paternal disapproval. The eyes reflect back his own guilt for desiring women, all of whom he tends to see as his forbidden mother. His pictures reveal a complex relationship between the provocative and audacious nose—representing his masculine drive and sexual desire—and the seductive but retaliatory eye—representing desirable women but also his disapproving father. He displays his nose before the female eye but fears the eye's Gorgon-like destructiveness. His fear of his nose's being stared at seems to have resulted in his withdrawal from almost all social contact and his complete inability to relate to women.

It is unfortunate that only a small sample of this patient's pictures can be presented here. Although, as is not surprising, there were included in the series a large number of pictures of faces—some of which were of great interest—it is perhaps the pictures depicting the entire human figure that were the most revealing.

In his sessions with his psychiatrist the patient spoke almost exclusively about the face. In his pictures he makes clear the way his face fitted into his relationships with other people. The pictures would have provided an excellent vehicle for extending the range of discussion and for incorporating into it the interpersonal difficulties that were obviously his real problem.

Part IV

SYSTEMATIC INVESTIGATIONS IN ART THERAPY

The Psychiatric Patient and His "Well" Sibling: A Comparison Through Their Art Productions[1]

JULIANA DAY

and HANNA YAXA KWIATKOWSKA

A recurrent question raised regarding environmental theories of mental disorders is: How is it that only one sibling becomes ill? Or, if the "well" sibling is seen as having personality problems: How is it that he too is not hospitalized?

In the course of our work with families at the National Institutes of Health we became intrigued with such questions when we began to notice certain rather unexpected similarities between the well siblings in different families and also unexpected psychological difficulties which did not match the reputations they had in their families. These findings could not be fully explained on the basis of constitutional differences or differing life experiences —the usual types of explanations given for the "wellness" of a sibling.

We are here concerned in a very general way with the interpersonal forces within the family which create a family culture and assist in shaping the personalities of family members through role differentiation and integration. More specifically, we shall acquaint the reader with the offspring of some of these families we have met; particularly we shall compare the "well" offspring and their patient siblings in their impact upon us and upon their families.

---

[1] This article is based on material presented at the Annual Meeting of the American Psychiatric Association, Atlantic City, New Jersey, May 1960.

Figure 1

The enigma of these "well" siblings may be illustrated pictorially, by the drawings of two sets of siblings in two families in which there was a schizophrenic and an ostensibly well sibling. These drawings were made in the course of art therapy with families in our project.[2] Throughout this paper the drawings are presented not merely as examples of individual performance but especially as vivid symbolic representations of the total functioning of an individual—his ego strength and his defenses under differing circumstances.

Figures 1 and 2 are the productions of two sisters, ages 20 and 17; the elder one is a schizophrenic who has been acutely ill for about a year. Each sister happened to choose a house as a central theme. In the elder girl's picture (Figure 1) each of the walls of the house is outlined in a different color; the door is yellow and there is an enormous green door-knob. What she describes as a "pot of gold" sits upon the roof. Next to the house a blue whirling waterfall descends from the skies and empties into a tiny blue puddle on the ground; it separates the picture into two parts. On the far left is a dark, rather amorphous area of blacks, greys and browns, which she describes as "the dark—this is to be afraid of." She pointed there to a ghost and a bear. The elements of this picture are incongruous and unrelated, as is often observed in paintings by schizophrenics.

The 17-year-old sister, who has had no overt psychiatric difficulty, drew another house (Figure 2), painted in a crude and childlike fashion. It has few components, just the house and tree solidly planted on thick green grass. There are two dense clouds above the house. The picture is well organized. Upon taking a closer look one notices something slightly odd or surprising:

[2] See Hanna Yaxa Kwiatkowska, "Family Art Therapy: Experiments with a New Technique." *Bulletin of Art Therapy,* Vol. 1, No. 3, Spring 1962.

Figure 2

Those clouds are *blue* and the sky colorless—and she calls the picture "The Haunted House."

Let us look at another family which includes a different sort of schizophrenic, a 25-year-old highly ritualistic young man, who considers himself something of a beatnik. Figure 3 represents several months' hard work. This

Figure 3

Figure 4

scene, outside the ice house, is from his favorite movie, "East of Eden." All the lines were drawn and redrawn hundreds of times. The resultant effect is of stiff, frozen figures, which seem not to relate to one another even though the scene attempts to represent a significant interaction. Figure 4, "Suspicion," was painted in a much later period of his work in art therapy when he was able to perform less rigidly and to produce some free compositions.

Figure 5 is his nonschizophrenic sister's; she is a young woman of 22 who ran away from home to marry a rather artistic and literary man. These delightful horses nudging one another are skillfully drawn and are a lively contrast to her brother's pictures. Let us look more closely; these horses are oddly incomplete, they seem to have stilts for legs—and there are but six legs for two horses.

Both of these "well" siblings' productions appear on first impression well-organized and integrated. Only upon scrutiny does one notice something incongruous, something unusual—and this can easily be dismissed.

We will next demonstrate something that is harder to ignore: What happens when these siblings have not chosen a definite subject, when, for instance, the art therapist specifically suggests and encourages non-representational free expression; for example, depiction of a mood or feeling. When the well sibling who drew the house was told, "Draw anything, just what you feel like" she produced Figure 6, a multi-colored conglomeration of scattered colors and shapes which have little relation to one another. She attempts to unify them by a line which encircles them like a frame and by the repetition of three similar vertical shapes. (In the original picture these are much less

Figure 5

prominent.) Nevertheless, this effort does not succeed, the unstable and confused quality remains; it is best described by her own title, "The Big Mix-up." The other sibling, who so skillfully sketched the horses, made a drawing, Figure 7, where the shapes bear no relation to one another. It remained disorganized even though here also an effort was made to unify the parts into a composition, this time by a certain repetition of color. A single, barely noticeable touch of red in the upper right corner, slightly resembling lips, gives the picture its surprising title, "The Smile." This picture has some of the features which have been observed in the pictures of schizophrenics: it is fragmentary and its title is inappropriate, peculiarly foreign to the overall feeling of the picture.

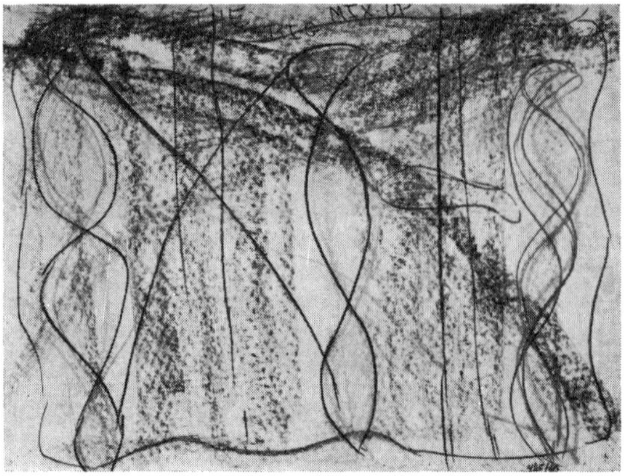

Figure 6

Figure 7

A sibling from another family, a 17-year-old younger sister of a paranoid schizophrenic, drew Figure 8 using a scribble of her own as a stimulus. In this "scribble technique," a person draws a free-flowing line and uses it to get an idea for a picture. How well that which develops out of the scribble is integrated into a picture or, on the contrary, how much it remains a conglomeration of fragments, indicates the integrative abilities of its author. This sibling makes no attempt to integrate the lines that she chose in order to convey a single idea. She accentuates and fills in certain portions of the scribble, a method often used to a more marked degree by some severely schizophrenic patients. The resulting picture looks in part like misplaced and skewed features of a face. Its rather hallucinatory title, "The Mouth Speaks," increases the impression of some weirdly distorted mask.

We have presented the siblings of schizophrenics in three different families. Their drawings show integrated functioning in well structured situations, except for easily dismissed minor details. Their productions become more fragmentary when the environment does not provide structure, but places the siblings in a situation where they must rely on their own inner experience. In this latter situation their performance approaches that of the schizophrenic. It is more confused, more fragmentary.

It is our primary thesis, therefore, that these siblings' health is in some way superficial or less than complete. We shall explore this enigma by enlarging our view of these siblings, describing first the impact they have on persons outside the family, and next their uninvolvement with the family as contrasted to the patients' experience. Finally we shall examine and define the psychodynamics underlying this enigma, using for illustration extensive material from a single family seen over some period of time in family psychotherapy.

This work with siblings is but one aspect of our long-term study of the family in mental illness, particularly schizophrenia; our interest has been focused upon the roles and relationships within the family. Briefly, the physical setting is a small open ward where patients with various psychiatric illnesses are hospitalized and participate with their parents and siblings in family psychotherapy, art therapy, and psychological testing. The patients are usually persons in their late teens or twenties. Of the approximately 35 families studied in which there were two or more offspring, about two-thirds of the families included a schizophrenic member and the other families had offspring with manic depressive, delinquent, obsessive or other psychiatric illnesses severe enough to warrant hospitalization.

Our curiosity about the sibling was aroused by two facets of the way he was perceived, in contrast with the patient. First, his reputation in the family: There was no question in the family's mind about the sickness of the patient or the wellness of his sibling. The latter was usually described as a paragon of health, strength and success. Second, our direct perception of the sibling differed oddly from his family reputation. When we tried to fill in the silhouette, he did not come to life. Despite the patient's desire to protect himself against relating, we usually found him to be a more complete

Figure 8

Figure 9

human being. We were untouched by the sibling. When we started to review what we expected to be a wealth of data on these offspring, we were puzzled by our finding: The material was sparse and barren despite the sensitivity of the interviewers. Their detailed descriptions failed to convey any depth or individuality.

Illustrative is the single art therapy session held with a young married woman of 32 years, one of the sisters of a 28-year-old chronic schizophrenic. She was the eldest child in a very intellectual and artistic family. Because the art therapist's first impression of this sibling was of an attractive person with a pleasant, somewhat eager and responsive attitude, the therapist expected this therapy session to be rewarding. Her expectation was not fulfilled; the session actually left her with a sense of frustration. This woman appeared to offer the possibility of a relationship: she seemed outgoing. Yet both in her conversation with the therapist and in her drawings there was a distressing shallowness. Neither the affective nor the representational aspect of her paintings conveyed anything very meaningful about herself. In a single hour she made a number of facile, superficial drawings. She did not try to develop or elaborate any of them. She never became absorbed in her task, never gave herself to it.

Figure 9 is the first drawing she made. These are graceful but conventionally stylized shapes similar to the designs she and her group use in pottery class; they are entirely impersonal. She made no creative effort; she didn't try to make the total picture express some meaning. Figure 10, "The Cat that Swallowed the Canary," produced in the latter part of the session, conveys rather amusingly her guardedness, the feeling that her inner experience is no one's business but her own. She calls the cat's expression "smug." The title of this picture should not be taken too literally, however. In this art therapy session, as well as in psychotherapeutic interviews and psychological tests, this young woman's inability to convey to another person the deeper aspects of her own personal identity was for the most part outside of her awareness.

As with the siblings mentioned earlier, when this young woman experimented with the scribble technique she was unable to carry over even the stereotyped yet esthetic quality of her first picture. She produced Figure 11, which seems rather empty and almost as disorganized as "The Big Mix-up."

Our inability to involve ourselves emotionally with these siblings had its counterpart within their families. These offspring seemed to be less involved with the family difficulties, more detached from the family's distress, than their hospitalized brother or sister. Some of them who participated in family therapy sat in silence, albeit an intense and watchful one. The schizophrenic's sister, whose solid house we described earlier, seldom contributed to the discussion with the family, but when she did, it was to dismiss the conflict the rest of the family experienced. For example, in a family session the mother was speaking haltingly of her own sister who had died that particular week; she described with difficulty how the death had something to do with a liver disease. Her husband indicated vaguely that his sister-in-law was morally responsible in some way for her own death and that this had to do with the way she had lived. The non-schizophrenic daughter interrupted the conversation to question caustically, "Why don't you say that your sister was an alcoholic and was running around with a married guy before she married him?" Although her comments were factually correct, her insensitive approach carelessly dismissed that which was of greatest moment to the parents. The aunt's death touched off something relating to the parents' own marital difficulties. Yet the quality of the parents' moral and sexual struggles, in

Figure 10

Figure 11

which the patient was anxiously and intimately involved, did not appear to affect the patient's sister.

Let us contrast this girl's casualness about family struggles with a schizophrenic patient's rather typical involvement with his family. Figure 12 illustrates a 23-year-old triplet's view of his family. He and his two brothers are schizophrenic, he the least ill of the three. There is a sister, six years older, who is married and has several children. In the upper part of the picture are the parents with a heavy wall between them. On the left is the mother, angry, hysterical and weeping, wielding a rolling-pin. Red tears are dripping from her eyes and a pool has formed at her feet. To the right of her is the "indifferent" father smoking a pipe, with his newspaper next to his chair where, at one depressed period of his life, he allegedly sat motionless for five years. The other brothers are below. On the left, one of them, red like the mother, is a devil, a toy gun is at his feet. The other, the most psychotic, is fat and infantile; he holds a toy train by a string. Caught between the pairs, both above and below, you can twice see a small black figure, the third of the triplets—the author of the picture. He is also seen outside the house, explaining "Everything from the outside calls me away, cars, buildings and people. I want out!" But an enormous magnet pulls him back, and a heavy wall next to the house holds him. There is a wealth of fascinating detail in his inscriptions, all expressing this patient's sensitivity to the family difficulties. This drawing is important in another respect—the elder sister, the well sibling, is not in the picture. This patient views her as outside the family conflict.

Reciprocal to the patient's or sibling's view is the parents' quality of involvement with their offspring. The mother of the ritualistic beatnik schizophrenic mentioned above stated, "John is my only living child." John was the patient. She had lost her first child in a miscarriage. Her daughter had left home; she had eloped. In another family a father was filling out a form for us, which requested a list of his children. He put down his schizophrenic daughter's name but omitted his son's, although this boy was living at home at the time.

Next we shall present in some detail a particular family which was engaged in family psychotherapy for several years. In order to examine the dynamics of the well sibling's apparent uninvolvement in the family conflict, or more precisely his disowning it, we shall contrast his experience with the patient's.

The family consisted of the two parents and two sons: Andrew, the patient, age 23, and his brother, Bob Jr., two years younger. Andrew was a borderline schizophrenic with severe obsessional features who was hospitalized; Bob was in college. Several excerpts from tape-recorded family sessions follow.

In one meeting Andrew, the patient, was hesitantly describing his difficulties as a child, his struggles, wanting to be on the team, to be a success, thinking he was never quite good enough, always feeling on the fringe and never free with his friends.

Bob, the well sibling, responded in an offhand manner to his brother's complaints:

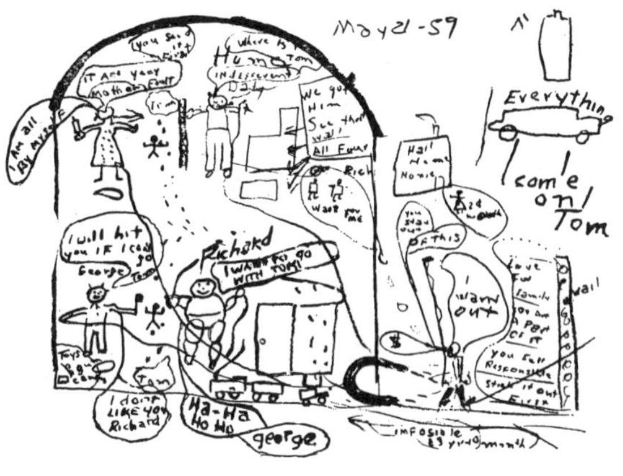

Figure . 12

> "I don't understand why it's so important. I remember one time in basketball I tried to make the basket. I shot the ball about 20 times and I could never make it . . . Lots of frustrations like that happen. I was never particularly friendly with anyone on the football team . . . I was never pleased with my grades at school, but I'm not setting my standards any lower just because I can't attain them."

Bob appears to feel no distress at being without friends, and getting poor marks. The rest of his family concurs, in this meeting, in representing him as a person who is without problems, satisfied to go his own way, unruffled and accepting his limitations comfortably. He is free of that which binds them unwillingly to one another. Yet at other times he does object to this bland view of himself. Could his annoyance also be a comment on the isolation his supposed uninvolvement bequeaths to him?

Bob spoke as follows of how his father's anger affected him.

> "I live in my own little world. I do things that will satisfy me in the future but if you blow up . . . it doesn't bother me . . . There are certain times when I have my shortcomings and this makes father mad . . . He expects . . . that if I want to be a successful businessman that I should change some of my ways . . . But it doesn't bother me at all. I just brush it off. And I try to gain from these different things that happen by improving myself."

The patient, Andrew, answers him:

> "And I live by a different law. When I consider an authority, like the law or my father . . . when they offer criticism I tend to take their word for it and try to please them rather than myself . . . I never happened to have any definite goals for myself . . . except by just getting things down to where I can visualize them, so I can know them to perfection."

Andrew is experiencing conflict, hesitancy and his wish to rely on others and yet please himself, while Bob insists upon his lack of involvement, and his freedom to solve his own problems.

Some time later when Andrew and his parents were still involved with the problem of dependency as against success, but expressing their roles more clearly, the father stated:

> "Something you said one day made me feel that you had come to the conclusion that you may as well have an AB degree. And I am sure that you and I would agree that a degree in itself is not a measure of education, but it is still accepted that way—in getting jobs."

Andrew replies:

> "I realize that this is an economic and social little piece of paper, or a ticket, but I just don't feel that mercenary about it . . . one of the big things that stops me from thinking about a degree very much is . . . this thought of, 'After college, what?' I don't picture myself as a mature person."

The struggle in which Andrew is involved relates to such areas of conflict within him as infantile dependency, competitiveness and masculinity. His

Figure 13

conflict has, as we see in the above discussion, its counterparts within the parents. The father is an active professional man, inclined to be artistic and also to deny this. He is a person for whom success is vital. He has continued to improve his position, yet always privately views himself as a failure. As a boy he was small, and skinnier than his contemporaries; his father would not let him swim or ride a bike for fear of his being hurt.

The mother is a healthy buxom woman of Norwegian descent. Her own mother felt that education was of overriding importance, and was greatly pleased when her daughter married a professor in a university. The mother's manner is aggressive and formidable, yet she was amazed, albeit somewhat pleased, when a therapist spoke of her in such terms.

The next excerpt illustrates the complement to Bob's dissociation from family conflict, that is, the hospitalized son's awareness and acceptance of conflict in contrast to the father's insistence upon a constricted view.

A painting of Andrew's was discussed in a family psychotherapy session by the father and son. At that time family art therapy had not been instituted as a part of the program; Andrew was the only member of the family who engaged in art therapy. Thus it is impossible to give any illustration of the brother Bob's functioning in this medium. In the course of Andrew's work in art therapy, to which he became increasingly responsive, painting became an extremely important mode of expression in which he developed an impressive creative power.

Unfortunately this oil painting (Figure 13) loses much of its effect through black and white reproduction. At the upper left is a deep menacing slate grey sky which gradually softens and merges toward the right into yellows and soft reds and ochres. In the middle distance are soft and verdant greens which seem to move outward, becoming more blue toward the horizon.

The sharp wall-like structure at the lower left is both strong and forbidding. It is deeply textured—black, brown and dark velvet red. Immediately to its right are soft greens and browns separated by a furrow of tufted browns from a field of warm browns and oranges, with the most vivid orange in the foreground.

The following is an excerpt from family therapy on the day in which Andrew brought this painting to the session:

Father: I greatly admire that technique up through there (the right). That whole area in there, but not down through here (the forbidding wall-like shape in the lower left). If you took and framed this part of the picture from there over and blanked that thing out up there (the threatening darkness in the upper left) I'd feel as though I was up in the sky, but not the way the earth is today, but a billion years ago. Here again it's like that dark earth down in there (lower right).

Andrew: I started from the top on that one and when I got down to the bottom I felt the whole thing just wasn't any good. I couldn't—something was keeping me in the same old form or routine. I couldn't escape from that . . . So I got very angry . . .

Father: Got any pieces of paper around here . . . I want to mat off this thing. (He puts typewriter paper along the left border of the painting, matting off the dark and threatening parts of it.)

Andrew: . . . I'll explain the process of the painting. I started on this and I worked on over and I was remembering things about Van Gogh and his orange colors. Then I came down here and this was all supposed to be an underpainting for another painting. Then I start thinking about things very far in the distance, lakes or green blobs or something in the mountains in a mist or something.

Father: Well that's exactly what it means to me.

Andrew: And somehow I was going to bring it into stronger colors down here, but . . .

Father: I've seen the Appalachians stick up above the cloud banks just like that. To me, when he got into this forceful sort of stuff right here, it takes you back a billion years.

Andrew: . . . This plain here (lower center) is so typical I didn't know what to do and I got very frustrated about the way it was turning out so I put this orange and the splash and that big damn thing in (lower right) trying to make something out of it. It wouldn't work.

Therapist: (To the father) What is it that you're matting off?

Father: . . . This (on the left) doesn't seem to add anything to it. This is my own personal taste. Sometimes in some of his work there are areas that are pretty good, then it gets over to an area where he loses control of it or loses interest in it.

Therapist: Loses control?

Father: Lose control of any intention of how you particularly wanted to paint this picture.

Andrew: That's quite right . . .

Father: I was pointing out to Andrew that Gauguin or Van Gogh worked with certain consistent techniques which they carried through consistently throughout the painting. Andrew will shift right from one technique to another, on the same painting practically . . . Of course your attitude is that of a sketcher not a painter . . . You're doing painting for amusement, aren't you? . . .

Andrew: When I'm doing a picture like that, the emotions and the struggles involved in it, putting the thing on, are very clear-cut and immediate to me . . . When you look at the picture, there's not much in there to indicate the fantastic struggle that's involved in getting to what I'm thinking about and getting what I want painted . . .

Therapist: I guess the struggle part of it is what you were matting out.

Father: Maybe I was. Yes.

This excerpt reveals several things about this father and son. Clearly the father both recognizes the threatening quality of this painting and wishes to deny it—to remove it. His interchange with his son also demonstrates his unusual sensitivity and his ability to react perceptively and personally to his son's painting. Yet he cannot allow himself to be overtly aware of his artistic sensibility. Although he is in an occupational field which might allow for some creative artistic expression he has chosen to work only in teaching and administration. He denies himself personal expression and in a sense rejects his son's paintings by recommending to him that he follow the techniques of the great painters. It is left for the son to identify with the creative, yet denied, part of the father and for him to carry alone the burden of experiencing and expressing in his paintings not only beauty but also turmoil.

This is a vivid example of how, when a parent has resolved conflict by dissociation, the child, through identification with the parent, will internalize the dissociated, as well as the manifest, aspects of that parent. The patient seems often sensitive to such conflict and yet unable to resolve it. It is likely that the parent will find objectionable that aspect of the child which represents what is dissociated in himself. The child who stays "well" identifies with those aspects of the parent which are within the parent's awareness, which resemble his recognizable and conventional self. The sibling's unawareness of the contradictions which give the parent's character some depth lends to his personality that peculiar constricted quality which we have noted.

Andrew, who identifies not only with his father's more obvious attributes of success and manliness, but with what is partially out of the father's awareness, his sense of failure and weakness, is acutely conscious of conflict. Bob, on the other hand, acts—albeit not quite convincingly—the man his father would wish him to be. He presents himself as insensitive, unlike the father, to the ambiguities of his role. The father's partial awareness of a sense of failure may be one reason Andrew is no sicker than he is.

Bob's singlemindedness had its effect upon his living. He married hastily a girl who was superficially attractive, but cold and distant, a much less lively woman than his mother. Their child arrived unwanted; it became distasteful for him to sleep with his wife. At present they are separated.

Perhaps not all the patients' siblings have had so much trouble in their lives as did the brother Bob in this family. However, when they were evaluated independently by projective tests—Rorschach, TAT, Sentence Completion, and Draw-a-Person—they all showed some disturbance varying from the schizophrenic to the mildly neurotic. Bob appeared as a moderately to severely neurotic person of obsessive type, relatively introversive although trying hard to be sociable. It was noted that the most differentiating test feature between Andrew and Bob was that Andrew blamed himself for failure and Bob blamed himself for guilty transgressions. The well sibling mirrored the father's pessimism and doubt that there is much real satisfaction in life, yet resolved to go ahead and try for success. He was willing to take blame in a penitent way, yet did not feel deeply that he had failed or was inadequate.

We return at this point to the question posed in a somewhat different way at the beginning: If the sibling is as psychologically disturbed as he appears in some ways, how is it that he functions as well as he does? Possibly the very constriction, which gave this offspring less of a subjective sense of conflict, allowed him to move out of the family emotionally at an early age. Also, since he was not a participant in the family's struggle in the same way as the rest of its members, he was able to make a fair number of childhood friends, unlike the patient. It is expected that these friendships would have the same shallowness which we have noted in our relationships with him. Yet, through pseudo-identification with his peers and imitation of them, the sibling may find some support outside his family; when he marries he does not have to rely on his parents.

To conclude, we may return to some thoughts about the first pictures we discussed. Perhaps those incongruous aspects of the pictures we remarked upon, the blue clouds, the hoofless horses, are out of the sibling's awareness. With the patient such aspects are very much "in the picture," though often fragmented, confused, and in conflict. The well sibling is free to move out of the home and into a job and marriage; all of this is at the expense of greater depth of character and personality, a depth which derives from the ability to perceive more of life's contradictory experiences.

A New Use of Art in Psychiatric Diagnosis*

ELINOR ULMAN

Nine years ago I began working in the psychiatric department of a general hospital. When I discovered that treatment was at that time almost nonexistent in a service whose main function was diagnostic, I felt indignant at first, then frustrated and secretly (though doubtless not secretly enough) superior. Here were patients of all ages, human beings obviously in need of help, whatever fancy psychiatric tag did or didn't apply to them. I held a deep belief that psychotherapy was the main avenue of help, and that I as an art therapist could contribute effectively to psychotherapy under medical supervision. Was I the only one who really cared, down there in the basement? (Activity departments in hospitals are traditionally situated below ground.) Were the well-paid psychologists upstairs just playing magical parlor games with ink blots, while the even better-paid psychiatrists treated live human beings merely as demonstration material for the young doctors-in-training they were teaching to be the psychiatrists of the future? That is how it looked to me from my underground eminence. I felt very virtuous, but also exceedingly lonely.

I knew better than to practice, by myself, the kind of therapy-through-art that aims at startling new insights. I did search for ways to make available the satisfactions of genuine artistic experience at any level where the patients could respond. It was hard, however, to nourish the hope that in the few hours they spent on art during the few weeks of their hospital stay some of the seeds I tried to plant had fallen on fertile ground. Thus my interest in diagnosis began quite frankly, even cynically, because it was the only way

* This article is based on material presented at the Syracuse University Summer Session Symposium on "Creativity for the Exceptional Individual," Syracuse, N. Y., July 1964.

I saw to get into the act that was going on above ground, to relieve, at least through an intellectual exercise, my own near-despair during a few of the 40 hours of the work week.

Gradually I learned how badly I had underrated the skill, care, and sensitivity that good psychologists put into their diagnostic work, and the seriousness with which the thoughtful hospital psychiatrist takes his awesome responsibility for decisions that may shape the course of a human life. The label "psychotic" officially affixed or withheld may determine whether an individual spends years in a mental hospital or leaves after his 30 days of "mental observation" to wander the world as freely as the rest of us. For another the alternatives may be a life snuffed out in youth by execution for a crime, versus hospital treatment which may eventually restore him to a satisfactory life in the community.

The philosophically minded may argue whether mental illness is or is not a myth, but my years of psychiatric hospital work leave me convinced that physically healthy and morally blameless people sometimes must be confined against their will for their own protection or for the protection of others. Therefore, anything that an art therapist can contribute toward making the psychiatrist's decision an enlightened one, based on all possible diagnostic evidence and prognostic clues, will at times help a patient as much as all the therapy an art therapist might offer him under other circumstances.

In addition, I learned that diagnosis was not the cold, clever effort to fit round human beings into square categories that I had supposed. The articulate psychologist analyzing data obtained through a battery of tests comes up with a penetrating description of an *individual,* full of lifelike shadings and complex contradictions. He assays not only the patient's sickness but his health, indeed often includes an estimate of his creative potential. So, having climbed up out of my physical basement, it was also a relief to climb down from my precarious spiritual pedestal. Not only were there others who cared about the patients' welfare at least as much as I did, but they knew a great deal more than I did about the job we were all there to perform. If, after learning from them, I could make some small, new contribution to this complex and fateful business of psychiatric diagnosis, I would have a legitimate source for my pride.

The Diagnostic Session

The hospital's chief psychologist helped me begin to think about what I saw in paintings and sculptures from a diagnostician's point of view. From him I learned the basic method of interpretation wherein a single moment of observed behavior is generalized as typical of the way in which a person responds to superficially differing yet fundamentally similar situations. In 1959 he began sending patients to me for a single session whose purpose was the quick, efficient accumulation of diagnostic information. Now, most of the psychiatric residents and staff doctors request such evaluation of an occasional patient. These are often patients who present a somewhat puzzling diagnostic picture, so many of their productions do not resemble the clear-cut, obvious examples that are usually selected to illustrate painting typical of patients falling in particular diagnostic categories.

The procedure I developed is as follows: The standard set of materials consists of grey construction paper, 18 by 24 inches in size, and 12 colors of hard pastels, including a full spectrum of colors, brown, black, and white. For uniformity and convenience the boxes of colors are arranged in spectral order, followed by the neutrals. A more or less full, open box of each color is provided, so that the range of colors is more conspicuous than it would be with only a single stick of each color. Before the patient is taken to a room where nobody else is present, a floor easel has been set up and the first sheet of paper has been tacked to a drawing board, but the board is not set on the easel, so that the patient will make his own choice whether to place it vertically or horizontally.

The task, which consists of making a series of four pictures, is presented as an assignment ordered by the doctor, much like going to X-ray or taking a psychological test. Surprisingly few patients refuse to do what they are asked to do. At first I was careful to use a room where there were no pictures to invite copying, but I have found that this is not important. Even when convenience dictates the use of the art room, where the walls are covered with paintings, very few people seem to notice them, and any tentative suggestion of copying one of them has been easily discouraged. Patients occasionally use real objects as models; this I do not discourage. The available objects consist of me, ordinary hospital furniture, and the views from one or more windows.

The first picture is made in response to the request "Please use these materials to make a picture." I offer as few suggestions as I can manage, but often I must give a good deal of encouragement. When a patient insists that he can't think what to draw, I try to rattle off so many ideas that they will cancel each other out, and if the patient adopts one of them it will be in a sense his own choice. I sometimes hear myself ending up weakly with, "Or it might be just a design," but most of the abstract patterns we get have been made by patients who did not ask me what they should draw. It is possible to derive a good many clues about personality through the form of pure design, just as from handwriting, but the addition of content enhances the likelihood that something about the source and style of a person's responses to life may be revealed.

Next the patient is directed in physical exercise involving movement of the whole body—pretending, without actually using the chalk, to draw sweeping straight lines across, then up and down, an imaginary wall or cliff. Then he draws large imaginary circles, swinging his arm from the shoulder.

These exercises and the "scribble technique" they lead up to are described in Florence Cane's book, *The Artist in Each of Us.*[1]

I ask patients to use their second sheet of paper to record the movements they have already made in the air, though of course they are restricted by the limited size of the paper. I watch carefully, and if necessary exhort the patient to move freely. Even this second sheet, produced in response to uniform, well-defined directions, reveals something about personal style, hints at such characteristics as conformity, rebellion, perseveration, degrees of tension, and investment of energy. Three markedly different examples are included among the illustrations (Figures 4B, 7B, and 9B).

These simple exercises constitute a drawing lesson, for they demonstrate in one's own body the relationship between movement and the production of lines. But they are more than that. They give a sense of liberation, make people feel exhilarated, even excited. Some people find the experience exceedingly pleasant; to others it does something that they dislike. Patients react to it in a wide variety of ways.

On the third sheet of paper, the patient is asked to make a rhythmic scribble with his eyes closed. I urge him to use the same kind of free-swinging movement from the shoulder that he used in the directed exercise. Often I compare the drawing board to a dance floor over which the hand moves to imagined music. I stop the scribbling at a point where the paper is fairly well covered with intersecting shapes, but before it is reduced to an impenetrable tangle of lines. The drawing board is then placed on the floor so that it will be easy to walk around and study accidental shapes from all four sides. This is done with a view to finding suggestions of imagery in these forms. Some people see many images, some are unwilling or unable to see any at all. At best, people are able to select one image or set of images that interests them. They are then asked to develop these into a picture right on the scribbled sheet. They are invited to use as many of the colors as they wish, and to add to, change, or obscure the accidental forms as much as they want to.

Images which are remarked upon but not used, and changes that occur during the course of the drawing, may contain much significance that is not apparent in the finished product. Frequently I feel free to take notes while a patient is working, because he does not seem to notice, or, if he notices, to care. If for some reason I do not feel so free, notes are made immediately after the session.

For the final drawing the patient chooses whether he will begin with another scribble or whether he will return to the more deliberate method of starting his picture on a blank sheet of paper. His choice in itself tells something about whether he has welcomed the liberating effect and imaginative stimulus of the scribble, or whether he is happier in situations where he can

---

[1] New York, Pantheon Books, 1951.

better exercise conscious control. But whichever procedure he chooses, the last drawing is apt to present interesting differences from the first one—and if it turns out not to be very different, that is interesting too.

Some examples will show the kinds of paintings that have been produced in response to this procedure. I shall try to tell what notions I derived about the painters and how I derived them. Had I ever fallen flat on my face in using this method, coming up with ideas incompatible with the findings of psychological tests and psychiatric observations, honesty would have compelled me to include at least one instance. So far I have not. At first this was a pleasant surprise, and I still wonder each time whether I will pull a complete boner. But by now I think I would be surprised if my findings were radically at variance with those arrived at by more established methods, and might even hang on to a stubborn notion that *I* was right and *they* were wrong.

Edward Berry

Usually name, age, and sex are the only advance information I have, and I prefer it so, feeling that my observations will not only be less biased but sharper if I must depend on them alone. But young Edward Berry was too famous a patient for that; by the time he had turned 16 he had been identified as the perpetrator of 12 rapes. Most of his victims were at least twice his own age. A public-spirited lawyer had requested his removal from jail to hospital. Kept in solitary confinement while awaiting sentence, he had begun talking to himself and beating his head against the wall. Figure 1 shows the drawings this tense, polite, manly looking boy made for me. He worked steadily for almost two hours, trying desperately to do the very best he could.

The drawings themselves, without regard to Edward's behavior and remarks, strongly indicate schizophrenia. The drawings deliberately made (A and C) suggest a paranoid trend—because of their strong, harsh color, areas which are rigidly separated by clear boundaries, and because of the sharp, aggressive forms, the many triangles some of which clearly suggest arrowheads. Drawing B, the one that resulted from projection of pictorial ideas into a scribble, indicates even more severe schizophrenic pathology, but it is not what would be expected from a paranoid patient. When Edward had been invited to abandon customary controls, he did not explode, but instead produced something weak and empty. The scribble at first suggested nothing to him but "handwriting." Schizophrenics often identify little besides conventional symbols, such as letters and numbers, when they are asked to project ideas into their scribbles.

The scribble drawing itself doesn't tell much about Edward as an individual, but through his associations it was possible to put together a good deal. The only thing Edward spontaneously added to his weak, jerky scribble was the word "Mother," more or less arbitrarily imposed on the accidental lines. Then he mentioned other suggestions: "an airplane . . . vines . . .

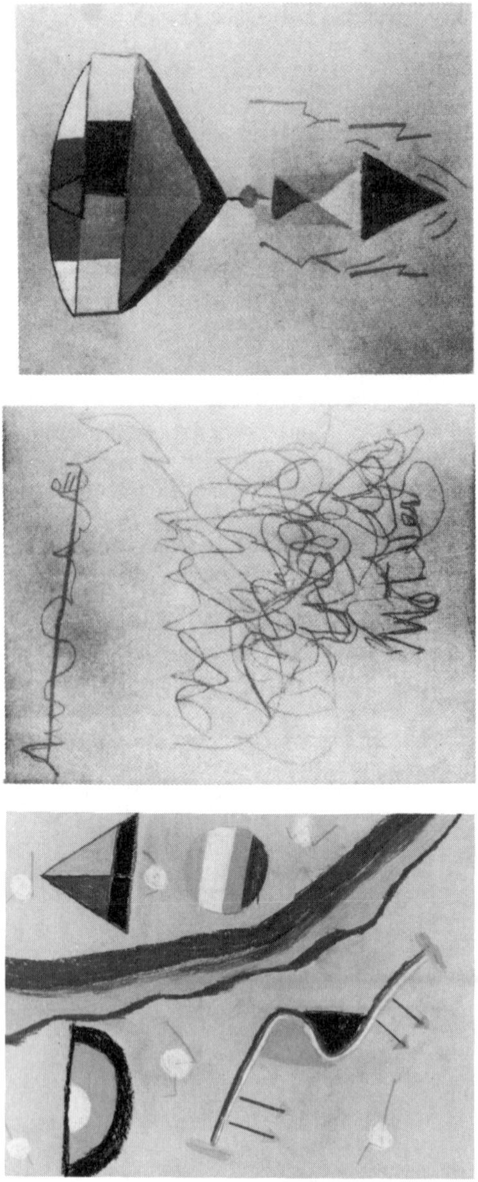

A B C

Figure 1

a boa constrictor . . . blast off and crash" (that last, he said, was an *American* missile) ". . . a weird monster . . . fighting . . . a diver." I was not able to see what parts of the drawing suggested these images to him, but I noted that while his ideas were both aggressive and frightening, he talked about them flatly, with no sign of emotion. "Blast off and crash," and the idea of diving, struck me as having orgastic overtones. I asked where the diver was, and Edward drew the straight line at the top of the sheet (which he referred to not as a diving board but as a "plank") and the weak suggestion of a little figure. I asked, "Can he swim?" and Edward answered "No. He's scared." This then was no pleasure dive; the little figure was rather "walking the plank" to his doom.

These were the observations on which I based the following statements in my written report: "Sexuality is closely tied to the idea of mother. Aggressively destructive impulses may initiate the sexual act, but it ends in self-destruction. It fizzles out prematurely, leading not to satisfaction but to inevitable and terrifying disaster—the ultimate castration of death." Obviously these ideas could not have been arrived at merely by looking at drawing B.

Edward's associations to his first and last drawings also entered into the conclusions I drew. In drawing A he saw "an ark; it's the beginning and end of everything." (I cannot say which shape suggests the ark.) "There's a sun, [the horizontally striped disc] and when it explodes, the colors from it go into the river" (diagonal striped form). Drawing C he called "a modern submarine, the submarine of the future." A floating ship (at the top of the picture) lets the submarine (below) down into the water. Something about the orange squiggles around the submarine reminded Edward of a "flower." He did not suggest that the submarine ever came back. This added strength to the idea that he feared the permanent loss of sexual potency. He called this last picture "pretty and modern, balanced, like an ink blot," and was very concerned about the chalk that had dirtied his hands and left a few spots on his clean pajamas. The last drawing is more unified and even more rigid than the first. I noted that "given a choice, the patient resumes his rigid defenses, his attempt to impose an arbitrary order, and to maintain a conventional façade."

The final summary reads in part: "This patient is prey to strong impulsive drives which he attempts to control by an obsessive-compulsive defense system. His unsuccessful effort to conform, his ineffective attempt to establish a connection with reality, leads to extreme tension and flattened expression of affect. While he was not overtly psychotic at the time the drawings were made, past psychotic episodes and/or a future psychotic break appear very likely."

These general findings tallied with those arrived at by a full battery of psychological tests. The suggestion of his feelings about the sexual act dramatically bore out his story to interviewing psychiatrists of the desperate frustration to which he had felt compelled to return again and again in his violent assaults on surrogates for mother. His moments of coition were over almost as soon as they began.

Mrs. Ziegler

Figure 2 shows the drawings made by a 35-year old woman, a patient whose private doctor from time to time found it necessary to have her spend a few days in the hospital. Mrs. Ziegler's attitude toward me and the materials and my initial request was the diametric opposite of Edward's. She was furious, and was especially repelled by the need to touch the "dirty" chalk whose dust might spoil the perfection of her grooming. Her willingness to go through the motions seemed to depend on her determination to defeat me by compliance; she set out to show just how stupid and futile the whole procedure was. By indirection, she was, at the same time, disparaging her doctor's efforts to help her.

Sneering that "my 5-year old daughter can do better" (and of course it's quite likely she could) she hastily made drawing A. I thought to myself that the contemptuous expression on the "face" of the big house reflected Mrs. Ziegler's attitude toward me, and that the pathetic, frightened, almost weeping expression of the little house might have something to do with her underlying feelings about herself. She denied that she saw or cared about any suggestion of facial expressions in her houses; if she thought about them at all it was only to wonder how many rooms they had inside. But she half denied my response that apparently she was a "practical" person.

The first scribble drawing (B) she insisted on doing with her eyes open, and, still antagonistic, she quickly drew in the outline of a whale that was the only thing she could see in the scribble except for repetitions of the letter "L." Then, to my surprise, she volunteered to make another scribble, this time with her eyes closed, and in it she saw real imagery in the *shapes,* not conventional symbols accidentally suggested by the lines. She chose to draw the grinning, toothy jack-o-lantern (C) because, she said, it was easier than the other things suggested to her by the forms, and while she was doing it her mood shifted suddenly and dramatically. Laughing with childlike delight at her own performance, she said that the jack-o-lantern brought back memories of her childhood. "This is *fun!*" she exclaimed.

She was happy to make one more picture, and decided not to start this one (D) with a scribble. But comparing her last picture with her first one, it is evident that her relaxed mood and friendly attitude have made a great difference. The subject matter is just as conventional and even more infantile, and the disposition of forms is as immature, but she has worked with some care, and the suggestion of feeling is relatively calm and idyllic. She asked me whether there were any smudges on her face, but was now unconcerned about her thoroughly dirtied hands, and she did not repeat an earlier request that nobody should see her pictures.

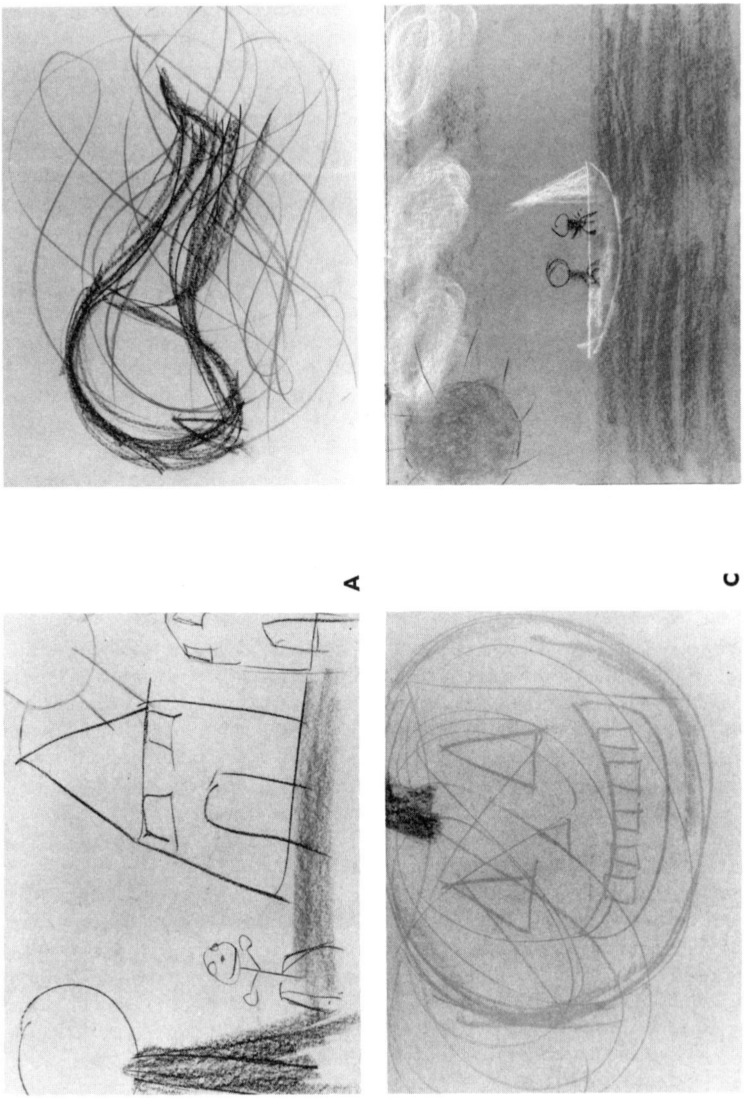

A B C D

Figure 2

See also color plate XV.

While my idea about Edward derived largely from his interpretations of what he drew, with Mrs. Ziegler the drama she played out in relation to me and the process of picture-making was on the whole more important. It was on the basis of this drama, plus the general childishness in style and content of the drawings, that I described her as a deeply depressed and very angry young woman. Her effort to control her anger results in a very constricted style of life and behavior, made even more constricted by her attempts to avoid failure by not trying to do anything that might be beyond her capacity (remember her remark about her 5-year old daughter).

What terrifies her most is her own babyish wish to fill unmet dependency needs. She bottles up whatever intellectual ability she has, and almost all her capacity for genuine feeling, in trying to look very competent and grown up, in command of herself, of others, of all situations. She tries hard to hang onto a rational view of the world around her, but this is hard since she cannot allow herself to recognize her own feelings, or those of other people. Therefore her perceptions are superficial and hollow; under stress she might easily get seriously confused, especially about people and their motives (remember her refusal to consider that there might be anything human about the expression of her houses).

Since she is able to let a fair amount of resentment dribble out (certainly a good deal had dribbled out on me, at first) she is probably less afraid of a violent explosion than of falling apart, becoming like a helpless, fussing and fuming infant. While she is compulsively clean, she can relax when she momentarily relinquishes the need to keep up the correct, lady-like, grown-up front (as she showed at the end of the session).

While she was drawing the straight lines and circles, I had suggested that she think of dance movements in order to perform with greater relaxation and freedom. "But when I dance, somebody *else* moves *me,*" she said. Putting this together with her initial reluctance to relinquish control, I concluded that (to quote again from my report) "she alternates between a pseudo-feminine compliance and passivity, and a pseudo-masculine show of domineering control over those around her."

One specific association to the pictures provided a very important clue. When I asked her who the two figures in the boat (picture D) were, she answered, "Could be me and my husband." This was interpreted on the basis of a generalization made by Loretta Bender about the drawings of very young children. The ocean, Dr. Bender stated, stands for the amniotic fluid in which the embryo once floated so comfortably, and the first two figures to appear represent the child and his mother. I therefore speculated that Mrs. Ziegler in her relationships with men secretly wants a male mother. As a result she belittles men, for she cannot forgive them for being neither mothers nor babies to her.

Not only was Mrs. Ziegler's physician impressed with the completeness and accuracy of this report, but he saw in the last two drawings a new ray of hope. This was the first time in the years he had known her that his patient had enjoyed *anything*. Furthermore, psychological tests had revealed the full extent of her pathology but had not disclosed even so small an indication of positive potential. The doctor wanted her to start private outpatient art therapy sessions; I predicted that she would refuse, and I was right. However, a few months later during another brief sojourn at the hospital, she came willingly to a single art therapy session, and maintained the mood of her last diagnostic drawing. She poked gentle fun at her rather sad, lonely paintings for being "childish," but she was happy for staff members and other patients to see them, and worked with obvious pleasure.

Sarah Buchanan

Sarah Buchanan's drawings (Figure 3) tell their own story of agitation, torment, and despair. The first two, both of which were drawn in quick succession in response to my initial request, show some remnants of rigid control. The work was done in November, the month she has designated in the picture of the body hanging from the tree (A). "The happiest day of my life" (B) features a tombstone in a labeled "cemetery" (bottom, left).

There was no formal exercise. Miss Buchanan never spoke to me except to answer questions in whispered monosyllables, and I found myself unable to go through my usual routine. The rhythmic scribble alone, however, was enough to enable her to use a graphic language much more successfully (C) than in her previous, contrived production of semi-literary symbols. Starting with the prominent, staring eyes, she completed the face, put some red in its cheeks, then almost entirely obscured it with black, finally crossing it out with red.

I asked whether she liked red; it is very hard to converse with someone who is almost mute. By gestures she indicated her preference for the cooler, milder colors that predominate in her other drawings. The only generalization concerning color that I have found valid is that the hot colors are associated with strong feelings and impulses, and the cooler ones with deliberation and control. When I remarked that the girl in her last drawing looked trapped, Miss Buchanan smiled, her only smile during the 45 minutes we spent together. I later learned that she saw various kinds of traps in many of her responses to the Rorschach ink blots.

These drawings were obtained the day before a staff conference at which Miss Buchanan's immediate fate was to be decided. She was only 23 years old, but she had already had numerous abortions, experienced a brief, unhappy marriage, been arrested for stealing a car, made several suicide attempts, and spent two periods in mental hospitals. During much of her childhood she had lived in institutions because her family was unable to cope with her periods of withdrawal, when she seemed to be almost completely unaware of

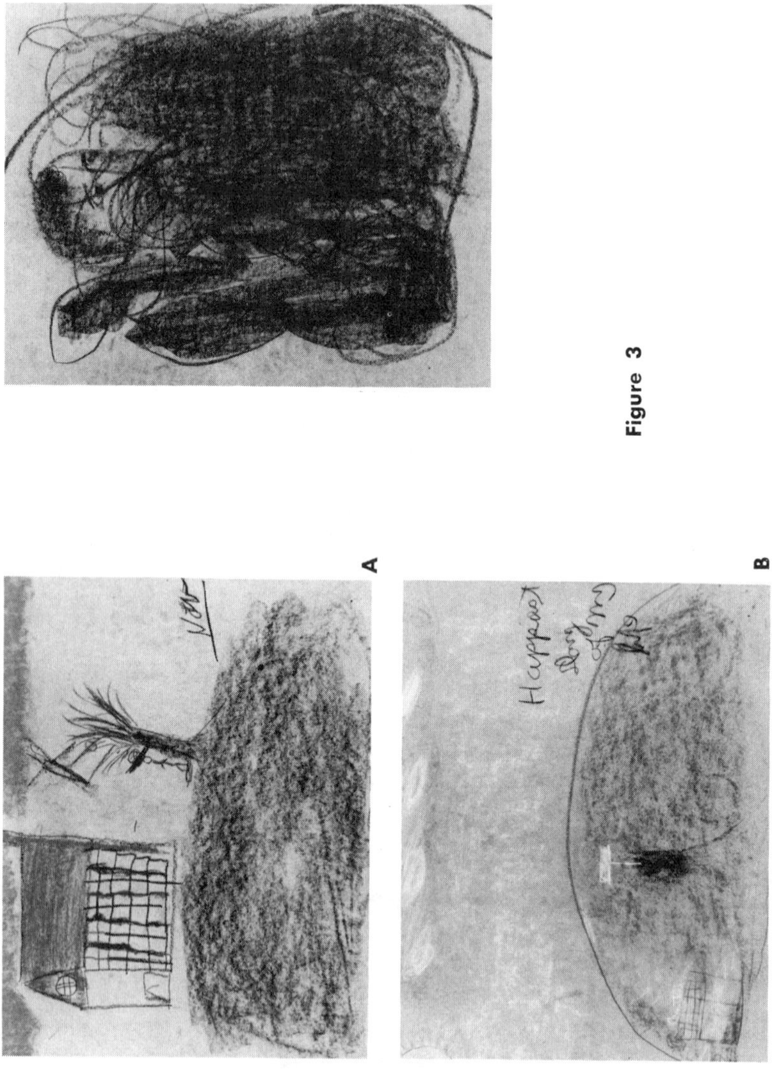

A

B

C

Figure 3

what was going on around her. She reported that she had been molested or seduced by older men several times while she was still a child, but there was no corroborating evidence that these incidents had actually occurred. She had many somatic complaints, prominent among them being laryngitis which, the psychologist noted, usually followed periods of extreme tension that had ended in angry outbursts. She had occasionally, and with remembered pleasure, killed small animals when she was a child. So far, she had not harmed another human being, but she spoke of feeling the impulse to kill others as well as herself.

Psychological tests indicated signs of paranoid schizophrenia, which I felt were borne out by my experience with this patient. In addition to the prominent, staring eyes of the last picture, there were the labels she had mixed into her other pictures. She had been exceedingly alert to outside noises during the session, and her only complete sentence was the whispered question "What is this supposed to do?" Although the first two drawings might conceivably have been hysterical dramatizations, the anguish in the last drawing looked altogether genuine. As she violently obliterated the girl she had created on the paper, the symbolic acting out of self-destruction seemed blatant.

Clinical impressions, however, won the day. In spite of all her emotional handicaps, Miss Buchanan had not only completed high school but had almost finished training as a laboratory technician. At her best, she was an attractive, well-dressed, articulate young woman. Only the day before her mute performance with me, she had been chatting intelligently with doctors and medical students. They dismissed her muteness as due to laryngitis, interpreted as a strictly physical condition. Despite her history, despite previous diagnoses of psychosis, and the psychologist's recent findings, and despite the drawings, she was promptly discharged from the hospital. Within a matter of weeks she was back, following a suicide attempt that this time almost succeeded.

Ellen Miller

Ellen Miller's problems have some resemblance to Sarah Buchanan's. When Ellen was sent to me for help with diagnostic evaluation, she was 20 years old. I had not been able to avoid hearing that she had given birth to two illegitimate children who had immediately been placed for adoption; she has since given birth to a third.

The drama Ellen played out with me was the opposite of Mrs. Ziegler's, for she started out in an amiable manner, even eager to show off her prowess in drawing. She is very pretty, and was carefully dressed and made up in a sexy style. She had studied singing, she told me, and had been enrolled for a short time in an art school.

Her first picture is more or less typical of her figure drawing as I had seen it displayed in the day room of her ward. When she portrayed female figures, either the middle of the body lacked the clarity and detail characteristic of her style, or the figure seemed about to break in two at the hips despite her fairly well-developed ability to visualize anatomical structure. Here (A) she depicted a pose where the body folds sharply at the hips and the genital area is completely hidden.

When I asked her to record the line and circle exercises (B) she suddenly became challenging, angry, and suspicious. By the time she developed the double-faced image from her scribble (C) her brittle poise had given way to cold fury. She hated the scribble because the things she saw in it were not "pretty," and "beauty," she told me, is all she really cares about. She icily refused to make a fourth drawing.

Ellen's *behavior* during the drawing session was enough to tell me that she has paranoid attitudes, and suffers from great anxiety about losing control, about having anyone penetrate inside her shell. The glaring eyes in her last drawing strengthen the impression of paranoia. The possibility of schizophrenia was at least suggested by the two-faced mask she developed from her scribble. I based some speculations about her sexual attitudes on the symbolic forms in the scribble drawing, as well as the weakness in the genital area of her figure drawings. Note especially the mouths of the mask-faces: one knife-like, the other agonized, readily suggesting a vagina, and barbed. I concluded that she is much preoccupied with sex; is probably frigid and finds sexual intercourse painful. She would like to take revenge by hurting and injuring men. In summary I thought that while she is not now psychotic, this last drawing made it appear likely that she may move toward a schizophrenic break.

My speculations about Ellen's sexual attitudes were borne out by clinical reports. It is noteworthy that her performance on projective psychological tests was more successfully guarded.

Ellen left the hospital the day after these drawings were made, and did not follow up the suggestion of outpatient treatment. Within six months she was back, again pregnant. It seems that she is somewhat contented only when her inner emptiness is symbolically filled by pregnancy.

Our staff remained undecided whether Ellen should be looked upon as suffering from a character disorder with hysterical features, or as a latent schizophrenic. Although she is intelligent, fairly well educated, and comes from a very respectable family, she not only has had a succession of illegitimate children but she periodically indulges in shoplifting, making little effort to get away with it or to defend herself after she is caught. Her behavior perhaps suggests personality disorder rather than schizophrenia. On the other hand, like Sarah Buchanan she has made suicidal gestures, and there were times when she believed she had a supernatural power to control other people's minds. I felt that the drawings lent some weight to the likelihood of latent schizophrenia, which was also suggested in the psychological findings.

After giving birth to her third child, Ellen has again been discharged from the hospital. Only time will tell whether there is indeed a schizophrenic

A B C

Figure 4

Figure 5A

process at work in her. She apparently forgave me for the diagnostic session, for during her second admission she was a regular member of our art therapy group. In a distant way she was always friendly to the art therapy staff, so long as she was allowed to go her own way in her drawing and to treat us, a trifle condescendingly, as equals.

John Bigelow

The drawings shown in Figure 5 were made by a 56-year old man, John Bigelow. This example is included mainly as a warning about how deceiving drawings taken by themselves may be. These look very like the work of a mental defective, with the added suggestion of psychotic-like withdrawal; despite two attempts, Mr. Bigelow could make nothing of his scribbled forms. In his fifth and last picture (B) he made very concrete use of the objective environment (easel, door, electrical outlets).

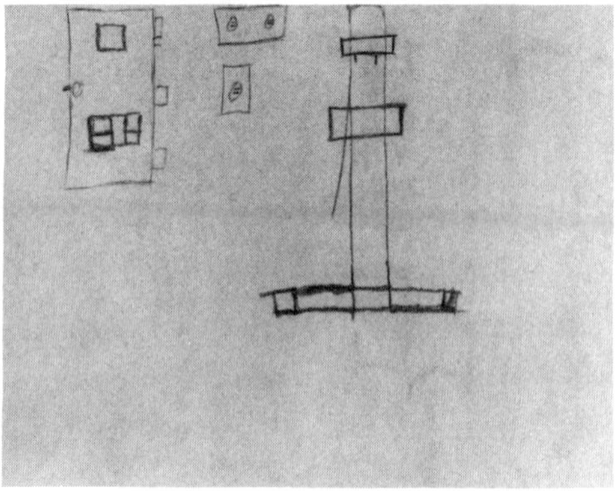

Figure 5B

Mr. Bigelow's talk and behavior, however, made it obvious that he was neither mentally defective, nor, at the time, psychotic. My report, which checked out well with the findings of the others, was arrived at in an effort to explain the discrepancy between the drawings and the impression Mr. Bigelow as a person made on me. His extremely limited use of resources, both external resources (typified by the material offered him) and the internal resources, intellectual and emotional, revealed by his conversation, had to be explained on the basis of unconscious defensive maneuvers. Specific but heavily veiled verbal clues further revealed that he is a schizoid person, passive, dependent, and deeply ambivalent about his dependency. (For example, he wished above all that he could paint a portrait of his long-dead mother but said, "I mustn't even try it, because it would be terrible to mess up her face.") Even his fantasy life is impoverished, but he does permit himself a few modest paranoid explanations of his disappointments with himself and the world.

Mr. Simpson

Figure 6 shows contrasting work of another middle-aged, depressed man. Mr. Simpson had always lived with his parents, and when they died in quick succession he became unable to work and began to suffer from numerous, unexplained physical symptoms. We see that the scribble technique enabled him to get away from his very conventional attempts to please (see drawing A) by conforming to the world's supposed wishes. The formal symbolism of his third and fourth drawings (B and C), confirmed not only by Mr. Simpson's verbal associations but by the intermittent physical complaints he made while he was working, suggested a good deal about his conflicts in the areas of sexuality, dependency, and aggression.

In considering the sexual issues only, we see in drawing B numerous phallic protrusions, but the obvious opportunity to portray a body opening (the mouth) has been rejected. Drawing C, also developed from a scribble, abundantly makes up for this lack. Whatever fills this strange vessel is brown, the color of feces, the light yellow shading that produces the shiny effect readily suggests urine. Mr. Simpson obligingly volunteered that "It's some kind of a giant cup . . . a loving cup;" and that the shading, "looks like a liquid . . . like water . . . something shimmery." The protruding form at the bottom is a second "handle" which "fits in a hole in the table—if you had a table." You can lift the cup with either handle to pour its contents out.

Mr. Simpson referred to a cloud in drawing A and the ear in drawing B as "upside down," and each time immediately complained of a choking sensation or a "nervous feeling" in his throat. References to "rolls of fat in a person" (drawing B) and "the gloss on a person's hair" (drawing C) were followed by fits of dizziness that made him stop drawing and sit down. His doctor and I surmised that he is in a state of near-infantile confusion

Figure 6A

over the distinction between destructive aggression and sexual activity. Although his actual sex life has been meager, unconscious conflicts center on masturbation, homosexuality, mouth-genital contact, and fears about the fragility of the sex organ. He has never completely outgrown the sexual connotation of every body opening, common among very young children.

Mr. Simpson was no more intelligent, perhaps only a little more talented,

Figure 6B

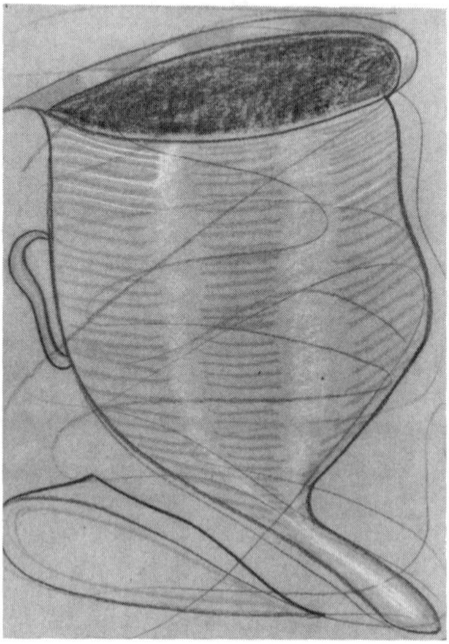

Figure 6C

See also color plate XVI.

than Mr. Bigelow, but his defense system was flexible enough to permit much freer expression of fantasy without any danger of his losing control. Because of this, his drawings served a practical purpose. The referring doctor came with key members of the nursing and junior medical staff to review the drawings with me. Mr. Simpson is not the kind of patient who readily arouses the interest of budding young psychiatrists; his fairly gallant attempts to bear up under his hypochondria had won him no more than casual indulgence from the more maternal among the nurses. The drawings made the ward staff aware that Mr. Simpson had access to more intellectual and emotional resources than they had realized, and the quality of the attention he got therefore improved considerably.

Three Adolescent Boys

In arranging the illustrations I placed the work of very sick people on the earlier pages. Although no exact order is possible, the selection moves gradually toward productions by patients who were less disturbed. The drawings of Edward Berry, for example, appear at a glance less healthy than those of Mr. Simpson. Figure 7 is the first illustration showing work done by somebody who had never been a mental patient.

At age 18 Richard Lewis had a speech difficulty and part of his vocal cords had been removed in the effort to correct it. The speech therapist, noting that at times Richard could speak up loud and clear, suspected that this problem had a psychological rather than a physical basis. She sent him for evaluation in the hope that, if her hunch was confirmed, the surgeons would be prevented from snipping away further at Richard's vocal equipment.

I could judge little directly about the speech problem because, although he was very polite and responsive, Richard scarcely uttered a word. Therefore I was thrown back entirely on the drawings, and to a large extent on general ideas about symbolism, in making some estimate of his personality. (Fortunately the John Bigelows are rare, and Richard is not one of them.)

I made speculations about Richard's relationship with his parents by assuming that the house (drawing A), with its light windows and the broad path leading to its door, stood for the mother; and that the small sun partly hidden by a cloud represented the father. From these I correctly deduced that he had an enveloping but at least superficially warm mother, and that the paternal figure had been rather distant, unreal, and weak. The conventionality of this first picture indicated that, to quote from my report "Richard seeks and probably attains approval by conforming to the demands and expectations of his environment." If the origin of his speech problem was indeed psychological, his lapses into inaudibility may have represented a very covert rebelliousness underlying his outstandingly sweet, compliant attitude.

The fairly successful realism of drawing A indicated that Richard's intelli-

Figure 7A

gence is at least average, probably higher. From the smiling, open-mouthed "dog" (drawing D, upper left, white) and the articles of food (chicken, fruits) in the same drawing, I derived the idea that he tends to look passively for mothering and nurture. He chose to make a second scribble; this showed that he had welcomed a new opportunity. His ability to make use of this stimulus improved, even though he did not demonstrate much ability to organize the forms into a unified whole. This led me to write that, "Apart from successfully maintained conventional controls, he has little developed capacity to organize his emotional resources, but has a rather childlike openness to his world of feeling and fantasy."

I took the big nose (drawing C) with its relatively weak attachment to the face as a phallic symbol. Richard chose to stay on and make a conventional

Figure 7B

Figure 7C

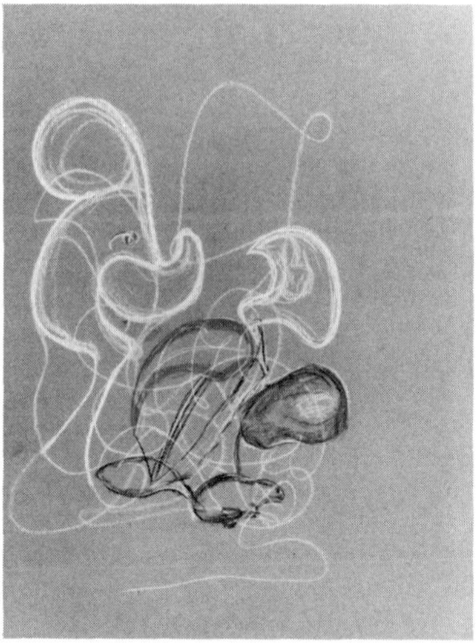

Figure 7D

tempera painting of the Washington Monument, and this too entered into my speculations about his sexual attitudes. Down the years I have come to call this "Washington's Favorite Phallic Symbol." I concluded that Richard is unsure of his own maleness, and somewhat preoccupied with concern about it.

Figure 8 shows, for comparison, the work of a 16-year old boy who also has never been a mental patient. Drawing A is not unlike Richard's first picture in its subject matter and realism. The two boys appear about equally intelligent, but Joseph could find nothing in his scribbles, and when he returned to deliberate drawing (B) the intervening experience had reduced rather than enriched his powers. His grip on the outside world is more tenuous than Richard's and unlike Richard he has to sacrifice spontaneity and access to his feelings in order to hang onto his intellectual and social controls.

In Joseph's case intelligence was the main issue. His school performance was poor and a psychologist in a foreign country had evaluated him as mentally deficient. The drawings indicated that he was of at least high average intelligence, and this was later borne out by expert psychological testing. Instances have been reported where mental defectives draw like bright, talented adults, but I have never run across any such discrepancy, and believe it must occur very seldom.

Figure 8A

As a final contrast, Figure 9 shows the drawings of a boy only a little younger than Joseph, but one who is fast turning from juvenile delinquency to adult crime. I worked with Willie on the ward because he was too unpredictably violent to come to the art room.

From the start (A) his drawings are concerned with fighting and destruction. When first asked to scribble he appeared to draw deliberately with closed eyes (C), a course of action often chosen by schizophrenics. Willie may have been merely defying me by disobeying instructions; he readily admitted that he had not really scribbled. The submarine (D) is another aggressive, warlike symbol, derived from his first actual scribble. In his final drawing (E) we see that the loosening process of the exercise and scribbling has had a marked effect, even though the picture was started on a blank sheet. There is none of the static quality of the first picture, and color areas (sharp yellow, bright brown) have been introduced, with devastating effect. Willie

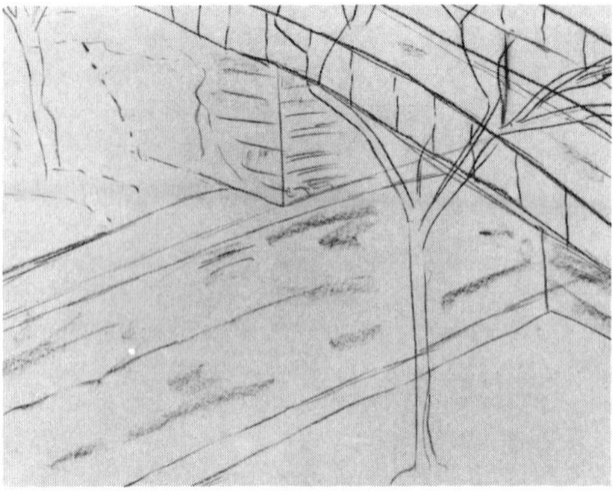

Figure 8B

Figure 9A

Figure 9B

Figure 9C

Figure 9D

explained that the soldier is both killing and being killed. It looks rather as if he is being showered with feces, or else is spewing them forth.

The Role of Diagnosis in Psychiatry

The distinction between diagnosis and treatment is much clearer to the staff than to the psychiatric patient. It is right that we should make the distinction even artificially clear, for we must never pretend to be healing when primarily we are investigating. But in truth the experiences of the patient during the course of diagnosis may open up avenues of treatment for him—as we saw at least suggested in several of the cases illustrated. Therapy, on the other hand, may be conceived as a way of gaining, for both doctor and patient, an ever clearer picture of individual psychodynamics, in effect a continuing diagnostic process.

Figure 9E

In branches of medicine other than psychiatry, correct diagnosis has a clear-cut bearing on treatment; sometimes it is only the skills of the diagnostic consultant that determine whether lifesaving measures will be taken in time. Even some doctors look upon psychotherapy, on the other hand, as an undifferentiated treatment for an undefined illness. But this is not quite the case. For example, most believers in psychoanalytic principles would not hold that every mental patient should be encouraged to abandon his customary defenses and express hidden feelings in order to better understand himself, his desires, and frustrations. Such uncovering techniques may at times be useless, even dangerous. Some psychotic or borderline patients can function within limits but the structure of personality is so fragile that it is better to leave defenses intact, however crippling they may appear. Others less severely ill who might, under ideal conditions, profit from insight and cathartic emotional expression, must not be deliberately subjected to such experiences, whose effect would be mainly destructive in the absence of needed help toward rebuilding the personality on firmer foundations. Even though some trial and error may always remain necessary, the enlightened decision rests on sensitive diagnostic appraisal of psychological weaknesses and strengths.

I recall an alcoholic patient whom I first met almost 13 years ago in a clinic whose staff was dedicated to psychoanalytically oriented psychotherapy. Thomas was our bright hope; he had not only stopped drinking but had expressed genuine insights and seemingly progressed toward a much richer social and personal life. In art therapy, too, he was rewarding to work with. I noted in passing that some of his paintings, highly elaborated symmetrical designs made up of myriad dabs of color, resembled text-book reproductions that were labeled as typically schizophrenic; and his portraits almost invariably had the hard line quality and fixed, hypnotic stare associated with the work of paranoid patients. I found these phenomena interesting, but assumed that, since Thomas was so healthy, his pictures merely showed how wrong the generalizations in the books could be.

By the time I left the clinic four years later, Thomas had again taken intermittently to drink; he had withdrawn to a great extent from his new-found social contacts, and his love affairs had ended unhappily. His painting too had regressed from a high point of freedom and grace into harsh rigidity. But he was still attending psychodrama, and being encouraged to cathartic emotional expression and self-analysis in group and individual psychotherapy sessions.

A few years later I learned that a recent repetition of the Rorschach test had revealed that Thomas was not, as had been thought six years earlier, a compulsive neurotic, but was tottering on the bring of a paranoid schizophrenic psychotic breakdown. The psychologist recommended that all therapeutic efforts should be directed toward helping Thomas strengthen the compulsive defenses that were all that now stood between him and overt psychosis.

I last saw Thomas several months ago, in the elevator of the city hospital where I now work. He was on his way to a state mental hospital. It is impossible to say how much he might have been spared had I and the rest of the Clinic staff taken seriously the warning signals that appeared in his paintings more than 12 years ago, and 6 years before they became apparent in his responses to psychological tests.

By now many other experiences have convinced me that diagnostic clues appearing only in patients' art products ought to be considered important even in the face of divergent clinical observations and psychological test results. Probably only a few psychiatrists and a slightly higher percentage of psychologists share this conviction. In statistics-conscious America nothing short of statistical research and validation will lend widespread respectability to any new kind of diagnostic material.

The Value of The Diagnostic Drawing Series

In the procedure described in this paper, the first drawing in each series tends to demonstrate a person's habitual modes of response. The exercise and scribble technique make for a lowering of defenses and the emergence of stronger feelings and more unconscious material. As the illustrations show, this experience may be welcomed, may induce near-panic, or may be rejected out of hand. In the final drawing, some people return with relief to their stereotyped pattern; others continue to exercise their new-found freedom; and still others show that they have integrated the new experience even though they choose to use a more deliberate, controlled approach, as in the first drawing.

Of course, established psychological tests, such as the TAT, the Rorschach, and several simple, standardized drawing procedures likewise reveal the underlying structure of the personality as well as its current, more superficial manifestations. Does this new kind of diagnostic drawing series contribute something unusual, beyond its obvious cheapness and speed?

One art therapist described free painting as being "less scientific but more accurate" than projective psychological tests. Our first drawing offers the patient more space, richer materials, and more freedom of choice than do such familiar procedures as prescribed figure-drawing. The dynamic stimulus of exercise and scribble opens up further possibilities for letting us know not only where a person is at the given moment, but where he is likely to go, what possibilities are open to him, and how they may be made more available.

Pathology may show up very early in drawings of this character, giving them a high predictive potential, but at this juncture such clues seldom gain widespread credence. Today, therefore, the likelihood of demonstrating strengths is perhaps more important. Through this procedure we have discovered hidden capacities in some of our patients that neither clinical observation nor projective testing had revealed.

Art for the Mentally Retarded: Directed or Creative?[1]

JAMES W. CRAWFORD

On the assumption that retardates lack the ability for creative self-expression, they traditionally have been given tasks such as basket-weaving, sewing, and drawing where emphasis is placed on following carefully and repeating a prescribed pattern. The concern has been with teaching a skill, the final product, and the retardate's supposed satisfaction with this kind of accomplishment. Since his possible need for individual expression was not considered, it did not matter that the products all looked very much alike.

Most art educators believe, however, that the real value of arts and crafts comes from the activity itself and that the primary aim, whether for retarded or normal children, is self-expression and personal adjustment. They feel that self-expressive art activities help the individual symbolize his experiences in such a way as to make some of them less threatening. The area of the self available for the pupil's own examination is thus expanded, and he may assimilate into the self-structure experiences previously denied to awareness. Realistic self-knowledge and broadened acceptance of experience reduce psychological tensions and make for better personal adjustment.

The drive toward personal adjustment is generally assumed to exist in the mentally retarded as well as in others, but it is not taken for granted that retardates have the resources for solving their own problems. Many people question the retarded child's ability to work in an imaginative and creative manner and to attain better personal adjustment as a result of such experiences.

Creative Methods Used with Mental Defectives

Lowenfeld [2] offers the teacher excellent guidance for understanding how expressive art can be made useful to the handicapped. Teachers need, he says, to become aware of "a therapy specific to the means of art education." He stresses the vital importance of the body image, which may be expressed and developed through art activity. Intense motivations are needed; however,

---

[1] This investigation, conducted at Laurelton State Village, Pa., was supported in part by a research grant (M-2121) from the National Institute of Mental Health, U.S. Public Health Service.

[2] Viktor Lowenfeld, *Creative and Mental Growth,* 3rd edition. N.Y., The Macmillan Co., 1957.

"a motivation used in art education therapy differs from any other art motivation in degree and intensity but not in kind." There is an important distinction between this and other methods of using art in therapy, methods based on the interpretation of symbols. Lowenfeld cautions teachers against attempting the latter kind of diagnosis or therapy, which is foreign to their entire preparation and background.

Schaefer-Simmern [3] has emphasized the importance of "visual conceiving," stating that the need for creative experience is natural to man and that this need is satisfied through artistic activity that encourages a natural unfolding. He has tested his theory with good success on various kinds of people, including two groups of mental defectives. Through successive translations of the same topic, these retardates were led step by step to visually conceive more and more of their world. As they mastered stages of conception, they also acquired a belief in their own worth and at the same time achieved better personal and social adjustment. Schaefer-Simmern criticizes mere mechanical manipulation as having no therapeutic value for retardates and states that it may even have adverse effects: ". . . the patient may attain control over his hands, he may even learn manipulation of a tool, he may become so used to this occupation that he is able to execute it without personality participation in it, he may even feel at ease in doing it, but the compulsory attention and concentration repeated over and over will throw him into a mental and emotional rigidity worse than before. He may become more or less adept at making things, but his personal relationship to them remains external because the work does not have its origin within him; it does not reflect himself."

[3] Henry Schaefer-Simmern, *The Unfolding of Artistic Activity.* Berkeley, University of California Press, 1948.

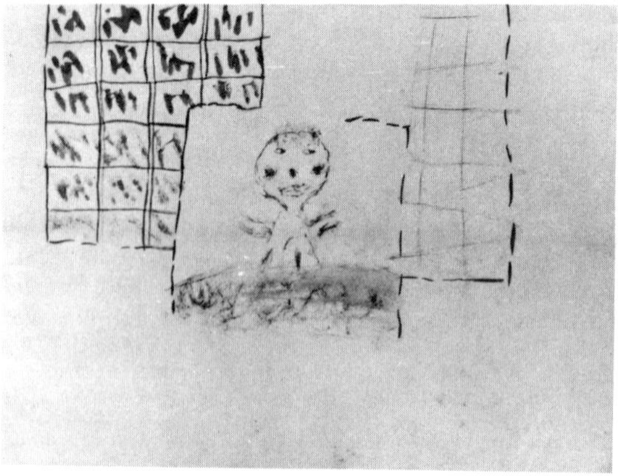

Figure 1

Painting by a 16½-year-old girl with I.Q. of 69, made at the first session.

Figure 2

By the same girl as Figure 1, made at the last session.

An Experiment with Retarded Girls

The present study was undertaken in order to assess the retardate's potential for engaging in and profiting from creative art activities. An effort was made to compare the effectiveness of creative art activities and directed art activities in developing a greater awareness of self, more realistic self-concepts, and generally healthier self-attitudes. The experiment was conducted for a period of ten weeks with 75 institutionalized adolescent girls. These were mental retardates, whose IQ's ranged from 50 to 80. A "Creative Group" was involved once a week in activities which provided opportunity for expression of feelings, wishes, and the body image. A "Directed Group" used patterns and repetitious procedures. The third group of 25 was designated "Control" and had no art experiences. All lessons were taught by the writer, who made a sincere effort to eliminate bias or expression of preference for either method.

Results were evaluated through observation of the groups in action, as well as independent judgment of the art products from the Creative Group. Two measures of self-concept,[4] chosen because they were constructed particularly for use with retardates, were administered to all three groups at the beginning and again at the end of the experiment. The Verbal Self-attitude Scale requires agreement or disagreement with statements such as: "I feel left out of things"; "A lot of jobs are too hard for me"; "The future looks dark." The Pictorial Test of Self-evaluation requires the respondent to indicate in which of two pictures the person is doing the "best thing" and,

[4] A. Butler, G. Guthrie, and L. Gorlow, "A Study of Self-attitudes, Emotional Adjustment, and Learning in Mental Retardees." *Progress Report, NIMH Study,* Laurelton State Village, Laurelton, Pa., January 1960. Further partial report, *American Journal of Mental Deficiency,* September 1961.

in pairs of pictures representing similar situations, which person is most like herself. The Verbal Scale tends to measure self-satisfaction and dissatisfaction in relation to common standards of what is socially desirable, while the Pictorial Test measures the discrepancy between the self as perceived and the self-ideal. On both measures, a score of zero indicates complete self-satisfaction; a score of fifty indicates complete dissatisfaction. Since a realistic person will probably admit to some shortcomings, the desirable score is not definite but lies somewhere between the extremes.

Contrasts between Directed and Creative Activities

In the earliest lessons the Creative Group was more reluctant than the Directed Group. The girls were afraid to express themselves and seemed to miss the security or the success assured by the directed lessons. It was obvious to the observer, however, that members of the Creative Group improved in their ability for self-expression. The Directed Group, on the other hand, had no opportunity for self-expression or self-examination. Enthusiasm, involvement, and originality also increased in the first group, but girls in the Directed Group grew more antagonistic as the experiment progressed. Especially important were the indications of growth of self-awareness in the Creative Group, evidenced by an ability to throw themselves into the work and to express individual experiences.

The most successful lesson from the standpoint of creative thought and freedom of expression was the puppet project. In this lesson, the students in the Creative Group constructed hand puppets from papier maché and used odd bits of yarn, buttons, corks, and scraps of cloth, as well as poster paint, to produce highly individual creations. Many chose to depict particular people, and apparently derived pleasure from distorting certain features. While the fact that this lesson was one of the last probably contributed to its

Figure 3

Painting by a 15-year-old girl with I.Q. of 72, made at the first session.

Figure 4

By the same girl as Figure 3, made at the last session.

success (by then the students had become much less inhibited), puppets by their nature seem to offer an especially good opportunity for self-expression, both in the process of construction and in their later use. During the last part of the lesson the girls were invited to hold conversations with their puppets and with other puppets. This part of the lesson was not formally organized, since it was felt that the more spontaneous it was, the better. All the girls joined in with enthusiasm, and voiced personal feelings very freely.

Clay modeling, during the fourth meeting, also provoked interesting reactions. There were many references to forbidden interests in body parts and body functions. Most girls were reluctant to handle the moist clay, but were very relieved once the move was made. This medium stimulated intense feelings, and appeared to promote more personal release than any other during the course of the experiment.

Several of the lessons were devoted to painting with poster paints. The students were more hesitant in these meetings, but in the course of them developed a great deal of self-awareness, awareness of others and of environment (see illustrations). Each painting session began with an intense motivation; it was found that there were advantages in approaching bodily and other intimate personal feelings indirectly. Sometimes aspects of the body image were better expressed through such subjects as animals, trees, machines, or the wind, than through the portrayal of a person. Especially for the very inhibited group members it was easier to express strong emotions through substitutions of this kind.

The Directed Group worked entirely with patterns or according to step-by-step directions. A demand was made that instructions be followed exactly, and the importance of the final product was emphasized. Typical projects were pre-punched sewing cards and silhouette cut-outs. A lesson in modeling was also taught, but with very definite methods, using clay coils and clay balls. This was the fourth meeting, and during this lesson there was a great deal of resistance. This session appeared more frustrating than any other. Enthusiasm and interest decreased rapidly in this group and it became very difficult to enforce attendance. In contrast to the Creative Group, these girls were very pleased to have the meetings and the experiment end.

Evaluation of Drawings and Test Results

The first and final drawings of each girl in the Creative Group were compared and evaluated by a group of art educators. Their judgment confirmed the impression of a significant gain in self-concept, self-involvement, and expressive ability (see illustrations). The final drawings contained more depictions of the self, more indications of social interaction, and greater inclusion of environment. Without a doubt the most dramatic change was in the completeness of the body concept. In the first drawings, figures were often shown with only a head and arms or head and legs. Features were often omitted. The last drawings gave evidence of richer concepts, in addition to showing more body parts and details.

The two tests administered were not equally sensitive to the kinds of change that resulted from the creative art experience. Responses to the Verbal Scale were not significantly different as between the three groups or between the creative group before and after the experiment. The Pictorial Test, on the other hand, indicated that the creative activities had an effect on self-attitudes. The second testing of the Creative Group showed less tendency toward the extremes of self-satisfaction and dissatisfaction as compared with the other two groups and with their own responses before the series of art lessons.

The nature of the measures themselves has an interesting relation to these test results. The desirability of certain responses is assumed in the Verbal Scale; the test questions themselves thus encourage the subject to equate success with conformity. In the Pictorial Test, social norms play less part. The subject first makes her own assignment of value, which thus may be determined by underlying needs rather than social desirability. Directed art contrasts with creative art much as the two tests contrast with each other. Creative art activities encourage, not conformity, but responses determined from within the individual.

This study indicates that art methods for the mentally retarded should provide creative opportunities. Contrary to still widely held assumptions, the retarded have creative ability and resources that can be mobilized as a result of self-expressive activities.

An Experimental Approach to the Judgment of Psychopathology from Paintings

ELINOR ULMAN and BERNARD I. LEVY

In view of the widespread belief that paintings can be used as a basis for psychiatric diagnosis, it is remarkable that so little experimental work has been undertaken to test the underlying assumption. By far the larger part of the literature devoted to diagnostic aspects of pictures painted by psychopathological subjects is based upon the authors' personal observation, description, and interpretation. Most of the early work was concerned with paintings by schizophrenics, and consisted of attempts to correlate stylistic features of the paintings with various facets of the schizophrenic syndrome.[1]

Later studies have treated the relationship between paintings and a broader range of pathological states and aspects of personality.[2]

---

[1] See for example: C. Lombroso and M. du Camp, "L'arte nei pazzi." *Archivio di Psichiatria, Antropologia Criminale e Scienze Penali,* Vol. 1, 1880.

M. Simon, "L'imagination dans la folie: étude sur les dessins, plans, descriptions et costumes des alienés." *Annales Medico-Psychologiques,* Vol. 16, 1876.

H. Prinzhorn, *Bildnerei der Geisteskranken: ein Beitrag zur Psychopathologie der Gestaltung.* Berlin, Springer, 1923.

F. Reitman, *Psychotic Art.* New York, International Universities Press, 1951.

[2] Among such studies are: *Psychoneurotic Art,* by Margaret Naumburg (New York, Grune & Stratton, Inc., 1953) to which Adolf G. Woltmann contributed a "Correlation of the Patient's Rorschach and Other Tests with the Patient's Art Productions"; and "The use of spontaneous art in analytically oriented group therapy of obese women," by Margaret Naumburg and Janet Caldwell (*Acta Psychotherapeutica,* Supplement to Vol. 7, 1959).

See also: Hanna Yaxa Kwiatkowska, "The use of families' art productions for psychiatric evaluation," *Bulletin of Art Therapy,* Vol. 6, No. 2, Oct. 1966; and Elinor

A much smaller number of workers has attempted systematic or experimental diagnostic investigations,[3] but as far as is known, the present study constitutes the first forthright test of the ability of judges to diagnose psychopathology from paintings.[4] Unless the crudest diagnosis—patient or normal—can be made with sufficient precision, the assumption that paintings and drawings contain data related in regular ways to psychopathological categories lies open to serious question.

The Experiment

Paintings were collected under reasonably controlled conditions from members of two groups, normal and patient. Independent observers were then asked to identify group membership through judgments based on the paintings alone.

The Paintings

Of 105 paintings, each by a different adult, 51 were made by acutely ill hospitalized patients most of whom were diagnosed as schizophrenic. The normal group consisted of medical, nursing, and clerical members of a hospital staff, vocational rehabilitation clients, and a variety of students of the health professions. None of these had a known history of psychiatric hospitalization. The difference of age between the two groups was not statistically significant.

One of the authors, an art therapist, collected all of the paintings. Subjects painted in rooms where there were no pictures to be seen. They worked either individually with the therapist or in groups of two or three. When several people painted together they were placed so that they could not see each other's work without making an effort. The therapist strove to give the same directions and to maintain a neutral, supportive attitude throughout the experiment. Each painter was supplied with the same materials: an 18-inch by 24-inch sheet of gray construction paper tacked to a drawing board (placement of the board in horizontal or vertical position on a floor easel was left to the painter's choice); and an assortment of hard-pastel sticks (10 colors, black, and white), sufficient for complex color mixtures. Sticks of each color were

---

Ulman, "A new use of art in psychiatric diagnosis," *Bulletin of Art Therapy,* Vol. 4, No. 3, April 1965.

[3] See for example: A. Anastasi and J. P. Foley, "An experimental study of the drawing behavior of adult psychotics in comparison with that of a normal control group," *Journal of Experimental Psychology,* Vol. 34, 1944.

E. F. Hellersberg, "The Horn-Hellersberg test and adjustment to reality," *American Journal of Orthopsychiatry,* Vol. 15, 1945.

T. Waehner, "Interpretation of spontaneous drawings and paintings," *Genetic Psychology Monographs,* Vol. 33, 1946.

[4] This study was reported in the *Journal of Abnormal Psychology,* Vol. 72, No. 2, 1967: "Judging psychopathology from paintings," by Bernard I. Levy and Elinor Ulman. An account of statistical methods used and the results of statistical analysis was included in that report.

massed in a separate box so that the colors available to choose from showed up clearly.

The therapist avoided making suggestions about content and technique. The only help she offered was through her encouraging attitude, and some acutely psychotic patients needed a great deal of encouragement before they could paint. When the paintings were complete, the therapist administered a brief information test [5] known to provide a reliable estimate of intellectual functioning at the time of testing, which here coincided with the time of picture-making.

The 96 paintings used in the study were selected so as to provide an equal representation of patients and normal subjects, and an equal number of paintings done by men and women in each of these categories. (The nine remaining paintings were used as samples during the experiment proper.) The paintings were photographed in color, and, finally, were presented to the judges in the form of projected transparencies.

The Judges

There were 84 judges who made the diagnoses required of them in this study. Of these, 26 were professional mental health workers (including four art therapists); 30 were student mental health workers; and 28 had no mental health experience. The last-named group included 17 artists and 11 people with no experience in either art or the field of mental health.

The Judgments

The judges were asked to diagnose each subject from his or her painting as it was exposed on the screen for approximately three seconds. They were told that the paintings were the work of adult patients with various psychiatric diagnoses, and of people with no known psychiatric hospitalization, and that there was a wide range of intelligence among the painters. They were shown the first nine paintings, without further comment, as samples to accustom them to the task. Their judgments were to be entered as either P (patient) or N (normal) in the appropriate space on the data form.

Results of the Experiment

The data were approached with four questions in mind: (1) How accurately do judges make the diagnoses? (2) Are there characteristics of judges which influence their diagnoses? (3) Are there characteristics of the painters other than mental health or illness which are related to the diagnoses? (4) Are some paintings easier to identify correctly than are others?

Accuracy of Judgments and Characteristics of Judges

Statistical analysis of the judgments confirmed the hypothesis that judges

[5] W. D. Altus, "The validity of an abbreviated information test used by the Army," *Journal of Consulting Psychology,* Vol. 12, 1948.

can distinguish to a significant degree between paintings by psychotic patients and paintings by normal subjects. There was no statistically significant difference in accuracy of judgment on the part of judges with much, little, or no experience in the mental health field. Apparently, experience with psychiatric patients does not make for special sensitivity to the patient-normal distinction as revealed by paintings.

Although amount of contact with psychiatric patients appeared to be unrelated to diagnostic *accuracy,* it occurred to the investigators that it might make a difference in diagnostic *tendency:* that is, judges with professional experience in psychiatry might see more psychopathology than would others. Analysis did not bear out this supposition; it was, however, found that *all* judges saw more paintings as done by patients than by normals in a sample that in fact was equally divided between the two categories. Considerations related to our third question, which will be discussed below, may help to explain this tendency.

Another possible difference among groups of judges is related to our fourth question; as will be described in detail further on, we did indeed find that 36 of the paintings could be described as "difficult to judge" (see page 7, categories (2) and (3)). Each judge within each of the three groups was given a score for his correct diagnosis of these 36 "difficult" paintings, and here also it was found that professional experience did not appear to sharpen the judges' ability.

Outside of the experiment proper, six physicians who acted as judges at the beginning of their first year of psychiatric residency were asked to judge the slides again almost a year later. During the intervening months they had viewed the art work of numerous patients and taken part in discussion of some of these products after they were presented at conferences by the art therapist with her comments. In addition, they had attended approximately 10 training sessions where they themselves produced pictures and discussed the psychological implications of their own and each other's work.

It was found that this year's experience had no influence whatever on their capacity to perform the assigned task of judging the paintings. Scores had changed a point or two, but to no significant extent, and the ranking of the six in their ability to judge accurately remained the same.

No attempt was made to correlate accuracy of judgment with amount of experience in art. A cursory inspection of the judges' records makes it appear unlikely that experience in this area has any more influence on accuracy than has experience in the mental health field. For example, the four art therapists, the only judges with experience in both fields, as a group exhibited no superiority.

Subject Characteristics

While professional training and experience of the judges do not seem to influence their responses, the intelligence of the people who produced the paintings displays a strong relationship to the judgments. A mean intelligence level of 117.8 was found for painters to whose pictures the judges responded with a significant number of "N" (this includes 21 normals correctly diagnosed and three patients incorrectly diagnosed as normal). Conversely, those correctly (39) and incorrectly (17) judged to be patients had a mean IQ of 83.3.

Clearly, the more intelligent the painter, the more apt is a judge to call the painting the work of a normal person. The normal group included a number of mentally retarded but psychiatrically normal individuals; this helps to account for the actually normal painters having been judged incorrectly more frequently than were the actual patients. A further possible explanation, not, of course, subject to analysis, might lie in the sickness of the patients being better guaranteed than was the health of the normals. Our working definition of "normal" on the whole was equivalent to "not a patient in this hospital at this time," and the sample may well have included some subjects with serious psychopathology. Figure 6 is typical of the work by normal painters with very low IQ's.

Sex of the painters was the other characteristic studied; it was found that male and female painters were diagnosed with equal accuracy by the judges.

Characteristics of Paintings

The paintings were divided into three categories according to the correctness with which they were judged: (1) Paintings to which a significant proportion of judges responded *correctly* beyond chance expectation (Figures 1, 2, 3, and 4). With a total of 84 judges, statistical standards demanded at least 55 correct judgments for a painting to be placed in this category. (2) Paintings to which a significant percentage of judges responded with the *incorrect* diagnosis (Figures 5 and 6). (3) Those to which the majority response was not significantly different from chance; the last-named were termed "ambiguous."

In the group of 48 paintings by normals, 21 were judged correctly, 10 were ambiguous, and 17 were incorrectly judged to be the work of patients. Of the 48 paintings by patients, 39 were judged correctly, 6 were ambiguous, and 3 were judged incorrectly. The 60 "correctly judged" paintings were hung on a wall in two groups, patient and normal, and each group was arranged in order of the frequency of correct versus incorrect judgments (Figures 1 and 4 show the extremes and figures 2 and 3 the center of this continuum). Thus the two groups could be compared and the characteristics of the paintings in each group could be isolated and described.

Observing the total range, one is impressed with the dramatic disorganization and unrealistic quality at one end of the series as contrasted with the opposite end where we find pictures that are well integrated and, usually, realistic in color, shape, and perspective. Some paintings obviously dictate a judgment of health; others, of illness.

The similarity of paintings within each group is startling. In the normal

Figure 1. Most obvious picture by a normal painter, correctly identified by 82 out of 84 judges. IQ 110. No art training, very little art experience.

group, most of the paintings are landscapes. The entire page is filled with solidly colored shapes, numerous colors are used, and colors are mixed or blended. Linear and atmospheric perspective are frequently evident. Most of the normal painters tried, within the limits of their skill, to make the pictorial content as realistic as possible. The few abstractions show organized use of the entire available surface, and tend to refer to real objects whose shape and

Figure 2. Least obvious painting recognized as being by a normal painter, correctly identified by 55 out of 84 judges. IQ 90. No art training, a little art experience.

Figure 3. Least obvious picture recognized as being by a patient, correctly identified by 55 out of 84 judges. Diagnosis: schizophrenic reaction, chronic undifferentiated type. IQ 105. Trained as a draftsman, some experience with sketching.

proportions have obviously been observed with considerable objective accuracy.

In the patient group, the paintings tend to be abstract, contain shapes which are symbolic, often labeled, usually unintegrated with each other and unrelated to the page as a whole. Of the few attempts at perspective, most are ineffectual. Graphic chaos prevails.

At this point, some comment on the relationship between these paintings

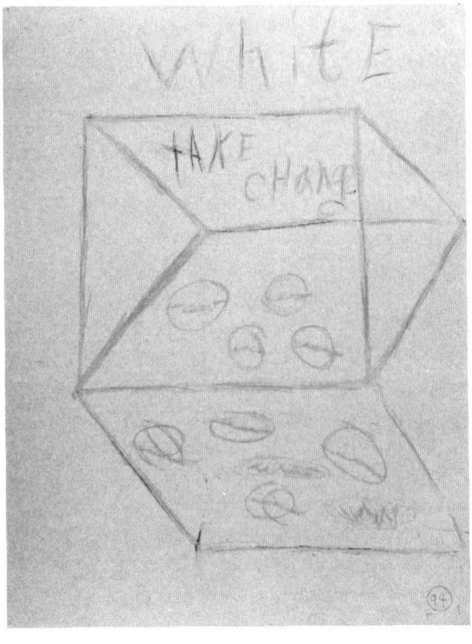

Figure 4. Most obvious picture by a patient, correctly identified by all 84 judges. Diagnosis: schizophrenic reaction, paranoid type. IQ 67. Had art course in high school, no further art experience.

Figure 5. False positive: by a patient, incorrectly identified as normal by 63 out of 84 judges. Diagnosis: paranoid schizophrenic. IQ 118. One semester of training at an academy of art, further experience in oil painting.

and the work of professional artists seems to be called for. In particular, the paintings of cubists, surrealists, nonobjectivists, expressionists, abstract expressionists, and action painters are easily associated with the paintings of mental patients in the minds of many people. Paintings of these schools express either emotional experiences or theoretical conceptions. They tend to be either abstractions or exaggerations of realistic forms, or, in the extreme, completely nonrepresentational.

Paintings by patients share many of these characteristics. However, the striking difference seems to lie in the implication of a graphic logic behind the products. Patients impress one as expressing disordered logic. Professional painters on the other hand, no matter how exaggerated, abstract, or nonrepresentational the content of their paintings, usually reveal a relatively systematic, orderly, and well integrated formal structure in their work. To paraphrase Reitman,[6] the artist presents us with a *re*organized version of reality while the psychotic painter offers a *dis*organized one.

The similarity between patients' graphic endeavors and those of artists seems greater when characteristics are listed than when the paintings are actually seen. When paintings by acutely psychotic patients look at all like the work of professional painters, they are usually in the nature of primitive caricatures. The same is true of the frequently mentioned likeness among the

[6] *Op. cit.*

works of psychotics, true primitives, and children. Graphic characteristics accurately enough denoted by the same words do not necessarily produce the same impression. The works of adult psychotics, for example, frequently contain many "childish" elements, but they seldom really look like the work of children.

Artistic talent and artistic training are factors lying outside the scope of this study, but in our sample we saw signs that they may complicate the use of paintings for diagnosis. Only one patient in our experimental group had studied art; her estimated IQ was high and her painting (Figure 5) was among those incorrectly judged as the work of a normal. Artistically gifted mental patients, whether or not they have had artistic training and experience, sometimes retain part of their ability for integrated graphic expression even, at times, when clinically they are in the midst of an acute psychotic episode. And of course there is no guarantee against psychosis in professional artists. There are recorded instances where acute mental illness has diminished but not destroyed an artist's integrative powers, and where, in the course of a chronic psychosis, such powers have progressively deteriorated.

Summary and Conclusions

While this study indicates that observers can discriminate between the paintings of patients and those of normals, it must be noted that mentally retarded subjects who are otherwise psychiatrically normal appeared to the judges to paint in much the same way as patients. In addition, paintings of efficiently functioning and very intelligent patients tend to be misdiagnosed as normal. It appears that judges can distinguish most efficiently paintings by subjects whose intelligence ranges from dull average to bright average.

We found that familiarity with deviations and distortions in the thinking of patients as expressed in words does not sharpen sensitivity to signs of

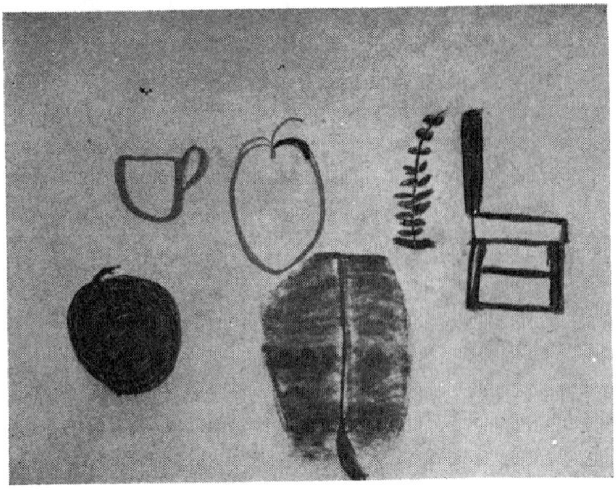

Figure 6. False negative: by a normal painter, incorrectly identified as a patient by 72 out of 84 judges. IQ 58. No art education or experience.

mental illness as expressed in graphic productions. Mental health workers, including art therapists, have no greater ability than others for the diagnostic task required in this study. Some individuals, independent of specialized training in either psychiatry or art, are better diagnosticians through pictures than are others. Correct diagnoses on the part of individual judges ranged from a low of 50 to a high of 73.

Future research might well concern itself with isolating the formal elements of graphic productions and studying their relationship to personality. For example, clinical judgments such as those in the present study might be validated by listing the objective characteristics of the drawings (e.g., number of colors used, percentage of paper covered with color, and so on) and finding out whether drawings scored on the basis of these elements would yield the predicted results. Eventually such formal elements might be more exactly distinguished and their association with the subtler aspects of personality studied.

In the past we have been much concerned with *content* and its symbolic implications. Our present study suggests that research centered on *form* and its correlation with personal characteristics may point the way toward greater reliability in the use of paintings for diagnostic purposes.

Contributors

John Birtchnell is a member of the scientific staff of the Medical Research Council, Clinical Psychiatry Unit, and honorary consultant psychiatrist at Graylingwell Hospital, Chichester, Sussex, U.K. He graduated in medicine at the University of Edinburgh in 1959 and was awarded an M.D. at the same university in 1966. He obtained the diploma in psychotherapy of the University of Aberdeen in 1967 for a thesis entitled "Psychodynamic Aspects of the Face." He is an associate member of the British Association of Art Therapists and is currently a part-time lecturer in the remedial art course at St. Albans College of Art, Hertfordshire.

James W. Crawford was formerly associate professor and chairman of the Art Department at Frostburg State Teachers College, Maryland. He is now on the faculty at Humboldt State College, Arcata, California, and is working with retarded children in the schools of that area.

Penny Dachinger is a recent graduate of The George Washington University Master's degree program in art therapy. As a graduate student, she was a member of the American Art Therapy Association's Student Committee, and also served as the program's representative. Formerly a consultant to the Pinecrest State School, Pineville, Louisiana, Ms. Dachinger now teaches at the University of Northern Colorado in Greeley.

Juliana Day, a research psychiatrist, works in the Section on Family Studies at the National Institute of Mental Health, Bethesda, Maryland. Since joining the NIMH staff in 1953, Dr. Day has been co-author with Drs. Lyman C. Wynne and Irving Ryckoff of many psychiatric papers concerned with the family as a unit. She is a graduate of Bryn Mawr, received her medical training at Tufts College Medical School, served as a psychiatric resident at Johns Hopkins Hospital, and is at present a candidate in the Washington Psychoanalytic Institute.

James M. Denny is a clinical psychologist and coordinator of intern training in clinical and counseling psychology at the Counseling and Testing Center of the University of Hawaii. He is also in the private practice of clinical psychology.

Irene Dewdney started practicing art therapy with her husband, Selwyn Dewdney, in 1956 at Westminster Hospital, London, Ontario. From 1962 to 1967 she worked at St. Joseph's Hospital and at the Ailsa Craig Boys' Home near London and then resumed her formal art training at the Artist's Workshop of London. She has been art therapist at the London Psychiatric Hospital, and since 1970 she has also served as art therapy consultant at the Western Ontario Therapeutic Community. In the course of their work together, the Dewdneys have pioneered a new form of art therapy, the picture-centered group session.

Selwyn Dewdney is currently involved full-time in field, laboratory, and museum studies of aboriginal hide, bark, and rock pictography in Canada. His career as an art therapist began in 1947 at the Psychiatric Institute of Westminster (Veterans') Hospital in London, Ontario. He was joined in this endeavor by his wife Irene in 1956, and continued to work there until 1972. Mr. Dewdney's interest in rock art research began in 1957; he is at present a research associate in pictography, art, and archaeology at the Royal Ontario Museum in Toronto, and is a senior associate of the Canadian Rock Art Research Associates.

Josef E. Garai is director of the Graduate Art Therapy Program and professor of psychology at Pratt Institute, as well as a lecturer at the New School for Social Research in New York. He received both his B.A. and Ph. D. from New York University. With his wife Selma E. Garai, he works conjointly in family and group art therapy. At present, Dr. Garai is writing a book on creative-expressive modalities in therapy and education.

Lena L. Gitter was educated in Vienna, where she studied the Montessori Method. She has lectured and written extensively on this educational system, her most recent publication being *A Strategy for Fighting the War on Poverty: The Montessori Method as Applied to the Brookhaven Project*, which is based on her wide experience in special education. At present she serves the American Montessori Society as consultant, lecturer, and evaluator.

Miriam Goldberg, a psychiatric social worker, has practiced social work in Baltimore, Maryland, at the Department of Public Welfare and the Board of Education, and at an outpatient clinic of the Veterans Administration since receiving her M.S.W. degree from the University of Pennsylvania School of Social Work.

Edith Kramer—painter, sculptor, and author of *Art as Therapy with Children*—takes part in the training of art therapists in the graduate program of The George Washington University, Washington, D.C. She specializes in art therapy with young people at the Albert Einstein College of Medicine and the Jewish Guild for the Blind, and teaches courses in art and art therapy at the New School for Social Research and the Turtle Bay Music School, New York City.

Hanna Yaxa Kwiatkowska heads the Art Therapy Department at the National Institute of Mental Health. Her sculpture won wide recognition in Europe and South America before she came to the United States, where she was associated with the Sculpture Center in New York. She has organized art therapy exhibits for national and international psychiatric conferences, and is well-known not only in New York and Washington but in the psychiatric centers of Brazil for her illustrated lectures on psychoanalytically oriented art therapy.

Erika Lehnsen studied art and the teaching of applied art in Berlin before leaving for Central America to escape the Nazi regime. Her own paintings have been exhibited in group and one-woman shows, as have art works made by children and adults with whom she has worked. In the United States she received her M.A. in psychology from the New School for Social Research in New York City, and studied art therapy with Edith Kramer. Her long experience as art teacher and art therapist includes work with all age groups, and has provided material for lectures presented in this country and abroad. She has worked in school, community, and hospital services and has conducted a private practice.

Bernard I. Levy is a professor of psychology and heads The George Washington University's Department of Psychology. At the time that the article included here was undertaken, Dr. Levy was chief psychologist at the District of Columbia General Hospital, Washington, D.C.

Al. Marinow is director of the Psychiatric Hospital in Bela/Russensko, Bulgaria.

Margaret Naumburg is recognized internationally as the leading figure in the field of art therapy and has published three books on the subject, the most recent being *Psychoneurotic Art: Its Function in Psychotherapy*. She is a certified psychologist and a practicing psychotherapist, specializing in analytically oriented art therapy. She was the founder and the first director of the progressive Walden School in New York, and has recently returned to the field of education, teaching graduate courses in the Department of Education at New York University.

Sandra Pine is at present associated with a new day-treatment center at the Bronx Municipal Hospital Center of the Albert Einstein College of Medicine; she was formerly a teacher-therapist in the preschool unit of the Mental Retardation Institute of the Flower Fifth Avenue Hospital, New York City. She has taught art in a public elementary school, also in New York; has been art therapist at a residential treatment home for severely disturbed children; and, as a psychotherapist, has used art at Brooklyn Psychiatric Centers, New York. She earned a Master's degree in special education with emphasis on art therapy at the Bank Street College of Education, and she has studied art therapy with Edith Kramer.

Irving Schneider is director of the Arlington Mental Hygiene Clinic, Arlington, Virginia. He did undergraduate work and graduate work in sociology at the University of Chicago before taking his medical training at New York University. Dr. Schneider is assistant clinical professor of psychiatry at the Georgetown University Medical School and a candidate of the Washington Psychoanalytic Institute.

Myer Site has taught art in the Baltimore public school system since 1926, where his experience ranged from working with accelerated classes to conducting special classes for slow learners and academically retarded children. He has also taught summer classes for community groups, for patients at the University Hospital Psychiatric Institute in Baltimore, and for staff at the Crownsville State Mental Hospital, Crownsville, Maryland.

Joachim H. Themal, art instructor at Pleasantville Cottage School, Jewish Child Care Association, Pleasantville, New York, is an artist whose work is represented in a number of American art museums as well as in the State Department's collection of paintings that hang in foreign consulates. He studied painting in Germany, has been the recipient of numerous awards and fellowships, taught school in Cyprus, and was a housefather at the Cottage School before taking up his present work.

Elinor Ulman is editor of *The American Journal of Art Therapy* and coordinator of the Master's degree program in art therapy conducted at The George Washington University. For ten years, she served as the director of the art therapy program she had initiated at District of Columbia General Hospital, and earlier she led an art group and supervised a program of occupational and recreational therapy for patients of the Alcoholic Rehabilitation Clinic, District of Columbia Department of Mental Health.

Harriet T. Voegeli, an art therapist, served her apprenticeship in art therapy at the District of Columbia General Hospital. Mrs. Voegeli studied art at the Houston Museum of Art and at Carleton College and is a graduate of The George Washington University.

Diana Wittenberg, a registered art therapist, practices art therapy with adolescent inpatients at Roosevelt Hospital, New York City, as well as with the young residents of the Veritas drug-free therapeutic communities; she has previously conducted art groups in neighborhood centers, a summer camp, a hospital, and residential centers for children. She is an exhibiting artist who received training in Vienna, Paris, and the Art Students League in New York. She has also studied art therapy with Margaret Naumburg, Edith Kramer, and in workshops with Janie Rhyne and Elaine Rapp.

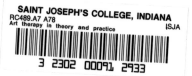